Deep Calls To Deep

Deep Calls To Deep

Transforming Conversations Between Jews and Christians

Compiled and Edited by
Tony Bayfield

scm press

© The Contributors, 2017

First published in 2017 by SCM Press

Editorial office
3rd Floor, Invicta House,
108–114 Golden Lane,
London EC1Y 0TG

Hymns Ancient & Modern

Hymns Ancient & Modern® is a registered trademark
of Hymns Ancient and Modern Ltd

SCM Press is an imprint of Hymns Ancient & Modern Ltd
(a registered charity)
13A Hellesdon Park Road, Norwich,
Norfolk, NR6 5DR, UK

www.scmpress.co.uk

All rights reserved. No part of this publication may be reproduced, stored in a retrieval system, or transmitted, in any form or by any means, electronic, mechanical, photocopying or otherwise, without the prior permission of the publisher, SCM Press.

The Contributors have asserted their right under the Copyright, Designs and Patents Act, 1988, to be identified as the Authors of this Work

The process of dialogue reflected in this publication was assisted by the Council of Christians and Jews (CCJ). However, the views, opinions and ideas reflected here are those of the individual contributors and in no way reflect those of CCJ, nor necessarily of other contributors.

British Library Cataloguing in Publication data
A catalogue record for this book is available
from the British Library

978 0 334 05512 9

Typeset by Regent Typesetting
Printed and bound in Great Britain by
CPI Group (UK) Ltd, Croydon

Dedication

This book is dedicated to the memory of:

The Revd Dr John Bowden, a publisher who brought Christian–Jewish dialogue to his list, a theologian who asked challenging questions of all three Abrahamic siblings, mentor and companion in transforming conversations.

Sir Sigmund Sternberg KC*SG, a survivor of the Shoah who dedicated his life to collaboration between religious, political and business leaders in order to eradicate senseless hatred and build constructive relationships between communities.

Contents

Acknowledgements xi
Contributors xiii
Foreword xix

A Dialogical Roadmap Tony Bayfield 1

1 **The Third Dialogue Partner: How Do We Experience Modern Western Culture?** 19

  Liberating Individuals and Challenging Communities 21
    Elli Tikvah Sarah
  Time, Space and the Possibility of God 36
    Stephen Roberts
  Further Reflections 51
    Tony Bayfield

2 **How Should Christians and Jews Live in a Modern Western Democracy?** 57

  Inside Out or Outside In 59
    Steve Williams
  Democracy and Its (My) Jewish Discontents 72
    Jeremy Gordon
  Further Reflections 85
    Tony Bayfield

3 **How Do We Cope with Our Past?** 91

  Coming to Terms with the Past: Introduction 93
    David Gillett and Michael Hilton

	'The Jews' in John's Gospel Michael Hilton	95
	William of Norwich and Echoes through the Ages David Gillett	103
	Holocaust Memorial Day Michael Hilton and David Gillett	119
	Coming to Terms with the Past: Conclusion David Gillett and Michael Hilton	128
	Further Reflections Tony Bayfield	129
4	**The Legacy of Our Scriptures**	135
	Beyond the Wilderness: Transforming Our Readings of Jewish and Christian Scriptures Alexandra Wright	137
	Reading Together: Receiving the Legacies of Our Scriptures Today David F. Ford	153
	Further Reflections Tony Bayfield	167
5	**Religious Absolutism**	173
	Rethinking Revelation, Exclusivity, Dialogue and Mission Alan Race	175
	A Jewish Theology Embracing Difference Debbie Young-Somers	189
	Further Reflections Tony Bayfield	202
6	**What Does Respect between People of Faith Mean?**	207
	The Heart of How Things Ought to Be Wendy Fidler	209
	Negotiating the Complexities of You and Me Joy Barrow	222
	Further Reflections Tony Bayfield	237

CONTENTS

7 **Christian Particularity** 241

Incarnation and Trinity 243
    Patrick Morrow
Friendship and Respect in the Face of Impenetrable Doctrine 264
    Vivian Silverman
Morrow, Maimonides and Torah in Translation 270
    Natan Levy
Response to Patrick Morrow: We Are the Louse in Your Fur 276
    Michael Hilton and Victor Seedman
Further Reflections 286
    Tony Bayfield

8 **Jewish Particularism** 291

Spying on Israel: Morality of a Promised Land 293
    Natan Levy
Christians, Jews and the Land 308
    Teresa Brittain
Further Reflections 320
    Tony Bayfield

Concluding Thoughts David F. Ford 325

Glossary 331

Acknowledgements

I would like to thank SCM Press for the enthusiasm with which it has embraced publishing this book and David Shervington, Rebecca Goldsmith, Hannah Ward and Joanne Hill, for their support, advice and prompt professionalism. Alan Race and I were particularly keen that SCM should be the publisher – in part because we've both been published by SCM but largely out of gratitude and respect for the late Editor and Managing Director of SCM Press, the Revd Dr John Bowden, to whom the book is dedicated. That leads me also to thank:

- The Revd Dr Marcus Braybrooke, former Director of the Council of Christians and Jews (CCJ), for more than 30 years my partner and guide in dialogue theology.
- Sister Margaret Shepherd and the Sisters of Sion for seeing to and from the heart.
- The Rt Revd Nigel McCullough, former Bishop of Manchester and immediate past Chair of CCJ, who commissioned this book.
- The 16 members of the CCJ Theology Group who have given so unstintingly of themselves, their deepest commitments and questions and their time over a five-year period. Never have I had the privilege of chairing such a rewarding group of people.
- Dr Steve Innes who has supported the publication process on behalf of CCJ with such calm skill. Steve has also prepared the Glossary (along with Rabbi Dr Michael Hilton) and developed educational materials to accompany the book and facilitate its use.
- Professor David Ford who was volunteered as Vice-Chair in the early days of the Group when there were some challenging personnel issues and who knows the difference between pouring oil on troubled waters and sweeping important issues under the carpet!
- Victor Seedman, so insightful and knowledgeable when we urgently needed assistance from outside the Group.
- Rabbis Michael Hilton and Natan Levy for contributing to the section on Christian particularism as well as their own chapters.

ACKNOWLEDGEMENTS

- Rabbi Yuval Keren for setting the vowels in the Rabbinic Hebrew texts.
- My former PA Laura Moss who, despite receiving multiple copies of every essay and endless revisions, managed to present me with a flawless text for final editing.
- And finally, my beloved partner Jacqueline Fisher who not only prepared the final manuscript for SCM and later proofread the book, but gave each of my personal contributions the benefit of her love of English and extensive teaching and writing. If my contributions are grammatical, lucid and accessible, that is her doing. The questionable theology is entirely my responsibility.

Contributors

Joy Barrow gained a degree in Theology and taught Religious Studies in London secondary schools for 25 years, during which time she obtained an MA from King's College, London, and a PhD from Leeds University. She has been actively involved in interfaith relations since 1980. After leaving teaching in 2005, she was Director of the International Interfaith Centre in Oxford, then Inter Faith Relations Officer for the Methodist Church in Britain. A committee member of the Hillingdon Branch of CCJ and Hillingdon Inter Faith Network, she currently volunteers at the London office of CCJ as Branch Liaison Manager.

Tony Bayfield CBE is a former President of CCJ. He began his association in 1983, embarking on a dialogue project co-convened with CCJ's then Executive Director Marcus Braybrooke. This led to *Dialogue with a Difference* (1992), *He Kissed Him and They Wept* (2001) with Sidney Brichto and Eugene Fisher, and *Beyond the Dysfunctional Family* (2012) with Alan Race and Ataullah Siddiqui. He was awarded a Lambeth Doctorate in 2006 and is Professor of Jewish Theology and Thought at Leo Baeck College. A widower with three children, his younger daughter Miriam Berger is a graduate of Leo Baeck College and, like her father, a Reform Rabbi.

Teresa Brittain is a member of the Roman Catholic Congregation of the Sisters of Our Lady of Sion and taught for a time in state schools in London. She studied Theology at King's College, London, and then worked full time in parish ministry. Since gaining a Master of Literature in Theology at Birmingham University she has worked on the integration of the new relationship with the Jewish people with Roman Catholic Catechesis. Presently residing in Manchester, she works in Jewish–Christian relations in the local area with the Jewish community and for the Catholic Diocese of Salford and is involved in retreat-giving and different forms of adult education.

Wendy Fidler MBE can't remember a time when she didn't have an interest in interfaith matters. Following a career as a scientist in the health service, she undertook a Master's degree at The Woolf Institute in Cambridge and has recently completed a PhD at Southampton. A leading figure in the Oxford Jewish community, she is involved in interfaith activities locally, nationally and internationally. She is a Trustee of CCJ and a member of its Advisory Council as well as chairing Oxford CCJ.

David F. Ford OBE is a Fellow of Selwyn College and Regius Professor of Divinity Emeritus in the University of Cambridge. He is a co-founder of the interfaith practice of Scriptural Reasoning and holds the Sternberg Foundation Gold Medal for Inter-Faith Relations and the Coventry International Prize for Peace and Reconciliation. His publications include *The Drama of Living*; *Interreligious Reading after Vatican II*; *Theology: A Very Short Introduction*; and *Christian Wisdom*. He is married to the Revd Deborah Ford and they have three children.

David Gillett now serves as Honorary Assistant Bishop and Interfaith Adviser in the Diocese of Norwich. Before that he was Bishop of Bolton, following 11 years as Principal of Trinity Theological College in Bristol, having previously been a vicar in Luton, and a leader in a reconciliation centre in Northern Ireland. He has had a long involvement and interest in interfaith relations, both academically and in local and national life. He was the first Chair of the National Christian Muslim Forum and is presently a Trustee of the Council of Christians and Jews.

Jeremy Gordon is Rabbi of New London Synagogue, the community where he grew up. He is a graduate of Cambridge University and the Jewish Theological Seminary of America. He is the author of the recently published *Spiritual Vagabondry and the Making of a Rabbi* and has been active in a number of cross-communal and interfaith endeavours. He is married and the father of three children.

Michael Hilton is Rabbi of Kol Chai Hatch End Reform Jewish Community, London. He lectures at Leo Baeck College and is an Honorary Research Fellow of the Centre for Jewish Studies, University of Manchester. His academic work explores ways in which the history of Jewish customs has been influenced by surrounding faiths and cultures, and his books include *The Christian Effect on Jewish Life* and *Bar Mitzvah: A History*.

CONTRIBUTORS

Natan Levy is the Head of Operations for Faiths Forum for London. He received his rabbinical ordination in Israel from Rabbis Brovender and Riskin in 2006. Rabbi Levy was the Environmental Liaison to the Chief Rabbi, Lord Sacks, and the co-author of *Sharing Eden: Green Teachings from Jews, Christians and Muslims*. He was formerly the Jewish University Chaplain for the West of England and Wales, and the interfaith and social action consultant to the Board of Deputies of British Jews. He holds an MA in Jewish Studies from King's College, London, and is pursuing a doctorate in environmental theology at Bristol University. He lives in London with his wife and four children.

Patrick Morrow is an Anglican priest, in parish ministry in Chelmsford Diocese and a mental health chaplain in North London. After a first degree in Theology (Durham University) he gained an MPhil in Ecumenics (Irish School of Ecumenics, Dublin) and an MA in Jewish–Christian Relations (Woolf Institute, Cambridge). As well as extensive engagement with CCJ UK, he is a member of the Theology Group of the International CCJ. He has published on the theologies of Pope Benedict XVI and Karl Rahner, and Christian attitudes to the Hebrew Scriptures and its difficult texts. He is also a writer of poems and liturgy.

Alan Race is Rector of St Margaret's Church, Lee, in South London. He has published widely in the Christian theology of religions and interfaith dialogue, including the book *Christians and Religious Pluralism* (1983), which defined a typology on Christian responses to religious pluralism and which contributed to shaping a debate on the subject for a generation. He is Chair of the World Congress of Faiths and Editor of the international journal *Interreligious Insight*. He has combined pastoral work with the theological study of interfaith dialogue for most of his ministerial career.

Stephen Roberts is Senior Lecturer in Modern Theology at the University of Chichester where he teaches Christian theology and interreligious dialogue. He is currently investigating ways in which theology and dialogue relate to wider conversations in the public sphere. An ordained Anglican, he has served in parishes in the Diocese of London, worked as a university chaplain and, prior to his current role, was Vice Principal of St Michael's College, Llandaff, the Church in Wales' theological college in Cardiff. He has been engaged in Jewish–Christian dialogue for more than 20 years, primarily through his involvement with CCJ.

Vivian Silverman was born in Liverpool but spent his teenage years in Ilford. He earned both semikhah (Rabbinic ordination) and a London University Semitics degree at Jews College. He undertook further studies at the Rav Kook Yeshivah in Jerusalem before taking up a ministerial position at Ilford Synagogue. He later served for ten years in South Africa, returning to the UK in 1987. For the last 20 years he has been Rabbi of the Hove Hebrew Congregation, actively involved with the wider Jewish community and playing a significant role in developing Jewish–Christian relations in Brighton.

Elli Tikvah Sarah is a graduate of LSE (1977) and Leo Baeck College (1989). She is Rabbi of Brighton and Hove Progressive Synagogue, Liberal Jewish Chaplain at Sussex and Brighton Universities, and a pioneer of LGBT equality within Liberal Judaism. A member of the Manor House Abrahamic Dialogue Group, she contributed to *Beyond the Dysfunctional Family: Jews, Christians and Muslims in Dialogue with Each Other and with Britain* (2012). She is co-editor with Barbara Borts of *Women Rabbis in the Pulpit: A Collection of Sermons* (2015) and author of *Trouble-Making Judaism* (2012).

Steve Williams is Co-Chair of the Manchester branch of CCJ, Secretary of Greater Manchester Faith Community Leaders, and Inter-Faith Adviser in the (Church of England's) Diocese of Manchester. These are roles he has combined since 2005, from his home, St Gabriel's Parish Church, Prestwich, where he has been priest-in-charge since 2001 – a parish whose population is 50 per cent Jewish and 10 per cent Muslim. His roots are in Liverpool, where he grew up and was ordained. For eight years, he was Religious Affairs Producer for BBC Radio Merseyside and, since 2012, has been on the rota of presenters for BBC Radio 4's *Daily Service*. He is an Honorary Canon of Manchester Cathedral.

Alexandra Wright is the Senior Rabbi of the Liberal Jewish Synagogue, St John's Wood, London. Ordained at Leo Baeck College in 1986, she has been involved in Jewish–Christian dialogue for over 30 years and is a member of the National Council of Imams and Rabbis and a founding member of Pathways, a Jewish–Christian–Muslim clergy group in Central London. Her special interests include translating some of the work of Rabbi Judah Loew ben Bezalel, the sixteenth-century mystical philosopher, and writing liturgy.

CONTRIBUTORS

Debbie Young-Somers is a Buber Fellow of Paideia, the European Centre for Jewish Studies, Rabbinic graduate of Leo Baeck College, and currently Community Educator at the Movement for Reform Judaism. She became involved in Jewish–Christian dialogue as a teenager, going on to chair the International Council of Christians and Jews Youth Council, working for the UK CCJ in Youth Dialogue, and joining the Lambeth Jewish Forum. She was responsible for interfaith activities at her first pulpit at the West London Synagogue where she established Peace by Piece, a Jewish–Muslim teen programme. She remains engaged in grass-roots and clergy dialogue.

Foreword

TONY BAYFIELD

This is a book intended for a wide readership, not least all those Christians and Jews who want to engage with each other on a level deeper than polite acknowledgement. Who are you as a Jew, as a Christian? What part does identity and faith play in your life? What exactly do you believe? Where does that leave me in your eyes?

The contributors are either specialist academics or full-time practitioners – or both. What we've endeavoured to do is maintain the highest academic standards but not clutter the pages of text with scholarly apparatus. All sources are given; the many books cited can be followed up and the Glossary consulted for clarity and further information. But nothing, we hope, stands in the way of going straight to the challenges involved in engagement at depth.

As well as an individual readership, the book is intended for use by those on religious studies and theology courses and at seminaries. It's also written with group study and discussion in mind – and to that end the Council of Christians and Jews is publishing educational materials concurrently with the publication of the book.

In editing with maximum accessibility as the priority, I've had to face up to some considerable non-theological challenges!

- As far as translations of New Testament passages are concerned, these are all taken from the Fourth Edition of the New Oxford Annotated Bible (NRSV). Passages from the Hebrew Bible, Rabbinic texts and commentaries are more denominationally sensitive and I've stayed largely with the translations provided by the contributors. I'm personally unequivocally committed to gender-inclusive language and, in particular, to avoiding the translation 'Lord' for the Tetragrammaton but, after Group discussion, have left these issues to individual discretion and theology. The biblical Hebrew is taken from the Biblia Hebraica Stuttgartensia (1990), Stuttgart: German Bible Society; Westminster Seminary.

- Transliteration of Hebrew terms has proved particularly difficult. I've opted for giving priority to preventing mispronunciation by those unencumbered by knowledge of Hebrew. In the main, I've followed the system adopted by *Encyclopaedia Judaica* but used *kh* (as in the Scottish for lo*ch*) for the Hebrew letters *khet* and *khaf*. However, I've also used just *h* for words beginning with a *khet* such as *H*asidism where *Kh*asidism would simply have looked odd. I've also often used an apostrophe where an *e* might otherwise have been pronounced *e* as in b*e*d. I fully acknowledge the inconsistencies.
- In the context of orthodox/Orthodox, liberal/Liberal and the like, we distinguish between a mode of thinking (lower case) and denomination (upper case). 'The Rabbis' and 'Rabbinic Judaism' refers to the teachers and exponents of the Judaism born at much the same time as Christianity, and this usage has been continued to cover Mishnaic, Talmudic and classical midrashic literature. The lower case – rabbinic Judaism and rabbis – is used to denote the Judaism and teachers of the last millennium, irrespective of denomination. Rabbi as title is, however, capitalized – all Rabbi Levys are Rabbi Levy regardless of their century and affiliation!

Whatever the technical issues involved, the solutions underline the wide-ranging importance of the subject matter and the intention that as many people as possible will feel empowered to engage in dialogue at depth.

A Dialogical Roadmap

TONY BAYFIELD

*Take care of your own soul and another person's body.
Not of your own body and the other person's soul.*
                                        Menachem Mendel of Kotzk[1]

This book was conceived at a meeting held in a room at the House of Lords with the then Chair of the Council of Christians and Jews (CCJ), Nigel McCulloch, Bishop of Manchester, and David Gifford, CCJ's Chief Executive. The location was chosen because of its convenience for an overworked, commuting senior cleric but it also provides a telling metaphor for formative aspects of the relationship between Christians and Jews in Britain today.

Although the presence of a handful of bishops in the House of Lords is little more than a token of the power once wielded by the Lords Spiritual in Britain, it illuminates a history of the Church which renders Christianity an ineradicable part of the landscape and soundscape of this green and pleasant land. Britain is historically, culturally[2] and numerically[3] a Christian country. That's something I, and the overwhelming majority of British Jews, accept and respect. But the meeting place said something else as well. I've never lost the sense of privilege from being invited to the House of Lords – or driving through the gateway into the forecourt of Lambeth Palace. It makes me wish my great grandparents from Holland, a remote corner of the Austro-Hungarian Empire, Poland and Russia could see me now, on first-name terms with two successive Archbishops of Canterbury! Being recognized by the gate-keeper at Lambeth fosters feelings of acceptance which do more than disclose the deferential dimension to my personal psychology. Christian–Jewish dialogue has played a significant role in making British Jews – despite continuing anti-Semitism and the Islamist threat – feel, albeit insecurely, at home in Britain.[4]

CCJ, said Bishop McCulloch, was anxious to enter the field of theology. Since its foundation in 1942, a more pressing agenda had held sway. This was the need to affirm a loving relationship with Jews, to acknowledge the role of the Church in fostering anti-Judaism, and to begin the process of reconciliation in the face of the horrifying, unfathomable news emerging from Europe. As the years and decades rolled on, the corresponding Jewish agenda had become more and more apparent – to expose the continuing connection between Christian teaching and anti-Semitism, to extract acknowledgement and repentance, to find a relationship which could be trusted to ensure 'never again'. In recent years the agenda was broadened through the leadership of Chief Rabbi Jonathan Sacks; collaboration on social policy reached previously unimagined heights. But Lord Sacks was inhibited from taking part in *theological* dialogue; he is a student of Rabbi Joseph Soloveitchik, one of America's greatest Orthodox Jewish thinkers, who was opposed to *theological* engagement.[5]

I represented – after nearly 70 years – a possible way forward. In 1973, I'd struck up a friendship with Marcus Braybrooke, about to take up the post of Executive Director of CCJ. By a quirk of fate, Marcus and I had both been undergraduates at Magdalene College, Cambridge – at that time as unlikely an *alma mater* for ground-breaking theology as one could imagine. Conscious of potential problems, the dialogue the two of us set up took place on my turf – the newly established Manor House Centre for Judaism in Finchley, North West London – where I'd been given a free programming hand (provided only that I didn't spend any money). With some good fortune and by trial and error, Marcus and I found a formula for theological dialogue. We identified a group of Jews and Christians who we were fairly sure shared the same appetite that we had for talking about issues of doctrine and belief – trying to understand what defines us and has been the cause of nearly two millennia of antagonism and worse.

We were clear the members of the group were not representatives and would be there to speak for themselves alone. Yet we had a sense that to confine membership to people denominationally and temperamentally like ourselves would be too self-indulgent. From the start, the Manor House Dialogue Group included an Orthodox rabbi as well as Reform and Liberal; the Christians included Catholics as well as Anglicans – and, at least as if not more important, women as well as men. One of our members, Richard Harries, was soon appointed Bishop of Oxford and later became Nigel McCulloch's predecessor as Chair of the Council of Christians and Jews. Alan Race, a contributor to this book, had just published *Christians and Religious Pluralism* with SCM Press,[6] whose remarkable editor and managing director, the late John Bowden, was also a member of that group.

We quickly fell into a pattern of meeting, not frequently – two full-day meetings at the Manor House and one two-day residential a year – but regularly. Attendance rates remained high with membership constant and we developed over a period of no less than ten years relationships of trust. I wasn't the only member of the group who found that, in this context, I could explore my own personal theology in a way I hadn't felt able to do with exclusively Jewish colleagues. If you'll forgive the slightly twee metaphor, I came to discover that Judaism and Christianity are adjoining gardens, shaped differently and not planted identically. By being taken on a tour of the Christian garden, I learned new things about horticulture, recognized weeds in my own garden – and was motivated to dig deeper. Dialogue is not, in my experience, threatening to one's own faith but it does have a knack of prompting self-criticism[7] and making one explore more seriously attitudes and beliefs one had simply taken for granted.

Marcus and I set up the Manor House Group *lishmah*, for its own sake, coming to realize that it didn't need a purpose beyond meeting. We'd each be changed by the experience and our changed selves would impact on our work in the wider world. But after some years, when the group seemed to be nearing its natural end, we decided on a book. *Dialogue with a Difference: The Manor House Group Experience* was published – by SCM Press, of course, and under John Bowden's supervision – in 1992.[8] Bishop McCulloch and David Gifford were aware of *Dialogue with a Difference* and said they wanted a second volume for the next ten or twenty years. I was the candidate to produce the new book.

For decades, CCJ had five Christian Presidents but only one Jewish President, the Chief Rabbi. That was a consequence, at first, of the realities of the Jewish community but later of intra-faith tensions, which will not be unfamiliar to Christians! However, Jonathan Sacks and I had been friends in our undergraduate days, maintaining our friendship through several turbulent decades. We were quietly determined to help the community travel forward in a more cohesive and collaborative way. One of the obvious places was around the CCJ Presidents' meeting table at Lambeth Palace when I became a second Jewish President. Nigel McCulloch and David Gifford thought I could take CCJ into the area of theology without embarrassing the United Synagogue.

At the time of the House of Lords meeting in 2010, I was approaching retirement as Head of the Movement for Reform Judaism and thinking seriously about the next stage of my working life – old rabbis never retire but they do go on and on! I wanted to write a systematic theology of Reform Judaism and was also toying with a concluding book on the theology of Jewish–Christian relations. Preparing for the meeting at the House of Lords, it became clear to me this book had to embody the understanding of dialogue and dialogue theology that I'd developed. Over 20 years, I'd been involved with three dialogue theology projects, all leading to books – *Dialogue with a Difference*, which contained the voices of a group of people who'd engaged in dialogue for a decade; *He Kissed Him and They Wept*,[9] the product of a dialogue between scholars from the World Union for Progressive Judaism and the Vatican; and *Beyond the Dysfunctional Family*,[10] the fruits of a Jewish–Christian–Muslim dialogue group on which I'd worked with Alan Race[11] and a courageous Muslim academic, Ataullah Siddiqui. It had taken even longer than *Dialogue with a Difference*.

It became apparent that the CCJ book needed to be written more quickly but something of the methodology had to be retained and I soon produced a proposal. When first drafting this roadmap four years later, I went back to that document and was gratified to find we'd been able to make adjustments as we went along but the original proposal had proved to be robust.

David Gifford and I assembled a 'team' of 16 – eight Christians and eight Jews. I identified eight topics which would enable us to explore key issues for the theological underpinning of Jewish–Christian relationships over the next decade. The 16 would form eight pairs and each pair would produce two papers. These, however, would not be 16 essays allocated to people writing in isolation. The papers would be written in dialogue both between their authors and between the pair and the Group. They would be open to constant revision – even when the complete text of the book, provisionally edited, was considered by the entire Group at a final residential. I have a habit of being wildly ambitious about process, only realizing how much work I've given myself when it's too late to turn back.

The 'CCJ Theology Group' bedded down at an initial residential, tweaked the topics, agreed to pairings and identified a pattern of working. We would meet three times a year, for one-day sessions, alternating between Christian and Jewish venues. At each session a pair would read the first draft of their papers. The Group would then go into detailed interrogation and discussion. The first pair would benefit from three years in which they could revise and revise – but with the disadvantage of not benefiting *ab initio* from subsequent papers and the process itself. Conversely, the last pair had to wait a long time to be heard and received less feedback than others. Nothing is perfect.

We soon realized that Professor David Ford brought something special as a founder and pioneer of Scriptural Reasoning. His essay partner, Rabbi Alex Wright, was gripped by his methodology from the beginning and a session of Scriptural Reasoning was built into the programme for each day, proving to be of incomparable help in developing openness and interaction within the Group. Studying together, we learned, is a *sine qua non* of true dialogue.

From the outset my role was to chair the Group and edit the book. Beyond that, we were uncertain but the process soon provided clarity. Previous experience had taught me that dialogue doesn't work if people give papers surveying Christian or Jewish teachings on a particular subject. First, Christianity says/Judaism says is a fundamentally flawed concept – there is no such thing as one Christianity[12] or one Judaism historically or geographically. Second, survey papers are deadly dull. What is essential to dialogue theology is the personal: this is what *I* believe (or question). None of the contributors to this book are spokespeople; it is what each brings personally that's decisive. My task has therefore been to offer a setting for the individual contributions, place the arguments in the context of recent dialogue in Britain and America and highlight areas for further debate and discussion – 'further reflections'.

The Group began its work with a residential in 2011; it signed the work off at a residential in June 2015. That meeting was, for me in particular, extremely exciting. All the people round the table felt they had been participants in an innovative experience. The process had enabled them to encounter the other at depth and engage in transforming conversations. In discussing possible titles for this book, one participant sought to reflect the depth of the Group's theological engagement with the words of Psalm 42: 'deep calls to deep'.[13] Others added that crucial notion of 'transforming conversations'. All agreed that genuine theological dialogue is a dynamic, face-to-face process but one that can yield outcomes communicable in a book.

From the beginning – the first draft of the first pair of essays – we demanded of each other thinking with a sound academic basis but not encrusted with inaccessible academic niceties or excessive caution. We also realized that wherever this book is used collectively – in churches, synagogues, CCJ branches, theological colleges, university departments and interfaith courses – it would be enhanced by dedicated educational materials. These will appear concurrently with the publication of this book to make both the ideas and methodology as widely accessible as possible.

Let me now introduce the eight pairs of essays, which, each with a 'further reflection', become eight chapters. But, first, a brief preface to them all.

The 300 years between the Maccabean Revolt against Greek rule and the expulsion by the Roman emperor Hadrian are truly formative for all the descendants of Abraham and Sarah.[14] The Land or Holy Land witnessed unprecedented upheaval – not just physical but political, ideological and religious. Of the many groups who formed in that period, only two have survived.

Rabbinic Judaism emerged from the 'party' of the Scribes and Pharisees. Its unparalleled achievement was to transform the pillars on which biblical Judaism rested. The Temple, a special building in a special place, gave way to the synagogue[15] and the priests to lay teachers called rabbis.[16] The Temple rites were replaced by daily prayer services, and a portable Judaism – Rabbinic Judaism – enabled Jews to live Jewish lives though they'd been expelled from the Land.[17]

Christianity emerged from the same biblical Judaism and milieu but with a radically different focus. It sought to respond to the revelation discerned in the Jew Jesus Christ and came to understand that his teachings and values were for all humanity.[18] For some time both dimensions of biblical Judaism lived together and the parting of the ways[19] was more gradual and uneven than once was thought.

1 The Third Dialogue Partner: How Do We Experience Modern Western Culture? Rabbi Elli Tikvah Sarah and the Revd Dr Stephen Roberts

Despite their separation, Jews and Christians continued to live side by side. But the context was empire – Roman, Holy Roman, Christendom – which dealt in categories and classes with differential power structures, making the group dominant over the individual.[20] There was interaction with, as Michael Hilton rightly insists, periods in which social relationships were formed and during which Christianity influenced Judaism as well as the other way round.[21] The eleventh and twelfth centuries in Europe reveal considerable theological, socio-economic and political contact when Jews – to quote the Cambridge historian Anna Sapir Abulafia – played a significant part 'in the service of Medieval Christendom'.[22] But the following century, characterized by the legislation of the 1215 Lateran Council, ushered in five centuries during which exclusion and isolation predominated.

When Jews began to emerge from the ghettos of Western Europe and, later, *shtetlach* of Eastern Europe, they entered the modern western world – an evolving environment to which Judaism, Christianity and Islam, as well as Greece and Rome, had all made considerable contributions. Interaction increased but not always in a way comfortable for Jews and Judaism. Jews found integrating as distinctive equals elusive almost to the point of mirage and Judaism learnt about warring denominations from Christianity. That world then imploded, precipitating a paradigm shift[23] as a result of the traumas of the twentieth century – not the least the 20 desperate years from the election of Hitler to the death of Stalin.

In Britain, in this postmodern world, Jews and Christians live side by side as never before. We are born and brought up within it. We inhabit the same environment, are immersed in the same culture. We live, breathe, study, work and die together. Twenty-five years ago, Rabbi Norman Solomon – Orthodox Rabbi and longstanding participant in the work of CCJ – observed that when Christians and Jews meet and talk, they do so in the presence of a third dialogue partner: (post-)modern western culture.

When Jacob and Esau were reconciled, Genesis tells us that Esau kissed Jacob and they wept.[24] But they then went their separate ways,[25] which isn't possible for us: the world is utterly changed. We share the terrain and are immersed in the same cultural environment with its daunting challenges but – and this is not always acknowledged – with opportunities at least as great.

'What do you make of the modern or postmodern world?' we asked Elli Sarah and Stephen Roberts. What's it like? What are the implications for Judaism and Christianity? Elli – the more recently liberated – is exhilarated and surfs the waves. Stephen is part of a tradition that has known the modern western world since its sixteenth-century beginnings and seen the process of evolution from the inside. The Canadian Catholic author of *A Secular Age*, Charles Taylor, shows just how intimately Christianity is involved with the seemingly irresistible emergence of a competing ideology: secularity.[26] Jewish and Christian responses to modernity have much in common but are also, like the traditions themselves, separate and distinctive.

2 How Should Christians and Jews Live in a Modern Western Democracy? The Revd Canon Steve Williams and Rabbi Jeremy Gordon

The second chapter confronts issues of power. Christianity in Britain today lives with a legacy of relatively recent disempowerment. For the last 370 years, since the Peace of Westphalia, the power of the Church within the State has gradually been pushed back to the point today where only historic vestiges remain. Judaism, however, comes from a very different experience. The American historian of Jewish secularity, David Biale, in *Power and Powerlessness in Jewish History*, examines the strategies Jewish communities adopted to manage their precarious situation as unenfranchised minorities in countries the world over.[27] Biale's portrait underplays the extent of the periods of disastrous impotence but the conclusion he offers is nevertheless profound:

In this dialectic between power and vulnerability, the long history of the Jews may unexpectedly serve as a beacon to the nations. From Biblical times to the present day, the Jews have wandered the uncertain terrain between power and powerlessness, never quite achieving the power necessary to guarantee long-term security, but equally avoiding, with a number of disastrous exceptions, the abyss of absolute impotence. They developed the consummate political art of living with uncertainty and insecurity; their long survival owes much to this extraordinary achievement. Jews today must struggle to come to terms with this history in the light of their present power, to see both past and present through a realistic lens, neither inflating their power nor exaggerating their powerlessness. The lessons this history can teach are necessary for their own continued existence and are equally relevant to the continued existence of mankind.[28]

Isn't it revealing that a major American Jewish commentator, living in a longstanding liberal democracy, sees all minorities in that precarious light? Nevertheless, very different histories are visible in the ways in which Christians and Jews respond to democracy in Britain today.

Another American academic, Ivan Strenski, is particularly enlightening in the distinction he draws between *potestas* and *auctoritas*.[29] Although the late fifth-century Pope Gelasius 1 tried to separate the roles of the Holy Roman Empire and the Church, the two became fused. This allowed Christianity to play a major part in the governance and development of society but it could also be coercive and corrupting. *Auctoritas* describes 'a non-coercive power that works by way of mutuality, recognition [and] acceptance'.[30] Steve Williams is the Christian who turns away from the tradition of *potestas* and finds Christian *auctoritas* in working on the margins of society with the disempowered and dispossessed. But even if deeds speak more eloquently than words, how does Christianity articulate its values in the public square[31] and play the role one would expect of Britain's major religious influence and tradition in a modern democratic society?

Jeremy Gordon, rooted in the Jewish community, comes with very different memories and experiences. Still today, the leadership of British Jewry negotiates directly with government in order to secure the position of a small and vulnerable minority. But Jeremy's dominant question is far larger. Jews have lived through the unravelling of democracy, its subversion by the demos, the people who established it and its descent into ochlocracy, mob rule. Who is to say that it cannot and will not happen again? And what is the relationship between the secular majority and religious minorities in a mature and sophisticated democracy? What space is there for us 'to do our own thing' – within our own families and communities or among the poor, the widow, the orphan and the stranger?

3 How Do We Cope with Our Past? Rabbi Dr Michael Hilton and the Rt Revd David Gillett

Let's return to the challenging beginning of our narrative. Rabbinic Judaism and Christianity emerged at the same time from the same place – Roman-occupied Judea. From the earliest stage there was mutual suspicion and rivalry. Our shared history has been scarred from the beginning. There were, undoubtedly, periods and places where ordinary Christians and Jews were able to live in harmony. Michael Hilton is among the pioneers in demonstrating that Christianity influenced Judaism in a productive way. However, the history of the relationship makes grim but unavoidable reading.

A Christian friend, at the vanguard of reconciliation, once expressed his extreme frustration: 'Jews hold me responsible for everything that's happened to them in the past. Now, along come the Muslims and make the same accusation.' It's tough being a Christian[32] because the past clings even to the most open and reflective. The early twentieth-century historian Salo Baron – an American Jew born in Galicia[33] – is famed for rejecting the 'lachrymose' account of Jewish history. Yet today, Simon Schama's second volume of *The Story of the Jews*[34] is delayed as Schama struggles with even more tears than he'd first imagined. Jewish history – so much of it spent as a precarious minority in Christian and Muslim lands – suggests that belief in conciliation and collaboration represents the triumph of hope over experience. But, as the late Rabbi Hugo Gryn's father said to him in Lieberose Concentration Camp: 'You and I have seen that it is possible to live for up to three weeks without food. We once lived almost three days without water; but you cannot live properly for three minutes without hope.'

It's a very painful experience for sensitive and honest Christians to confront the history of Christian–Jewish relationships over the last thousand years – even in Britain. It's one of the reasons why David Gillett's essay is so outstanding. Patiently, unflinchingly, he probes the blood-libel of William of Norwich, uncovering not only anti-Semitism but wider failings which challenge the very integrity of Christianity in one of its ancient, glorious cathedrals. Jews have to resist impatience at how long the task is taking and avoid cynicism. Full acknowledgement by Christians of their part in our calamitous history demands patience from us – and something else as well. We Jews have endured so much pain, so much prejudice, so many slurs – still a feature of contemporary life even in tolerant, democratic Britain. Can we respond appropriately to those courageous Christian leaders who won't stop digging in their own backyards until what lies beneath the surface has been revealed, identified and acknowledged for what it is? It's hard to let go of anger, suspicion and fear, but friendship and collaboration – demonstrated by the imaginative way in which their task is conducted and accomplished – between a bishop and a rabbi are exemplary, moving and encouraging.

4 The Legacy of Our Scriptures. Rabbi Alexandra Wright and Professor David F. Ford

Our starting point is an American Jewish academic, graduate of Yale and the Jewish Theological Seminary, Peter Ochs. He was one of a handful of American scholars who started what has become known as Scriptural Reasoning – Jews, Christians, Muslims and others reading their sacred Scriptures together and exploring the meanings that each other finds. The society for Scriptural Reasoning was founded by Peter Ochs, David Ford and David's father-in-law, the late Daniel Hardy. Ochs is doubly interesting. A disciple of the American pragmatist philosopher Charles Peirce,[35] he finds a way forward for dialogue which bypasses the problems raised by historical criticism and the obstacles it creates for many Orthodox Jews, Christians and Muslims.

Ochs also identified a new school in Christian thought, termed 'post-liberalism', in which he hails David Ford as a pioneer. It is telling that, as a result of dialogue, an important Jewish scholar should write a book on Christian theology[36] in which he clearly finds points of similarity with his own theological position. As mentioned earlier,[37] David and Alex enabled Jews from four denominations to study Torah and New Testament together in a way seldom witnessed before in this country. Their two essays also make use of Scriptural Reasoning and are equally important in opening up dialogue through reading the Scriptures of the other, discovering the meanings that the texts hold for our respective dialogue partners.

A second enabling figure is Mary C. Boys – Professor of Practical Theology at Union Theological Seminary in New York – pivotal to Sister Teresa Brittain's essay in the final chapter of this book. Professor Boys is a contributor to a remarkable publication, *Christ Jesus and the Jewish People Today*.[38] The book carries a Preface by Walter Cardinal Kasper, former President of the Pontifical Council for Promoting Christian Unity and of the Pontifical Commission for Religious Relations with the Jews at the Vatican – yet Mary Boys is still permitted to ask pointed questions of her own Catholic Church about crucifixion by the Romans and the shift in blame to the Jews displayed by the Gospels.[39] Reading together doesn't preclude critiquing together. Doors are being opened on both sides of the Atlantic, making it possible for Christians and Jews to walk through together.

5 Religious Absolutism. The Revd Dr Alan Race and Rabbi Debbie Young-Somers

The book which, more than any other, provided a framework for my thinking about Judaism and Christianity is *Rebecca's Children* by the American historian Alan Segal.[40] Segal's starting point is the text in Genesis which describes Esau and Jacob struggling for supremacy even in their mother's womb. Rabbinic commentators had long seen Jacob as the Jew and Esau as the Gentile. What Segal did was to equate the two with Rabbinic Judaism and Christianity. They were not mother and daughter but siblings. That changes everything. Not the least by making the Hebrew Scriptures a *shared* inheritance – a huge challenge to the traditional Jewish sense both of exclusive ownership and of being the senior faith.

But the metaphor has its limits. Though born in the same place and at the same time, Judaism and Christianity are not identical twins. To think in such terms is to reinforce a painful and costly misunderstanding – that the two should be the same and any departure from the norm represented by 'us' is a deviation by the 'other': in so far as you conform to me you are as you should be and in so far as you differ you've gone wrong. No one understands that better than Alan Race. Judaism and Christianity are not identical twins but siblings – related but sometimes very different, as is the case with children, particularly if they've been brought up for much of their lives in different circumstances. Even more importantly, Alan understands how claims to be the best or the one in the right are not just unnecessary but a barrier to a reconciliation between equals. Absolutism, Alan argues, is the root of religious violence, not least the historic religious violence visited by Christians on Jews for more than a millennium.

Debbie Young-Somers agrees and her approach underlines just how different the two siblings are. It has been said that, even in 'religious America', rates of atheism are higher among Jews than any other group. The events of the hundred years from 1914 have shaken Jews and Judaism to the foundations; we live in a world of fragments, repairing and constructing anew as best we can. So Rabbi Young-Somers brings, first and foremost, herself and her own personal experience to the table. There's a strong inference that, whether we like it, admit it or not, that's true for all of us. In Debbie's essay, we come closer than anywhere else in this book to the exposure of personal faith. One day, a successor group to ours will have the trust and space to explore our individual and collective relationships to the One God. The rewards could be revelatory.

6 What Does Respect between People of Faith Mean? Dr Wendy Fidler and Dr Joy Barrow

Wendy Fidler says that her first reaction to being allocated 'respect' was that she and Joy had been 'let off lightly'. She goes on to discover this not to be true – and it may be that this is an area where we got the sequence wrong. Perhaps 'respect' should have come before rather than after a consideration of religious absolutism. But no matter: what Wendy Fidler and Joy Barrow achieve, from different starting points and in different ways, is highly significant.

My earliest experiences of dialogue taught me that, however warm, friendly and genuine the encounter, the spoken was often accompanied by the unpalatable and therefore unarticulated: 'There are many things to admire in Judaism that have been lost from Christianity – it's such a pity that you're missing out on the Greatest Truth of all.' 'Christians have given so much of value to society and continue to do so – what a pity it's all founded on a mistaken understanding of an unremarkable Jew.' It seemed to me then, and I'm even more convinced now, that the reservations – unspoken or not – are incompatible with respect. The outcome may be polite, courteous, well-meaning, but it's not respectful. For me, the reservations are also incompatible with the existential reality of the life and faith of many whom we encounter, particularly in dialogue.

For Wendy and Joy, respect comes before anything else and doctrine dissolves in the face of that imperative. It means regarding the honour of the other with the same weight as one's own, giving priority to sensitivity and standing in the shoes of the other over pressing one's own agenda.[41] Wendy and Joy enlarge on an exchange I came across some years ago:

> Do you love me?
> Yes.
> Do you know what causes me pain?
> No.
> Then you don't love me.

Or, I would add, respect me.

Absolutism, denying the other even privately to oneself, is completely incompatible with respect. Wendy makes this point in the context of the Jewish–Christian relationship; Joy takes a wider perspective. Do they both run the risk of a feeble relativism which is clearly not part of the thinking of the Group, even those who would identify themselves as liberals? Not at all. Faith must always be tested by ethics; God never commands us to behave unethically towards our fellow human beings whatever their faith or none – or accept their unethical behaviour. Respect means respect for both body and soul but it doesn't require us to respect unethical teachings and deeds – within any tradition including our own.

7 Christian Particularity. The Revd Patrick Morrow, Rabbi Vivian Silverman, Rabbi Natan Levy, Rabbi Dr Michael Hilton and Victor Seedman

Here, more than anywhere else, we began to struggle. This is immediately apparent from the trinity of Jewish respondents in place of the expected one. At first we couldn't understand quite why we were thrashing about to so little effect. Yet it is, with hindsight, obvious. To engage with Christian particularism is to encounter the otherness of the other, their distinctiveness, the ways in which our sibling is different from us.

I once had a long conversation with a government minister responsible for community relations. He presented me with his department's new mission statement about finding common values, using shared bricks to build a home together. I suggested it was a noble vision but distinctiveness was at least as important. The differences prompt self-examination, exploration of what has been taken for granted in one's own faith and lead to growth. It turned out to be a rewarding challenge because the minister responded with a helpful analogy – that of choral music, his non-political passion. The true joy and beauty, he said, comes not from singing in unison but from the harmonies emerging from the alignment of the different parts. I didn't add then, as I do now, that one must, however, be prepared for a considerable amount of discord which is more conducive to change and growth even than the carefully arranged harmonies.

Patrick Morrow brings something which is, at least on the surface, very different from the approach to dialogue so familiar to me as a dyed-in-the-wool dialogical liberal. He offers an orthodox (Anglican) voice but one familiar with dialogue and sensitive to the needs of his closest sibling. What is so illuminating is that it is neither absolutist nor disrespectful but, rather, a courageous attempt to explore Christian particularism using language he knows from experience will be accessible at least to some Jews. Equally illuminating was how difficult his approach was for many of the other Christians in the Group. I've never been more aware of the variety of Christian interpretations and the fuzziness surrounding use of the term 'metaphor' than when the Group discussed the final draft of Patrick's paper!

Rabbi Vivian Silverman brought to the Group a lifetime of patient and tolerant experience. An orthodox believer, like Patrick Morrow, he's committed to friendship and collaboration. For three years Vivian listened attentively but, in the end, acknowledged there was still a great deal with which he couldn't engage. The practice of dialogue is very dear to him; the theology of dialogue remained unfamiliar and impenetrable. He sees Patrick as, perhaps, Jacob saw Esau – his brother, but who, in many respects, has been rendered a stranger by decades of living apart and seeing the world differently. We needed to explore whether different responses to distinctive Christian beliefs were possible and two other members of the Group were volunteered to try – Orthodox Rabbi Natan Levy and Reform Rabbi Michael Hilton.

Natan draws on different experiences of encounter and learning from Vivian, not the least that gained through his work at the coalface of the Jewish–Christian relationship with the Board of Deputies of British Jews. He offers a response – the imperative of engagement – which is profoundly encouraging.

Michael Hilton chose to team up with Victor Seedman, an academic steeped in the theology of Jewish–Christian dialogue. Together they provide familiarity with Patrick's conceptual language and historical reading. They shift the focus from the challenge of certain doctrines to a crucial underlying difference – doctrine is of greater importance to Christianity than Judaism. The particularity, the otherness of the other, is what challenges us most – as we were to find out again when playing the reverse rubber.

8 Jewish Particularism. Rabbi Natan Levy and Sister Teresa Brittain

The Council of Christians and Jews was founded in 1942, just as news of the extent of the European catastrophe was beginning to emerge. It was both right and inevitable that anti-Judaism and anti-Semitism would dominate the agenda of CCJ for decades. I first drafted this passage only days after the horrific terrorist attack in Paris took the form not just of an attack on a satirical magazine but also on a kosher grocery. On 10 January 2015, *The Times* published a disturbing article by experienced journalist Roger Boyes reflecting on the persistence of anti-Semitism in France:

> Paris is arguably Europe's capital of antisemitism. There are antisemitic political parties in the parliaments of Greece and Hungary but there is something very unfiltered about French establishment attitudes to Jews and something uncontrolled about the fierce hostility of French based Arab immigrants ... There is nothing unique to France about this, but it seems more pervasive there.[42]

Whether or not Boyes is correct in singling out France, there is no doubting the appalling and disturbing persistence of anti-Semitism – even in 2017 America.

No one with any experience of Christian–Jewish dialogue could fail to acknowledge the truth of Sister Teresa Brittain's observation that, whatever the topic and objective of a meeting organized by CCJ today here in Britain, most Christians present want to talk about Israel.[43] However much this feeds Jewish insecurity still further, one suspects that neither the horrors of Paris themselves nor the *Times* article will make any difference to that phenomenon. Why?

Why is Israel the almost obsessive concern of so many 'rank and file' Christians? To what extent does it relate to the observation with which I began the previous section of this roadmap – that it is the difference, the distinctiveness, the particularity of our sibling that we find so difficult to deal with? Working on interfaith matters for the Board of Deputies of British Jews, Rabbi Natan Levy has much experience of the Israel issue. What he offers in response is very different from standard Jewish apologetics. The pragmatic, moral, historical and legal rights to the Land – or part of it – are taken as read. Rabbi Levy addresses the *theological* issue head-on, using the traditional rabbinic technique of close and creative reading of the text of the Torah, deploying commentaries from classical sources and also from the Lithuanian-born French philosopher Emmanuel Levinas.[44] There's no flinching from confronting the issues and he gives a profound response, both theological and ethical. Israel as Land is of the essence of Jewish particularity.

Sister Teresa responds in exactly the way that a highly charged and painful situation demands. The utter transformation of the role of the Sisters of Sion – from praying and talking about Jews to walking alongside us – becomes a metaphor for the radical response needed from Christianity if the stubborn refusal to accept Jewish otherness is finally to be vanquished. Let us – Christians and Jews – walk side by side in the Land, exploring the meanings of our holy places together, Sister Teresa tells us. We must leave old securities behind and resume an even older, but, hopefully, familiar journey towards we know not quite where.[45] It is the best possible note on which to end this book.

Notes

1 Hasidic Rebbe (1787–1859), Poland.

2 Think of the rhythm of the calendar or where people, though not regarding themselves as 'practising Christians', turn to mark life-cycle events.

3 There are between 270,000 and 300,000 Jews in Britain. According to the 2012 Census the number of Christians is 33.2 million. We must never lose sight of this disparity as a major physical and psychological factor in dialogue between the two faiths.

4 An important distinction: the overwhelming majority of British Jews feel at home in Britain. But that doesn't mean they feel secure. Anti-Semitism persists, though not at levels some suggest; history magnifies the insecurity. The Brexit vote shocked many within the Jewish community: how far have we actually come? What still lies beneath the surface, threatening not just us but our vision for secular, collaborative, democratic societies which respect each person and community as multifaceted, equally valued participants?

5 Jonathan Sacks, 'Perspectives', *L'Eylah* 21, Pesach 5746, p. 47.

6 Alan Race, 1983, *Christians and Religious Pluralism: Patterns in the Christian Theology of Religions*, London: SCM Press.

7 Among the many things John Bowden taught me was the importance of self-criticism in religious thinking.

8 Tony Bayfield and Marcus Braybrooke (eds.), 1992, *Dialogue with a Difference: The Manor House Group Experience*, London: SCM Press.

9 Tony Bayfield, Sidney Brichto and Eugene Fisher (eds.), 2001, *He Kissed Him and They Wept: Towards a Theology of Jewish Catholic Partnership*, London: SCM Press.

10 Tony Bayfield, Alan Race and Ataullah Siddiqui (eds.), 2012, *Beyond the Dysfunctional Family: Jews, Christians and Muslims in Dialogue with Each Other and with Britain*, London: The Manor House.

11 See List of Contributors, p. xv.

12 See John Bowden, 1988, *Jesus: The Unanswered Questions*, London: SCM Press.

13 Psalm 42.8.

14 *Infra* p. 22.

15 Although the synagogue may well go back to the time of the Babylonian exile, it was transformed into a place of meeting, worship and – above all – study.

16 Those who merited the title rabbi (my master) explored the text of the Torah and derived, through interpretation, practices and religious insights suited to a very different society from that to which the Torah was addressed. They were intellectuals, teachers who interrogated Torah, debating their conclusions in the synagogue – and, being Jewish, often disagreeing!

17 *Infra* p. 00.

18 It is in no way to decry Christianity's universal message to point to the book of Jonah, written many centuries earlier, in which the reluctant Jonah is sent by the

God of all humanity to bring a message of repentance to Israel's arch enemy and persecutor, Nineveh, capital of the Assyrian Empire.

19 James J. D. Dunn, 1991, *The Partings of the Ways: Between Christianity and Judaism and Their Significance for the Character of Christianity*, London: SCM Press. The plural, partings, highlights the complexity and relative gradualness.

20 See, for instance, Friedrich Heer, 1962, *The Medieval World*, London: Weidenfeld and Nicolson.

21 Michael Hilton, 1994, *Christian Effect on Jewish Life*, London: SCM Press.

22 Anna Sapir Abulafia, 2011, *Christian–Jewish Relations 1000–1300: Jews in the Service of Medieval Christendom*, Harlow: Pearson Education.

23 The term originates with the American Jewish philosopher Thomas Kuhn who defined it as change both inherent in the old yet totally new.

24 Genesis 33.4. But note that in the vocalized Hebrew text, dots have been placed over the word for kiss, indicating that kiss can also be read as bite.

25 Genesis 33.7.

26 Charles Taylor, 2007, *A Secular Age*, Cambridge, MA: The Belknap Press.

27 David Biale, 1986, *Power and Powerlessness in Jewish History*, New York: Schocken Books.

28 Biale, *Power and Powerlessness*, p. 210.

29 Ivan Strenski, 2010, *Why Politics Can't Be Freed from Religion*, Malden, MA: Wiley-Blackwell.

30 Strenski, *Why Politics Can't Be Freed*, p. 97.

31 Public square, as distinct from public sphere, refers to those places in a democracy where issues of public policy are discussed and debated.

32 A Yiddish song declares: 'Shwer Tsu Ziayn A Yid', it's hard to be a Jew.

33 Galicia, the most north-easterly province of the Austro-Hungarian Empire, now split between Poland and the Ukraine.

34 Simon Schama, 2013, *The Story of the Jews: Finding the Words, 1000BCE–1492CE*, London: Bodley Head, vol. I.

35 Peter Ochs, 1998, *Peirce, Pragmatism and the Logic of Scripture*, Cambridge: Cambridge University Press.

36 Peter Ochs, 2011, *Another Reformation: Postliberal Christianity and the Jews*, Grand Rapids, MI: Baker Academic.

37 *Supra* p. 4.

38 Philip A. Cunningham *et al.* (eds.), 2011, *Christ Jesus and the Jewish People Today: New Explorations of Theological Interrelationships*, Grand Rapids, MI: Eerdmans.

39 Cunningham *et al.* (eds.), *Christ Jesus*, pp. 59f.

40 Alan F. Segal, 1986, *Rebecca's Children: Judaism and Christianity in the Roman World*, Cambridge, MA: Harvard University Press.

41 Joy writes about Pakistani Christians within a Methodist church and leaving them out of the church's dialogue with Muslims because their experience of persecution is so raw. That's both kind and respectful.

42 Roger Boys, *The Times*, 10 January 2015, p. 6.

43 *Infra* p. 308.

44 Born 1906, Kovno (present day Kaunas), Lithuania, died 1995, Paris, France.

45 Genesis 12.1.

I

The Third Dialogue Partner: How Do We Experience Modern Western Culture?

Liberating Individuals and Challenging Communities

ELLI TIKVAH SARAH

Before exploring how we experience modern western culture, a little unravelling is in order. What do the words, 'modern western culture' connote? From a historical perspective, 'modern western culture' developed over the course of the nineteenth century following the French Revolution of 1789. With the demise of feudal societies, a new social compact emerged in Western Europe, rooted in the new values of *liberté, egalité* and *fraternité* and framed by the spirit of rational enquiry that had marked the dawn of the Enlightenment a century earlier.

However, that is not the end of the matter. In an important sense, 'modern western culture' describes a specific epoch in European history that was eclipsed by the horrifying, destructive events of the first half of the twentieth century. Those events – principally the First World War and the Shoah – defied 'reason' and, also, modernity's optimistic assumptions concerning human progress. So, arguably, the inhabitants of Western Europe have lived since that time in a postmodern world, characterized by an eclectic array of ideas and ways of life – by multiplicity, diversity, subjectivity and relativity. But postmodernity, by definition, is not absolute. Modernity survives as a dimension of contemporary existence. When we use the word 'modern' today, we mean, simply, contemporary living and thinking by contrast to the 'old'.

So, how do Jews experience the modern world? In order to address this question, I would like to unpack some assumptions about 'Judaism' and 'Jews' by examining these two words.

Judaism and Jews

What is Judaism? The great twelfth-century Jewish philosopher and codifier Moses Maimonides[1] argued that it was only possible to speak about God in negative terms – by articulating what God is *not*.[2] In some senses the same can be said of 'Judaism'. Judaism is not a faith; it is not a religion – it is not even 'Judaism'.

I will return to the issue of Judaism not being a faith or a religion. But, first, the word 'Judaism' itself. The term is a misnomer. It is, at the very least, misleading; a made-up word, with its roots in two related Hebrew words, *Y'hudah* – Judah and *Y'hudi* – Jew. *Y'hudah* was the fourth son of Leah and Jacob. We read in Genesis 29.35 that when Leah conceived and bore a fourth son in succession, she said: 'This time I will praise (*odeh*) the Eternal. Therefore she called his name *Y'hudah* ...'[3]

Subsequently, when the descendants of the sons of Jacob became the 12 tribes of Israel, Judah became a tribe. Later, after the majority of the tribes occupied the land to the west of the Jordan (*c.* 1250 BCE), Judah denoted an area of land. Later Solomon's kingdom was divided, following his death (*c.* 930 BCE), between his son Rehoboam and Jeroboam, the son of one of Solomon's officials. The latter led a revolt against him and became king of the new Northern Kingdom of Israel. After Israel was destroyed by the Assyrians, *c.* 722 BCE, Judah, with its centre in Jerusalem, remained until it was overrun by the Babylonians in 586 BCE. But Judah was not destroyed completely. When the Persians defeated the Babylonians, King Cyrus allowed the exiles to return (*c.* 538 BCE) although many chose not to. Later, when the Greeks held sway following the conquest of Alexander the Great (*c.* 333 BCE), Judah became known as Judea. And the name was retained during the brief period of independence following the Maccabean Revolt (*c.* 140 BCE). So: Judah designates a son, a tribe, a land.

What of the word, *Y'hudi*, Jew? The plural, *Y'hudim*, is found in 2 Kings 16.5–6, where it is recounted that during the reign of King Ahaz of Judah: 'King Rezin of Aram and King Pekah son of Remaliah of Israel advanced on Jerusalem for battle. At that time King Rezin of Aram recovered Eilat for Aram; he drove out the *Y'hudim* from Eilat ...' It is clear from this reference that the term *Y'hudim* refers to the people of Judah. In Jeremiah 34.8–9 we find the earliest singular usage of the word *Yehudi*, 'Jew' – but, then again, it is clear from the context that the reference is to individual residents of Judah:

> The word came to Jeremiah from the Eternal after King Zedekiah had made a covenant with all the people in Jerusalem to proclaim liberty for them – that everyone should set free his Hebrew slaves, both male and female, and that no one should keep his fellow Judean enslaved – *l'vilti avod-bam bihudi akhihu ish.*[4]

It is not until much later, in the first century CE, that the word 'Judaism' emerges. For example, in 2 Maccabees 2.21 we read concerning the purification of the Temple and the rededication of the altar following the war against Antiochus Epiphanes, of 'the celestial manifestations that came to hearten the brave champions of Judaism'. However, since 2 Maccabees was originally written in Greek, it is not possible to cite this text as the first example of a word approximating to 'Judaism' appearing in Hebrew. In fact, the Hebrew equivalent, *Yahadut*, is very rarely found in Jewish sources. It does not appear in the Hebrew Bible; there is no mention of the word in Rabbinic literature. Louis Jacobs writes: 'It is a truism that Judaism is centred around the Jewish people. This is expressed in the very names for the religion: Judaism derived from the Greek, and *torat yisrael* or *dat yisrael* in Hebrew.'[5]

Judah Maccabee and his fellow freedom fighters fought to restore the practice of the teachings of the Torah – *torat yisrael*. That is what is meant by 'Judaism' in 2 Maccabees 2.21. They did this by engaging in a struggle which involved recapturing the Temple desecrated by the Seleucid Greeks and, eventually, regaining national independence for the *Y'hudim* – the people of the kingdom of Judah.

So, Judaism: the teachings and practice of the Torah by the people of Judah. But this is not a very satisfactory definition for understanding what is meant by Judaism in the context of a modern western society. The kingdom of Judah has not existed since the Romans conquered the region in *c*. 65 BCE. When we speak about 'Judaism' we are talking about a living phenomenon. And that is precisely the point: 'Judaism' has changed over time.

To review the major transformations:

Leviticus describes teachings and practices during the Second Temple period when 'Judaism', for want of a better word, took the form of a system of sacrificial worship conducted by a hereditary priesthood.

After the Temple was destroyed by the Romans in 70 CE, the Rabbis, the teachers who first emerged in the form of 'scribes' during the period of the Babylonian exile, reinvented 'Judaism'. Drawing on the teachings of the Torah, the Rabbis formulated an entirely new way of putting the Torah into practice, centred on the home and the synagogue, and on the individual's responsibility for keeping the *mitzvot* – the commandments – originally outlined in the Torah, which the Rabbis interpreted and made practicable in the context of daily life. It is possible to describe what the Rabbis created as 'Judaism', although they didn't use this word. Rather, the Rabbis spoke of the halakhah – based on the Hebrew root, *heh-lamed-kaf*, 'to go' or 'to walk' – which in the Aramaic form used in the Talmud, *hilkhata*, came to mean 'law'. So, in this context, 'Judaism' was about following the law, set out in the Torah and expounded by the Rabbis. Judaism became a way of life, not a 'faith' or a 'religion'.

But this is not the whole story. For the Rabbis, formulating a way of life was not confined to establishing law. While the halakhah satisfied the need to ensure and regulate Jewish practice, the sages were also engaged through exegetical methods including the telling of stories and parables – aggadah – with exploring the ethical and theological dimensions of Jewish existence. Over time, halakhah came to dominate aggadah, leading to a distortion of the Rabbinic enterprise. Modernity challenges both: as individuals are empowered to work out their own relationship with Jewish life and teaching, they generate aggadah that reflects their concerns with meaning-making in the here and now, and also engage with halakhah in the context of their own lives. The result is a continually creative aggadah and a halakhah that returns to the root, a framework for 'going' along the way, rather than a means of asserting communal control.

Judaism, Jews and change

This understanding of Judaism as a way of life held sway in all the lands where the descendants of the people of Judah – the Jews – lived for 1,800 years. At the same time, while the Rabbis created a framework for Jewish living in *every* place, Jewish practice also *varied* from place to place depending on the cultural context in which different Jewish communities lived. At the Festival of Pesach (Passover), while the Torah and subsequent halakhah is absolute about the removal of *hametz* (leaven), Sephardi Jews continue to eat rice, a staple food in Mediterranean Middle Eastern countries, while for Ashkenazi Jews, living in Northern and Eastern Europe, the *minhag* (custom) is for rice not to be eaten because it belongs to a class of foods known as *kitniyyot*, 'legumes', excluded because of the swelling properties that make them similar to *hametz*.[6]

As we can see, 'Judaism' is not a monolithic, static, unchanging entity. To explore how we experience modern culture it is essential to acknowledge that Judaism has responded to modern culture in different ways, depending on the particular circumstances of different Jewish communities, and that societal change has prompted new and varying Jewish responses. If we take the French Revolution of 1789 as a watershed, it is possible to discern three principal Jewish responses – none of which existed before the dawn of modernity: Progressive Judaism (encompassing Liberal and Reform varieties);[7] Conservative Judaism; and Orthodox Judaism (an umbrella term encompassing differing approaches from the modern stance of Samson Raphael Hirsch through ultra-orthodox forms of expression).[8] Broadly speaking, Progressive Judaism responded positively, both to enlightenment and to political emancipation, embracing democratic values and the empowerment of the individual. Meanwhile, Conservative and modern Orthodox Judaism, which both developed in Germany in the 1850s as a reaction to the more liberal religious positions taken by Progressive Judaism, endorsed a form of Jewish life whereby an individual could be 'a Jew at home and a human being in the street'.[9] Ultra-Orthodox Judaism, by contrast, in the absence of the ghetto walls, sought to strengthen 'the fence round the Torah',[10] in an attempt to insulate Jewish life and protect it from erosion by the wider society, which had become more open and accessible.

So, different varieties of Judaism experience modern culture in different ways. Nevertheless, the very fact that the dawn of modernity gave rise to different forms and denominations of Judaism is a testament to its impact on Jewish life. I would now like to explore that impact more closely.

Encountering modernity

For the Jews of Central and Eastern Europe, the collapse of the *ancien régime*, following the French Revolution of 1789, precipitated over the course of the nineteenth century a complete transformation in the circumstances of Jewish life. Having lived for the most part in segregated communities,[11] barred from the medieval guilds and from owning land, individual Jews now had the opportunity to participate in wider society, gaining access to 'secular' education and the professions – and also, to citizenship.

As soon as one mentions 'individual Jews', the implications of modernity become clear. The pre-modern world was characterized by a fixed hierarchy of social strata, with peasants at the base and absolute rulers at the apex. It was also characterized by the complete control of the individual by the group or community. Just as a particular group in the hierarchy knew its place, so each individual's life was determined by communal mores and expectations. Pre-modern Jewish life was no exception. Since the halakhah dictates that the observance of the *mitzvot*, the commandments, devolves on the individual, individuals have no choice but to fulfil their prescribed roles – which are, of course, divided by gender. From the age of 13, for males, and 12 for females, becoming bar and bat mitzvah respectively, individual Jews are bound by the obligations that determine their lives from that moment onwards.[12]

A segregated ghetto existence ensured Jewish communal stability and continuity by supporting a system of social control inherent in the practice of halakhah. Then modernity came along and disrupted the social order by bringing down the ghetto walls and introducing a new agent into society: the empowered individual. As Jewish communities were no longer required to dwell alone and apart, so individuals were free to roam beyond the confines of Jewish life and explore new opportunities to realize their personal hopes and dreams.

Of the threat to traditional Jewish life, modernity's challenge to communal authority over the lives of individuals had the potential to wreak the greatest havoc. It is not surprising that one powerful response was the development of Orthodox Judaism – an attempt to limit the threat of modernity by reinforcing the limits and boundaries around Jewish life. This response remains powerful and effective to this day. Indeed, it might be argued that after more than two centuries of flux and change and the continuing generation of a multiplicity of choices for individuals, Ultra-Orthodoxy, in particular, has become an attractive and safe solution to the complexities of modern life for those individuals who seek to orientate their lives and find a coherent path in the face of a plurality of options, ideas and truths.

The resurgence of orthodoxy also has something to do with the underside of modernity, the assault on meaning and traditional approaches to meaning-making. Alongside the new opportunities, open vistas and stimulating developments in human knowledge – in particular, the scientific revolution – modernity has also brought in its wake a materialist impulse that has threatened to reduce human existence to material factors and a plethora of forms of measurable data. Of course, the lives of people in modern culture have benefited hugely from advances in technology and material prosperity. But as individuals have been transformed into consumers, driven to accumulate more and more must-have products, paradoxically increasing consumption has generated an existential sense of emptiness. In 1976, four years before his death, Erich Fromm, a Jewish psychoanalyst and social reformer, who was born in Frankfurt in 1900 and emigrated to the United States in 1933 when Hitler came to power, published a book entitled *To Have or To Be?*[13] Fromm argues that people in today's world no longer say 'I am', but rather 'I have'. It's not just that our material possessions dominate our existence, having is also the way we relate to the people we know and the people we love. Fromm points out that, in Hebrew, there is no verb to express 'having'. If I want to say 'I have', I must say, *yesh li*, 'there is to me'.[14] He suggests that the word for 'to have is absent ... in societies with predominantly functional property, that is, possession for use'.[15]

Fromm's observation about language hints at the trauma that people experienced as the mode of existence shifted from 'being' to 'having' at the beginning of the Industrial Age. In 1844, as the new industrial order was reaching its zenith, Karl Marx argued in his *Economic and Philosophic Manuscripts*[16] that with the advent of mass production, workers, who were no longer engaged in creating things with their own hands from start to finish, became alienated from their human essence as creative beings. Before the advent of manufacturing, the objects that people made were extensions of themselves, bearing the stamp of each person's individual personality. In my view – and I imagine that Jews from across the denominations might agree – during the past 200 years, since the rise of modernity, human beings have become so estranged from ourselves that it is now almost impossible to imagine what it would be like to come home to ourselves; to be able to say 'I am', instead of making sense of ourselves mostly in terms of what we have and what we consume.

Opportunity: equality

Stephen's reflections on 'time' and 'space' in the context of contemporary globalization are extremely helpful in articulating the impact of modernity on human existence. It has been very interesting and illuminating for me to write my essay, the first in this book – and so the one that has benefited least from the four-year-long process of encounter in which this book has been written – and then return to it, at the conclusion of that process and read it alongside its companion essay. While my approach to modernity emphasizes the implications for the lives of individuals, Stephen's focuses on the impact on the religious traditions and, while my essay is more preoccupied with the liberating aspects of the loss of the old ways, Stephen's is more orientated to the problematic dimensions of contemporary life. Nevertheless, as my analysis here indicates, I too acknowledge the troubling challenges of modernity, in particular for individuals. All in all, both of us recognize our differences in focus and emphasis as integral to our efforts towards responding to the question of how we experience modern western culture – both as individuals and as active participants in our religious communities. It is important in this regard to make clear that neither Christianity nor Judaism are monoliths, and that no individual Jew or Christian, or particular group of Jews or Christians, can represent an entire religious civilization. While being aware of other streams within Jewish life, I reflect and write as a Progressive Jew, who participates in and is influenced by a progressive 'take' on modernity.

That being said, Jews of all persuasions would no doubt readily acknowledge that Progressive Judaism by definition encapsulates the most positive response to modernity. From its inception in Germany at the beginning of the nineteenth century,[17] of all the Jewish denominations Progressive Judaism articulated the most enthusiastic and positive response. At the dawn of the twentieth century, two of the founding figures of Liberal Judaism in England, the Honourable Lily Montagu and Dr Claude Montefiore, expressed their determination to adapt Judaism for the modern era. In 1899, Lily Montagu, writing about 'Spiritual Possibilities of Judaism Today', declared: 'Together we must sift, with all reverence, the pure from the impure in the laws which our ancestors formulated in order to satisfy the needs of the age ...'[18]

Shortly after the establishment of Liberal Judaism's first incarnation, the Jewish Religious Union, in 1902, Claude Montefiore argued in one of his early Shabbat sermons, entitled 'Religious Education':

> Religion needs the mind; it needs thought and study, as well as ardour and love ... Where Jewish students, or rather Jewish teachers, so often fail is that they learn the answers of past ages to past problems, but hide their ears and envelop their minds from the questions and problems of today.

Even after two world wars, including the horrors of the Shoah and nuclear devastation, had demonstrated the lethal power of technology to destroy life, the third founder of Liberal Judaism in Britain, Rabbi Israel Mattuck, remained firmly committed to the notion of the onward march of human progress. He wrote:

> Judaism cannot for all time be confined in a form given it in the past. It must develop as life changes and human thought grows ... Judaism ... was always a developing religion. Rabbinic Judaism developed out of Biblical Judaism; the Bible itself records a development of Judaism. Liberal Judaism is its latest development.[19]

Claude Montefiore became the first president of the World Union for Progressive Judaism when it was founded in 1926 and Lily Montagu was appointed Honorary Secretary. Although she did not become a rabbi, as a lay minister, Lily Montagu led Shabbat and Festival services and also conducted life-cycle ceremonies, including weddings and funerals.[20] She demonstrated one of the core principles of Progressive Judaism that was a direct response to the modern age: gender equality.

Opportunity: diversity in gender and sexuality

Since the time when Lily Montagu lived and worked, Progressive Judaism has continued to respond to 'the needs of the age' – a landscape that, since the 1960s, has been transformed by the women's and gay liberation movements – and, more recently, by acknowledgement of the lives and relationships of lesbian, gay, bisexual and transgender people. In the 1970s, Progressive Judaism's theoretical commitment to gender equality was put to the test, as women began to apply to Progressive seminaries to train as rabbis.[21] In the late 1980s, the first 'out' lesbians also sought rabbinic training.[22] Within the next two decades more women and lesbians – as well as gay men – decided that they wanted to become rabbis, so that by the first decade of the twenty-first century, half the Progressive rabbinate in Britain had become female, and by 2014, 20 per cent of rabbis were lesbian or gay.[23]

The arrival of women and lesbian and gay rabbis has had a profound impact, not only on the rabbinate, but also on Progressive Judaism. Progressive Judaism has been challenged to become more egalitarian and inclusive in its treatment of individuals, couples and families – and in its approach to liturgy, ritual and the interpretation of sacred text. Rabbis whose experiences range beyond exclusively male and hetero-normative values have brought difference and diversity to the teaching and practice of Progressive Judaism.

Opportunity: responding to consumerism and globalization

While responding to transformations in the arena of gender and sexuality in the wider world, Progressive Judaism has also responded to the emergence of other issues in society at large. These include concern for the impact of consumerism and our ever-expanding material wants on the environment, as well as concern about the negative impact of the global economic capitalist system on small economies dependent on the production of single crops like cocoa, coffee and bananas. Liberal Judaism's policy as stated in *Ethical Eating*[24] is a good example of a response to 'the needs of the age' that brings commitment to fair trade, animal welfare and organic food production, together with a reinterpretation of the Jewish dietary laws that emphasizes ethical and universalistic values while maintaining a distinctive Jewish approach.

Opportunity: individual meaning-making

The way in which Progressive Judaism continues to respond to 'the needs of the age' is not confined to the development of new teachings and practices. From its inception, as I have indicated, Progressive Judaism acknowledged modernity's greatest revolution: the empowerment of the individual. Once the individual is free to choose, it is no longer possible to speak about the experience of modern culture exclusively in communal terms. For individuals in the twenty-first century, living in a modern culture generates a host of possibilities for ways of living and for meaning-making. As a consequence, individuals who are born Jewish may develop multiple identities and personal allegiances. In this context, each individual is free to create their own Judaism as well as their own particular Jewish identity – and she or he is also free not to be a Jew at all.

All streams of Judaism are challenged by the phenomenon of individual autonomy. For Liberal Judaism, 'informed choice' has been the watchword, emphasizing the role of education in enabling individuals to make Jewish choices. In recent years, I have explored the issue of individual autonomy with my articulation of three key 'compelling commitments' that bridge particularistic and universalistic concerns, as a way of focusing on the task of engaging individual Jews with the core values and practices of Jewish teaching.[25] Meanwhile, Tony Bayfield, examining the challenge of autonomy from the perspective of Reform Judaism, speaks of 'responsible autonomy' as a process of negotiation between the needs of the individual and the demands of community and Jewish life.[26] For Conservative, and in particular, for Orthodox denominations, rooted in a more traditional understanding of halakhah as 'law', responding to the needs of individuals and their power to choose is yet more challenging.

Threat: opting out

Of course, contemporary life is dynamic. Perhaps, at the dawn of modernity, when the ghetto walls came down, some individuals exercised their new freedom in a deliberate way. Over 200 years later, the full integration of most Jews in modern societies means that without making conscious choices, an individual's sense of Jewish identity may become marginal for them. After all, modern culture holds so many fascinating possibilities for human endeavour. One of the major ironies of the inclusion of Jews into modern society is that, with the exception of the Ultra-Orthodox who keep themselves apart, the majority of Jews today, whatever their denomination, while being highly educated in the secular sense – in a variety of disciplines – may know very little about their Jewish inheritance. We talk of modern British society becoming 'multicultural', but in the multicultural mix, in Britain at least, there is not much evidence of an overtly *Jewish* contribution. Of course there are counter-indicators, too. During the past 30 years, the cross-communal adult study phenomenon that is Limmud has played an important role both in bringing Jews together from across the Jewish spectrum and in stimulating Jews to engage in Jewish learning.[27] But judging by the 2011 Census figures, the numbers of people identifying themselves as 'Jewish' continues to decline.[28] It seems that for many Jews, modern culture has become the perfect environment in which to adopt allegiances that do not include living and learning as a Jew.

Opportunity: tailor-made Jewish identity

Nevertheless, alongside birth Jews for whom their Jewish identity may have become marginal, modern society has also enabled individual Jews to be Jewish in their own ways. In addition to denominational allegiances which are much broader than the three main types I have mentioned, there are secular Jews, humanist Jews, socialist Jews, Zionist Jews, Buddhist Jews,[29] New Age Jews, renewal Jews,[30] eco-Jews, and so on – many of whom cross-fertilize from these different varieties of ways of being Jewish, as they forge their own sense of what it is to be a Jew. Then there are also Jews who are not born Jewish, who choose to become Jews, as well as those who are not Jews, either by birth or choice, but who choose to walk along some of the paths of Jewish life and engage with their own selection of Jewish teaching and practice.[31] Each year, in the course of my work as a congregational rabbi, a range of different individuals, with different backgrounds – Jewish, Jew-*ish* and non-Jewish – and with their own personal aspirations and orientations to the world and its plural possibilities, come to see me to talk about their particular journeys and why they wish to engage with Jewish teaching and/or Jewish life. For some individuals, all they want is a chance to talk, before continuing their journey. For others, however they define themselves and make sense of their personal identity, that conversation is the catalyst for a new journey into congregational life and a deeper engagement with Jewish teaching and practice.

Impact on community

Of course, it is not possible to disentangle Jewish communal responses and individual responses and file them neatly into separate categories. In my experience, the differences that different individuals bring to Jewish life as they make their journeys are in the process of transforming Jewish communal life. For example, Brighton and Hove Progressive Synagogue today is a very different phenomenon from the congregation I encountered when I became the rabbi in December 2000. While the differences partly reflect the way in which my particular interests and concerns and changes in Liberal Judaism have impacted on the congregation, they also reflect the differences that individuals – Jewish, Jew-*ish* and non-Jewish – who have got involved have brought with them.

So, Jewish congregations that open their doors to individuals are in the process of change. Where will these changes lead? Will multiple expressions of Jewish life give rise to multiple Judaisms? Has 'the Jewish people' already become 'many Jewish peoples'? The impact is not only internal – internal to the synagogue, internal to the Jewish world. Those who come in from the outside, as it were, bring more than themselves, as individuals, to congregational life. They also take the world within with them outside – and create bridges between the congregation and wider society. So, as the congregation looks outwards, engagement and alliances with other communities become possible – with different religious, spiritual and faith groups, with people with different ethnicities, with a variety of organizations and interest groups. Of course, the universalistic values within Jewish teaching, emphasized by Progressive Judaism from its inception, both motivate and underpin the development of relationships with other communities. But a theoretical framework is not the same thing as a living reality – and a living reality is dynamic. The consequences for allegiances and a sense of identity, of Jewish individuals and congregations engaging with others, are varied, complex and multifaceted.

Opportunity for alliances

Take me as an example. I'm aware that, as a result of participating in interfaith dialogue since I became a rabbinic student in 1984, in certain crucial contexts my sense of allegiance as a 'liberal' to liberals of other faiths and cultures can feel stronger than my allegiance as a Jew to Jews of other denominations. These crucial contexts are very telling. As I have indicated, the rise of modernity generated different Jewish responses. The birth of Progressive Judaism saw the emergence of a form of Judaism that was positively committed to engaging with wider society and embracing the new ethos of personal liberty, social equality and democracy. When considering the 'authority' of Scripture and whether or not it is open to reinterpretation in the context of contemporary circumstances, or when issues arise about gender equality and about equal access to religious leadership for women and lesbians and gay men, my allegiance, unreservedly, is with liberal Christians and liberal Muslims, with whom I share a commitment to transform the teachings of our respective traditions to meet 'the needs of the age'. I don't think I'm alone. Taking another, very different, example: when lesbian, gay, bisexual and transgender Jews were trying to organize the World Pride March in Jerusalem in 2005, not only was the reaction of Ultra-Orthodox Jews extreme, to put it mildly, including rioting in the streets, but events at that time included the unprecedented spectacle of the traditionalist leaders of the Jewish, Christian and Muslim communities joining forces and meeting together to condemn homosexuality and decry 'the spiritual rape of the city'.[32]

One of the prevailing assumptions underlying much of what is called 'interfaith dialogue' is that the dialogue that takes place is between the members of each particular 'faith' – for want of a better word. However, in my experience – principally, of Jewish–Christian–Muslim and Jewish–Christian dialogue settings – when we meet together, the interfaith exchange becomes interwoven with another layer of dialogue between those representing a liberal approach and those representing an orthodox approach to their respective traditions. A related assumption is that the challenge of dialogue centres on the challenge of encountering the 'other' faith, while, in practice, the most challenging aspects of the interchange that takes place may often revolve around a clash between liberal and orthodox values and approaches. In this clash, both parties not only express allegiances that transcend religious divisions, they continue to play out the battle between the old and new worlds ushered in by the rise of modernity. The ultimate outcome is unknown and unknowable. What is clear is that, whatever side you're on, modern culture is a real presence, and with the exception of religious denominations that withdraw completely from society, none of the forms of Judaism or Christianity extant today – or any of the other faiths for that matter – would be the same without it.

Notes

1 Moshe ben Maimon ('Maimonides'), b. 1135, Spain, d. 1204, Egypt.

2 Moses Maimonides, translated by Shlomo Pines, 1963, *The Guide of the Perplexed*, Chicago, IL: University of Chicago Press, Part 1, ch. 59, pp. 137–43.

3 *Odeh* comes from the Hebrew root *yud-dalet-heh*, meaning 'to praise'.

4 In one of the last books to be included in the Hebrew canon of the Bible, Esther, Mordecai is referred to as 'a Jew' – *ish Y'hudi* (2.5a). Also, at 10.3: Mordecai the Jew – *ha-Y'hudi*. At 8.1: Haman is referred to as an 'enemy of the

Jews' – *ha-Y'hudim* – and again in 8.3. While the setting of the book of Esther, a novella rather than a chronicle, is the Persian Empire, *c.* 486-465 BCE, during the reign of Xerxes I, some scholars date the book later, to the early Hellenistic period (third to fourth century BCE). See *The New Oxford Annotated Bible*, 2010, Oxford: Oxford University Press. Either way, the book constitutes the first diaspora context for the word, *Y'hudi*.

5 Louis Jacobs, 1992, *Religion and the Individual*, Cambridge: Cambridge University Press, p. 1: *Torat*, teaching; *dat*, religion.

6 *Kitniyyot* include rice, corn, soya beans, string beans, peas, lentils, mustard, sesame seeds and poppy seeds.

7 Progressive Judaism is a generic term. The World Union for Progressive Judaism, founded in 1926, is the international body that encompasses a variety of movements designated as 'Liberal' and 'Reform'. In the USA, a third Progressive movement known as 'Reconstructionism', founded by Rabbi Mordecai Kaplan (1881–1983), emerged in the late 1920s.

8 German Rabbi Samson Raphael Hirsch, b. 1808, Hamburg (then in France), d. 1888, Frankfurt am Main, is best known as the intellectual founder of the *Torah im Derech Eretz* (Torah with 'the way of the land') school of contemporary Orthodox Judaism.

9 This expression is attributed to Yehudah Leib Gordon (1831–92), the most important Hebrew poet of the nineteenth century and a leading figure of the Russian *Haskalah* (Jewish Enlightenment).

10 See *Pirkey Avot*, The Sayings of the Sages, 1.1 (appended to the Mishnah, order *Nezikin*, edited *c.* 200 CE).

11 The English term 'ghetto' is an Italian loanword, which actually comes from the Venetian word 'ghèto', slag. (See: etynline.com – the online etymology dictionary).

12 *Bar mitzvah* means, literally, 'son of the commandment'. *Bat mitzvah* means, literally, 'daughter of the commandment'. *Bar* is the Aramaic word for 'son'; *bat* is the Hebrew word for 'daughter'.

13 Erich Fromm, 1979, *To Have or To Be?*, London: Abacus.

14 Fromm, *To Have or To Be?*, p. 32.

15 Fromm, *To Have or To Be?*, p. 32.

16 Karl Marx, *The Economic and Philosophic Manuscripts of 1844* (also known as *The Paris Manuscripts of 1844*). First published in 1932.

17 For an account of the rise of Progressive Judaism, see Michael A. Meyer, 1988, *Response to Modernity: A History of the Reform Movement in Judaism*, Oxford: Oxford University Press.

18 Published in the *Jewish Quarterly Review*, 1899.

19 See Israel Mattuck, 1962 [1947], *The Essentials of Liberal Judaism*, London: Routledge & Kegan Paul, p. 140. Israel Mattuck, who trained in the United States, became rabbi of the newly established Liberal Jewish Synagogue in St John's Wood, London, in 1912.

20 For an account of Lily Montagu, see Margaret Jacobi, 'Lily Montagu – A pioneer in Religious Leadership' in Sybil Sheridan (ed.), 1994, *Hear Our Voice: Women Rabbis Tell Their Stories*, London: SCM Press.

21 The first woman to be ordained was Fräulein Rabbiner Regina Jonas on 27 December 1935. She was deported to Terezin in November 1942 and then to Auschwitz in October 1944. See ch. 4, 'Fräulein Rabbiner Regina Jonas and

the Mysterious Disappearance of the First Woman Rabbi', in Elli Tikvah Sarah, 2012, *Trouble-Making Judaism*, London: David Paul Press. The first woman to be ordained after the Second World War was Sally Priesand (Hebrew Union College, 1972). The first woman ordained in Britain was Jackie Tabick (Leo Baeck College, 1975). See Barbara Borts and Elli Tikvah Sarah (eds.), 2015, *Women Rabbis in the Pulpit: A Collection of Sermons*, London: Kulmus Publications.

22 Sheila Shulman z"*l* and I were ordained on 9 July 1989 (Leo Baeck College).

23 Regarding female rabbis, see 'Women Rabbis Ordained under the Auspices of Leo Baeck College', in *Women Rabbis in the Pulpit*. As of 2014, 15 LGBT rabbis had been ordained by Leo Baeck College in London, and a further four had become involved in the Progressive movements in Britain, who were ordained elsewhere. See Elli Tikvah Sarah, 'Have Lesbian and Gay Rabbis Found Equality? *Jewish Chronicle*, 11 July 2014.

24 Rabbi Janet Burden, 2007, *Ethical Eating*, London: Liberal Judaism.

25 Initially published as a MANNA Essay, *Bridging Choice and Command*, MANNA 78, Winter 2003. See also 'Compelling Commitments: A Radical Re-think of Liberal Judaism?', in David J. Goldberg and Edward Kessler (eds.), 2004, *Aspects of Liberal Judaism*, Portland, OR and London: Vallentine Mitchell; *Compelling Commitments: A New Approach to Living as a Liberal Jew*, 2007, London: Liberal Judaism; 'Compelling Commitments and the Impulse for Engagement', in Sarah, *Trouble-Making Judaism*, ch. 10, pp. 196–207.

26 Tony Bayfield, 1993, *Sinai, Law and Responsible Autonomy: Reform Judaism and the Halakhic Tradition*, London: Reform Synagogues of Great Britain.

27 See 'The Jewish Family is Dead: Long Live Jewish Families!', in Sarah, *Trouble-Making Judaism*, ch. 10, pp. 225–32.

28 According to the Humanist Association, the 2001 UK Census proves that those of no religion are the second largest belief group at 15.5 per cent of the population: www.humanism.org.uk/campaigns/religion-and-belief-surveys-statistics. The figure for Jews in the 2001 Census was 266,740: https://en.wikipedia.org/wiki/British_Jews. According to the Institute for Jewish Policy Research document, *Key Trends in the British Jewish Community: A Review of Data on Poverty, the Elderly and Children*, published in London in April 2011, the figure was 270,499.

29 See Roger Kamenetz, 1994, *The Jew in the Lotus*, San Francisco, CA: Harper.

30 The Renewal Movement first developed in the United States. See the homepage of ALEPH: Alliance for Jewish Renewal: https://www.aleph.org/.

31 See 'Living as a Jew in a Multicultural Society', in Sarah, *Trouble-Making Judaism*, ch. 13.

32 On 30 March 2005, Israel's two chief rabbis, the patriarchs of the Roman Catholic, Greek Orthodox and Armenian Churches, and three senior Muslim prayer leaders attended a news conference, where they expressed their public condemnation of the proposed World Pride Parade scheduled for 18–28 August in Jerusalem. See www.christiantoday.com/article/christian.jewish.muslim.leaders.unite.in.campaign.to.halt.jerusalem.gay.festival/2457.htm.

Time, Space and the Possibility of God

STEPHEN ROBERTS

As Elli's paper indicates, religious identity is a complex phenomenon and part of that complexity relates to the relationship between individuals and religious communities. If Elli's paper has been more concerned with the benefits of modernity for many individuals, then this paper pays particular attention to the challenges of modern life experienced by some Christian faith communities. Christianity, like Judaism, is a richly diverse set of beliefs and practices that cannot be succinctly described let alone reduced to simple definition. Again like Judaism, part of the diversity in Christianity lies in a range of responses to modernity. Unlike Judaism, however, the tensions between conservative and progressive approaches to the challenge of modernity run through rather than between denominations.

In relation to the churches deriving from the Reformation, Friedrich Schleiermacher[1] is often described as the 'pioneer of modern theology'[2] because he was one of the first Protestant theologians to embrace the challenges posed to Christian faith by distinctively modern questions. He did this by developing a theology that put human experience centre stage, making religious experience the key to his theology. His was an approach that placed religion alongside other dimensions of human culture, and theology alongside other forms of intellectual enquiry. The subsequent liberal theology that stands in the tradition established by Schleiermacher has been strongly rejected by others, most notably – among Protestant theologians – by Karl Barth. Barth's abandonment of the nineteenth-century liberal theology he was taught in Berlin was influenced in part by the experience of the First World War and reinforced by his involvement with the Confessing Church's opposition to Hitler. The Kingdom of God as encountered in what he referred to as the strange new world of the Bible was something very different from the modern belief in human progress embraced in liberal theology.

While the effects of modernity on Roman Catholic theology have been experienced differently, a similar tension between different approaches is seen in the Catholic modernist crisis of the late nineteenth and early twentieth centuries, with Alfred Loisy and George Tyrell being the key figures advocating an approach to Scripture and doctrine that was open to the historical-critical method inspired by modernity. While still not uncontroversial, the Second Vatican Council can be seen as a more measured opening of the Catholic Church to the needs and challenges of the modern world. What this means is that, as well as the historical diversity of different Christian traditions – Catholic, Protestant, Orthodox – there is the further diversity generated by different responses to modernity leading to the dynamic that Elli speaks of in her paper.

Yet it is not only religious traditions that are both complex and multiple: cultures are too, and this is what makes the third dialogue partner as frustrating, elusive, inconsistent and stimulating as the other two. How to describe the times in which we live? Is it late modernity, high modernity or postmodernity that we inhabit? Or should we rather speak of multiple modernities[3] alongside the multiple Judaisms of which Elli speaks and the multiple Christianities to which I can equally attest? In fact it is even more complicated than this. Religious traditions and modernity are so intertwined that different conceptions of modernity are as much influenced by religion as vice versa. In a recent discussion within the context of the discourse of multiple modernities, Anthony Carroll has argued that modernity as understood by the late nineteenth-century German sociologist Max Weber was in fact a distinctively Protestant modernity and that a Catholic modernity would be described differently.[4]

In the light of this background there could be many ways of exploring the experience of modern western culture, as indeed of describing more precisely what is meant by this constellation of terms. I want to take a slightly different way into the question by starting with a poetic reflection on the experience of contemporary life. As is so often the case when faced with such challenging subjects, poets encapsulate what more analytical forms of prose can struggle to convey. Micheal O'Siadhail is an Irish poet who, in recent work on the experience of life today published as *Globe*, effectively conveys something of what modern western culture has become. The final sequence of *Globe* is called 'Angel of Change' and begins with 'Overview':

> Giddy world of shuffle and hotchpotch
> Criss-cross planet of easy mix and match.
> Keyboards tap a galaxy of satellites
> And monies shift in nervous kilobytes
> Across a grand bazaar of cyberspace.
> Migrants roam our busy market-place.
> Noise and anguish of an age. Free-range.
> Freewheeling. Nothing endures but change.

Given a globe where borders leak and flow
A violin pleads beside a sitar and koto
As nightly starving Sudanese now stare
Out of the tube. And no hiding unaware
Or folding out again an old cocoon.
No turning back. We've reached the moon.
Adam, atom-splitter, rider in space.
Is this our earth's frail and wispy face?[5]

So much is expressed and evoked in these few lines, which in short span communicate so many dimensions of modern western culture as lived reality. What I want to take from them, though, are two themes that are central to contemporary experience: globalization and speed, the related themes of space and time. Following an exploration of these two themes I will move to a related discussion of the possibility of God in modern western culture, clearly a critically important as well as often difficult question for religious communities.

Time

Giddy world of shuffle and hotchpotch ...
Nothing endures but change.

Fast food and instant credit, one-click ordering with next-day delivery, instant communications and continual change: speed is one of the marked features of modern life, the 24/7 consumer culture of which Elli speaks. Some find this exhilarating, creating a world full of possibility, while others find it exhausting and challenging. But what effect does this have on religious life? How is this pace of life experienced by religious communities?

According to the central character of Yann Martel's *Life of Pi*, Christianity should be quite at home in this world of speed and movement:

> Christianity is a religion in a rush. Look at the world created in seven days. Even on the symbolic level, that's creation in a frenzy. To one born in a religion where the battle for a single soul can be a relay race run over many centuries, with innumerable generations passing along the baton, the quick resolution of Christianity has a dizzying effect. If Hinduism flows placidly like the Ganges, then Christianity bustles like Toronto at rush hour. It is a religion as swift as a swallow, as urgent

as an ambulance. It turns on a dime, expresses itself in the instant. In a moment you are lost or saved. Christianity stretches back through the ages, but in essence it exists only at one time: right now.[6]

It may appear this way from a Hindu perspective, but the relationship to time in Christianity is rather more complex than this suggests. There is the measured experience of the liturgical calendar with the annual cycle of festivals resonating with the seasons: no rush here as each moment of the Church's year moves inevitably on to the next and then round the cycle again. But the very liturgical celebrations that mark this cyclical routine point to other relationships to time. There is the making present of past time in *anamnesis*,[7] the remembrance that lies also at the heart of Passover; and there is the eschatological anticipation of future time. These last two – *anamnesis* and eschatology – are encountered particularly but not exclusively in the Eucharist. The Christian experience of time, liturgically mediated, is potentially a very rich one; but that richness is compromised by aspects of contemporary life. Both the modern mythology of progress, so undermined by catastrophic events of the twentieth century, and the present blurring of time through speed pose a challenge to the Christian relationship to time, particularly as expressed and experienced in worship.

At one level this challenge to the liturgically mediated experience of time is very straightforward. Religious minorities like Judaism have long faced the challenge of negotiating their liturgical celebrations around a calendar set up to favour the majority tradition. Now, though, in a post-Christian society the Christian churches are finding that Sunday morning is no longer time culturally demarcated for worship and so the numbers gathering to experience liturgical time in its different aspects are decreasing. People are spending their time on other pursuits.

But the challenge goes deeper than this and can be seen as a theological issue. It is not just that new speeds of communication, travel and change have been made possible by technological advance and that this has had an impact on the way we live our lives. It is that; but it is more than that and concerns the nature of time in modernity, in which time comes to be seen as an undifferentiated linear progression lacking any sort of religious meaning, such as that provided by the messianic 'now time' that the German Jewish intellectual Walter Benjamin[8] describes,[9] time in which 'every second of time [is] the strait gate through which the Messiah might enter'.[10] Prior to modernity, time was given meaning by a story of divine involvement in human history. Modernity called that religious narrative into question but still told a story that imbued time with meaning: the narrative of human progress. Postmodernity calls into question the very narratability of time and human history. Scott Bader-Saye, a Christian theologian involved in Jewish–Christian dialogue, puts it like this: 'while modernity gave us a story without an author, postmodernity has given us a world without a story', the effect on time being that 'Life is "just one damn thing after another".'[11] Or, referring again to Benjamin, he says that the 'homogenous, empty time ushered in by the modern era continues to reign supreme, but now without the optimistic assumption that human beings could imprint order on its pristine sands. All moments become interchangeable.'[12] Time, then, is practically and theologically problematic in modernity and postmodernity, however these are conceived. How might religious traditions respond?

One of the most striking responses to the contemporary challenge of time that I have encountered in fact comes from a Muslim writer. Hasan Askari is writing in the context of a dialogue about ultimate goals in faith traditions and suggests that the affirmation of faith in God connects the believer to a reality that transcends the breakneck speed of contemporary life, indeed transcends time itself. He bears quoting at some length to convey the full force of his evocative vision:

> To utter the word God is to regather all the threads of the universe, and to return to its centre, the hidden peace and stability behind all discord and change. To believe in God is to reaffirm freedom from the finality of the world, and to reaffirm freedom is to again mistrust the medium of our existence, namely, *time* ...
>
> The modern city is the embodiment and artifice of pseudo-eternity. People within the city run on and on *panting* for time. It is like running a long race – the track is of course long, stable and continuous (just like time which is there, and will continue endlessly) but the runner constantly gasps for breath.
>
> Alienation is exactly this breathlessness, panting and gasping for time, while freedom is the ability to run fast. The very thing man has supposedly conquered, recoils against him.
>
> To utter the word God is to raze the edifice of pseudo-eternity to the ground, to declare again that man is free.[13]

It is the pseudo-eternity of speed that can seem so inimical to religious life in the modern world. But not just religious life. As Askari implies, the freedom promised by the mastery of time through speed is oppressive to the experience of human being whether religious or not. It is simply that religious traditions offer a different account of the human relationship to time that becomes more difficult to appreciate against the background of this pseudo-eternity.

Something of this different experience of time is expressed very effectively in Christian terms by R. S. Thomas in 'The Bright Field',[14] which likens the sun illuminating a field to the pearl of great price in Jesus' parable (Matthew 13.45–6). It is worth everything to possess this pearl, described in terms of a present encounter with eternity shining through the brightness of the illuminated field. This almost sacramental encounter with eternity in the present moment is in stark contrast to the restless chasing after a future that never arrives or the nostalgic longing for a past that never was. The attention to the present moment in which eternity is encountered is not one that is encouraged by the emphasis on freedom through the mastery of speed. In the sense of eternity conveyed by R. S. Thomas, Yann Martel's Pi is right to see Christianity as existing 'right now'. But does the urgency of the 'now' mean being in a rush? Certainly not in the 'now' of 'The Bright Field'. But there is another sense in which the 'now' of God's liberating presence and purpose, as experienced in the Exodus tradition, compels to urgent action. The transformation of Jewish–Christian relations over the past 60 years is a valuable example of such urgent action. Time that is seen as marked in some sense by providence offers a meaningful context for such action.[15] When Jews and Christians meet together the painful past of enmity and persecution is present and awaits transformation by the experience of present and anticipation of future friendship. Meaning is given to time not by the triumph of one story over another but by the weaving together of different narratives into a story that marks time differently, even pointing, however tentatively, to a redeeming of lost time.

The relation to time in Christianity, then, is a complex one, from the eschatological intensity of the earliest period in which the return of Christ was expected imminently, through the fourth-century reconciliation to time,[16] to the changing experience of time in (late/post/high) modernity. The contemporary experience of time is one that some individuals and some faith communities find liberating, but that can equally present challenges for religious traditions shaped by very different understandings of time. The nature of the challenge, a challenge on which Jews and Christians may usefully reflect together, is further explicated by a discussion of the changing experience of place.

Place

Criss-cross planet of easy mix and match ...
A violin pleads beside a sitar and koto

The effects of globalization on the places we inhabit are every bit as significant as the transformed experience of time. Place is important in different ways in Christianity and Judaism, from the Land of Israel (the subject of future papers), through the shrines associated with Christian saints to the gathering places in use for worship today. Historically and still today some of these spaces are hotly contested either in terms of ownership or in terms of significance. But my questions about place are more to do with how our (religious) experience of place is being transformed in modern western culture. For many today the geographical 'community' in which they live holds much less significance for their life and identity than it would have done even a generation ago. High streets are replicated around the country with fewer and fewer marks of distinctiveness, and shopping malls could often be anywhere in the world. There is a blurring of place as there is of time. The rise of the global village means that on one level everybody is everybody else's neighbour, while on another level nobody is anybody's neighbour any more. Social networking connects us with people on the other side of the globe while those living a few doors away may remain strangers. As with the effects of our changing experience of time, so with the experience of place, the local church sometimes suffers from the declining significance of the local in the face of changing social patterns and the wider effects of globalization.

Zygmunt Bauman,[17] the renowned sociologist, has used the metaphor of 'liquid' to describe the current experience of modernity, speaking of a transition from modernity's solid phase to a liquid phase, which is particularly associated with the release of capital from ties to particular locations, with global corporations having roots in no specific place. Bauman's conception of liquid modernity is a rich and nuanced sociological reading of the contemporary socio-economic context with many aspects to it. Not least of these is the effect on place, articulated in relation to the city. Bauman speaks of two lifeworlds inhabiting the same space of the contemporary city, creating a two-tier experience of city life today, with the urban elite being much less attached to the local:

> The secession of the new elite (locally settled, but globally oriented and only loosely attached to its place of settlement) from its past engagement with the local populace, and the resulting spiritual/ communication gap between the living/ lived spaces of those who have seceded and those who have been left behind, are arguably the most seminal of the social,

cultural and political departures associated with the passage from the 'solid' to the 'liquid' stage of modernity.[18]

What this suggests is a problematization of the local in the experience of modern western culture today with many, particularly among the powerful, identifying more strongly with fluid networks than fixed local structures. One Christian response to this changed perception of place has been to embrace a liquid account of church in which (virtual) networks are more important than the traditional liturgical practices of *gathering* together in one place at one time.[19] Another response to the effects of globalization on place, though, is very different. As some religious thinkers have been critical of the relationship with time that is engendered in modern western culture, seeing that culture as offering a pseudo-eternity, so within Christian theology there has been a critique of globalization as distorting our experience of place.

William Cavanaugh, writing as a Christian theologian who is critical of aspects of modernity, argues that the liturgical practice of gathering the faithful together in one place stands as a challenge to what he calls the 'false catholicity' of globalization.[20] According to Cavanaugh's critique, globalization 'enacts a universal mapping of space typified by detachment from any particular localities'.[21] This has a damaging effect on local communities and individuals, leading to fragmentation and the undermining of genuine catholicity. His critique here is an extension of his critique of the modern nation state in which complex space is flattened and homogenized.[22] In his account of this process the changing experience of place is related to the experience of time:

> Advances in the management of time have made possible the extension of the universal mapping of space to a global level. The speed with which information and people can travel across space has overcome spatial barriers and shrunk the dimensions of the world.[23]

But the description of this using the homely language of 'the global village' masks the more negative effects of globalization, which Cavanaugh describes as a detachment from the particularity of specific places which have to mould themselves to the requirements of global capital in order to compete.[24]

Against the background of this assessment of the false catholicity of globalization, Cavanaugh draws out the significance of the Eucharist for understanding the significance of the local in contemporary Christian life. 'The Church gathered in the catacombs', he writes, 'was as catholic as the Church that would ride Constantine's chariots to the ends of the known world.'²⁵ It is this emphasis on the catholicity of the gathered community that enables an overcoming of the tension between local and universal. This is where we see the contrast with the false catholicity of globalism because the 'action of the Eucharist collapses spatial divisions not by sheer mobility but by gathering in the local assembly'.²⁶ One of the notable features of this gathering in its earliest form is that it broke down social barriers and Cavanaugh concludes his book with an example of that same local expression of catholicity in operation in a contemporary context. Fr Rutilio Grande was killed by a death squad in El Salvador following a homily in which he preached on the Eucharist as 'a communion of sisters and brothers that smashes and casts to earth every sort of barrier and prejudice and that one day will overcome hatred itself'.²⁷ Archbishop Oscar Romero, against much opposition from the elite, declared that the only Mass to be celebrated in the Archdiocese that Sunday would be the funeral Mass, such that those from all social backgrounds would be gathered in one space. Cavanaugh concludes by noting from this example:

> ... the power of the Eucharist to collapse the spatial barriers separating the rich and the poor, not by surveying the expanse of the Church and declaring it universal and united, but by gathering the faithful in one particular location around the altar.²⁸

There is here a contemporary Christian theological critique of the effects of modernity on our experience of place with a liturgical and theological response. As with time, then, so with place, there is an ambivalent relationship between faith communities and modernity. Without denying the benefits brought by modernity, there are costs; and the diminishment of place is one such cost.

Against this background, what of Jewish–Christian relations? It strikes me as significant that the predecessor of the Group producing this collection of papers was rooted in and named after a place, the 'Manor House'. The book produced by that group notes the importance of that place in facilitating their gathering.²⁹ Places have featured negatively in the previous history of Christian–Jewish relations: one need only think of the ghettos. Can we see the gathering of Jews and Christians in the same place as – at some level – redeeming the exclusionary places of past relations? At one level the work of this Group could have been carried out virtually through the exchange and circulation of papers by email. But as the place of meeting is important for each community, so is the place of interreligious encounter. The significance of place for the Group has been implicitly noted by our recognition of the importance of meeting in both Jewish and Christian spaces.

The possibility of God

In the background of our discussion of the contemporary experience of time and place from a religious perspective has been lurking the underlying question of the possibility of religious life today. The place of religious faith and practice in the contemporary context is a complex and contested question. But it is one that must be addressed in thinking about Jewish–Christian dialogue, especially where that dialogue is a theological one. What can we say about God in the context of religious pluralism? What can we say about God in a secular society? What can we say about God after the Shoah? Perhaps more fundamentally, *can* we speak of God outside of our faith communities today? And if we can, then what, in particular, can Jews and Christians talking *together* say about God in the modern, late modern or postmodern world?[30] This final question is one that will be addressed in different ways in later papers. In order to set the context for these further reflections I will consider two approaches to the question of the current possibility of God-talk: the 'post-secularism' of Jürgen Habermas[31] and the 'anatheism' of philosopher Richard Kearney.[32]

The fact of church decline, in terms of attendance and influence, has been explained in various ways: scientific advance and trends in intellectual history ultimately stemming from the Enlightenment; and social forces such as individualization and rationalization. However understood and explained, a consensus has been emerging that religion as a significant social force is at least on the wane, if not on the way out completely. Against this background the rise of fundamentalism and of various forms of (New Age or alternative) spirituality are seen either as the exceptions that prove the rule, or as facets of the processes of decline rather than evidence against them.[33]

With the decline of traditional religious practice being such an accepted fact of life, some form of secularization thesis is at least implicitly taken for granted by religious and non-religious alike. The tide, however, may be turning. In 2001 Jürgen Habermas, a leading secular philosopher, was awarded the annual peace prize at the Frankfurt Book Fair. In his acceptance speech he generated some surprise by arguing that secular societies needed to engage in dialogue with religious believers. In the decade following that statement he has come to be one of the most influential exponents of the view that we are entering a post-secular society and of the important contribution that religious believers can make to the wider public conversation.

When he speaks in terms of a post-secular society it is important to be clear what he does and does not mean. He continues to recognize the effects of a process referred to as 'the functional differentiation of social systems' whereby 'churches and other religious organizations lose their control over law, politics, public welfare, education and science'.[34] This in turn leads to a withdrawal of religion into the personal domain and a growing individualism in religious practice, something which can be experienced positively for personal religious identity, as Elli's paper argues, as well as challenging collective religious identity. So Habermas is not rejecting the secularization thesis in its entirety. But he is recognizing that the impact of this in terms of the decline of religious influence has not proceeded as anticipated.

One of Habermas's most important contributions to this debate comes in an article on religion in the public sphere,[35] although his dialogue with Pope Benedict may be more well known.[36] In the former he notes the surprising turn of events that seem to buck the trend of declining religious significance and argues that religion must be taken more seriously in the public conversation. In this context he engages another significant philosophical voice, that of John Rawls, who in his later work argued that religious reasons could be introduced in public debate with the proviso that they were subsequently translated into the language of public reason, meaning a reason that all can accept. Habermas pushes the translation proviso further by saying that the burden of translation doesn't just fall on those using the religious arguments but on those using secular reason, thus setting up an important conversation between secular and religious thought. He begins to develop this conversation in his dialogue with Pope Benedict and continues it in his dialogue with philosophers from the Jesuit School for Philosophy in Munich, published under the suggestive title of *An Awareness of What is Missing*.[37] Here he articulates not only the allowability but the *necessity* of religious reason in the public conversation. So to answer one of my earlier questions: according to Habermas, God-talk is not only possible but desirable. He speaks here of 'post-secular society's awareness of the unexhausted force of religious traditions'.[38] It is only as the post-metaphysical thinking associated with modernity (secular reason) comes to terms with this unexhausted force of religious thought that modern reason can overcome 'the defeatism lurking within it'.[39] In this way, theological thinking comes to be seen as important for his central project of reclaiming the possibilities of reason against its postmodern detractors.

The fact that such an influential philosopher not only observes but embraces the abiding significance of religious thought, despite not being religious himself, suggests that this particular aspect of the experience of modern western culture is undergoing significant change. A notable feature of Habermas's understanding of the post-secular context is the important place of dialogue in negotiating a pathway through it. As with time and space, there is the potential for a distinctive Christian–Jewish approach to the possibility of God in a context described as post-secular.[40]

Some other contours of what that approach might look like are sketched out in recent work by Richard Kearney and his advocacy of what he describes as *anatheism*, or 'returning to God after God'.[41] Bewailing the dominance of equally uncritical religious fundamentalism and aggressive atheism, Kearney offers a third way of a dialogue between the religious and the secular, the questioning believer and the open-minded agnostic or tentative atheist. He seeks to create a space for hospitality instead of hostility as the response to the stranger, and it is a space that is populated by artists, philosophers and religious believers, as well as being a space that can be experienced in daily life. The philosophical tradition that Kearney draws on for this work, that of French postmodern thought, is one that has Christian and Jewish influence at its heart: the Christianity of Ricoeur,[42] the Judaism of Levinas and the Jewish influence on some of Derrida's thinking.

Here too, in Kearney's *anatheism*, is an awareness of what is missing, a divine absence that needs to be acknowledged. What is particularly significant about this is the place of interreligious encounter in that acknowledgement. I use the word 'encounter' rather than 'dialogue' at this point for a reason. It is about something more fundamental than talking together: it is about how we respond to the stranger who disrupts our world and calls us into question. Interreligious encounter is a particularly significant context for such meetings with strangeness and we can respond with hostility or hospitality. Jewish–Christian dialogue is a hospitable response and one that, therefore, creates an important place for the returning to God after God of which Kearney speaks.

For Kearney, though, this possibility of return is not just found in religion and he traces the renewed possibility of God as a phenomenon in twentieth-century literature, thus rooting anatheism in the space between religion and modern western culture more broadly. The 'return of the sacred' that Kearney also describes in terms of 'sacramental aesthetics' is illustrated through the work of Joyce, Proust and Woolf, who '(e)pitomize ... a sacramental imagination that celebrates the bread and wine of everyday existence'.[43]

A particularly significant feature of this example of a post-secular turn is that it complements some of the critique of modernity earlier in this paper. In offering that critique I have not wanted to cast modernity in wholly negative terms from a Christian perspective. As Elli attests, there are many positive features of modernity, not least the ability of individuals to forge their own religious identities freed from oppressive religious authority. Kearney's work is evidence of the rich literary tradition in modern western culture, one in which such identities can be explored and celebrated. It is also evidence of a greater openness to the possibility of God in the postmodern world and, therefore, of a more hospitable environment for religious belief and practice.

Time, place and the possibility of God

In this paper I have tried to explore the experience of modern western culture by looking at the contemporary experience of time and place from a Christian and interreligious perspective and then by considering the post-secular, post-atheist turn in which there seem to be new possibilities for religious thought opening up in the public sphere. Modernity has issued, and continues to issue, a range of challenges to religious life and thought, and different Jews and different Christians have responded variously to these challenges. Modern western culture is neither good nor bad: it is where we live and we engage with it critically and collaboratively from within. Interreligious dialogue in general and Jewish–Christian dialogue in particular is an important contributor to that engagement.

Taking seriously the challenges of modernity, I argue that there is a time and a place in which the possibility of God is at its most tangible. This is the time and place of dialogue in which Jews and Christians inhabit a particularly significant space where the remembered past and the anticipated future are present. The gathering of Christians and Jews in one place *as* Christians and Jews has been central to the work of the Council of Christians and Jews in the 75 years of its existence. In such gatherings the participants are not simply a group of individual citizens who happen to be Jewish and Christian; but nor are they defined purely by their collective identities as Jews and Christians. They are not standing together *against* modernity, but neither do they embrace modern western culture uncritically. They model a way of being together that is precisely the third alternative advocated by Habermas between the communitarian identity politics of the radical multiculturalists on the one hand and the difference-blind assimilation of the hard-line secularists on the other.[44] Instead of these options, Habermas advocates 'complementary learning processes'[45] between religious and secular. In Jewish–Christian dialogue we learn, model and develop such approaches to mutual learning, and not just between our religious traditions, because the debate between religious and secular runs through our traditions and is not something external to them. Following Kearney, I have suggested that it is in such hospitable and dialogical approaches towards other traditions of faith and life that we discover the possibility of God in modern western culture. This has been my own experience: the challenges to the possibility of belief today have been most effectively addressed not by apologetics and argument, but by dialogue with those of other faith and those of none. The possibility of faith and religious life today, then, is an interreligious possibility which is critically and creatively rooted in its particular modern context.

Notes

1 Friedrich Schleiermacher, b. 1768, Silesia, d. 1834, Berlin.
2 Keith W. Clements, 1987, *Friedrich Schleiermacher: Pioneer of Modern Theology*, London: Collins.
3 S. N. Eisenstadt, 2000, 'Multiple Modernities', *Daedalus* 129:1, Winter.
4 Anthony J. Carroll, 2007, *Protestant Modernity: Weber, Secularization, and Protestantism*, Scranton, PA: University of Scranton Press.
5 Micheal O'Siadhail, 2007, *Globe*, Bloodaxe Books, p. 92.
6 Yann Martel, 2002, *Life of Pi*, Edinburgh: Canongate, p. 57.
7 The Greek word *anamnesis* means 'remembrance' but can mean more than simply the remembering of a past event: it is the making present of that event.
8 Walter Benjamin, b. 1892, Berlin, d. 1940, Spain.
9 For further discussion of this, see Scott Bader-Saye, 'Figuring Time: Providence and Politics', in Randi Rashkover and C. C. Pecknold (eds.), 2006, *Liturgy, Time, and the Politics of Redemption*, Grand Rapids, MI: Eerdmans, p. 93. In his discussion, which arose as part of a Jewish–Christian conversation on the nature and significance of liturgy, Bader-Saye draws on Walter Benjamin's discussion of Messianic time.
10 Walter Benjamin, 1999, *Illuminations*, London: Pimlico, p. 255.
11 Bader-Saye, 'Figuring Time', p. 94.
12 Bader-Saye, 'Figuring Time', p. 95.
13 Hasan Askari, 1974, 'Unity and Alienation in Islam', in Stanley Samartha (ed.), *Living Faiths and Ultimate Goals: Salvation and World Religions*, Maryknoll, NY: Orbis Books, pp. 54–5.
14 R. S. Thomas, 2003, 'The Bright Field', in *Selected Poems*, London: Penguin, p. 114.
15 This is the burden of many of the papers in Randi Rashkover and C. C. Pecknold (eds.), 2006, *Liturgy, Time, and the Politics of Redemption*, Grand Rapids, MI: Eerdmans.
16 'As the church came to feel at home in the world, so she became reconciled to *time*.' Dom Gregory Dix, 1945, *The Shape of the Liturgy*, London: Dacre Press, p. 305.
17 B. 1925, Poznań, Poland.
18 Zygmunt Bauman, 2007, *Liquid Times: Living in an Age of Uncertainty*, Cambridge: Polity Press, pp. 78–9.
19 Pete Ward, 2002, *Liquid Church*, Carlisle: Paternoster Press.
20 William T. Cavanaugh, 2002, *Theopolitical Imagination: Discovering the Liturgy as a Political Act in an Age of Global Consumerism*, London: T & T Clark.
21 Cavanaugh, *Theopolitical Imagination*, p. 98.

22 Cavanaugh, *Theopolitical Imagination*, pp. 99ff. The changing relation to space is articulated in dialogue with Michel de Certeau's distinction between itineraries describing particular routes through local places and maps that 'survey a bounded territory from a sovereign centre' (p. 101). The effect on space is described using the now familiar description of McDonaldization (p. 105).
23 Cavanaugh, *Theopolitical Imagination*, p. 105.
24 Cavanaugh, *Theopolitical Imagination*, pp. 106ff.
25 Cavanaugh, *Theopolitical Imagination*, p. 112.
26 Cavanaugh, *Theopolitical Imagination*, p. 113.
27 Cavanaugh, *Theopolitical Imagination*, p. 122.
28 Cavanaugh, *Theopolitical Imagination*, p. 122.
29 Tony Bayfield and Marcus Braybrooke (eds.), 1992, *Dialogue with a Difference: The Manor House Group Experience*, London: SCM Press, pp. vii–viii.
30 There is not space in this paper for a detailed discussion of the different ways of describing our relationship to modernity today, but it is important to acknowledge that this is a contested topic. Habermas, who is discussed below, defends modernity as an unfinished project but describes the current experience of modernity as 'modernization threatening to spin out of control' in his 'An Awareness of What is Missing', in Jürgen Habermas *et al.*, 2010, *An Awareness of What is Missing: Faith and Reason in a Post-Secular Age*, Cambridge: Polity Press, p. 18.
31 B. 1929, Germany.
32 B. 1954, Ireland.
33 See Steve Bruce, 2002, *God is Dead: Secularization in the West*, Oxford: Blackwell, for a sustained defence of the secularization hypothesis.
34 Jürgen Habermas, 2008, 'Notes on Post-Secular Society', *New Perspectives Quarterly* 25:4, p. 19.
35 Jürgen Habermas, 2006, 'Religion in the Public Sphere', *European Journal of Philosophy* 14:1, pp. 1–25.
36 Jürgen Habermas and Joseph Ratzinger, 2006, *The Dialectics of Secularization: On Reason and Religion*, San Francisco, CA: Ignatius Press.
37 Cavanaugh, *Theopolitical Imagination*, p. 122.
38 Habermas, *Awareness of What is Missing*, p. 18.
39 Habermas, *Awareness of What is Missing*, p. 18 This is a reference to his ongoing debate with postmodern philosophy (Derrida, Foucault *et al.*) in which he sees reason undermining itself: this is the intellectual aspect of 'modernization threatening to spin out of control' that I quoted in note 30.
40 The interreligious practice of Scriptural Reasoning is a significant example of the sort of dialogue that has the potential to generate such insights. See the paper by David Ford, *infra* pp. 153–66, especially pp. 158–60.
41 Richard Kearney, 2010, *Anatheism: Returning to God after God*, New York: Columbia University Press.
42 Paul Ricoeur, French philosopher, 1913–2005.
43 Kearney, *Anatheism*, pp. 101–2.
44 Habermas, 'Notes on Post-Secular Society', pp. 24–9.
45 Habermas, 'Notes on Post-Secular Society', p. 27.

Further Reflections

TONY BAYFIELD

At the end of an earlier Christian–Jewish dialogue project, Rabbi Dr Norman Solomon[1] made the following incisive observation:

> The members of our dialogue group, as well as others who joined us from time to time, came together on the pretext of participating in a bilateral dialogue, of Jews and Christians. We were all sufficiently sophisticated to know that there could not be a dialogue between abstractions, between Judaism and Christianity, but only between individuals. We knew also that not only was none of us a perfect representative of his or her faith, but that both faiths had developed such complex and varied resources that the very concept of a perfect, 'authentic' representative was suspect.
> Still, there were two sets of us, a set of Jews and a set of Christians, so the dialogue was bilateral. Or was it?
> The first circumstance that might have alerted us to the presence of an invisible guest was that we were all speaking English, our common native tongue. Now, English is not the language in which either Judaism or Christianity was formed, and the group was sufficiently aware and expert that we scurried back to our Hebrew and Greek texts whenever some sensitive scriptural text was cited. But if we were talking and thinking English, then we were mediating our Hebrew and Greek traditions through another culture (for language is the articulation of culture). It was this shared culture that made the dialogue possible. But it did not – could not – provide a neutral medium. Rather, it was the 'third presence' in the dialogue, a presence whose profound influence was so all-pervasive that it was in danger of not being noticed.
> Three cultures – even three civilizations – met. A Christian civilization, a Jewish civilization, and the third civilization, in which all of us Jews and Christians live and find our identity, and which was mediated through the English language. This third was the civilization of modernity, or of enlightenment.[2]

Both Elli and Stephen acknowledge this truly Solomonic insight. Jews and Christians alike are born into modern western culture – whether they live in Britain, the United States, Rome or Jerusalem. We breathe it, are educated within its institutions, live our lives within its embrace – and die in its shadow.

Some, within both the Christian and Jewish worlds, go to great lengths to evade it, by building educational and social walls to shut it out. But they're a small minority and this book is not for them. For all the contributors, such a response is neither possible nor desirable. Instead, we recognize and acknowledge the third dialogue partner, the culture within which we've chosen to minister. Sharing our responses is a feature of religious life today, characteristic of the three-way exchange that Rabbi Solomon identified a quarter of a century ago.

I won't forget the meeting of our Group when Elli gave the first draft of her paper. It caused consternation, widely expressed in terms of the paper being 'unrepresentative'. Of course it isn't representative. It's my task to place it within the spectrum of Jewish responses to modern western culture, modernity or postmodernity. But what Elli did then – and does in the essay you've just read – is open up the subject with characteristic spirit and forthrightness.

What Elli says could not be put more clearly. The Jews of Western Europe entered the modern world when the French Revolution and the Enlightenment brought down the ghetto walls and accelerated a process already begun in Jewish intellectual circles in the second half of the eighteenth century. I would quibble with Elli about where modern western culture begins. For me the sixteenth-century cosmologists, Copernicus, Kepler and Galileo – and the response from the Catholic Church – are decisive. They brought about a shift from God-centred to human-centred thinking – Descartes in philosophy and Newton in science – and an (unnecessary) oppositionalism between religion on the one hand and science and reason on the other. That conflict has persisted into the twenty-first century but the closing section of Stephen Roberts' essay, particularly the discussion of the contemporary German philosopher Jürgen Habermas, suggests that there are now glimpses – in post-secularism – of a way beyond.

Certainly for Jews, the nineteenth and twentieth centuries were transformatory, just as Elli says. She goes on to emphasize what may well be – for Jews *and* Judaism – the most decisive feature of modern western culture, its emphasis on the individual. I want to put this in as neutral, non-judgemental terms as possible. Jews had been living within communities which structured their lives, provided a distinctive pattern of behaviour and placed them in the context of a system of duties, obligations – to the community and to each other. As Louis Jacobs points

FURTHER REFLECTIONS

out in his book *Religion and the Individual: A Jewish Perspective*,[3] the 'pre-modern' (Jewish) individual was profoundly respected – each of us unique and created in the image of God. But, says Jacobs:

> Stress on the Jewish community has provided Jews with the fortitude to survive and it has freed the individual Jew from a morbid retreat into egotism and selfhood. Yet it cannot be denied that it has often resulted in a marked imbalance in which the needs of the individual Jew, both material and spiritual, tend to be relegated to the background of Jewish life, if not completely ignored.[4]

Modern western culture unyoked the Jew.[5] Each individual became 'autonomous', as Elli says. Autonomy is not, however, a theological category. It's sociological – no longer feeling the constraints of community and society. It's psychological – 'I'm free to make choices; no one can take away from me that choosing.' It's also philosophical. Canadian Catholic academic Charles Taylor, in his massive study of secularity,[6] characterizes the contemporary individual who espouses a philosophy of self-realization as a person who says: 'You only live once and my first duty is towards myself and living my own life to the full.' But that isn't a *theological* category. Elli, like me, suggests that we aren't sovereign selves but situated selves,[7] which means, for Jews, situated in the context of a people, a tradition, an ethic/theology to which we have obligations.

If modernity is a tide – rolling in where Matthew Arnold's 'sea of faith' has receded – Elli rides the rollers with greater relish than most, Jews or Christians. She is perhaps best understood as more recently liberated than many of us – it's only in the past 30 years that Jewish lesbians have come out of their social ghettos and become actively involved in the mainstream Jewish community. She rejoices in Jewish liberation from the oppression of patriarchy. She celebrates the diversity of expressions of Jewish identity. She attempts to build community within a riptide sweeping significant numbers of Jews away from previous anchorages, throwing them a line and offering support. She stands at the opposite end of the spectrum to that noted by Louis Jacobs – those sections of community which so stress community and its rules that the needs of individuals are largely ignored.

You don't have to be Elli in order to recognize the nature of modern western culture as she describes it – both its positive and negative features. It sets the context for what the rest of this book addresses – particularly when seen through the eyes of Jews, a people with a tradition that goes back three millennia and is struggling not just to survive but renew itself amid the extreme turbulence of the twenty-first century.[8] The straight male Jews in the Group came out of their ghettos and entered the sea of modernity 200 years ago and our enthusiasm is, perhaps, more muted – alive to the liberation of the individual but more troubled by the diminished responsibility to community. Stephen Roberts, reflective of an environment with which Christianity has engaged for five centuries and, according to Charles Taylor, played a decisive role in creating, is not surfing the rollers. He understands Elli, but reminds me of a Jew in a story I first heard told by Rabbi Lionel Blue. A huge tidal wave is heading for Tel Aviv. Muslims rush to their mosques and pray that Allah will intervene. Christians flock to church imploring Christ to save them. Even the secular Jews of Tel Aviv go to synagogue and pray: 'Dear God, it's going to be difficult living under ten metres of water.' Stephen starts with the undeniable fact of long-endured Christian immersion – under the swirling waters of modernity – and begins to address the difficulties. They've become still more challenging since the terrible events of the twentieth century, shaking to their foundations the confidence and certainties of the modern world, bringing about the paradigm shift to the postmodern world in which we all now live.

It was David Ford who introduced the Jews in our Group to Micheal O'Siadhail; Stephen selects lines which marvellously express the exponential, disorientating rate of change sweeping the globe. How do we cope? More particularly, what is there in our respective traditions that we can bind ourselves to without behaving like King Cnut? For all of us in the Group, the task is not to declare the past unchangeable but rather to build a sturdy ship out of both traditional and modern planks and sail the sea that way. We criticize and collaborate with postmodernity, perhaps in equal measure.

Stephen is an understated man and so is his writing. It's easy to overlook the way in which he draws on Jewish thinkers – Walter Benjamin, Zigmunt Bauman – in a way that many Jews are less open to doing with their Christian counterparts. Benjamin's 'weak Messianism' offers untold potential for theological dialogue in a Jewish–Christian setting. Similarly, Bauman's critique of the globalization of western economics provides an excellent framework for Christian–Jewish discussion of the individual and their true worth.

Stephen Roberts' reflection on time and the way in which postmodern western society fills time with an ever more demanding treadmill of activity only to leave an emptiness at its heart – what's all this striving and busy-ness for? – underlines the limitations of secularism and the challenge to religion to offer meaningful answers. I was reminded of the ancient Jewish tradition of inaugurating the Sabbath over a cup of wine – kiddush. Time is *hol*, ordinary; Shabbat is the taking of 25 hours[9] of that something ordinary and setting it aside for a different, special purpose. Asking 'for what purpose?' is one way Jews and Christians can begin to grapple with the task Stephen has highlighted.

Stephen's insight into the effect globalization and the virtual world have had on place – making it seem petty, parochial and irrelevant – is a luminous insight into the challenge that postmodernity had posed to the physical gathering of Christians and Jews in churches and synagogues which has sustained our respective faiths and been their hallmark for two millennia. It doesn't solve one of the greatest challenges we face, but understanding the challenge better – and seeing it as an urgent, shared problem – is both a fruit of and agenda item for dialogue.

Stephen refers us to the recent work of Jürgen Habermas. Interestingly, Habermas comes from the Frankfurt School, so much part of twentieth-century European Jewish thought. In recognizing that religion and its values – rooted in community rather than in individual choice – have much to contribute in the public sphere, Habermas may signal an end to the privatization and exclusion of religion. Perhaps there is light at the end of a long, dark tunnel and a post-secular age will begin to dawn. Both Elli and Stephen welcome such a possibility with enthusiasm.

Academics in Britain, notably Professor Steve Bruce of Aberdeen and his school of the sociology of religion, declare that 'God is dead' as a result of 'secularization in the West'.[10] Not so, says Stephen Roberts – there's a vital role both in time and place for religion in a post-secular age but it's a role which should be rooted in 'anatheism', returning to God, conscious of the recent past. Many old understandings were destroyed in the disasters of the twentieth century – disasters not directly of God's making but ours – and, in penitence and humility, Christians and Jews must renew a journey on which collaboration rather than conflict is essential.

Notes

1 B. 1933, Cardiff. Former United synagogue Rabbi. Author of 1991, *Judaism and World Religion*, London: Macmillan, and 2012, *Torah from Heaven*, Oxford: Littman Library of Jewish Civilization.

2 Tony Bayfield and Marcus Braybrooke (eds.), 1992, *Dialogue with a Difference: The Manor House Group Experience*, London: SCM Press.

3 Louis Jacobs, 1992, *Religion and the Individual: A Jewish Perspective*, Cambridge: Cambridge University Press.

4 Jacobs, *Religion and the Individual*, p. 1.

5 The Rabbinic phrase *ol mitzvot*, yoke of Torah, implies obedience rather than oppression. But it is obedience to something other than the self and its promptings.

6 Charles Taylor, 2007, *A Secular Age*, Cambridge, MA: Harvard University Press.

7 The attribution of the two phrases 'sovereign self' and 'situated self' is examined by Jonathan Boyd in Jonathan Boyd (ed.), 2003, *The Sovereign and the Situated Self*, London: UJIA, p. 1. He writes: 'the sovereign self describes the state of identity in much of the western world, certainly in the decade leading up to 11 September 2001. Sociologists and thinkers such as Robert Putnam, Robert Bellah, Zigmunt Bauman and Steven M. Cohen have written extensively about the notion of radical individualism.' He goes on to attribute 'the situated self' to 'British Chief Rabbi, Professor Jonathan Sacks'.

8 Our Group didn't engage with what it actually feels like to be an 'endangered species' – as equally it didn't get to grips with the swirling emotional complexities of being a Christian in today's very changed and rapidly changing British society. Peeling away at layers always exposes new layers.

9 25 not 24 hours because, traditionally, Shabbat begins roughly 20 minutes before sunset and ends about 40 minutes after sunset when three stars are visible.

10 Steve Bruce, 2002, *God is Dead: Secularization in the West*, Oxford: Blackwell. Steve Bruce is Professor of Sociology at the University of Aberdeen.

2

How Should Christians and Jews Live in a Modern Western Democracy?

Inside Out or Outside In

STEVE WILLIAMS

Introduction

My mother enjoys seizing the moment when face to face with election candidates in her local constituency. Just when each has promised the earth to their audience, she says – with great authority – 'I support increased spending on international aid. What's your view?' They flinch. She enjoys seeing each candidate try to win her vote while appealing to the self-interest of everyone else in front of them.

That's the problem with democracy. We all have a natural interest in our own flourishing. Yet the system only seems to make sense if we live by a code of values where we look out for the interests of our neighbours and behave with decency, integrity and a basic trustworthiness. It has to be 'something greater than two wolves and a sheep voting on who will be for dinner'.[1]

Democracy fuelled by an appetite for self-interest alone fails to appreciate the moral framework of duties and values which honour the rights that govern the way we live. 'Active citizens who meet their duties thereby secure one another's rights,' argues the philosopher Onora O'Neill, Baroness O'Neill of Bengarve, who chairs the Equality and Human Rights Commission.[2] She quotes, as an example, the right to a fair trial, which is 'mere rhetoric unless judges have duties to give fair decisions, and witnesses have duties to testify honestly'.[3]

'Trust' makes these relationships work – trust in others, in effective institutions, in the obligation of law and good governance.

What is 'trust' but 'faith'? So it should come as no surprise that communities defined by faith should have played a major role in shaping the moral culture of responsible choice within today's democracies. Yet these same faith communities face a problem. They have interests of their own as well as inspiring those within the body politic to look to the interests of their neighbour.

Does a distinct faith community provide moral leadership in a world of many voices? Or does it seek to protect itself from all that threatens its identity and practice? Which comes first – love of neighbour or need of self? The proactive word of the prophet or the defensive strategy of the victim? Engagement or self-preservation?

Both a faith community's sense of 'self', and the 'self' of a nation's body politic, are heirs of history. The two are distinct. But the way in which they relate, or even overlap and inter-react, may have profound implications for the future of them both.

'I wouldn't start from here if I were you ...'

The Christian community has grown by the need to name and define itself. Usually, this has been in opposition to an 'other'.

In the Gospel of John, the 'others' are the Jews who dispute with Jesus, and the 'world' which is incapable of receiving the Spirit of God. Yet the community begins as a largely Jewish phenomenon – and it delivers a message intended for the world God made.

'The more the Christian community becomes a society within a society, or a state within the State, the more conscious it becomes that it is bound up with concrete social problems,' wrote Ernst Troeltsch in his seminal work, *The Social Teaching of the Christian Churches*.[4]

Christians begin with a strong sense of being the 'Hebrew' – the outsider, the critic, the prophet.[5] But their development presents a paradox. They become part of the social order against whom they define themselves. The Christian prophet finds herself in opposition to the Christian Prince. We are the Church of the Borgias as well as Mother Teresa.

Government of which people, by what people, for whose people ...?

Our working definitions of 'democracy' are themselves historically conditioned, too.

When Abraham Lincoln delivered his memorable statement – 'Government of the people, by the people, for the people' – in the Gettysburg Address of 1863, he spoke before the days of universal suffrage. With whom did the power really lie? Who were the people entitled to vote? Whose voices were the ones that were heeded by the decision-makers? Whose were the interests that had someone to represent and promote them? And who were the lesser citizens – those who, without the vote, possessed a voice that was quieter and interests that required the advocacy of another if they were to be heard?

There was an assumption of accountability beyond oneself – which today is expressed in the language of human rights. 'The point on which the ancients were most nearly unanimous is the right of people to govern, and their inability to govern alone,'[6] declared Lord Acton, speaking as both a Catholic and a political Liberal, in his influential lecture, *The History of Freedom in Antiquity*, delivered in 1877.

From here comes the notion of living under the rule of law, an independent judiciary alongside an executive that owed its position to popular consent. Acton saw this as an ancient virtue, quoting Solon: 'It is the essence of Democracy to obey no master but the law.'[7]

Of course, the law itself could be manipulated in the interests of wealthy, articulate or blindly privileged powers. But the principle of accountability remained an important bulwark against the 'tyranny of the majority', the ochlocracy or mob rule that served only itself. In Rowan Williams' words: 'A legitimate democratic polity is one in which no interest goes unchallenged, but equally no interest is denied a voice.'[8] There will always be occasions when, through ill health or dependence upon others, we need somebody to speak for us. 'We shall always have to have our own good secured by others, as we are also invited to secure the goods of our neighbour.'[9]

The Torah is the quintessential example of a communal law expressing the mutual performance of duties and responsibilities that secure the welfare of the vulnerable. The Torah is a duty-based system. The landowner has a duty not to cut the corners of the field and that gives rise to a correlative right on the part of the poor to glean.[10] Modern human rights owe a great deal to Christian natural law thinking. The two concepts – one duty-based (applauded by Onora O'Neill) and the other rights-based – offer a helpful partnership of perspectives.

This is inescapably moral. Michael Sandel, most recently, has indicated this means that contemporary democracy cannot remain agnostic or neutral about 'the good life' in the public sphere: 'Arguments about justice and rights are unavoidably arguments about the moral meaning of the goods at stake.'[11] This is done by recognizing that human beings grow in responsibility for one another's welfare by engaging in the democratically representative process.

As the soul requires a body, so these values require visible expression: the State.

Defining the State

The State's role in the body politic has a Dr Jekyll and Mr Hyde quality to it.

The 'hard' Mr Hyde definition is still Max Weber's classic statement: 'A state is a human community that (successfully) claims the monopoly of the legitimate use of physical force within a given territory.'[12] And you may ask who is blessing the guns, leading prayers in Parliament and anointing the Monarch ...

The 'soft' Dr Jekyll definition is no less important. Advocates of a 'pluralist' theory of the State included such varied figures as the late twentieth-century English priest-theologian David Nicholls; the monk, historian and philosopher J. N. Figgis, a student of Lord Acton whose life spanned the Victorian and Edwardian eras; and the influential socialist economist of the inter-war years, Harold Laski. They defined it as 'a particular cluster of smaller political communities negotiating with each other under the umbrella of a system of arbitration recognized by all'.[13] These are 'first-level' associations, such as trade unions, ethnic and cultural groups, churches and faith groups, that have their own way of life without taking over the whole public arena. This can be the engine room of the just society – where 'We need people to speak up and speak from their situation: women to be women, men to be men, and Jewish people to be Jewish.'[14] David Nicholls' work would indicate that it is a mistake to suppose that a healthy or just society can survive where there is an attempt to restrict religious ('first-level') identity to the private sphere. Rather, these associations are a partner in the negotiations of public life.[15]

Christian self-understanding – the confident outsider?

Christians clearly were 'critical outsiders' of the State in the first 300 years of the Church's life. The State had a Godly function: to keep 'the world', the arena of human fallibility and sinfulness, in order, for the sake of the common good. Paul affirmed the ruling authorities as, in the singular, 'God's servant: an agent of justice'.[16] There was no authority except from God. The State was to uphold order and punish the wrongdoer. Christians should pay taxes, and honour the ruling authorities as God's ministers.[17] But the State could not command the devotion of the worshipper's heart. St Paul wrote of 'our citizenship which is in heaven'.[18] Justin Martyr expounded this dual citizenship:

If we looked for a human kingdom, we should deny Christ ... More than all other men, we are your helpers and allies in promoting peace ...

To God alone, we render worship but in other things we gladly serve you, acknowledging you as kings and rulers.[19]

Rowan Williams, in his David Nicholls Memorial Lecture of 2005, noted how Nicholls and Figgis observed that the Roman State was hostile to an unlicensed association, such as the Christian Church, that refused this form of ultimate allegiance.[20] But, in the long run, this led to an erosion of the State's claim to sacredness.

It was this Christian resistance – affirming that the State had a proper, but not a holy, power – that prepared the way for future secular scepticism about its terms of reference.[21]

The paradox is that this happened through the unexpected appropriation of the Christian Church *by* the State.

Christian self-understanding – the reluctant insider?

Constantine I won the Battle of Milvian Bridge on 28 October 312 against Maxentius in his quest to be the sole ruler of the Roman Empire. He believed '[t]he Christian God – a god of battles – had been on his side'.[22] This had precious little to do with the itinerant carpenter of Nazareth, preaching love of enemies. Constantine told of his vision of the cross superimposed on the sun, bearing the words, 'In hoc signo vince' – 'Conquer in this sign'. Believing this to be responsible for his victories, he showered privileges upon the Christian Church: building the new Church of St Peter in Rome and the Church of the Holy Sepulchre in Jerusalem. Others, such as Justinian, might have done more to develop this relationship. But one outcome was clear. The Christian Church accepted the favours.

The fact that the 'hard' State sought its blessing was significant. Herein lies the root of Establishment. But more significant were the roles that the Church began to fulfil – as part of the 'soft' State. It was entrusted with the distribution of the corn or bread dole, 'the major form of statutory relief'.[23] Churches became public buildings. Christian communities were sources of welfare.

This, also, was a sign of Establishment – where bishops became, effectively, civil servants, the qualities of Roman citizenship and Christian discipleship became 'two facets of a single reality', and visions developed of exclusively Christian cities that had no mission to those outside them (e.g. Constantinople).[24]

It is from here that we have to trace the love–hate relationship that follows between Christianity and the State. Is the Constantinian settlement a Faustian pact? Or is it an opportunity for principled Christian leadership to be exercised in the corridors of political power?

The story of what happened next is too rich and dense to examine in a short paper. But we live with the effects of a majority Christendom culture that, while bearing the name of the Christian Christ, bore the face of the 'God of Battles' whom many Christians sought to critique or oppose.

There are many expressions of the Christian Church today that will have nothing to do with State power in a formal sense, believing this form of appropriation to be a fatal compromise of their integrity. A Catholic priest is normally forbidden from serving as a Member of Parliament, whether in the Commons or the Lords. Those who serve in governments of other countries are disciplined. Free and Catholic Churches look askance at the degree of government interest in the appointment of bishops in the Church of England. Where there is a history of persecution or efforts at government control, many churches will understandably resist State requests to register themselves with them.

Christendom has left a legacy. Today, government is accountable to universal expressions of law and human rights. In past ages, this accountability was directed towards law, an order beyond itself – expressed in terms familiar in Christendom. Government alone could not change the terms of engagement.[25] But this approach had its toxic blind spots, too – especially in its failure to recognize the 'other' – demonstrated in Christendom's appalling blindness to the needs of the Jewish community. Examples abound. The expulsion of the Jews from England by Edward I in 1290[26] was the first of its type in the world, and widely emulated.

Christian critiques – secularism's unwitting midwife?

Christian attempts at offering critiques of Christendom had the effect of unleashing forces that bear the label 'secular' today.[27]

Martin Luther's notion of the two kingdoms – of God and Man – was an attempt to challenge the division between secular and sacred, but, instead, intensified them.[28] R. H. Tawney reckoned Luther had proposed a theory '[w]hich emptied religion of its social content and society of its soul'.[29]

Today's market state may laud Reformation emphasis on individual piety for the effect it had on individual economic activity and entrepreneurial ability – to the consternation of the ascetic Puritan and Methodist divines who promoted it. Margaret Thatcher quoted, selectively and with approval, John Wesley's maxim, 'Gain all you can, save all you can, give all you can.'[30] Wesley, though, gave due attention to the context. In an age of possessive individualism, he wrote: 'Christianity is a social religion. To turn it into a solitary religion is indeed to destroy it.'[31]

It would be instructive to trace the origins of many contemporary, apparently secular, concepts of justice, human rights and equal opportunities legislation to see just how rooted they are in classic Hebrew and Christian texts.

We thus have the intriguing prospect of a Christian group in every age that has the sense of being in exile, of being the 'Hebrew' critiquing an establishment, or a conventional wisdom, that other Christian protagonists have had a hand in making. Some believe we should be naturally suspicious when interpreting the motives and claims of an establishment that has an interest in its own survival and eminence (a 'hermeneutic of suspicion'!).

Today, more than ever, Christians face the question of authentic identity – and have never quite learned to live with the taint of Constantine's approval.

Today's situation

Christian discomfort rests in the desire to be a Hebrew – a critical outsider – while the rest of the world tends to see us as a prince-bishop, an unelected power-broker. This reflects a dialogue within Christian circles too. There may be those who uphold the theological importance of order, while there are others who critique models within the Church of an absolute monarch who dictates the running of an organization.

Religious life and practice shapes the life of this State today – both 'hard' and 'soft' – far more than the secularist will allow. The language is predominantly, but not exclusively, Christian – as instanced by the Coronation of the Monarch, the Established Church, the role of the churches in primary and secondary education, chaplaincy in the armed services and the NHS, Remembrance Sunday, and significant rituals for the marking of birth, marriage and death.

The clearest expression of this is the notion of Establishment – the history and effect of having an Established Church. Of course, this does not speak for the whole variety of Christian experience and commitment within the nation. The hermeneutic of suspicion, or just plain old dissent, is important to stress. But there was a time that the Established Church did purport to speak thus – theologically, as the church of the nation, and politically, as the Christian expression of citizenship, the qualifying condition for entry to university and significant public life. Of this, the Jewish community would be the more aware. Only in 1861 could a Jewish MP recite an oath, with no ambiguity, that admitted him to serve in full integrity according to his identity.[32]

'Establishment' is a phenomenon of both the 'hard' and the 'soft' State. The Church is 'by law established', not 'established by a law'.[33] Just as there is no written constitution, so the Established Church is woven into many aspects of national life that cannot be unravelled through the passing of a single piece of legislation.

However, Christians find that their faith, practice and identity is challenged in many aspects of public life – through, for example, human rights, employment and 'equal opportunities' legislation issues; public inhibition in recognizing one religious identity for fear of upsetting another religious community; and the simple if weary declaration of Tony Blair's spin doctor Alastair Campbell: 'We don't do "God".'

There are a number of factors at work here. There is the democratic virtue of ensuring that the rights of the minority, and of the conscientious objector, are protected. There is the desire to manage difference by seeing all religious discourse as essentially private, not a matter for, say, a borough or city council ('Season's Greetings' rather than 'Happy Christmas'). There is the search to discover, through law, an appropriate mechanism for regulating behaviour and contractual obligation when there is a 'plurality of goods', to use the phrase coined by the influential and much-lauded political twentieth-century philosopher and historian of ideas, Isaiah Berlin.[34]

Of course, not all Christian comment in this country is refracted through the lens of the Church of England. Catholic and Free Churches contribute to public debates with confidence as proponents of insights they believe are applicable to wider society, from their own theological perspective and without either the obligation or the encumbrance of being the nation's 'Conscience Laureate'. Good examples are 'The Common Good and the Catholic Church's Social Teaching', the statement by the Catholic Bishops' Conference of England and Wales in 1996 that presaged the General Election the following year;[35] and 'The Lies We Tell Ourselves: Ending Comfortable Myths about Poverty', published in 2013 by the Methodist, United Reformed and Baptist Churches, and the Church of Scotland.[36]

Nor need this be seen as esoteric activity that only has meaning for the faith community that produces it. In an important dialogue on 'rethinking secularism', while viewing religious language differently, the philosophers Charles Taylor and Jürgen Habermas (Taylor a practising Catholic, Habermas a self-described 'methodological atheist', already cited by Stephen Roberts[37]) agreed that Martin Luther King's imperative religious language had meaning for those who did not share his religious convictions. Habermas said: 'Listening to Martin Luther King, it makes no difference whether you are secular or not. You understand what he means. He is speaking in public and was killed for that.'[38]

Unusually, it is within this context that the Established Church is looked to increasingly as, in some sense, a guardian of the *pluralist* sacred conscience. It is often the Church of England that mediates multi-faith representation at Remembrance ceremonies. Bishops are lobbied to speak for other faith communities' interests in the House of Lords. Some Church of England Voluntary Aided Primary Schools have a majority-Muslim intake. Far from withering on the vine, the Established Church is becoming a new hybrid plant, within a society that acknowledges religious pluralism yet lacks public confidence to engage with it consistently in the civic arena. All this is happening while some Christians also believe they are treated as a minority or special interest, having to rely upon appeals to the European Court of Human Rights, for example, for freedom to express or follow their faith.[39]

This is fundamentally about identity – and where the impassioned plea for a recognition of embodied identity, made in Rabbi Jeremy Gordon's paper, is to be heard.

The questions to face

Human rights legislation, at domestic, European and international level, has become our standard of belonging. We choose to recognize ourselves accountable to it. This is today's way of saying that the people cannot govern themselves alone. But it too is historically conditioned. We need to keep articulating and addressing the *values* that govern engagement with public and civil society, be confident of their origin, and of our capacity to engage, even though we cannot determine the outcome.

The values under scrutiny at the moment are the following.

1 The freedom to declare and live one's identity

Faith communities have positive qualities to contribute towards the flourishing of a civic society, through respect given to their identities. The North West Development Agency commissioned an Economic Impact Survey, published in 2005, pricing the value to the local economy of unpaid voluntary-based care work by faith communities, which was sufficient to give them a seat at the Regional Development Agency table.[40]

There is pain in the Christian community when it is rendered invisible, for instance by local authorities who fail to see it as a faith community among faith communities, when it is challenged, for instance, for holding awkward ethical views that demand conscience clauses in employment practice, or simply when its contribution to the history and well-being of a society is ignored.

In its most extreme form, this pain identifies itself as Christianophobia, a term coined by Metropolitan Hilarion Alfeyev, who serves the Patriarch of Moscow, Kirill Gundiaev. Just as Pope Benedict XVI mourned the European Union's failure to affirm its Christian heritage in its latter-day constitutional statements, so Metropolitan Alfeyev laments: 'The removal of Christian symbols from the public sphere, the denigration of Christianity and refusal to recognize the Christian heritage of Europe, the persecution of people who openly express Christian convictions and who choose to live according to Christian moral standards.'[41]

2 The freedom to engage with one another

Faith communities have positive qualities to share with one another within a pluralist civic society, secure in their identity without needing to define themselves against an opponent. The common cause made by Muslim and Jewish communities over *sh'khitah* and *halal* meat labelling in the European Union is an example.[42]

3 The freedom to engage critically with those who seek to regulate the public sphere

There is a need to examine further the values governing the relationship of law, culture and identity.

One needs a sense of history in order to challenge any voice that declares the debate is now closed on any particular issue. The most critical exchanges are likely to concern the reading of Articles 9 and 14 of the European Convention on Human Rights.[43]

For example, is Article 9 an 'enabling' piece of legislation, allowing you to declare your religious identity in most reasonable circumstances, or a 'restrictive' one, assuming that a significant number of people in the public sphere are at risk of being offended if you do?

Why it is important

I therefore find myself in agreement with Jeremy's paper. The health of the public realm depends upon the ability of faith communities to engage with it, and with one another, secure in their identity, especially where each may define themselves in ways difficult for the others to understand. The Christian habit of defining oneself 'against' another (who I am not, rather than who I am) has delivered a troubled legacy.

I also agree that this may involve a proper understanding of the other's suffering, and that this may require a mutual vulnerability. The Koine Greek[44] of the Christian Scriptures includes the word *makrothumia*, 'long-suffering', translated as 'patience'.[45]

Lord Acton argued that religious liberty was the foundation of all liberty. For it meant that the State was prepared to recognize that it could be accountable to values determined beyond itself. 'Liberty is the essential condition and guardian of Religion,' he argued.[46] Once the State attempted to see itself as sacred, totalitarianism lay ahead. It is that eternal accountability beyond ourselves to which we bear witness that guards our freedom. We may meddle with the vocabulary. Woe betide us if we lose the syntax.

Notes

1 James Bovard, attributed.

2 Onora O'Neill, 2002, *A Question of Trust*, Reith Lectures. Lecture 2, 'Trust and Terror', p. 4, retrieved from: http://downloads.bbc.co.uk/rmhttp/radio4/transcripts/20020410_reith.pdf.

3 O'Neill, Reith Lectures, pp. 2–3.

4 Ernst Troeltsch, 1911, *The Social Teaching of the Christian Churches*, Germany and London (1931): George Allen and Unwin; New York: Macmillan, vol. 1, p. 50.

5 See Jeremy Gordon's essay following, the section that begins 'Being the Hebrew', p. 74.

6 Lord Acton, 1877, *The History of Freedom in Antiquity*, an address delivered to the members of the Bridgnorth Institute, 26 February, online at: www.acton.org/research/history-freedom-antiquity.

7 Acton, *The History of Freedom in Antiquity*.

8 Rowan Williams, 15 June 2012, 'Sovereignty, Democracy, Justice', Magna Carta Lecture, at: www.archbishopofcanterbury.org/articles.php/2527/.

9 Williams, 'Sovereignty, Democracy, Justice'.

10 Leviticus 19.9–10; 23.22.

11 Michael Sandel, 2009, *Morality in Politics*, Reith Lectures. Lecture 2, 'A New Citizenship', 16 June.

12 Max Weber, 1919, *Politics as a Vocation*. First delivered as a lecture at Munich University, 1918: www.studymore.org.uk/xweb.htm.

13 Summarized by Rowan Williams, 2012, 'Law, Power and Peace', in *Faith in the Public Square*, London: Bloomsbury, p. 50.
14 See Jeremy Gordon *infra* p. 79.
15 Williams, 'Law, Power and Peace', p. 53.
16 Tom Wright's translation of Romans 13.4. Tom Wright, 2011, *New Testament for Everyone*, London: SPCK.
17 Romans 13.6.
18 Philippians 3.20.
19 Justin Martyr, *Apology*, 1.2–4, 7, 11, 12, 14; 17.1.
20 Williams, 'Law, Power and Peace', p. 52 – the starting point for which is David Nicholls, 1975, *The Pluralist State: The Political Ideas of J. N. Figgis and His Contemporaries*, London: Macmillan.
21 Williams, 'Law, Power and Peace', p. 52.
22 Richard Fletcher, 1997, *The Conversion of Europe*, London: HarperCollins, p. 19.
23 Robert M. Grant, 1978, *Early Christianity and Society*, London: Collins, p. 144.
24 Fletcher, *Conversion of Europe*, pp. 22–5.
25 C. Insole, 2004, *The Politics of Human Frailty: A Theological Defence of Political Liberalism*, London: SCM Press, pp. 1–14.
26 Edward I issued an edict expelling the Jews of England on 18 July 1290 (corresponding to 9 Av 5050). Every Jew had to leave the country by All Saints' Day, 1 November.
27 Charles Taylor, 2007, *A Secular Age*, Cambridge, MA: Harvard University Press.
28 J. Atkinson, 1968, *Martin Luther and the Birth of Protestantism*, Harmondsworth: Penguin, p. 125.
29 R. H. Tawney, 1938, *Religion and the Rise of Capitalism*, Harmondsworth: Penguin, p. 196.
30 John Wesley, 'The Use of Money', in Paul A. Welsby (ed.), 1970, *Sermons and Society*, Harmondsworth: Penguin, pp. 187–93.
31 John Wesley, 1872, *Works*, 5.296, in J. W. Bready (ed.), 1938, *England: Before and After Wesley*, London: Hodder & Stoughton, p. 197.
32 http://en.wikipedia.org/wiki/Emancipation_of_the_Jews_in_the_United_Kingdom.
33 A useful explanation and discussion of this important point can be found in Peter Hinchliff, 1966, *The One-Sided Reciprocity: A Study in the Modification of the Establishment*, London: Darton Longman & Todd.
34 Rowan Williams, 2012, 'Pluralism – Public and Religious', in *Faith in the Public Square*, London: Bloomsbury, p. 126. Berlin was, of course, a Jewish refugee/emigrant from Latvia.
35 http://www.catholicsocialteaching.org.uk/wp-content/uploads/2010/10/THE-COMMON-GOOD-AND-THE-CATHOLIC-CHURCH_1996.pdf.
36 http://www.jointpublicissues.org.uk/wp-content/uploads/2013/02/Truth-And-Lies-Report-smaller.pdf.
37 *Supra* p. 45.
38 Editors Jürgen Habermas and Charles Taylor in conversation, 2009, *The Immanent Frame*. Available at: http://blogs.ssrc.org/tif/2009/11/20/rethinking-

secularism-jurgen-habermas-and-charles-taylor-in-conversation/ (accessed 22 September 2014).

39 For example, the case of Nadia Eweida, whose freedom to wear a silver cross necklace as a sign of her Christian faith while working in British Airways' check-in was upheld by the European Court of Human Rights in one of four judgements that demonstrate the complexity of these situations. See European Court of Human Rights, case of Eweida and others v. the United Kingdom (Applications nos. 48420/10, 59842/10, 51671/10 and 36516/10), judgement, Strasbourg, 15 January 2013 – published 27 May 2013, at: http://hudoc.echr.coe.int/eng?i=001-115881#{"itemid":["001-115881"]} (accessed 19 July 2016).

40 North West Development Agency, February 2005, *Faith in England's Northwest: Economic Impact Assessment* – to be read in conjunction with *Faith in England's Northwest: The Contribution Made by Faith Communities to Civil Society in the Region*, November 2003.

41 Alfeyev, 'Bishop Hilarion speaks about Christianophobia with the European Commission President José Manuel Barroso', *Europaica Bulletin*, 137, 25 January 2008.

42 www.shechitauk.org/ and http://www.muslimjewish.org.uk/Past-events/Kosher-and-Halal-statement-11-May-2014.html.

43 Article 9 declares the person's right to freedom of thought, conscience and religion, to express it in public, subject to law and a democratic society's understanding of public order, safety, health, morals and the rights and freedoms of others. Article 14 declares that all the human rights in the Convention shall be secured without discrimination on any ground whatever.

44 Koine or common/shared Greek was the Greek of the Eastern Mediterranean during the Hellenistic and Roman periods.

45 For example, Galatians 5.22.

46 Acton, *The History of Freedom in Antiquity*.

Democracy and Its (My) Jewish Discontents

JEREMY GORDON

Definition

By democracy, I mean a theory driven by etymology, a practical reality and an associative imagination.

- Etymologically the word derives meaning from the Greek words *kratos*, power, and *demos*, people. As a matter of theory, democracy is power exercised by the people.
- Democracy as a reality requires mechanical structures – a constitution. How is power to be allocated? How is the will of the people to be measured? Who counts?
- Then there is a western tendency to use the term 'democracy' as a shorthand to refer to everything good in civil society – the right to hold elected officials accountable, due process, human rights etc. Democracies are imagined as 'good' – theocracies, oligarchies, monarchies, dictatorships and the rest are imagined as 'bad', even if the democracy is rotten and the dictator benevolent.

Outnumbered

I am a husband and father of three. I am outvoted four to one regularly. If democracy suggests (minimally) the mandate to compel or (extravagantly) that privilege accrues to majorities, I admit a wariness verging on a complete rejection of its value and importance. Actually a four-to-one minority massively over-represents the amount of sway I should expect to exert on society as a Jew. Jews are a mere 0.5 per cent of the population of the United Kingdom, or 0.2 per cent of the global population.

Being at home in minority, or, perhaps more accurately, being disinterested as to claims made in the name of majorities is, I would argue, both healthy and characteristically Jewish. This disinterest vouchsafes Judaism while the fashionable opinions of the day ebb and flow – at least in theory. In the United Kingdom it seems that claims made in the name of religion are no longer (to the extent they ever were) ushered through to become government policy with a doffed cap and tugged forelock. The difference that this makes to the work of this country's Established Church has been covered by Steve Williams, but I'm not sure what difference multiculturalism or burgeoning secularism should make to the Jewish community. We are a diaspora community entirely used to being dis-established and outnumbered; ignored, at best, or subject to populist whims that have through time led to far worse.

For me, as a Jew, the notion 'power exercised by the people' elicits a particular and particularly deeply rooted reaction. It's hard to explain to those whose faith and national history isn't as scarred as my own. The phrase 'power exercised by the people' makes my stomach tighten. The collective memory of mobs of Russian peasants ripping through the *shtetlach*, Jewish villages of my ancestors, merges in my mind's eye with images of some vast Nuremberg rally all cheering and saluting. Hitler, after all, was a democratically elected Chancellor even as an anti-Semitic demagogue. In a technical sense, I can't help but fear the way democracy – the power of the masses, albeit theoretically constrained by controls and cross-checks – can and has so often descended into 'ochlocracy' (power exercised by the mob).[1] I know some, including some Jews, consider this an outdated neurosis but I can't transcend Monty Python; the Jews of Spain (brutalized and exiled in 1492) never saw the Inquisition coming. It wasn't funny then and the continued experience of Jewish suffering at the hands of mobs in every place where Jews are present (we were, of course, exiled from Britain in 1290) prevents scabs healing. It's not that I don't recognize the huge steps that have been taken, for example by the Catholic Church in the decades since *Nostra Aetate*, among many other profound examples of self-reflection from across Christianity. I am touched deeply to receive Jewish New Year greetings from current and former Archbishops of Canterbury (what an extraordinary moment in which we live!) and I cherish deeply the spirit of companionship that has animated the creation of this book, forged as it is in dialogue between Jew and Christian. But it's going to take longer than the blink of an eye that has passed since the Jews were last exiled/oppressed/annihilated, before the fear of the masses truly fades from my *kishkes* (the Yiddish for gut). Most of the time I am a comfortable and proud Briton, but the veneer, below which I am wary of the masses, even in this 'green and pleasant land', is thin.

That said, my Jewish scepticism when addressing the claims of the majority is not merely an anthropological reflection of Jewish history, it's also existential and touches on the nature of humanity, as understood in Jewish thought.

Being a Hebrew

My lack of love for that part of democracy which over-privileges the will of the masses is quintessentially connected to what it means to be a Hebrew. In the Rabbinic imagination[2] God's call to Abraham, the first Hebrew, brings our patriarch into conflict with the society which surrounds him. He is thrown into a furnace for his refusal to accept the claims of the masses in the land of his birth. From Abraham to Moses and beyond, my faith has called me to stand on the other side of the arguments of the masses if my faith leads me to believe those arguments are incorrect. Indeed, in Hebrew, to 'stand on the other side' is etymologically the same thing as being a Hebrew. Both senses are conveyed by the Hebrew root *'ayin-vet-reish*.[3] What is known in non-Jewish circles as 'playing devil's advocate' is, or at least was, in Jewish culture, holy (and ubiquitous). Perhaps the greatest challenge of increasing secularization among Jews living in a society which seeks to downplay religious difference is the diminution of this *davkanik*[4] essence – a diminution of a wilful desire to take the opposite side.

The individual expression of desire

At the heart of an ideological commitment to democracy, surely, lies a faith in the decisions of the masses. It believes that, in the privacy of the nation's voting booths, a people will 'do the right thing'. Here, again, I have a Jewish problem.

Traditional forms of Judaism – and I am a traditional Jew – approach statements and actions driven by personal desire sceptically. While we believe all humans are created in the image of the Divine and are, in that lovely phrase from Psalms, 'a little less than angels',[5] we acknowledge also an inbuilt fallibility and malleability. Rabbinically there is a sense that our actions, and even the conscious awareness of our will, is forged in a battle between two parts of an internal spiritual constitution – the good and evil inclinations. In Rabbinic thought the evil inclination – *yetzer hara* – is inbuilt into the human condition from its very first moment.[6] There is nothing un-human about our evil inclination. It's just that we will sometimes want that which is not good to want and sometimes do that which is not good to do.

The phrase 'and each person did what was good in their own eyes' is a leitmotif of several biblical books, most notably the book of Judges. What is perhaps remarkable to those who read the Bible through modern liberal lenses is that the phrase denotes a failing, it's not good. Following personal desires is perceived as selfish and self-aggrandizing at best and idolatrous or wanton at worst. In traditional forms of Judaism – and I claim no uniqueness for Judaism in this regard – the responsibility to do good trumps any supposed right to do what one wishes.

Who decides what is good?

The doctrine common to some liberal thinkers, which suggests that the self is the only appropriate obligating agent, is antithetical to my understanding of Judaism and the nature and role of human life. The Hebrew word *hov* is one of the most significant words in traditional Jewish life. It means a debit, just as one would find in any commercial transaction. It also means a religious obligation. The obliged Jew has to pay off the credit of their life and their life as a Jew. So completely does this sensibility infuse traditional observance that one could drown in examples, but these verses from Deuteronomy are typical. Following the mandate to observe Shavuot, Pentecost, we are told:

> You shall rejoice before the Lord your God, you and your son, and your daughter and your manservant and your maidservant and the Levite within your community, and the stranger and the orphan and the widow who are among you at the place which the Lord your God will choose to establish his name. You shall remember that you were once a slave in Egypt; you shall observe and carry out these statutes.[7]

The Jews' release from slavery (all those years ago) compels not only their (my) recognition of the gift of freedom, but also compels recognition of the need to bring celebration to the lives of the powerless, the landless and the economically bereft. In the terms of Isaiah Berlin's seminal 'Two Concepts of Liberty',[8] the freedom from slavery has become – in Rabbinic thought – the obligation to appoint God, as understood through centuries of Rabbinic enquiry, as One who compels us in liberty. I claim, as Berlin offers, this freedom – a freedom in which I accept an external obligator – as a more appropriate path for the Jew than the over-concentration on liberty as the removal of all fetters and external demands.

Of course there are dangers in an over-preoccupation with obligated freedom. If a person believes someone or something should be telling others what to do, they are liable to elide themselves into either that commanding entity or – only a small step away – the spokesperson for this commanding entity. The problem is especially concrete for rabbis who believe Rabbinic wisdom is central to an understanding of the ways a Jew should behave! At best those who dare articulate the commands of an external obligating agent must plead guilty of being paternalist, at worst we become fascists. But I believe in Rabbinic Judaism. Rabbis, of course, can be deceitful, shameful and cruel – there is no magic dust in ordination – but the rabbis of religious imagination, and so many of the rabbis I know, are wise, compassionate and knowledgeable. I feel more comfortable turning to them for guidance than allowing myself to be swept along by the norms of the masses or pursuing that which is right in my own eyes.

Theory and practice

The Platonic notion of a philosopher-monarch ruling a utopian *kallipolis* is not a theoretical conception that disturbs me. Plato's ideal form of government was leadership provided by lovers of truth and wisdom, motivated by a love of justice, kindness and decency – that sounds close to my conception of the rabbinic leader. The key is the desire to aspire to values beyond human desire. But – and this is where we leave the world of the theoretical to enter the world of the practical – where might one find such a person, and what if today's shining lover of wisdom becomes tomorrow's despot?

For all my theoretical dissatisfaction I do, as a Jew, love and appreciate enormously the gifts of living in an open liberal democracy. It's hard to imagine a British Jew not signing up wholeheartedly to Churchill's oft-quoted observation: 'Democracy is the worst form of Government except all those other forms that have been tried from time to time.'[9] While I have no ideational tie to democracy, practically I wouldn't want to live in any other form of society.

It is perhaps helpful to reflect, if only briefly, on what happens in the contemporary State of Israel where Jews are in the majority. At the beginning of this paper I suggested that democracy is, first, power exercised by a majority and, second, constitutional checks and balances. By both these measures Israel is a robust democracy. Elections are held and executive power is distributed between the victors in those elections according to their electoral success. Since the establishment of Israel in 1948, parties and their leaders have risen and fallen on the whim of the people. The constitutional mechanics of democratic existence have been running well. Indeed, the extent to which these checks have corrected abuse of executive and legislative power in Israel is extraordinary. Presidents have been prosecuted, prime ministers have been imprisoned and countless parliamentary-approved measures have been struck down by the Israeli Supreme Court. So far, so democratic, and, especially in the context of other countries formed in the years after the Second World War, so far, so impressive.

I also suggested that democracy is shorthand to refer to everything good in civil society. Here matters become more complex and contentious. Is it possible for Israel to be a pure democracy by dint of the first two counts, and still fail to achieve 'everything good in civil society'? Yes. Does having a strong democratic constitution and powerful checks and balances ensure a society is fair and just in its treatment of all? No. Indeed, the concerns I've expressed around democracies in which Jews are a tiny minority are the same concerns I experience when considering the one democracy where Jews make up a majority. I retain a sceptical attitude towards the acclaim often granted democracies even when the democratic majority is Jewish.

Despite this scepticism, democracy has much to commend it to my Jewish sensibilities. Rule of the majority, by definition, recognizes difference. For there to be a majority there needs to be a minority. Good constitutions protect and recognize the value of minority agitation. The party who comes second in a British General Election becomes the 'Loyal Opposition' – a term that bespeaks a certain (and impeccably Jewish[10]) attitude towards difference. It demands that different approaches be not only tolerated but supported and encouraged. That's good news if you do things differently, which, as a Jew, I do.

First tie up the camel

As a Jew, I find mechanisms of control embedded in democratic constitutions most attractive. Doctrines of separation of powers allow judges to deem politicians' acts illegal. Every once in a while politicians come and promise and every once in a while they are held accountable for their promises by an entire nation and, if they lose, summarily booted out of office. In practice, I find political claims that are scrutinized by electorates and executive actions that are overseen by a balance of powers safer than policy claims and actions defended as religiously inspired. I get nervous when presidents and prime ministers justify wars with reference to their religious faith. Most Jews, certainly outside of Ultra-Orthodoxy, would fully accept the Islamic prescription that a person should 'first tie up their camel and then put their faith in God'.[11] That is to say, the obligation to protect and foster decency is ours to worry about and perform. We don't abnegate that responsibility through submission in faith.

This responsibility to engage in protecting and supporting decency in the societies we have lived in has been a concern since Jethro consulted for Moses. There is an entire Talmudic tractate given over to setting up judicial systems and three more tractates combine to outline a civil legal system; close on 530 folios of Rabbinic discourse with maximum concentration on the human exercise of fairness and decency and minimum emphasis placed on submission to God's direct fiat in civil and civic affairs. The good society is built through human endeavour, argument and commitment to values. I want to hear the voices of holiness make contributions in these arguments but I don't want or expect these voices to hold sway simply because of their claims to speak on behalf of a Deity who has, I believe, empowered/left us humans to make our own decisions. In other words, while as a theoretical ideal I have misgivings about democracies, from a practical perspective I wouldn't want to live under any other kind of political system.

Making a contribution

Jeremiah chapter 29 commands Jews to pray for the states in which we live; we pray weekly for the leaders of the State in our synagogues. There is even a blessing to be said when one meets a bearer of civil power. Jews have a vested interest in the cities and states where we have found ourselves and this vested interest in the life of the public sphere drives a Jewish commitment to enter into the national discourse.

We live in a staggeringly multicultural society; how should the various cultures within Britain live together? It's one of the central questions of contemporary British life and it is a question Jews are ready to address. We are, of course, a refugee community – not just as refugees in this country. We have thousands of years of experience of seeing how awkward, different, potentially economically challenging newcomers should and can be included or what happens when they – we – are excluded. This is our story.

I was at a residential training programme with the community organizing group Citizens UK when a 16-year-old Somali refugee – living in the East End of London, just round the corner from where my grandfather lived – asked me if I minded him asking me a question. He wanted to know why there were so many Jews in the media. My hackles rose, but I didn't feel like brushing him off with the suggestion of anti-Semitism. Instead I told him I didn't know why so many Jews were in important positions in media, business, academia or the rest of it, but I did know that the parents or grandparents of these tycoons lived in the same streets – and in the same crummy housing – as he did. They experienced similar racism, had similar economic disadvantages, similar difficulties in getting health care, education – in many ways actually greater disadvantages – but had worked their way out of the ghetto. We ended up having a conversation about the importance of learning English, study, family values and the things a person can learn (and share) sitting on the edges of a host community.

It could be economics, welfare, ecology, banking, the penal system ... any of the big issues facing us today. As Jews, I believe, we have a distinct insight; we have a contribution to make. And I believe that society is increasingly interested.

Pulling back the veil of ignorance

It's not just that there is something unique about the value of a Jewish insight – even supposing there could be any kind of agreement as to what that insight might be. I also detect a shift in the contemporary culture of political philosophy which, as a Jew, I welcome. John Rawls suggested that if we wanted to know what a just society looked like we would have to put on a 'veil of ignorance'.[12] A person wishing to make a contribution to the public sphere would have to imagine themselves behind a veil where you wouldn't know if you would turn out male or female, black or white, rich or poor. In that ignorant space we would, Rawls imagined, determine a truly fair society because we wouldn't know how our life would manifest itself in the society so determined. It's a mighty idea, but it's been superseded by the mightier insight that suggests that because I am who I am, it makes no sense for me to imagine myself behind a veil of ignorance.[13] I'm never going to think like a woman, a black person, a poor person, a disabled person, so it's not particularly useful to pretend that I can. Instead, say thinkers like Reith lecturer and Harvard Professor Michael Sandel, we need to acknowledge we are 'situated selves' – we judge society as fair or unfair because we are who we are; in my case male, middle class and Jewish. And if we want to create a just society we need proud and clear-thinking representatives of the different constituent members in society fighting out the issues on their merits. We need women to be women, men to be men, black people to be black, white people to be white and ... we need Jewish people to be Jewish. To work out what a just society needs, we need people to speak up and speak from their situation, not pretend they can transcend it. If this is indeed a shift in how our society attempts to work out what is just, decent and true, that is good news not only for the minority that is Jewish, but for all minorities – and, indeed, we are all part of minorities in one way or another.

A protected quarter

So Jews are happy getting on with our own thing, as small a minority as we are.

We will look to play our part in this multicultural society, feeling cautiously optimistic as the society surrounding us seems to welcome the voices of minorities freed from an obligation to lurk behind Rawls' veil of ignorance.

But a paper like this would be incomplete without a reference to those areas of Jewish life where we, as Jews, demand protection from the masses, even as the protections we seek may make the masses feel hostile towards us.

There are several areas where, as a British Jew, I become nervous and want protection from what threatens to tip over into being a majority-held but oppressive perspective. Perhaps the Jewish relationship with Israel, as a land and a state, is such an area, but that will be the focus of another chapter. In this chapter I will address the Jewish commitment to *brit milah* – ritual circumcision of newborn boys. The other issue that is threatened in a similar manner is *sh'khitah* – ritual slaughter as a requirement in the preparation of meat for Jewish consumption. Both *sh'khitah* and *milah* are corporeal, literally bloody, and they both strike against a certain kind of 'do no harm' liberal approach that ebbs and flows in the opinions of 'the masses'. Both go right to the heart of what it means for a traditional Jew to practise as a Jew in this society. I'll focus on *brit milah* but some element of what follows would apply in the case of *sh'khitah* also.

The covenant of circumcision only includes men. Jewish women have always been accepted as fully covenanted members of the Jewish people. There is no sense that men are 'more Jewish' than women because they are subject to this particular obligation.[14] And there is no sense that female genital mutilation, only polemically called 'female circumcision', is anything other than appalling.

Milah is performed by a trained practitioner, a *mohel*, almost exclusively (outside of Ultra-Orthodox communities) also a medical practitioner and always with utmost care given to hygiene, best surgical practice and the medical well-being of the child. Subject to the newborn being in good health, it is performed on the eighth day of a boy's life and involves the surgical removal of the foreskin. Some Orthodox and almost all non-Orthodox *mohalim* use anaesthetic; those who don't claim that the procedure is so simple that the most painless way to perform it is directly, keeping all interference to a minimum. I was circumcised in this way myself and, as a father, friend and rabbi, have attended perhaps a hundred such procedures. The atmosphere is always tense. Emotions are intensely felt, particularly by mothers. The baby almost always cries as his nappy is removed and he is held securely (usually by a grandfather). But listening to the cries, it's rare to detect the moment when a cut occurs and, having been bandaged, the child is usually calm within minutes.

Exactly how much pain is felt is debated by those both with and without agendas. The extent to which being circumcised is a protection from HIV infection or has other medical or aesthetic advantages is likewise debated. The question of whether *brit milah* is a grievous mutilation comparable to castration and female genital mutilation makes the vast, vast majority of those circumcised as children shrug in bemusement – what's the fuss about? – but there are those who claim they have been so mutilated. Certainly the decision to perform a *brit milah* is taken by the parents – the opinion of the 8-day-old child is not sought, and this presents an insuperable challenge for those who place an absolute priority on a child's right to self-determination.

As a Jew living in Britain, I accept a certain level of broader British society's ('the masses') concern about infant circumcision. Certainly I don't accept parents have an unfettered right to injure their children in the name of faith. But I do demand that 'the masses' allow for the Jew (and the Muslim, of course, also) the space to practise such elements of our faith, culture and identity as we do, even if 'the masses' don't understand how important these strange practices are to us.

Broader society seems entirely committed to fighting anti-Semitism as long as the Jewishness being protected makes sense in the terms of the broader society. Contemporary society seems committed to vouchsafe some elements of religious commitment: the right to affiliate to one religion or another, and the right to have a private, spiritual, relationship with God, however a person might construct that relationship. And, indeed, Jews in this country enjoy full protection as far as the personal, spiritual and theological nature of our faith is concerned. However, traditionally Judaism is not – or at the very least is not primarily – about the personal, spiritual and theological. Judaism is rooted in action and is covenantal.

Rooted in action

Remarkably there is no Hebrew word for a person whose faith is entirely a matter of belief. Within more traditional denominations, one common Hebrew term used to describe someone 'religious' is *shomer mitzvot* – a keeper of the commandments. It stresses not the internal and reflective, but the practical. The term, in traditional Jewish circles, for someone who takes the Sabbath seriously is *shomer Shabbat*. It suggests not a weekly meditative spirituality, but a series of actions performed and avoided once a week. Thinking oneself Jewish, or believing oneself to be Jewish, even being internally delighted to have a Jewish child are less significant responses than Jewish action.[15] The corporeal nature of *brit milah* needs to be understood in the context of a general Jewish preoccupation with action, as distinct from internal or spiritual modes of affiliation.[16]

Covenant

There is, indeed, a founding biblical story and a religious imperative to circumcise, but I did not circumcise my sons as an act of superstition or as a gesture connected to a fundamentalist approach to the origin of the command. *Brit milah* – covenant of circumcision – isn't important to me as a superstition, it's a covenantal duty. It is how I understand the obligation to acknowledge the life gifted to me, as a Jewish parent. It is how I offer to my sons the chance to play a role in a covenant I trace back into the mists of time, a relationship with a people and a sense of the numinous that I have dedicated my life towards celebrating. I'm blessed with both sons and a daughter and I work hard to give my daughter both a sense of belonging and ownership over the Jewish aspects of her identity. There are many aspects of developing this identity and acknowledging the nature of this relationship, but for a son, *brit milah* goes to the heart of what it means to be a covenantal Jew. Quite how the covenant came to be constructed in this way is part of ancient history, but its centrality in Jewish life in an unbroken chain from ancient times until today makes it more than important. It makes circumcision an astoundingly significant element of my identity as a Jew and as a Jewish parent of sons. Circumcision is the paradigmatic covenantal act (to the extent that, in the Middle Ages, Christian anti-Semitic attacks alleged Jewish women weren't even part of the covenant – an allegation robustly rejected by the rabbinic scholars of the time[17]).

For me as a Jew, covenantal belonging is quite possibly the greatest gift I hope to share with my children – more important than the ability to speak French or know their seven times table. Just as I don't allow my sons to decline to do their homework, so too I take, on their behalf, the decision to enter into the covenant of their (and my) people in this way. Circumcision is the centre of Jewish identity religiously, but also culturally and as an aspect of peoplehood. It's about history, about national and tribal memory. It's about who I am in every way. That might not make sense in terms of a religion less based around this embodied sense of peoplehood, but it would be a mistake to think of Judaism in such Christian terms.

For a Jew, with a Jewish perspective on Judaism, removing or even threatening to remove the possibility of Jewish action strikes deeply. Threats to ritual circumcision are not threats to remove an insignificant part of what it means to be a Jew, they are threats to the heart of who we are and what it means to be Jewish.

The test of a society's commitment to tolerate and support a minority such as ours is not whether the society will oppose oppression as it understands oppression – of course we should expect society to have no truck with anti-Semitic violence. The test is, rather, whether the society will protect the practice of a minority even when it doesn't understand, even when this practice seems strange and, to non-Jewish eyes, 'unnecessary'. Democracies such as our own like to think of themselves as tolerant. To conclude where I began, there is much to learn from etymology. The word toleration is derived from the Latin to bear or endure hardship, pain. We are only tolerant if we are in pain. If we insist that all minorities conform to such behaviour as causes us no discomfort, we abdicate the right to use the word.

Notes

1 I'm grateful to the Revd Patrick Morrow who suggested this etymological distinction would be helpful.

2 *Genesis Rabbah* 38.13.

3 The biblical root first appears in Genesis as Abraham's response to God's call to pursue a life lived outside of the comforts of the land in which he was born. God calls and Abraham 'crosses over' the river and stands on the other side (Genesis 12.6). Rabbinic examples of disdain for the majority are too frequent to list. One classic example can be found in Mishnah *Eduyot* 5.6 where Akavia ben Mahalellel refuses to follow the majority, even at the cost of not becoming head of the academy.

4 *Davka* is one of those Yiddish words that resist translation. It elevates contrariness into an art form. To be a *Davkanik* is to approach majority expectations with a smile and merry disdain.

5 Psalms 8.5.

6 The *locus classicus* is *Genesis Rabbah* 14.4 on Genesis 2.7. This whole field has had two recent major treatments: Rosen-Zvi, 2011, *Demonic Desires:'Yetzer Hara' and the Problem of Evil in Late Antiquity*, Philadelphia, PA: University of Pennsylvania Press; and G. Anderson, 2009, *Sin: A History*, New Haven, CT: Yale University Press.

7 Deuteronomy 16.11.

8 A. Quinton (ed.), 1967, *Political Philosophy*, Oxford: Oxford University Press, pp. 141–52.

9 Speech to the House of Commons, 11 November 1947, available at: http://hansard.millbanksystems.com/commons/1947/nov/11/parliament-bill#column_206.

10 The Bible uses the term 'help-mate against him' to describe the role of the first partnership between Adam and Eve. Classic Rabbinic texts were forged and are still studied in what the Rabbis refer to as a 'War of Torah' (Sanhedrin 93b), a debate between two study, or Chavruta, partners. 'O Chavruta O Matuta' teaches the Talmud (BT *Taanit* 23a), 'either debate as friends or die'. Good friends, good lovers and good societies are built out of principled tolerant debate not an over-insistence on homogeneity and uniformity.

11 Hadith, At-Tirmidhi. A Jewish version of the same idea can be found in the name of Rabbi Yannai who would check the ferry before crossing the river, BT *Shabbat* 32a.

12 Most significantly in John Rawls, 2005, *A Theory of Justice*, Oxford: Oxford Paperbacks.

13 See, for example, Michael Sandel, 2009, *Justice: What's the Right Thing to Do*, London: Allen Lane.

14 This matter has received the attention of the leading Jewish historian Shaye Cohen, 2005, in *Why Aren't Jewish Women Circumcised? Gender and Covenant in Judaism*, Berkeley, CA: University of California Press.

15 While many who identify with more progressive interpretations of Judaism are more inclined to emphasize internal modes of affiliation and less inclined towards performative ritual, adherence to the 'rooted in action' and 'covenantal' nature of *brit milah* is strong and dearly held across Jewish denominations. The history of the relationship between internal reflection and action in Judaism, especially in the early Modern period, has received the recent scholarly attention of Leora Batnitzky, Chair of the Department of Religion at Princeton University. Leora Batnitzky, 2011, *How Judaism Became a Religion: An Introduction to Modern Jewish Thought*, Princeton, NJ: Princeton University Press.

16 Exodus 24.7 is the central text on the issue for Rabbinic Judaism – God offers Torah to the Israelites who respond, 'We will do and we will understand.' Action is understood to precede understanding. The Talmud, *Shabbat* 88a, claims this wisdom as a secret previously known only to the angels.

17 See Cohen, *Why Aren't Jewish Women Circumcised?*

Further Reflections

TONY BAYFIELD

Modern western culture is immensely rich and complex, a tapestry to which many hands have contributed. The legacy of Greece and Rome is apparent everywhere – from philosophy to law, sculpture to town planning. While humanists have made a considerable contribution, people of faith have also played decisive parts. Islam – particularly in the areas of philosophy and poetry, mathematics and medicine – has left an indelible impression. A major aspect of Judaism is consistently downplayed. The contribution of Jews over the last two centuries is unmistakable; however, the influence of the Jewish past has often been overlooked and still is. The translation of the Bible into English meant that the 'Old Testament' could speak directly and not just through the 'New' and subsequent Christian interpretation. Yet leading cultural commentator Melvyn Bragg, both in his television celebration of 400 years of the King James Bible and in his subsequent book, ignored the influence completely.[1] No one disputes the overwhelming significance of Christianity. But it comes at a price to Christianity itself – as Steve Williams makes abundantly clear.

Christianity began in a way that is utterly faithful to the remarkable Jewish figure portrayed by the New Testament. Whatever the complications of texts written after his time and in the context of growing tension between Christianity and Rabbinic Judaism,[2] Jesus manifestly stands in the radical prophetic tradition of challenging power and advocating for the outsiders and outcasts of society, the despised and oppressed. Steve is faithful to that model, writing, teaching and leading his life in accordance with it as, in his own words, an outsider.

The adoption of Christianity by the Roman Emperor Constantine and its consolidation under Justinian was, as Steve indicates, fateful. It wedded Christianity to Empire and gave it a vision that extended globally, even beyond the parts that the Roman Empire couldn't reach.[3] The early Christians were, indeed, the powerless supporting the powerless. Under Rome, Christianity embraced power. In theory a balance between Holy Roman Empire and Pope was struck – but not maintained in practice.[4] Christianity combined religious and secular power; for a considerable time and in many places, it was the State. My teacher John Bowden emphasized the Peace of Westphalia in 1648 as the point at which the earthly power of the Church began to be pushed decisively back.[5] There is an inexorable progression from then to now and Christianity has come to function within the ambit of a modern, secular democracy. As the majority faith in Britain, it has considerable presence and voice but no longer a veto.

There were many pluses to the empowerment of Christianity – to which the landscape of Britain bears tribute. England would not be England without its churches, towers and bells, its ancient universities, the vast number of schools which began as church foundations, the hospitals which tell of their origin through their names. One could expand the list for many pages. Most Jews acknowledge that influential past and welcome its enduring presence.

But – there is an enormous 'but'. There is a great deal of truth in the dictum that 'all power corrupts and absolute power corrupts absolutely'. Later on in this book, you'll read David Gillett's searingly honest, deeply moving exploration of the story of William of Norwich, and the appalling use that was made of it – still with us today.[6] Jeremy Gordon articulates a watchfulness, wariness, fearfulness – to which I would add an enduring anger – widespread in the Jewish community, which 70 years of earnest and determined work by CCJ could not possibly be expected to allay.

Steve welcomes the relative disempowerment of the Church today and the opportunity to resume the role of outsider, the un-empowered (by the State) working among the dis-empowered (by the State and society). However, Steve's experience of our own Group highlights the need for a rider. In England, many Christians – Catholics, Nonconformists – were treated as outsiders by the State through the Established Church. Events surrounding Catholic emancipation in 1829 and the Religious Opinions Relief Act of 1846 are graphic illustrations. Christians have argued for generations about the desirability of Establishment. The 'Church', as the sum total of Christian believers, is a much more varied and diverse group of people than the media's portrayal of the Church of England would indicate. A modern secular democracy – which sees its function as that envisaged by the nineteenth-century constitutional theorist Walter Bagehot, of promoting debate and discussion[7] and then pursuing compromise among the conflicting interests and views[8] – is a blessing. Such a democracy is one to which Christianity can contribute, advocate for the dispossessed and be true to the person and teachings of Christ.

Jeremy would share the critique of ecclesiastical abuse of power advanced by Steve – and David Gillett – but his essay's sharpest focus is on a rejection of ochlocracy, mob rule. Perhaps you have to be a

Jew to fully appreciate the scepticism this gives rise to. Jeremy therefore questions democracy but not to the exclusion of Churchill's famous observation that all other forms of government are so much worse. What he forces us to do – Jews and Christians alike – is to probe the meaning of the term democracy, setting the bar far higher than oppression by the majority through the ballot box. A true democracy should be judged by how it treats the minorities which make it up – noting particularly that we are all multifaceted citizens with varying aspects of the self that place us both in a majority and in a minority.

But this is not a debate about political philosophy. The question which Jeremy raises is of enormous relevance to our Group. Within Britain today, there is wide consensus on certain values – the sanctity of human life, the avoidance of causing harm to others, the importance of all life forms in themselves and to the future of the biosphere. But – points out Isaiah Berlin – it is of the nature of the human being and human beings that they hold conflicting values and engage passionately with what are, in reality, uncertainties: 'What was distinctive was Berlin's emphasis on human dividedness: the self was torn by competing impulses; the ends and goals that human beings pursued were in conflict.'[9]

We have differing needs and interpret the goals of society differently. Religious groups won't always be four-square with the popular consensus. Indeed, we Jews see ourselves – in the language of the American Jewish theologian Eugene Borowitz – commanded to be creatively maladjusted,[10] or, in Steve's language, to be outsiders. In *The Heretical Imperative*, Peter Berger reminded us that the English word 'heresy' comes from the Greek verb *hairein*, to choose.[11] Modernity forces us to make choices in a way that the pre-modern didn't. The choices that Christians and Jews make will not always be the same as those of the majority – they will often be, in terms of the popular consensus, heretical. Jeremy expresses that passionately and graphically by affirming the right of the Jewish community to maintain *brit milah* and *sh'khitah*.

I would also offer a counterpart question to Christians and Jews alike. Very recently the British government flirted with the proposal that faith schools should have no obligation to teach about other faiths and could affirm absolutist positions. In a de facto *res publica* contract between State and faiths, which permits faiths to be themselves and do their own thing, what obligations fall on a faith with regard to the State and other faiths? And what attitude should the State have to the maintenance by faiths of absolutist positions per se?

Stephen Roberts noted the liberal–conservative tension and debate within each Christian denomination. The same is true within Judaism. Elli Tikvah Sarah quoted Louis Jacobs on the excessive stress on communal needs over the needs of the individual within a minority of British Jewry. Outside that context, however, the reverse is true – the individual member claims supremacy. This represents among the most profound impacts of modernity on the Jewish community. Ironically, it's most clearly articulated in Isaiah Berlin's political philosophy. Berlin famously debated long and hard with T. S. Eliot. His biographer Ignatieff writes:

> Berlin did not give ground on the substance of the difference between them. The divide was not merely between a secular Jew and a believing Anglo-Catholic, but between a liberal individualist and a conservative with an abiding conviction that individualism was corroding European civilisation.[12]

But such stress on the individual, welcome in the political sphere, is more complex when applied to Judaism – because Judaism has, from its very beginnings, tried to hold the needs of a people, a community in balance with the needs of the individual Jew. We are not 'sovereign selves', we are 'situated selves' – standing within the context of a people, a tradition and an ethical/theological triangle.[13] Jeremy's insistence on the importance of *brit milah* and *sh'khitah* is not just about Jewish rights within British society. It underlines the importance of peoplehood, tradition and theology in determining the balance between responsibility to the Jewish community and personal autonomy.

Steve and Jeremy were asked to tackle the implications for Christianity and Judaism of living in a modern western democracy. When I finished reading their essays, I realized there's a related subject for future consideration. A passage from the short Mishnaic tractate *Pirkei Avot* records: 'Rabbi Simeon says: There are three crowns, the crown of Torah, the crown of Priesthood and the crown of Kingship; but the crown of a good name excels them all.'[14] The fourteenth-century scholar Simeon Duran understands the passage to refer to the loci of power within a Jewish community. He associates the crown of Kingship with the powerful, philanthropic members of the community – the people who raise the money and pay the bills. It's clear that even in those distant days there were struggles over where power and authority lay. Today's Jewish communities exist within a democratic, egalitarian society and how synagogues – of whatever denomination – are established and led is by no means a simple or trouble-free matter. Jews are aware that a variety of structures and models are employed within the different Christian denominations. Many may also be experiencing expectations brought about by postmodern western culture and, in particular, the gradual evolution of democracy, including the impact of social media. Though

FURTHER REFLECTIONS

different in size and resource, Jewish and Christian communities may well benefit from sharing experiences and thinking ahead. What are the implications of democracy for the structures and power relationships within synagogue and church?

Notes

1 Melvyn Bragg, 2011, *The Book of Books: The Radical Impact of the King James Bible, 1611–2011*, London: Sceptre.

2 See, for instance, Michael Hilton, 'The Jews in John's Gospel', pp. 95–102.

3 Tom Holland, 2012, *In the Shadow of the Sword: The Battle for Global Empire and the End of the Ancient World*, London: Little Brown.

4 American academic Ivan Strenski cites the theoretical resolution proposed by Pope Gelasius I in the late fifth century: 'The priest is subordinate to the king in mundane matters that regard the public order' but 'the king is subordinate to the priest on spiritual matters'. But Gelasius' ideological balancing proved unsustainable and the Church became a 'compulsory, all-inclusive, and coercive society, comparable to what we call the state and, in its totality, well-nigh indistinguishable from it'. Ivan Strenski, 2010, *Why Politics Can't Be Freed from Religion*, Chichester: Wiley-Blackwell, pp. 75–7.

5 John Bowden, 2002, 'Secular Values and the Process of Secularisation', *Encounters: Journal of Inter-Cultural Perspectives* 8:1, March, pp. 29–43. He traces the process by examining the development of universities.

6 *Infra* p. 103.

7 See Amartya Sen, 2009, *The Idea of Justice*, London: Allan Lane, p. 3.

8 Rabbinic tradition, beginning in Babylonian Talmud *Sanhedrin* 32b, asks why the word justice is repeated in Deuteronomy 16.20. It responds by saying that complete justice is never possible and compromise is always required.

9 Michael Ignatieff, 2000, *Isaiah Berlin: A Life*, London: Vintage, p. 203.

10 Eugene B. Borowitz, 1924–2016, was Professor of Theology at the Hebrew Union College in Cincinnati. I first heard him use the phrase 'creative maladjustment' in a lecture in Toronto some 30 years ago.

11 Peter L. Berger, 1980, *The Heretical Imperative*, New York: HarperCollins.

12 Ignatieff, *Isaiah Berlin*, p. 188.

13 See Tony Bayfield, 1993, *Sinai, Law and Responsible Autonomy: Reform Judaism and the Halakhic Tradition*, London: RSGB, pp. 17–24.

14 *Pirkei Avot*, IV.17.

3

How Do We Cope with Our Past?

Coming to Terms with the Past: Introduction

DAVID GILLETT AND MICHAEL HILTON

The history of Jewish–Christian relations is littered with stories of prejudice, discrimination and persecution. It is easy, from a post-Enlightenment standpoint, to imagine that the relationship between our faiths before the modern era was always based on prejudice and hostility. But a moment's reflection will show that it cannot always have been that bad. The tiny Jewish communities scattered across England and Northern Europe in the twelfth and thirteenth centuries could never have survived if every Christian hated every Jew – in small towns with narrow streets where everyone lived cheek by jowl with each other.

There were plenty of intellectual exchanges, as well as business and social relationships. Evidence has been uncovered that Christian and Jewish Bible commentators were responding to each other from the second century onwards. There are elements of biblical interpretation found in the *Zohar* (late thirteenth-century Spain) which reflect Christian models. Judaism in early Ashkenaz showed extraordinary creativity, introducing new ceremonies and rituals such as Bar Mitzvah, Simkhat Torah and *yahrzeit*, celebrations and memorials which suited well – and were often adapted from – the surrounding Christian culture. Unable to take part in pre-Lenten carnivals, Jews began their own carnivals at Purim. Hanukkah was to become a time of children's games (including gambling!) at a season of Christian festivity. From the seventeenth century onwards, Christians began to visit synagogues and to write, often positively, about what they had seen. It also seems to both of us likely, though stating it is controversial, that it was the Crusades which gave rise to the idea in the Jewish heart that returning to the Land could be a practical reality, not just an End of Days vision. It follows from all this that to study Jewish history as if it were a discrete story is incorrect. In Britain and in Europe, the Jewish story is completely entangled with the Christian story.

The Council of Christians and Jews has, since its foundation in 1942, worked hard for good working relationships between our faiths. This

HOW DO WE COPE WITH OUR PAST?

cannot be done without attempting to cope with the past. Times of tension and danger from the ancient, medieval and modern worlds can still haunt us – from the ancient world through the study of history, from the medieval world through popular traditions and practices, and from the modern world through personal and collective memory. In this section of the book we have picked three examples which illustrate the difficulties – 'the Jews' in John's Gospel, William of Norwich and the blood libel, and Holocaust Memorial Day. We have chosen a biblical example because of the continued importance and vitality of Scripture in both our faiths; an example from a local community, to encourage readers to look at their own local stories; and a contemporary issue about how we understand and relate to a past which is still so present. Taken together, these examples demonstrate how historical events, be they ancient, medieval or modern, can have loud and disturbing echoes in our own time.

Some reverberations from past events surprise us. The Wars of the Roses ended in 1485. Yet recent controversy in England about where to rebury Richard III's remains show that passions can still run deep. The nuances of scriptural text are the bread and butter of Jewish and Christian life, but even here there has been little study of the particular impact of the *public* reading (as opposed to private or small group study) of such texts. With post-biblical historical events, the impact on our contemporary dialogue can be just as striking, but less apparent. We are all conditioned by our past and our religious traditions are products of their own past. If we are not aware of that, we place a stumbling block before our dialogue, because we may imagine that we meet with a shared narrative of particular historical events, when that may be far from the case.

'The Jews' in John's Gospel

MICHAEL HILTON

In my childhood, the Judaism I learned was based on honesty, loyalty and family, and on the cycle of the week and of the festivals. My frame of reference for my faith was not social, and, although there was certainly a cultural element, that was also less important to me than the core values and ideas. As far back as I can remember, from my early days, I lived in a Christian environment and compared my faith to that of my Christian teachers at school and later, with that of my fellow students. Compared to the Jewish services of my youth, Christian prayers were warm and tuneful; compared to the Jewish teachers of my youth, my Christian teachers seemed to me both more knowledgeable and more approachable. But I have no memories of ever being tempted to become a Christian.

I am sure that is largely because of references in the Christian Scriptures to the Jews, seemingly always as the villains of the story. I remember from the age of seven or eight watching the nativity plays the school presented every year at the church hall next door, in which the villain was always 'Herod, King of the Jews'. At a slightly older age, we were taught other stories from the Christian Scriptures, in which Jesus always got the better of 'the Jews' in debate. Did my Christian teachers mention that Jesus was himself a Jew? They did, but it was a truth that became used in a negative way. The thinking, as I remember it, was that Jesus had begun life as a Jew but had risen to something far more important, as the saviour of humankind. It was as if God had placed his Son among the worst of all possible peoples, to teach those miserable Jews a lesson. It was as if I was being asked to learn that lesson too. As a theological argument, it was totally counter-productive. It was hardly welcoming to hear that Jews were the villains of the story. It was perhaps the first significant act of rebellion in my life when it became clear to me, as a young child, that whatever else was to happen in my life, I was determined to remain a Jew. My early dialogue with Christians reinforced a commitment to Jewish life which was to blossom some years later as a young adult.

In my adult life, I have studied the Gospels in detail and co-authored a book comparing Gospel stories with parallel Rabbinic sources.[1] My work on that book made it clear to me that many of Jesus' teachings and those of our early Rabbinic tradition have a great deal in common, using the same techniques such as the *mashal* or parable. Such a clear and obvious common heritage brings into even sharper focus those passages in which Jesus speaks with hostility to the group repeatedly called 'the Jews'. The term is used in all four Gospels, but it is much more frequent and more problematic in John than in the first three. Much of John consists of speeches by Jesus in which he corrects misunderstandings which come from the Jews. From the time when they began to read seriously the Christian Scriptures in the late nineteenth century, Jewish scholars found John difficult. Writing in 1905, Kaufmann Kohler, a German-born American Reform rabbi, called John 'a gospel of Christian love and Jew hatred'.[2]

Pushing the boundaries of dialogue forward for the future means coming to terms with the past. For most Christians in the world today, who will never meet a Jew, their understanding of the term may well be linked to the Gospel stories. Coming to terms with such texts as are difficult for dialogue is therefore essential. Difficult texts require careful *explanation, contextualization* and *translation*.

The Council of Christians and Jews pioneered a way of coming to terms with such texts by publishing a substantial booklet in 1993 entitled *Hard Sayings: Difficult New Testament Texts for Jewish–Christian Dialogue*, written by Gareth Lloyd Jones.[3] To his credit, Lloyd Jones did not underestimate the difficulty. He points out that John 8.44, where Jesus says to the Jews 'you are of your father the devil', was taken up by the Nazis in 1936 in a picture book for children. A picture of a Jew carried the caption, 'The father of the Jews is the devil.' John uses the term 'the Jews' 70 times and in nearly half of those instances, the reference is derogatory. There is much in John which has the potential to exacerbate prejudice and hatred of Jews. The problem was described by Samuel Sandmel[4] like this:

> The Synoptics present, as it were, a record of the conflicts in Galilee and Judea within the career of Jesus, in this or that synagogue, in connection with healings on the Sabbath. In John the issues, though presented about the past, are in reality those of 'to this day.' In John Jesus is the spokesman for the view of later Christians about Jesus in conflicts with later Jews.[5]

Gareth Lloyd Jones draws on the work of scholars who have explained that 'the Jews' in John[6] may mean 'the inhabitants of Judea' or 'the Jewish authorities'. But his own solution is different and follows the pioneering work of Raymond Brown.[7] He suggests that the bitterness of the references conceals not as Sandmel suggests a dispute between later Christians and later Jews but a dispute between, in effect, two groups of Christians, who could also be thought of in a way as two groups of Jews – those who had come to believe firmly in the divinity of Jesus, and those who accepted the message of Jesus but wanted to remain within the Jewish fold. The dispute rose to a bitter crisis, which has been rewritten by John as a series of arguments and accusations between Jesus and the Jews. Therefore, John must be read in the context of the bitter arguments of his own day, and not as an expression of a global anti-Judaism. Texts from history need to be read in the correct historical context – in this case neither the time of Jesus nor the time of the reader, but the time of John.

This and similar solutions to John's Jewish problem depend on linking two primary sources, one Christian and one Jewish. The Christian source consists of three texts in John (9.22, 12.42 and 16.2–3), which talk about those who accept Jesus as the Messiah being 'put out of the synagogue *aposunagogos genetai*'. The Jewish source is *Birkat HaMinim*, the twelfth of the 19 blessings recited in the thrice daily Amidah prayer, for the punishment of heretics. The version used today in the Ashkenazi tradition reads:

וְלַמַּלְשִׁינִים אַל תְּהִי תִקְוָה, וְכָל הָרִשְׁעָה כְּרֶגַע תֹּאבֵד, וְכָל אוֹיְבֶיךָ מְהֵרָה יִכָּרֵתוּ, וְהַזֵּדִים מְהֵרָה תְעַקֵּר וּתְשַׁבֵּר וּתְמַגֵּר וְתַכְנִיעַ בִּמְהֵרָה בְיָמֵינוּ. בָּרוּךְ אַתָּה יְיָ, שֹׁבֵר אֹיְבִים וּמַכְנִיעַ זֵדִים.

> May there be no hope for slanderers and may all wickedness instantly perish, and may all your enemies quickly be destroyed. May you quickly uproot, smash, destroy and humble the insolent quickly in our day. Blessed are you Adonai, who smashes God's enemies and humbles the insolent.

But an older, uncensored, version discovered in the Cairo Genizah[8] reads:[9]

1 May there be no hope for apostates (*minim*).
2 And may you quickly uproot the insolent reign in our day.
3 And may the Christians (*Notzrim*) and heretics instantly perish.
4 May they be erased from the book of life and may they not be written with the righteous.
5 Blessed are you Adonai, who humbles the insolent.

This is really a curse, not a blessing, and more words have been spilled on its origin than on any other paragraph in Rabbinic liturgy. In the fourth century, Jerome accused Jews of cursing Christ in their synagogues, an accusation first made by Justin Martyr in the mid-second century. These statements are supported by the uncensored Genizah text, containing a curse against Christians which printed prayer books have removed.

The word *minim* in Rabbinic literature refers to those of heretical views, no doubt different groups at different stages of history. There is no evidence that in ancient times the blessing specifically mentioned Christians, but both *minim* and the later *Notzrim* could refer to Christians of Jewish origin. Therefore, linking this so-called blessing with John's reference to those 'put out of the synagogue' makes sense, even though John makes no mention of any prayer or curse. Some have suggested that the benediction was so worded to prevent anybody leading prayers who had heretical views, since they would then have to make a verbal condemnation of their own views. But it could be that the effect of the paragraph was to create a situation where the *minim* would simply feel unwelcome.

Over the past 20 years, speculation about the Jews in John's Gospel has continued. A 300-page volume was published in 2001, which reaches the conclusion that John contains anti-Jewish elements that are 'intrinsically oppressive' and 'totally unacceptable'.[10] One recent article concludes that 'the Jews' have a shifting identity within John, and reminds us that at one point Jesus himself is referred to as 'a Jew' (4.9).[11] Judith Lieu writes: 'The fourth gospel blurs the boundaries between the Jews of Jesus' day and the Jews of John's time.'[12] I feel sure this is correct but Lieu fails to realize the profound implication of her remark – that because John writes 'the Jews' of his own day back into the time of Jesus, he is inviting the readers of his Gospel to do the same, particularly when hearing John read aloud in church, without an explanation by a sympathetic preacher. The listener is being invited to identify the Jews of his or her own time as a pariah people, hostile to Christianity and the true word of God. This has been implicitly recognized by the Roman Catholic and Anglican Churches. Today the lectionaries of both Churches omit John 8.43–50 completely from lists of readings.[13]

But however much you try to explain it away with different identifications of the word 'Jew', the difficulty is still there. This raises the question of whether the translation of the word should be emended. Elli Tikvah Sarah's paper in this volume reviews the history of the word Jew and explains that originally it was linked to geography rather than faith. In many contexts John clearly means a Judean rather than someone like Jesus from Nazareth in Galilee. This was convincingly argued in 1978 by Malcolm Lowe.[14] Even where John is clearly referring to the Jewish leaders of his day, they are still leaders within the Roman province of

Judea. When the Roman senate designated Herod the Great 'King of the Jews' in 40 BCE, his title was confined to this and neighbouring provinces, and it did not mean he had title over those of the Jewish faith living in Rome. Here, too, 'Judeans' would be a better translation. Furthermore, as the prevailing trend in modern scholarship is to emphasize that John was involved in communal disputes and was not attacking the wider Jewish faith as such, the word 'Judeans' helps to support that context. John's readers may have been a small minority within a wider Christian community which was itself a small minority. John looks back to a time when Jesus challenged and argued with the authorities of his own time.

A change in the way the word is translated would also preserve a context in which the observance and theology of the faith of Israel at the time of Jesus was hugely different from the Rabbinic Judaism which inspired subsequent generations.

John wrote the Jews of his own time back into the story of Jesus. They became Jesus' combatants and enemies for an author who could not attack the Roman authorities directly. The problem for translators is that at the time of Jesus, the Greek term *Ioudaioi* could still carry a geographical designation – the people of the Roman province of Judea. John refers to the people of Samaria as 'Samaritans', the people of Galilee as 'Galileans', but in the English translation the people of Judea are called 'Jews'. The inaccuracy of this rendering is particularly evident in John 7.1, where we read: 'After this Jesus went about in Galilee. He did not wish to go about in Judea because the Jews were looking for an opportunity to kill him.' The Johannine ministry of Jesus begins in Galilee (1.43; 2.1), but the scene soon shifts to Judea. In the NRSV translation (2.11, 13): 'Jesus did this, the first of his signs, in Cana of Galilee, and revealed his glory ... The Passover of the Jews was near, and Jesus went up to Jerusalem.' From the beginning, then, Judea was the place of encounter with 'the Jews' and also the place where the festivals were celebrated. Similarly in 7.2 we find, 'Now the Jewish festival of booths was near', ἦν δὲ ἐγγὺς ἡ ἑορτὴ τῶν Ἰουδαίων, ἡ σκηνοπηγία. In all these cases, 'Judean' would offer a much clearer reading. There are a few instances in John where *Ioudaioi* carries a wider geographical reference, such as 4.9, where Jesus of Nazareth in Galilee is called a Jew by a Samaritan woman. But in the story he has just left Judea, and Jesus goes on to talk about Jerusalem, and say in 4.22 that 'salvation is from the Jews'. Even in these instances, the translation 'Judean' does no violence to the sense.

But by the time John wrote his Gospel, the Temple was destroyed and the autonomous local government of the province had come to an end. Jews lived across the Roman Empire and were now identified by their link to their ancient faith, no longer by the link to the Land. John's contemporary, Josephus, uses the Greek *Ioudaioi* both for Judeans and Jews, such as those living in Rome. But John is not writing of Jews outside the Land, and an accurate translation needs to place the narrative into the context into which the author set it, so 'Judeans' is the more correct term. Even for those living in later centuries in the Diaspora, the term continued to carry a sense of a link to the Land from which their ancestors had come – compare today's use of the term 'African Americans'.

I am, then, inviting Christian leaders to change the translations both used in church and by Christian readers. In the days when the Vulgate was the text used in Europe, there was no distinction between 'Judeans' and 'Jews', and that is indeed true of many modern languages also. But English translators are forced to choose between the two terms. In suggesting a change from 'the Jews' to 'the Judeans', I am following in the footsteps of some worthy Christian commentators. Writing in 1985, the Evangelical Lutheran pastor Norman Beck, in his book *Mature Christianity: The Recognition and Repudiation of the Anti-Jewish Polemic of the New Testament*, suggested that 'the Jews' in John be translated in different ways according to the context: 'the people', 'the leaders', 'some of the leaders', 'the authorities', and so on. Beck's suggestions, and some other phrases such as 'the Temple police' and 'the crowd', were actually used to translate *Ioudaioi* in the version of John published as the American Bible Society Contemporary English Version in 1995 (known as the CEV Bible).

The extent to which we should identify today's Jews or Christians with groups in ancient society is part of a wider debate which grapples with issues of ethnicity and conversion as well as spiritual heritage. The foundation documents of Rabbinic Judaism were compiled at the beginning of or later than the third century of the Christian Era, and the focus through subsequent centuries on details of personal observance and community practice represents a necessary adjustment by a group which had lost its Land, its Temple and its government. Even if John's 'Jews' could be shown to be a specific religious group, they would represent only one of many groups in first-century Judea, with allegiances to a Temple cult which was immeasurably different from the Rabbinic Judaism which developed later. It is relevant to note that John has no word for 'Judaism', only '*Ioudaioi*', and that the Hebrew Bible only rarely uses the term *y'hudim*, the normal designation in the Bible being '*b'nei Yisrael*' (the descendants of Jacob, whose name was changed to Israel). It is only when we turn to the Christian Scriptures that the designation 'the Jews' becomes common. Because that is the designation used today, it gives the narrative a more modern feel and increases the likelihood of the reader jumping to incorrect conclusions about Jewish attitudes in our time. If we are to move forward from past prejudices, the designation 'Judeans' gives a more accurate picture of a people still linked to a particular province of the early Roman Empire. The wider implication is that if Christians wish to discover Judaism, they should seek out rabbis and Jews today rather than opening their Bibles. It is my hope that working on this and other difficult texts will increase the impetus for local Christian groups to try to understand contemporary Judaism, work in which the Council for Christians and Jews can and does play a vital, positive role.

Notes

1 Michael Hilton with Gordian Marshall OP, 1998, *The Gospels and Rabbinic Judaism: A Study Guide*, London: SCM Press.

2 German-born American Reform Rabbi (1843–1926). Kaufmann Kohler, 1905, 'New Testament', in *The Jewish Encyclopedia*, New York and London: Funk and Wagnalls, 9.251.

3 Gareth Lloyd Jones, b. 1938, is Emeritus Professor of the Department of Theology and Religious Studies, University of Wales. He was Canon Chancellor of Bangor Cathedral.

4 Rabbi Samuel Sandmel (1911–79) was Provost of Hebrew Union College, Cincinnati, Ohio. In 1968–69 he was Visiting Honorary Principal of Leo Baeck College, London.

5 Samuel Sandmel, 1978, *Judaism and Christian Beginnings*, New York: Oxford University Press, p. 370.

6 John 7.1.

7 Raymond Brown (1928–98) was an American Roman Catholic priest and prominent biblical scholar.

8 For reasons that are unclear but fortunate for us, the Jewish community in Cairo retained vast numbers of Hebrew documents. These include sacred texts containing the Hebrew name of God – which are not destroyed by widespread tradition – but also family and commercial documents and fragments with no sacred connotations, simply anything written in Hebrew characters. Over several centuries, the store or Genizah was filled and then ceased to be used. Its presence came to the attention of western scholars in the early twentieth century and about three-quarters of it was brought to Cambridge by the German-trained Jewish scholar Dr Solomon Schechter. It has fuelled a remarkable scholarly industry, shedding light on the life of Jewish communities around the Mediterranean in the early medieval period.

9 Lawrence A. Hoffman, 1998, *My People's Prayer Book: vol. 2 – The Amidah*, Woodstock: Jewish Lights, p. 134.

10 R. Bieringer, D. Pollefeyt and F. Vandecasteele-Vanneuville (eds.), 2001, *Anti-Judaism and the Fourth Gospel*, Louisville, KY, and London: Westminster John Knox Press, pp. 32–3.

11 Stephen Motyer, 2008, 'Bridging the Gap: How Might the Fourth Gospel Help Us Cope with the Legacy of Christianity's Exclusive Claim over against Judaism?', in Richard Bauckham and Carl Mosser (eds.), *The Gospel of John and Christian Theology*, Grand Rapids, MI, and Cambridge: Eerdmans, pp. 143–67.

12 Judith Lieu, 'Anti-Judaism, the Jews, and the Worlds of the Fourth Gospel', in Bauckham and Mosser (eds.) *The Gospel of John*, pp. 168–82.

13 Similarly, many modern Jewish prayer books omit the final verses of Psalm 137 and other passages which call for revenge.

14 Malcolm Lowe, 1976, 'Who were the *Ioudaioi*?', *Novum Testamentum* 18:2, pp. 101–30. Malcolm Lowe is a New Testament scholar, resident in Jerusalem.

William of Norwich and Echoes through the Ages

DAVID GILLETT

Part one: Beginning in medieval Norwich

Responding to Michael Hilton's plea

I am one of those Christian clergy who attempt to speak on the text of John's Gospel in a way that helps people to understand the differences between the world of the first century and Christian relationships with Jews and Rabbinic Judaism today. I would strongly support a nuanced translation of certain New Testament texts to reflect more accurately the complexities of the first-century relationship between synagogue and church and the many differences in that relationship in the twenty-first century.

Beyond this, however, there is the huge challenge of how to 'come to terms'[1] with the countless incidents and long, troubled periods which have left deep scars on our relationship ever since the founding of Rabbinic Judaism and the writing of the New Testament. In facing this task we are, in some sense, replicating the process by which we in these islands have been dealing with our past – our imperial legacy, particularly its disreputable side; our prominent role in the African slave trade; our relationship with the island of Ireland; and our more recent lack of hospitality to immigrants from the West Indies and the Indian subcontinent. But in coming to terms with Jewish–Christian relationships, which began 2,000 years ago, we need to go back further than in any of the other cases. I want to look at 200 years during the Middle Ages, a period when Christians and Jews were living side by side in this country, a period which has left a legacy of abuse and persecution only relatively recently acknowledged – and even now, patchily at best.

I have chosen to focus my look at how we come to terms with our often painful history by focusing on medieval Norwich – on the principle that it is important to look in one's own backyard first before peering over into other people's gardens. I live in Norfolk and am currently an honorary assistant bishop in the Diocese of Norwich and its Interfaith Adviser.

As I began to write this, a search of the website 'Visit Norwich, The Essential Official Guide' has just yielded: 'Your site search for William of Norwich. Sorry, no results found.' Yet the story surrounding the murder of a young boy, William, in Norwich in Holy Week 1144 – a time when Christians were remembering the crucifixion of Christ – is the first recorded accusation of blood libel against a Jewish community anywhere in the world. The blood libel charged Jews with using the blood of a Gentile child when making unleavened bread for Passover. It began with an unexplained death, attributed it to the local Jewish community and added the dimension of mimicking the crucifixion of Christ. The accusation spread across Europe and down the centuries – adding a further spiral to anti-Judaism and anti-Semitism. The Norwich website informs visitors to the City of other notable local figures from history – Horatio Nelson, Edith Cavell, Elizabeth Fry, Julian of Norwich – but, maybe in part because there is very little for the tourist to go and see, the story of William of Norwich and its subsequent ramifications is passed over in silence.[2]

As individuals within both the Jewish and Christian communities in Norwich have remarked to me on several occasions: 'The City does not like to be reminded of this part of its history.' The words of Professor Miri Rubin echo a corresponding national amnesia: 'The accusation of ritual murder is an English contribution to the stock of anti-Jewish narratives told in Europe since the twelfth century, yet knowledge of it has all but faded from English consciousness.'[3]

The foundation stones for coping with the painful past of the relationship between our two communities are:

- knowing what has happened
- having an agreed understanding of its significance
- acknowledging its importance
- coming to a joint awareness of its contemporary impact
- developing resolutions which can inform good relationships in the present.

A legacy bequeathed by Norwich in 1144

Largely through the closely related network of priories and abbeys throughout Britain and mainland Europe, knowledge of the blood libel accusation made in 1144 in Norwich spread and led to similar accusations in Gloucester (1168), Bury St Edmunds (1181), Bristol (1193) and Lincoln (1255).[4] In Europe as a whole from the twelfth to the sixteenth century the number of known cases of the blood libel amount to nearly a hundred.[5] These contributed to the growing perception of the Jewish community as a danger to the Church. In 1215, the Fourth Lateran Council issued Canons against the Jews which forbad Jews to go out in public in the three days around Good Friday and required the wearing of a 'Jewish badge' to distinguish Jews from the wider population. Though grounds for blood libel accusations were largely eroded in Protestant theologies at the Reformation, the tradition survived in many forms of popular European culture as well as in certain Catholic, Eastern European and Russian traditions.[6]

As early as 1144 – only months after the episode in Norwich – a Somerset folk song appeared, 'Little Sir William', containing the line, 'The Jew's wife hath me slain.'[7] Seven hundred years later, in the nineteenth century, the Brothers Grimm included in their collection of German tales 'The Rock of the Jews', which recounts how a lowly Tyrolean farmer in 1462 was forced by Jews to hand over his small son who is taken to the rock, tortured, murdered and then hung on a birch tree. In Nazi Germany the edition of Julius Streicher's *Der Stürmer* (*The Attacker*) of 1 May 1934 concentrated on the blood libel accusation as part of a determined attempt to inflame anti-Jewish hatred. The front page of the paper displays a horrific blood libel cartoon and, elsewhere in this edition, Streicher reproduced an old engraving of four rabbis sucking the blood of a Christian child through straws.

The momentum begun in twelfth-century Norwich continues today – on anti-Semitic Arabic[8] and neo-Nazi websites and publications. It is understandable perhaps that Norwich would rather forget this period in its history, but part of dealing with our past inter-communal conflicts is to acknowledge the hurt and legacy they have left and educate for a better future: ignorance allows the myths to be relived and replicated.

The original story of Norwich, 1144

Let me go back to that first fateful accusation in twelfth-century Norwich, in my backyard. The basic facts are reasonably uncontested. William was born in February 1132, the child of a farmer, Wenstan, and his wife Elviva, whose sister Liviva was married to a Norwich priest, Godwin Sturt. William was baptized in the parish of Haveringland and, as an 8-year-old boy, was apprenticed to a skinner in Norwich. In the course of his work he had dealings with the Jewish community. On Tuesday in

Holy Week, 21 March, he was '[s]een by his cousin to go into the house of a Jew'.⁹ The next sighting of him was when his body was found on the following Saturday, Easter Eve.

Most of the Norwich Jewish community had arrived just over half a century earlier from Normandy and Lower Rhineland in the wake of the Norman Conquest. They had settled in East Anglia when the region was reaching its heyday as the most populous and prosperous part of the country, Norwich being the largest medieval city after London. The See for the region (covering both Norfolk and Suffolk) had transferred from Thetford to Norwich in 1094 and the City's cathedral was founded in 1096. Out of a total City population of 10,000, the Jewish community numbered about 200 (about 2 per cent).¹⁰ The Jewish quarter was situated between the marketplace and the castle, the seat of the Sheriff under whose protection Jews were placed.

As background to the story of William of Norwich – and as the impetus for its subsequent misuse – lies the generally poor but interdependent relationship between the Jewish and Christian communities in the City:

> The relationship between Christians and Jews in Norwich was never good, and became worse during the century and a half of the community's existence; this deterioration can be traced in the increasing gravity of the attacks to which the Jews were subjected by the local population.¹¹

This should be seen in the context of a growth in the underlying religious animosity towards Jewish communities in the twelfth century, which was actively encouraged by monastic writers of the period. They produced an outpouring of Marian legends in which Jews are portrayed as the enemies of the Church, cruel and sly people who attacked defenceless children (who often benefited from the miraculous intervention of the Virgin Mary). These tales became among the most popular in English medieval culture, were included in the round of Marian liturgies and figured prominently in popular preaching of the period. East Anglia was one of the main centres where these Marian, anti-Jewish legends were being promulgated, most notably through one of the greatest Benedictine abbeys within the land, which was situated in the Diocese of Norwich at Bury St Edmunds.¹²

However, given the unfavourable background for the Jewish community and the immediate accusations of blood libel made against them, the tale made remarkably little local headway until the arrival in Norwich of the monk Thomas of Monmouth. He joined the Cathedral monastic community in about 1150, five or six years after the event had occurred.

He went on to document, develop and embellish the story in his hagiographical work, *The Life and Passion of Saint William of Norwich*.[13]

Thomas was astonished that so little capital had been made of such a promising story. The consequences for the Jewish community in the intervening period had not been disastrous. Thomas saw his task as revisiting a cold case and making the story count in a way it had not done so far. He developed the 'evidence' – through new witnesses, stories of vision, dream and theophany – into a martyrology that would support the cult of St William and expand the numbers of pilgrims who flocked to the Cathedral, thus promoting its sacral esteem and enlarging its coffers. At the heart of his account, Thomas quotes the 'evidence' of the convert, then monk, Theobald of Cambridge, who said that a ritual murder was carried out annually in a town picked by lot in Spain and that, in 1144, this had fallen to Norwich.

Thomas's task was to establish that William was not just an innocent victim of murder but a holy martyr – for only as such could he become a saint and the focus of a miraculous cult with all its attendant pilgrimages and healing miracles. Consequently, as he developed his work, Thomas elaborated the story, making the Jewish community the villains of the piece but, more importantly from Thomas's point of view, enhancing William's status. His birth was now attended by biblical-style annunciations, his life and family were enhanced by divine manifestations, and his death was depicted as a Christ-like crucifixion. Miri Rubin observes, correctly: 'Thomas placed the drama of Christian-killing in the midst of mundane urban life. He turned Jewish neighbours – patriarchs, merchants, financiers – into bloodthirsty enemies.'[14]

But you can see the Jews in terms of collateral damage inflicted by Thomas in pursuit of his larger objectives. As the story gained credence and importance, William's body was moved from the monks' cemetery to the chapter house and, later, to the Cathedral itself. Subsequently, a shrine was erected in the Cathedral to 'St William the Martyr', which perpetuated the blood libel. William of Norwich was a locally recognized cult (as with so many such local medieval cults, William was never canonized by Rome), which from the late twelfth century onwards attracted many pilgrims with countless healings attributed to the saint until the abolition of the cult and the destruction of the shrine at the time of the Reformation.[15]

Given the determined and culpable contrivances of a member of the Cathedral community, together with the support of his bishop and many other colleagues, the blood libel accusation is a fact that weighs heavily within the history of the Cathedral in Norwich. The story has to be told, its shameful legacy to subsequent history acknowledged, and contemporary opportunities for education provided: a challenge to which Norwich has recently begun to respond more fully.

Part two: Four contemporary 'echoes' from medieval Norwich

One: a drama by a Jewish playwright with Norwich connections

The natural tendency, when dealing with the anti-Semitism of the past, is to look to the perpetrators to make amends, offer apologies or make restitution as appropriate. There are, however, examples where someone from the Jewish community takes a lead in helping the whole community to face up to past offences. Such has been the case in Norwich.

The Jewish playwright Arnold Wesker, who had previously lived and worked as a young adult in Norwich and married a local young woman, was commissioned to write a play based on William of Norwich for a new theatre opening in the city. In 1991, he wrote *Blood Libel*, which, following the delayed opening of the Playhouse, was eventually performed in February 1996. As he began to work on the play, Wesker was clearly conscious of the inter-communal and international significance of what he was writing: 'It is a locally based subject which has many parallels with the recent revival of anti-Semitism and religious prejudice all over the world.'[16]

A similar point was made by a reviewer of the play, Ian Shuttleworth, when he wrote for the *Financial Times*:

> *Blood Libel* undoubtedly acquires added potency from being performed, as it were, on the scene of the crime; nevertheless, its admonitions about the force of unfounded convictions and the perils of acquiescing to them for pragmatism's sake are universally trenchant.[17]

The contemporary relevance of the events was emphasized by an interpretative decision which Wesker made about the murder as a sexual assault:

> Since it was inconceivable that the attack was the work of any member of the small (and vulnerable) Jewish community I could only assume it was a sexually motivated attack by a psychopath such as is familiar throughout time up to the present day. Yes, therefore I took poetic licence.[18]

Wesker portrays the events of 1144 as the direct result of anti-Semitism but also sees the play as a metaphor for religious fanaticism in general. The content and flavour of the premiere in its 'host city' – as well as its historical faithfulness – is well conveyed in Shuttleworth's review as he describes how the play enacts

> twelve-year-old William's rape and murder, the town mob's rage against the Jews of Norwich (on the vacuous grounds that surely no Christian could have perpetrated such an atrocity), and the zealous campaign of the monk Thomas of Monmouth to have the boy canonised as a martyr.[19]

We are shown the fabrication of pro-William and anti-Semitic 'evidence', the product of both self-delusion and outside coaching, and the debilitating and ultimately vain struggle of Prior Elias to hold to a line of reasoned inquiry in the teeth of a fierce lust to believe. When his sceptical 'wisdom' is derided by Thomas as doubt, the enemy of blind faith, Elias replies, 'Faith without wisdom is mere superstition', but the superstition welling up from the townsfolk and marshalled by Thomas in the cause of 'my William' acquires the force of a juggernaut.

In an interview published in the *Eastern Daily Press* at the time of the premiere, Wesker gave his understanding of the significance of what he had written:

> I think it deals in values, and in poetic metaphor. In this case a metaphor that points to the ill-effects of religious fundamentalism. I'm making the audience look at religious hysteria, which must lead them to look at their own time ... I don't think anyone should ever write anything which doesn't reach out beyond itself.[20]

Wesker has made a significant contribution to the process by which a local community acknowledges the past, comes to terms with it and learns how to interpret it for the present. That process is a precondition for healthy relationships between the two communities. Alan Webster, a former Dean of Norwich Cathedral, wrote, after seeing the play: 'Many in the theatre audiences of Christians and Jews found that they were spellbound.'

It is, sadly, noteworthy that Wesker's play has never had another performance anywhere else in the world, even though its significance is much wider than for the 'host city' itself. Hopefully, there are those elsewhere who will yet discover the opportunity this drama offers to encourage an honest evaluation of the issue of anti-Semitism in both historical and contemporary settings, far removed from Norwich itself.

But there is still more that Wesker's play can achieve in Norwich beyond its initial outing. As Shuttleworth remarks in his review: 'It is mildly ironic that Arnold Wesker's play (completed in 1991) about St

William of Norwich has finally received its world première in one of the city's few arts/performance venues not housed in a converted church.'[21]

Two new books published in 2012 and 2014 presented Norwich – and other places – with a further opportunity. The play had long been out of print but a new edition of Wesker's historical plays has just been published, and includes *Blood Libel*.[22] We held a day conference in Norwich Cathedral in March 2014, which included a rehearsed reading of Wesker's play, together with consideration of Miri Ruben's forthcoming book on William of Norwich, published by Penguin and launched in Norwich Cathedral in December 2014. Both Jews and Christians from the local and wider community participated in the day. A notable feature were the joint groups from both communities who worked together on how the Cathedral and the city could most helpfully record these events and their consequences – within the Cathedral and in educational programmes for schools. It is hoped that other opportunities can be found when Wesker's play can be performed in our city and in other venues around the country as it confronts the audience with the need to examine our own responses to similar prejudice and abuse which is still so much a feature today.

Two: recognition in Norwich Cathedral

There is no place, of course, where there more needs to be an adequate reminder of the medieval blood libel than in Norwich Cathedral – in which it was celebrated with a saint's shrine for several centuries and from where the evil spread around the world. A reminder is needed which not only educates but provides the impetus for all who enter the Cathedral to renew a commitment to working for good relationships between the Jewish and Christian communities today. The Cathedral does already give interpretative help for those who visit, but even those who produced the material used for several years have regarded it as 'work in progress'. It must become an unambiguous opportunity for contemporary reflection and a spur to good community relations.

In the Cathedral's 'Chapel of the Holy Innocents' the following text seeks to deal with the historical event of William's death and the subsequent cult, centred on the Cathedral itself. However, the main context used is not the events from Norwich's own past but events in Bethlehem at the time of the birth of Jesus, no doubt seeking to give a wider context within a better known Christian story:

> The Holy Innocents were young Jewish boys who were slaughtered by King Herod (Matt. 2.16–18) in his determination to kill the infant Jesus who had already escaped with Mary and Joseph into Egypt.

WILLIAM OF NORWICH AND ECHOES THROUGH THE AGES

William of Norwich: William was a young Norwich boy who was found murdered outside the city on Mousehold Heath in Holy Week 1144. Members of his family and a monk from the Cathedral accused the Jews of Norwich of crucifying him, but this claim was not generally accepted. Saner heads at the Cathedral and in the town prevailed, and there were no reprisals against the local Jewish community. This was, however, the first recorded instance of the influential 'blood libel' against the Jews, taken up in other places with murderous consequences.

Despite the accusations against the Jews being discredited, miracles of healing were attributed to William's intercession, and he was honoured as a boy-martyr. His shrine migrated within the Cathedral from the Chapter House to near this chapel and finally to the Jesus Chapel. His cult was locally popular, and there are images of him to be found on rood screens in East Anglia.

Please use this Chapel as a place of prayer for the ending of intolerance and persecution and for the reconciliation of people of different faiths and of none.

O LORD, remember not only the men and women of good will but also those of ill will. But do not remember all the suffering they have inflicted upon us; remember the fruits we have bought, thanks to this suffering, our comradeship, our loyalty, our humility, the courage, the generosity, the greatness of heart which has grown out of this; and when they come to judgement, let all the fruits that we have borne be their forgiveness. Amen.[23]

These words clearly acknowledge the significance of 'William of Norwich' in the history of Christian–Jewish relationships, and seek to place that significance within a wider context of racial hatred. But they fail to acknowledge the nature of the accusations, which were entirely fictitious, promulgated from within the Cathedral community itself and subsequently used to the Cathedral's profit. Furthermore, linking the medieval events in Norwich with the Shoah of the twentieth century, while offering suggestions for meditation and prayer, has the effect of confusing the roles of the aggressor and the innocent, the perpetrator and the victim. Young William is acknowledged as a victim, one of the Holy Innocents, but not the Jews of medieval Norwich. Hopefully, ongoing reflection on these events in the present context will lead to a clearer acknowledgement of past culpability. Clarity as between victim and perpetrator in hate crimes will enable the pilgrim and sightseer to reflect and pray with greater insight about its contemporary relevance. The day conference mentioned above has produced guidance from both Jewish and Christian perspectives which should lead to a new set of words, more appropriately dealing with William of Norwich for today.

A few other cathedrals involved in similar events in medieval England have also acknowledged the darker truths of Christian dealings with Jews in the past. In 1255, 18 Jews were murdered in Lincoln as a result of the blood libel. Reflection in Lincoln Cathedral about 'Little Hugh of Lincoln' led to the unveiling of a new plaque in the Cathedral. Kaddish, the Hebrew prayer for the dead, was sung by a synagogue cantor at the close of the service. There was also a solemn procession to the site of commemoration, the shrine of Little Hugh of Lincoln, as an act of memorial. In 1990, York Minster was one of the sites in a series of similar Christian–Jewish acts of remembrance on the eight-hundredth anniversary of the massacre of Jews at Clifford's Tower in 1190. On this occasion there was a weekend of events, including lectures, a memorial gathering at Clifford's Tower led by Rabbi Dr Norman Solomon, a civic reception hosted by the Lord Mayor of York, a memorial concert, a dramatic presentation of *The Jews in Medieval Drama*, a Jewish Sabbath service, an interfaith Bible study session, and a commemorative interfaith service in York Minster.

These events, and others like them, provide valuable opportunities for celebrating our common heritage as Abrahamic faiths and renewing our commitment to positive, creative relationships today.

Three: a cold case television programme featuring Norwich

Television can be a great educator in the area of good inter-communal relationships and there have been many examples that have accurately and helpfully portrayed the issues involved in anti-Semitism. However, the tendency to sensationalize events can, as in a recent example affecting both the Jewish and Christian communities in Norwich, raise the temperature and create problems for both communities that weren't there before.

Such was the effect of a programme, *Cold Case*, first shown on BBC2 in June 2011. The format adopted was 'a forensic approach' – reopening a case long since closed where reaching a verdict using modern techniques might just be possible. In 2004, the remains of 17 bodies had been found at the bottom of a medieval well in Norwich. Eleven of the 17 skeletons were those of children aged between 2 and 15. The remaining 6 were adult men and women. The inference made in the programme was that these could have been victims of persecution. The programme ended with a somewhat dramatically contrived concluding scene, asserting that the most likely explanation was that those down the well were Jewish and were most probably murdered or forced to commit suicide. These conclusions were drawn by a group of forensic scientists who based much of what they said on DNA analysis that suggested a possible link with European Ashkenazi Jews. The forensic scientists involved were using expertise gained in unravelling cases of ethnic cleansing of Kosovan Albanians. The leader of the forensic team said: 'We are possibly talking about persecution. We are possibly talking about ethnic cleansing and this all brings to mind the scenario that we dealt with during the Balkan War crimes.'

This caused an immediate problem for a considerable number in Norwich's Christian and Jewish communities. Members of the church in whose parish the remains were discovered wanted to acknowledge and make some recompense for the previously unknown crime perpetrated against the Jewish community in their parish, to hold a service of reconciliation, and to mark such an event with a memorial in their churchyard. Leading members of the Jewish community immediately began to seek permission to recover the remains from the city museum, where they had been kept since their discovery, in order to give them a proper religious burial. There were calls from various groups of Christians for a significant, high-profile event to counteract the sense of shame and outrage some felt after the claims made in the television programme. Emotions had been engaged and a sense of urgency to 'do something' was evident among both Jews and Christians.

Very soon, however, doubts began to emerge about the conclusions reached by the programme. The geneticist, whose original DNA evidence was so crucial, said subsequently that it had become clear that the original and small amount of genetic evidence was even less secure than had been thought previously. Two academics interviewed in the programme, Dr Sophie Cabot, a local Norwich archaeologist, and Professor Miri Rubin said that they were unhappy with the conclusions of the programme and had no confidence that the tragic events had been perpetrated against members of the Jewish community. The outcome was ambiguity about the attribution of the remains, with the possibility (but no more) that they may be Jewish – but with both the Jewish and Christian communities wishing to bring some resolution to a medieval crime which had suddenly become a contemporary issue between them. Subsequently, a leader from the Jewish community and I negotiated with the museum authorities that the remains should be released for burial in the Jewish cemetery in the city. This service took place in March 2013. I had the privilege of giving the homily – which I used, in part, as an opportunity to address the persecution of Jews by Christians in medieval Norwich. Following this, negotiations have been held between various sections within both communities to find appropriate ways of memorializing this event within the city centre. This was a difficult process, revealing strong differences within the churches about how to deal with such historical events and some apprehension within the Jewish community that certain approaches could cause an anti-Semitic reaction. Eventually the shopping centre under which the remains were discovered agreed to the positioning of a plaque in a prominent position with the following wording, which has proved acceptable to all parties:

> In memory of six adults and eleven children
> whose bodies were discovered in a well shaft in 2004
> during the construction of the Chapelfield Shopping Centre.
> This plaque commemorates their burial
> by Jewish and Christian ministers together
> on March 19th 2013
> in the Jewish Cemetery in Norwich.
> The burial was also an act of reconciliation for the persecution
> of the Jewish community in medieval Norwich.
> 'Return, O my soul, to your rest.' Psalm 116.7

This 'cold case' is a reminder that precision and accuracy, which are the hallmarks of the best historical research, are especially necessary when dealing with possible tragedies from the past that affect two communities whose history is very much intertwined with their present.

Four: a medieval Jewish poet from Norwich worthy of recall

In our attempts to recover and understand past history we are often hampered by lack of evidence of any positive aspects of life within Jewish communities. Readily available evidence points to distress and suffering. But there is another side to the story which often requires more diligent research if it is to be unearthed.

In the years immediately prior to the expulsion of the Jews from England in 1290 – one of those facts which is at the forefront of historical memory – there was an accomplished Jewish poet living in Norwich whose memory and importance (particularly locally) is only now in the process of being recognized. This changes our one-dimensional picture of medieval Jewish communities. The story is not merely a tale of artisans, craftsmen, money-lenders and the occasional apothecary or doctor, who were all too often the subject of discrimination and persecution. There was also a flourishing cultural life and Rabbi Meir ben Elijah of Norwich needs to be recognized as illustrating this story. He documents, with poetic skill, the pain and suffering endured by many of his fellow Jews, particularly in the difficult years leading up to the expulsion – a time when a number of Jews in the city were massacred. His poetry, however, also reveals a deeper, richer vein to the story of medieval Jewry. The full story of the Jewish presence in Norwich includes the faith and hope which sustained the community, as well as the pain and persecution. Rabbi Meir is a striking example of the community's literary heritage and his poetry reveals a cultural and religious sensitivity well able to stand alongside many of England's more celebrated poets – like Chaucer who came a century later. Until relatively recently, scholars have assumed that the small communities of medieval English Jewry did not have the cultural sophistication to produce such examples of learning and literary merit as we can now see in Meir of Norwich. Today we can see how his poems are worthy of comparison with the better-known examples from Spain and elsewhere on the continent.[24]

Meir's poem, 'On the Termination of the Sabbath', gives us insight into the religious and liturgical life of the Jewish community in thirteenth-century Norwich. He not only celebrates the Sabbath – that gift of Judaism to western culture – but also affirms Jewish worth in the face of contempt and persecution. His mixture of a confident, communal and religious identity, together with an uplifting sense of faith in the face of a constant milieu of threat, provides an insight into the resilient pride of the small Jewish community in thirteenth-century Norwich. It encourages us to recover an understanding of the cultural and religious life of medieval English Jewry and appreciate that its breadth is far more than the negative story of exclusion, persecution and expulsion with which we are more familiar. As a central feature in coping with the past, it is important to celebrate the positives as well as lament and seek to make amends for the tragedies.

But, particularly as the thirteenth century drew to its close, the pain was often so clearly to the fore. Meir's words in the last three stanzas of his 'Ode to Joy' movingly portray the agony of the Jewish community in Norwich prior to the expulsion, together with a defiant note of faith which endures.

> We languish, suffering in the land
> And hear the brutes' insults,
> And steadfastly do we endure
> While waiting for the Light.
>
> Mighty art Thou and glorious
> Those in darkness dwelling

Thou dost surround with Light.
A heavy yoke on us they lay
Commanding and compelling
That we abandon and forsake
Our only hope and Light.

Our blood is shed on garments fringed
Our heart it is they covet
But may you ever comfort us
For this by holy Light.

From Rabbi Meir ben Elijah of the thirteenth century we have words that can help in our understanding of the past and provide a timely reminder today of the history that informs the way in which we seek to foster and build good community relations in Norwich.[25]

Notes

1 By 'coming to terms' I mean that Christians now, while not responsible for what happened centuries ago, have a duty fully to acknowledge the past and work at a productive and creative relationship in the present in order to build a better future together.

2 For those tourists who want to look more closely into Norwich's history, the Heritage Website does mention, albeit briefly, the blood libel of 1144 in the section on the Jews of Norwich, http://tinyurl.com/bojkuje.

3 Miri Rubin, 2010, 'Making a Martyr: William of Norwich and the Jews', *History Today*, June, pp. 49–54.

4 The accusations of blood libel, begun in the twelfth century, led on to those of host desecration in the thirteenth century and the poisoning of wells in the fourteenth.

5 According to R. Po-chia Hsia, 1988, *The Myth of Ritual Murder*, New Haven, CT: Yale University Press, there were 8 in the twelfth century, 14 in the thirteenth century, 16 in the fourteenth century, 23 in the fifteenth century and 26 in the sixteenth century. 'The seemingly low figure of the fourteenth century must be seen in the context of the massive pogroms associated with the Black Death of mid-century, during which entire Jewish communities in the Holy Roman Empire were destroyed' (p. 3).

6 Hsia, in *The Myth of Ritual Murder*, argues convincingly that the combination of blood libel, host desecration and child sacrifice, which for several centuries formed the mainspring of Christian anti-Semitism, was based on ideas of magic and sacrifice that dominated much of medieval Catholic thought. Swept aside by the Reformation, this particular theological rationale for anti-Semitism lost much of its force: 'There was a broad consensus in Christian society of the magical nature of Jews ... The murdered children, like Christ, became sacrificial gifts. The offering of their blood through the double sacrifice of Jewish murder and Christian vengeance was meant to create a bond of exchange between heaven and earth for

assuring the incessant flow of divine grace ... the Reformation proved to be a turning point undermining the foundations of late medieval piety ... In attacking late medieval magic and in advocating the study of Hebrew, the Reformation provided another force to undermine ritual murder discourse' (pp. 226f.). Various strands within Reformation Theology did, of course, provide grounds for other anti-Jewish theologies.

7 Whenever Peter Pears sang Benjamin Britten's arrangement of this song he altered the offending line to, 'The school wife hath me slain.'

8 In 1840 in Damascus, the Christian community levelled a blood libel accusation against a Jew. In fact, the murder had been committed by a member of the Christian community. This did not stop the spread of this form of anti-Semitism within the Arab world. It was consciously fanned and exploited in the twentieth century by Arab leaders who had sided with Nazi Germany against Britain.

9 We don't, of course, know when the cousin made the accusation – before or after the body was found.

10 Nationally it is difficult to be certain of numbers throughout the period from the Conquest to Expulsion in 1290 (because of the effects of both plague and persecution) but in 1290, out of a total population of 3 million there were about 2,500 Jews.

11 Vivian David Lipman, 1967, *The Jews of Medieval Norwich*, London: Jewish Historical Society, p. 49.

12 The Abbot, Anselm (nephew of the famous Archbishop of Canterbury), produced an influential new collection of Marian miracles based on ancient tales.

13 This manuscript was lost for many centuries (though parts of the story remained in other dependent works) but was discovered by Canon Augustus Jessop of East Dereham in Norfolk in Brent Eleigh in Suffolk in 1891 – *Prologus de vita et Passione Sancti Willelmi Martyris Norwicensis*. Canon Jessop subsequently collaborated with Montague Rhodes James to translate the Latin manuscript and publish it with explanatory notes as *The Life and Miracles of St William of Norwich*, 1896, Cambridge, digitally reprinted by Cambridge University Press in 2011.

14 Miri Rubin, *The Passion of William of Norwich*, a paper prepared for discussion at the Jewish History Seminar, Institute of Historical Research, University of London, 12 June 2012, pp. 27f.

15 A few medieval reminders remain, as with the rood screen picture at Holy Trinity, Loddon in Norfolk. It is important to remember, however, that by the time of the Reformation Jews had been long absent from Britain. It was not until the time of Cromwell and the second half of the seventeenth century that Jews began – very slowly – to return.

16 Reported in *Eastern Evening News*, 28 January 1991.

17 *Financial Times*, accessed at www.cix.co.uk/~shutters/reviews/96006.htm.

18 From correspondence between Sir Arnold Wesker and me, July 2012.

19 *Financial Times*, accessed at www.cix.co.uk/~shutters/reviews/96006.htm.

20 Quoted to the author by Arnold Wesker in correspondence.

21 *Financial Times*, accessed at www.cix.co.uk/~shutters/reviews/96006.htm.

22 Arnold Wesker, 2012, *Wesker's Historical Plays*, London: Oberon Books. It also includes his three other plays that deal with conflicts caused by religion, science and the Establishment: *Shylock* (1972), *Caritas* (1980) and *Longitude* (2002).

23 A prayer found on a piece of wrapping paper in Ravensbruck, the largest of the concentration camps for women in Nazi Germany.

24 The Hebrew manuscripts of 21 of his poems are housed in the Vatican archive in Rome, though how they got there is presently a mystery. They were originally discovered in the Vatican Library by Abraham Berliner (1833–1915) who was a German-based expert in Jewish history and literature. The Hebrew text of the poems can be found as an appendix in Lipman, *Jews of Medieval Norwich*. English translations of the poems (by A. M. Haberman) are available in a bound typed volume in the local studies section at the main library in Norwich. In 2013, a new translation and introduction to Meir's poems – by some from the city's Jewish community – was published in 2014: *Into the Light: The Medieval Hebrew Poetry of Meir of Norwich*, trans. Ellman Crasnow and Bente Elsworth, Introduction by Keiron Pim, Norwich: East Publishing.

25 In October 2002, to celebrate the sixtieth anniversary of the Council of Christians and Jews, the local branch of CCJ held a concert in Norwich Cathedral in which one of Meir's poems which had been set to music was performed.

Holocaust Memorial Day

MICHAEL HILTON AND DAVID GILLETT

Michael Hilton writes

In January 1997, Tony Blair, then Leader of the Opposition, went to the launch of a new Anne Frank Trust exhibition, 'A History for Today', at Southwark Cathedral. The Trust aimed to draw on the power of Anne Frank's diary to challenge prejudice, reduce hatred and encourage people to embrace positive attitudes, responsibility and respect for others. The Trust's exhibitions never focus on the Holocaust alone but always on current racism and prejudice as well. The exhibition that Tony Blair visited was no exception: there was a panel about Stephen Lawrence, the black teenager murdered in South London in 1993, and Tony Blair was introduced to Stephen's mother Doreen at the exhibition. Four months later, Tony Blair became Prime Minister; two months after that, he set up the Stephen Lawrence Inquiry, a step on the road to convictions in 2012, changes in the police force and a great deal of reflection about the nature of British society.

Holocaust Memorial Day (HMD), commemorated each year on 27 January, was, in part, another result of that Southwark Cathedral visit. Gillian Walnes, Chair of the Anne Frank Trust, recalls that at the exhibition in 1997, Tony Blair said there must be a commemoration day for the Holocaust in the UK.[1] In his public speech at the exhibition he said:

> We must never forget what the result of intolerance and racial bigotry can be. The persecution of the Jewish community and other minorities by the fascist regime in Germany has scarred our century. No-one who sees this exhibition and its pictures and testimonies can be in any doubt about that.[2]

On 10 June 1999, Andrew Dismore MP asked Prime Minister Tony Blair about establishing a memorial day for the Holocaust. In reply, Tony Blair also referred to the ethnic cleansing that was being witnessed in the Kosovo War at that time and said:

> I am determined to ensure that the horrendous crimes against humanity committed during the Holocaust are never forgotten. The ethnic cleansing and killing that has taken place in Europe in recent weeks are a stark example of the need for vigilance.[3]

In October 1999 Blair set up a task force to discuss the subject further. Gillian Walnes of the Anne Frank Trust became a member. The chain of events helps to explain why, from the start, HMD was not just about commemorating the Holocaust but included educational programmes on other instances of racist and religious prejudice. Officially, in addition to the Nazi destruction, the day commemorates genocides in Cambodia, Bosnia, Rwanda and Darfur. Despite campaigns by further groups, these have never been included by the UN or the UK – not even the Armenians, whose massacre by the Turks during and after the First World War led Raphael Lemkin to coin the word 'genocide'. Since 1996, 27 January had officially been *Gedenktag für die Opfer des Nationalsozialismus* (Anniversary for the Victims of National Socialism) in Germany. Italy and Poland have adopted similar memorial days. The date was chosen because it marked the anniversary of the liberation of Auschwitz by Soviet troops in 1945.

On 27 January 2000, representatives from 44 governments around the world met in Stockholm to discuss Holocaust education, remembrance and research. At the conclusion of the forum, the delegates unanimously signed a declaration. This declaration forms the basis of the Statement of Commitment later adopted for the UK Holocaust Memorial Day. It included these words:

> We recognise that the Holocaust shook the foundations of modern civilisation. Its unprecedented character and horror will always hold universal meaning. We believe the Holocaust must have a permanent place in our nation's collective memory. We honour the survivors still with us, and reaffirm our shared goals of mutual understanding and justice. We must make sure that future generations understand the causes of the Holocaust and reflect upon its consequences. We vow to remember the victims of Nazi persecution and of all genocide. We value the sacrifices of those who have risked their lives to protect or rescue victims, as a touchstone of the human capacity for good in the face of evil.
>
> We recognise that humanity is still scarred by the belief that race, religion, disability or sexuality make some people's lives worth less than others. Genocide, antisemitism, racism, xenophobia and discrimination still continue. We have a shared responsibility to fight these evils. We pledge to strengthen our efforts to promote education and research

about the Holocaust and other genocide. We will do our utmost to make sure that the lessons of such events are fully learnt. We will continue to encourage Holocaust remembrance by holding an annual Holocaust Memorial Day. We condemn the evils of prejudice, discrimination and racism. We value a free, tolerant, and democratic society.[4]

Most dictionary definitions of 'the Holocaust' state that the term applies to the murder of Jews by the Nazis and their allies. This is the definition adopted by the UK Holocaust Memorial Day Trust.[5] On their website,[6] educational material on the Nazi destruction of Jews is grouped together under the tab 'The Holocaust', whereas the slaughter of other victims is referred to as 'Nazi Persecution'. On the same website the historian David Cesarani acknowledges that there are different definitions of the term:

The Holocaust is the word that's most widely used to describe the Nazi persecution and mass murder of the Jews in Germany and the parts of Europe they conquered with the assistance of other countries that collaborated with them and collaborators in the countries that they occupied. Many people also see the other victims of Nazi persecution as falling under the heading of victims of the Holocaust. Some historians agree with this, others disagree, but it's very important to remember that the Nazis persecuted a very wide range of groups, for what we call racial and biological reasons.[7]

The precise definition is important because the word 'Holocaust' is used in the title of the day, and opposition has focused on the question of whether or not HMD is relevant to non-Jews. For Jews the lessons are obvious, though they have changed over time. David Cesarani has pointed out that in the 1940s the lesson was that Jews needed their own state; in the 1950s that democracy is vulnerable to totalitarianism; but in the 1960s, attention turned to blind obedience to orders. In the 1970s it was realized that awareness of the Nazi past could combat racism today. By the 1980s, as Holocaust survivors were growing older, a redemptive note entered Holocaust education, as it was realized that some could survive the most appalling experiences and rebuild their lives. In the 1990s the duty to intervene to prevent racism was added to the lessons to be learned, and in the 2000s awareness of the Holocaust has led many to spring to the defence of multiculturalism when it has been under attack.

The first UK HMD in January 2001 was opposed by a number of voices in the Jewish community. There were various concerns. Some felt the Holocaust was a unique act which should not be compared with other atrocities; others pointed out that the Israeli government had established an official day (*Yom HaShoah*) in 1953 on the 27 Nisan, and that nothing else was needed. Some felt the day would be ignored, or that pressure to commemorate it would be counter-productive. Jews were not the only ones who had their doubts. Objections were raised by Armenians and others who felt their own genocide was being ignored. From 2001 to 2007 the Muslim Council of Britain expressed its unwillingness to attend the main ceremony, arguing that such a day 'hurt and excluded Muslims'. In 2008 the Council decided they would participate, but have more recently moved towards organizing their own Genocide Memorial Day, which includes the killing of Palestinians by Israelis. One of the arguments against HMD used by Muslims is that participation imputes responsibility where there was none: no Muslims were involved as perpetrators of the Holocaust. Furthermore, to privilege Jewish suffering is a profound mistake, which obscures the centrality of racism in western culture.[8]

Some Jews too have continued to have their doubts about the day. In an article entitled 'Too Little, Too Late', first published in 2004, the Jewish academic and modern historian Tony Kushner argued that HMD would miss the point if it failed to include more recent genocides, and that the world's failure to accept sufficient Jewish refugees in the 1930s and 1940s needed to be reflected in a different kind of HMD material calling for more liberal asylum policies today. He suggested that some areas of contention remained unexplored in HMD in order to provide a palatable narrative of Britain and survivors of the Holocaust, and to help to perpetuate the myth that Britain would always allow in genuine refugees.[9]

In 2005, the United Nations designated 27 January as the annual International Day of Commemoration in Memory of the Victims of the Holocaust and, in 2007, reiterated its objection to attempts to deny the Holocaust happened. The 2005 resolution made it clear that non-Jewish victims of the Nazis should also be included under the term 'the Holocaust': 'The Holocaust, which resulted in the murder of one third of the Jewish people, along with countless members of other minorities, will forever be a warning to all people of the dangers of hatred, bigotry, racism and prejudice.'[10] This is a helpful wording which deserves to be more widely known when the merits and impact of the day are discussed.

Every year since 2001 in the UK, the commemoration has adopted a particular pattern. There has been a main national event, plus events organized by local authorities across the country and events held in and for local schools. The HMD Trust publicizes an annual theme and prepares videos, educational and school assembly resources.

HOLOCAUST MEMORIAL DAY

I attended my first Holocaust Memorial event in 2003, organized by the London Borough of Harrow at Whitchurch Junior School in Stanmore, Middlesex. The main speaker was Gena Turgel who spoke very movingly of her own experiences in the death camps: 'My story, the story of a survivor, is a story that six million others cannot tell.' Gena's talk showed the immense power of personal testimony given to a live audience by a survivor. Following her talk, representatives of different faiths spoke briefly, and it was clear that many of them were visibly moved by what she said.

Unfortunately, Harrow Council did not follow up this event in the following years and confined HMD to much smaller events held during the day in the council chamber, mainly for councillors and staff. As Harrow has a large Jewish population, I started lobbying for more to be done, and larger evening events were reintroduced in 2009. However, the more recent events, although well attended, have attracted few from outside the Jewish community and so the wider aim of Holocaust education is not being achieved. The Jewish community recognize that HMD is not primarily for them, but feel an obligation to support it: other communities feel this is an event mainly for Jews and give insufficient support. Finally, in 2015, Harrow Council expressed a willingness to spread the message more widely. HMD on the ground is clearly patchy and a work in progress.

The HMD Trust has worked very hard to get the message out to schools and has over the years provided much excellent material, particularly videos, not just about the five official genocides, but about the consequences of racism in general. Unfortunately, however good the educational materials, where they are used without sufficient commitment from teachers or without personal testimony (live or recorded), they will fail to make the intended impact. A Jewish teacher in a non-Jewish school reported his upset at the school's HMD assemblies, which were presented as if the Holocaust was 'just another event'. Only when he took time out of his own lessons to tell the children the story of his own family did a real impact begin to make itself felt. In many schools, where there is only a brief assembly divorced from the history syllabus or from real life stories, he suggested that it is hardly worth the effort.

However, there are some shining examples of what can be achieved. In an area with a tiny Jewish population, the annual events organized by Neath Port Talbot College, presented with readings, music and drama, have brought in many local schools to well-prepared and moving events. In an area with a high Jewish population, the annual seminars run jointly by Northwood and Pinner Liberal Synagogue and Northwood United Synagogue bring in up to 2,000 secondary school children each year for a full half-day programme.[11] Whether or not other genocides are included, the message of combating prejudice and racism today is always there. In 2016 there were a record 5,590 local HMD activities across the UK, increasing year by year from 2,400 in 2014, of which 157 included young people as speakers or organizers. Back in 2006 there were only 266 local activities. Events take place in prisons and police forces as well as in schools, universities and other public buildings. HMD is growing year by year. It is up to all of us to make sure it is as effective as possible.

David Gillett writes

My real Holocaust education began in the early 1970s when I was watching a graphic television documentary about the Nazi atrocities with a group of my students. One of these students was from a non-observant Jewish background and was, by then, in training for ordained ministry in the Church of England. Up to that point he had always identified fully with his Christian peers and, indeed, occupied a prominent position within a close group of friends. As far as he knew, he had no family murdered by the Nazis and was not nervous about the prospect of watching the documentary in my flat with a group of his Gentile friends. But as the programme showed scenes from the concentration camps, he found the situation deeply traumatic, not only because of the horrors it portrayed but because it awoke within him a deep sense of distancing and alienation from those who were his closest friends. He had to withdraw from the room; he could not sit with the rest of us and watch.

I realized then, and have often reflected subsequently, that I and many of my generation are from similar backgrounds. We were born in the UK with no experience of the War and raised in increasingly affluent times. We do not inhabit history to anywhere near the extent of many within the Jewish community – the few whom I knew then and the many more who have since played a significant part in my life. When, a few years later, I was working in a reconciliation centre in Northern Ireland at the height of the 'Troubles', I was aware of similarly powerful historical narratives going back several hundred years, which were part of the present experience and ongoing formation of most of my Protestant and Roman Catholic friends there. Increasingly, I understood what Dutch Catholic priest and theologian Henri Nouwen referred to as the 'orphaned generation'. He used that phrase to describe the worst features of the atomized alienation of so many in our fragmented society for whom life has to find its entire meaning in the stark, unrelated experience of the present moment. For many this can lead to a deep sense of rootlessness or an illusory freedom from the shadows of the past.

Later, as I became involved in Holocaust education with groups of Christians, I was aware how the issue of whether or not one consciously inhabits a powerful history affects how we learn and process these issues. With groups of Christians who have little or no contact with the Jewish community (which, in the UK, is the majority), engaging with them about the moral and religious dimensions of the Holocaust requires much more groundwork than when one is with Christians who have friends within the Jewish community. In the former category, though to generalize is inevitably unfair to certain people, there is the need to create connections both with their own history and that of the other. In the latter category those connections have often already been made through their friendships and discussions with Jewish friends over the years. I have, more latterly, noticed these factors affecting how effective the events of Holocaust Memorial Days have been for different groups with whom I have been involved.

I have participated in HMD events in differing contexts – for several years in Greater Manchester with events organized largely by Orthodox Jewish communities, with minority involvement from representatives of the wider community; events organized by the Education Department, involving a wide representation from a diverse community including a significant number of Jews; events organized by a borough's interfaith group for the wider community, which included significant numbers of Christians, Muslims and Hindus but no Jews; and now, in Norfolk, an event organized for the City Council by the local branch of CCJ which takes the form of a Jewish–Christian civic service jointly conducted by Jewish and Christian ministers.

When HMD was first introduced in this country, I saw it as a valuable context for extending and deepening Holocaust awareness as well as leading to a more informed engagement with broader and even more contemporary issues of genocide, asylum seekers and the like. I believe much of value has been achieved but it has also revealed the need for extending such educational opportunities – particularly to adults who have not had the benefit of a school syllabus that included significant elements of Holocaust education.

It has become clear to me that the value of HMD for those who attend – largely those who already support its values – must not lull us into imagining it has had a major impact on the population as a whole. A survey in 2012[12] revealed that over 80 per cent of the population has only the vaguest awareness of the existence and meaning of HMD; 20 per cent has never heard of it at all. It can also prove difficult to lead on to wider consideration of the issues of other genocides or our own country's often ambivalent attitude to asylum seekers. One of the greatest problems is the failure to attract significant Muslim participation. Given the widespread availability, particularly to younger members of the community, of Islamic/Islamist websites that preach Holocaust denial, this is a major failing of the programme.

The ongoing, unresolved situation in Israel–Palestine has also had an impact on how Holocaust education is perceived and achieves its aims. Even in the best of times the two issues, Land and Holocaust, are seen as intimately connected. One of the major impulses that led to the UN vote in favour of partition was Nazi atrocities against Jews. The longer the problems continue between Israelis and Palestinians, the more attempts at Holocaust education are compromised in the eyes of many. It is an unpalatable fact I deeply regret that, year by year, the default position for an increasing number of Christians and for many within the wider community is becoming anti-Israeli and pro-Palestinian. This, in turn, leads to a lack of sympathy with Jewish–Christian reconciliation and, at worst, exposes a latent anti-Semitism; for some it also leads to a questioning of the legitimacy of the State of Israel.

This is the prism through which many now see the Holocaust. The discourse that arises from it inevitably causes major offence to the Jewish community; in particular, the growing use of 'holocaust' to describe the situation in Gaza, and 'apartheid' to characterize the State of Israel. Such deeply offensive use of language puts a responsibility on the Church to challenge the narratives that demean the Jewish community by declaring them historically untenable and gratuitously offensive. Given the place of the Holocaust as part-catalyst in the establishment of the State of Israel and continued threats to its existence from some surrounding nations, the increasing tendency of many to view Israel as the aggressor and the Palestinian as the victim skews the narrative so unfairly that it makes it impossible for many to engage in rational consideration of the issues. This only underlines the urgent need for HMD and other extended opportunities for Holocaust education while recognizing its increasing complexities.

Finally, turning to the position within the churches, it is clear that the majority of those who attend worship Sunday by Sunday never attend a Holocaust memorial event. I believe this means we need to find specific opportunities for Holocaust education (in the broadest understanding) as part of the normal Sunday programme. There are some among regular churchgoers who react against reference to the Holocaust with irritation and dismissal because they experience this as an attempt to create a sense of guilt for something for which they feel no connectedness or

HOLOCAUST MEMORIAL DAY

responsibility. In the main, such reactions occur when there is no significant opportunity to engage with the issue at greater depth. For these reasons I believe that churches need to build on the start that HMD has made for a minority of the population; we need to encourage the use of material provided for HMD within a Sunday worship context.

One final step is needed so that churches do not experience in any one year the Holocaust as the only major window through which to view Judaism and the Jewish community. At the very least this can produce an unbalanced view of another faith community which significantly fails to acknowledge its ongoing contribution within the community in a whole range of ways and also misses the opportunity to be consciously enriched by the Judaic roots of Christianity and the historic interaction emphasized by Michael. We need to think in terms of 'Holocaust education plus'. CCJ could well play a leading role in helping to develop other liturgical and celebratory material that can provide a focus for affirming the Church's connectedness with Judaism – and, wherever possible in practice, to include participation by members of the Jewish community.

Notes

1 hmd.org.uk/resources/podcasts/partner-organisations-anne-frank-trust-weiner-library-and-surf (accessed June 2014).

2 Speech given by Tony Blair, January 1997, Southwark Cathedral.

3 See *Hansard*, 11 June 1999.

4 Declaration of the Stockholm International Forum on the Holocaust, also known as the 'Stockholm Declaration'.

5 The HMD Trust base their own definition on that of Yad VaShem, the Holocaust/Shoah commemoration institution in Israel. Olivia Marks-Woldman (Trust Director), personal communication.

6 www.hmd.org.uk.

7 www.hmd.org.uk/resources/podcast/professor-david-cesarani%E2%80%99s-introduction-holocaust-part-one.

8 Philip Spencer and Sara Valentina Di Palma, 2013, 'Antisemitism and the Politics of Holocaust Memorial Day in the UK and Italy', in *Perceptions of the Holocaust in Europe and Muslim Communities*, Muslims in Global Societies Series, vol. 5, pp. 71–83.

9 Tony Kushner, 2004, 'Too Little, Too Late? Reflections on Britain's Holocaust Memorial Day', *The Journal of Israeli History* 23:1, pp. 116–29.

10 www.un.org/en/holocaustremembrance/docs/res607.shtml.

11 This programme has its own website: www.northwoodhmd.org.uk.

12 Holocaust Memorial Day Trust – External Evaluation 2012, p. 5. Available for download at http://av.hmd.org.uk/HMD_2012_Evaluation.pdf.

Coming to Terms with the Past: Conclusion

DAVID GILLETT AND MICHAEL HILTON

John's Gospel, read by Christians or heard in church, continues to give a particular unhelpful portrait of 'the Jews'. The local story of William of Norwich has emerged from its twelfth-century origin, surfacing in contemporary culture in surprising ways. The memorialisation of the Holocaust raises many contemporary issues between Jews, Christians and Muslims. These are but three small examples of 2,000 years of Jewish–Christian relations and the deep scars they caused. What the three have in common is the way each of them still reverberates in our time. The past always provides echoes in the present. If we are to continue our dialogue and proclaim the value of two equally important faiths living side by side in a free society, we cannot simply ignore those echoes. Learning from the past is not easy, but the study of history can and should lead to policy and recommendations. Our three essays all have specific suggestions for ways to proceed and to deal with the outstanding issues.

The relationship between Judaism and Christianity has shifted dramatically over the last century. The study of the history of Jewish–Christian relations as a formal discipline is much more recent, and is still an academic branch of study in its infancy. In particular, the general awareness that Jews and Christians in Europe have shared in local cultures and influenced each other for the better is very new, and can balance the legacy of tragic misunderstandings. The Psalmist said in Psalm 11.3: 'When the foundations are undermined, what can the righteous do?' The answer repeatedly given by the Scriptures is the building of trust.

Further Reflections

TONY BAYFIELD

Let me give a particular account of our shared history.

It starts with two historically insignificant people,[1] Abraham and Sarah. Their individuality is set against the broad panorama of humanity's emergence from the womb and its development, painted in vivid theological and ethical colours by the first 11 chapters of Genesis. That will always be the background and context for Abraham, Sarah and their descendants.

The account begins with journeying – forward, into the unknown, in the presence of God. *Hithalekh l'fanai ve'h'yeh tamim*, demands God. 'Walk with me' – in my presence, even 'before me' (the Hebrew is characteristically elusive, multi-layered), 'and find integrity' – discover what it means to be complete, whole, sound, healthy in spirit.[2] The many journeys of Abraham and Sarah, their children and grandchildren finally take them – refugees from famine – down into Egypt where they settle. But fertile Goshen becomes a forced-labour camp and the narrative of journeying one of flight – the Exodus from Egypt of the descendants of Abraham and Sarah, along with a 'mixed multitude'.[3] Soon liberation from slavery becomes freedom to accept the covenant at Sinai.[4] The Children of Jacob-become-Israel[5] are now the People Israel.

Israel journeys on and on. The best loved of all Jewish Bible commentators, the eleventh-century teacher known as Rashi,[6] explores the various uses of the Hebrew root for journeying in Torah. He observes that even when they pitched their tents, that too was part of the journeying.[7] The journey reaches the Promised Land. Canaan proves not to be Utopia or Shangri-La but the Land on which the journeying continues. It has many twists and turns in which Egypt and Babylon – in their many guises – play major parts, until we find ourselves in Judea under first Greek and then Roman occupation.

If journeying is a constant reality defining Jewish theology, so too is bifurcating. Abraham has two sons, Ishmael and Isaac. They go their different ways. So too, Esau and Jacob. Jewish–Christian relations are dominated by a process of differentiation which took place in the Land, during two centuries of Roman occupation.[8] Once again the journey bifurcates. Out of the party of the 'Scribes and Pharisees' emerges Rabbinic Judaism, the religious tradition to which all the Jews in our Group are heirs. In the same place and at the same time a Jew by the name of Jesus was born, lived his life and was cruelly crucified. From his followers Christianity emerges. Both faiths are the children of Abraham and Sarah; both are heirs to a tradition that, even then, stretched back considerably more than a millennium. Though the journey has bifurcated, the two journeys will criss-cross endlessly.

The understanding that Judaism and Christianity share Abraham and Sarah as parents I owe to the American Jewish historian Alan Segal.[9] Segal turns to the account in Genesis of the birth of Abraham and Sarah's grandchildren, Esau and Jacob.[10] The two boys struggle with each other for supremacy not only in Rebecca's womb but throughout their lives. The metaphor was not lost on Rabbinic Judaism and Segal demonstrates how well it applies to the relationship between Jacob and Esau, Judaism and Christianity, both born in the Roman world.

It's important to acknowledge at this point one particularly challenging way in which, from the Jewish perspective, the historical journey appears to have departed from the biblical paradigm. Genesis 25.23 promises: 'Two nations are in your womb; two peoples will be separated from your body; one people will be stronger than the other people and the elder [Esau] shall serve the younger [Jacob].' There's a curious motif which runs through Genesis – of 'Judaism' transmitted through the younger sibling. So, Isaac is favoured over Ishmael and Jacob over Esau. Earlier in the narrative, God promises Abraham that his descendants will be as numerous as the stars in heaven and the grains of sand on the sea shore.[11] For many years I found that promise difficult to equate with just 14 million Jews in the world – 0.2 per cent of the population of the globe. Now the logic of Segal's observation makes it clear. There are more than 2 billion Christians and almost as many Muslims.[12] They're also the children of Abraham.[13]

It's a profound understanding of who we are – siblings – children born in the same place, at much the same time, with the same parents. It provides the illuminating insight that if even archetypal parents like Jacob get into grave difficulties by showing favouritism, it must follow as day follows night that the Good Parent never has favourites. In only one respect does the understanding fail us or, rather, highlight a false understanding of each other. We're not identical twins. We have much in common as siblings always do. But we're each our own selves – distinctive both in appearance and personality. Wanting our sibling to be exactly like us, denying the separate identity and unique individuality of Christian and Jew, has long haunted our relationship.[14]

We Jews and Christians have arrived at a point of meeting shackled to chains so heavy that they threaten to immobilize us and so long they stretch shamefully back through times we can scarcely understand. The difficult history not only holds us but has become part of us, our self-understanding as well as our narrative. In assigning to David Gillett and Michael Hilton the task of telling us how to cope with our past, we handed them the poisoned chalice or kiddush cup par excellence! Their response is astonishing and could only come from two fine scholars who've devoted their lives to pastoral engagement, fully immersed in the local. We need to take careful note of Stephen Roberts' account of the cultural shift away from valuing the local.[15] What's essential to a major part of our work has become counter-cultural.

The Rabbi and the Bishop begin where the shackles were first forged. Michael offers a crucial insight into John's Gospel. While many Christians are attracted to St John as a lovable character, Jews are repelled by an angry man who denounces his fellows as the children of the devil. This hostile perspective proved a surprise even to some Christian members of our Group. It's far from clear, however, who 'the Jews' are whom John demonizes. Is it another group of emergent Christian-Jews? Is it the early adherents of Rabbinic Judaism? Michael shows that translating the word as 'Judeans' rather than Jews is not only philologically sound but leaves it open as to whom within the Judean population of his day – a period of fierce and passionate upheaval – John is at odds with. Above all, it's crucial to distinguish between John's opponents then and Jews today – language matters.

Our Group had several encounters with John during its lifetime. On one occasion, David Ford made a characteristically helpful comment: 'Maybe that's the nature of revelation – some understand and respect it, others do not. Those who do experience revelation feel profoundly rejected by those who do not.' What's clear is that John's anger and frustration is grounded in rejection. 'Why do you turn your backs on me? Why do you deny the Truth as I know it to be? Why do some of my Judean sisters and brothers [whoever they are] reject me?'

Our past is vast, endless and filled with the animosity of those too closely related for comfort. The last 900 or more years, since 1096 and the first Crusade when Rhineland Jewry served as collateral damage, have been particularly shameful. Michael makes the important point that we shouldn't see our interconnected histories as exclusively centuries of conflict – there have been times of productive social, economic and cultural interchange. David makes the equally important point that despite the disabilities of living within a hostile Christian world, Jewish communities lived spiritually, ethically and culturally rich lives. Had Judaism not been a rewarding faith, Jews would not have clung on to their Judaism so tenaciously and assiduously.

David Gillett will grant his Christian forebears, particularly their religious leadership, no alibi or pleas in mitigation. He says that one should start 'in one's own backyard' and, in so doing, produces a deeply moving, searingly honest study. He examines one small episode on the journey. The death of a child in Norwich was fanned into the blood libel, which led to the murder of Jews and the destruction of Jewish communities throughout medieval Europe and beyond both in time and geography.[16] He shows how the original account was ruthlessly manipulated in order to benefit the Cathedral in Norwich, enhance its reputation as a place of pilgrimage and fill its coffers. As a person of faith, I was physically shaken by his revelation of the cynical disregard for the truth and the exploitation of the other for sordid ends. As a Jew, I was humbled by David's fearless honesty. His injunction to start by digging in your own backyard graphically expresses just how much we *all* have to do. Such is his passion for truth[17] that we Jews are compelled to respond to something which follows ineluctably: if there are Christians – numbers of them – who are prepared to expose the shame of the past and own it yet want us to move forward together for God and for society and behave as siblings should, are we Jews not obliged to respond more generously than hitherto?

Michael Hilton and David Gillett shine their torches on a particular scriptural issue from 1,900 years ago, a tiny episode from the Middle Ages and a small, contemporary experiment. They turn finally to the establishment of Holocaust Memorial Day in Britain – its limited successes and the enormity of the task that still lies ahead. Continuing support on a national level, across boundaries of faith and ethnicity, is still required but leadership from the top, while essential, can only provide a framework. The real work must be done at the local level, unglamorous and under threat as passé and parochial. Only through local initiatives taken by churches and synagogues both working on their own members and reaching out into the community in which they live and function can progress be made. The local, the parochial, may be unglamorous and unfathomable but it must not be evaded.

Notes

1 'Insignificant' in the sense that you wouldn't expect to find records of them in the same way that there are records of contemporary rulers in the Ancient World.
2 Genesis 17.1.
3 Exodus 12.38. I added this reference because, from its beginning, the People is an open people, not an exclusive one. The journey is both of those descended from Abraham and Sarah and those who choose to join the journey – equally the children of Abraham and Sarah.
4 Jeremy Gordon makes this point *supra* p. 75.
5 Jacob's name is changed to Israel before his reunion with Esau. Israel means 'one who struggles with God', the Children of Israel are therefore the Children of Jacob.
6 Rashi is the acronym of *Ra*bbi *Sh*lomo *Yi*tzhaki or Shlomo ben Yitzhak, b. 1040, Troyes in Northern France, d. 1105.
7 Rashi on Exodus 40.38.
8 Roughly speaking, the first century BCE and the first century CE.
9 Alan F. Segal, 1986, *Rebecca's Children: Judaism and Christianity in the Roman World*, Cambridge, MA: Harvard University Press.
10 Genesis 25.20–28.
11 Genesis 22.17.
12 Muslims are the children of Abraham and Hagar not Abraham and Sarah. The word sibling includes children with only one shared parent. Tom Holland makes clear, in his controversial book *In the Shadow of the Sword: The Battle for Global Empire and the End of the Ancient World*, both the place and time of the birth of Islam are shared in their fundamentals with Judaism and Christianity.
13 The numerical disparity has left Jews with the strong feeling of being an endangered species, a significant factor in Jewish psychology.
14 Recognizing and accepting we are 'configured differently', differently shaped gardens with some similar and some distinctive plants is essential to the acceptance and respect addressed in Chapter 6.
15 *Supra* p. 42.
16 For instance the Damascus Affair of 1840.
17 My allusion is to A. J. Heschel, 1974, *A Passion for Truth: Reflections on the Founder of Hasidism, the Kotzker and Kierkegaard*, London: Secker & Warburg.

4
The Legacy of Our Scriptures

Beyond the Wilderness: Transforming Our Readings of Jewish and Christian Scriptures

ALEXANDRA WRIGHT

Introduction

It is a Shabbat afternoon in early December. Soon it will be Havdalah, the time to say farewell to the Sabbath with a simple ceremony of a lighted candle, wine and spice box. These are the ritual symbols of observance, bearing the memory of a day of rest, the additional soul given to the individual for the duration of Shabbat,[1] and signs of the creative potential of the new week ahead. The liturgy of Havdalah – the word comes from a Hebrew root meaning to separate or make a distinction – is more challenging, for the service is constructed around the idea of separation and difference: between holy and profane, light and darkness, the seventh day of rest and the six working days, and *Yisrael la'amim* – the Jewish people and the Nations. This is how Jewish liturgy, in its traditional form, remembers the Other, in a theological framework inherited from biblical literature – whether the Egyptians oppressing the Hebrew slaves, Israel's arch-enemy Amalek or the fictitious Haman of the book of Esther. As Ruth Langer has pointed out, 'The religious or political Other [of the Hebrew Bible] is almost universally a negative.'[2]

This is not a good starting point for a Jew and a Christian coming together to read their Scriptures, discovering their wisdom and truth and shaping a relational theology of meaning and interpretation. How do we move from that 'universally a negative' and oppositional to a reading that is more hospitable, generous, open and curious? To state the obvious, the Hebrew Bible is part of the Christian Scriptures; but the New Testament does not have the status of sacred text for the Jew. If I am at home in Tanakh and its commentaries, seeking to find ways in which to encounter the texts, to shape my own life and the life of my community by their teachings, laws and theology, where am I in relation to the New Testament? How do I listen, speak about, relate to the figure of Jesus who stands at the centre of Christian Scripture and faith? And how do I relate to the individual for whom Jesus is the embodiment of the word, 'in whom', as David writes, 'the light of the knowledge of God is seen'?[3] What can I learn from the texts of the New Testament – texts that remain outside the experience of Jewish liturgy and worship? Although we sit facing each other, with the same words on the page in front of us, I have a sense that I am standing in a doorway, overhearing the intimacy of another's conversation with his God.

> For it is the God who said, 'Let light shine out of darkness,' who has shone in our hearts to give the light of the knowledge of the glory of God in the face of Jesus Christ (2 Cor. 4.6).
>
> There, overwhelming darkness is met by the light and glory of God. The form this takes in our hearts is the face of Christ. All that goes on in our hearts is before this face. Jesus Christ is the focus of our core community. That is the meaning of his being Lord, friend, mother, brother, host, guest, and more.[4]

How am I to understand the grammar of faith that is built on these words? The Jew remains an outsider, a guest when studying the New Testament and must find a way of overcoming Jewish defensiveness and diffidence, of listening with grace from a place that is neither too contrived, nor too comfortable.

The legacy of Jewish Scripture – the Burning Bush

As behoves observant Jews on Shabbat afternoon, I am seated at my kitchen table, my not-quite-13-year-old nephew reading aloud from Exodus 3, his Bar Mitzvah portion. His twin brother will read the previous chapter – the birth story of a Hebrew infant, whose destiny, almost thwarted by a massacre of the innocents, is to become the saviour of the Children of Israel.

Both boys are musical and are chanting their *parashiyot* – their biblical portions – and must memorize, not only the vowels but also the musical phrases represented by the *n'ginot*, the notations which do not appear in the scroll:

וּמֹשֶׁה הָיָה רֹעֶה אֶת־צֹאן יִתְרוֹ חֹתְנוֹ כֹּהֵן מִדְיָן וַיִּנְהַג אֶת־הַצֹּאן אַחַר הַמִּדְבָּר וַיָּבֹא אֶל־הַר הָאֱלֹהִים חֹרֵבָה׃

And Moses, tending the flock of his father-in-law Jethro, the priest of Midian, drove the flock into the wilderness, and came to Horeb, the mountain of God.[5]

There is a composed simplicity in the syllabic enunciation of each word. Apart from four key words in the verse – 'Now Moses' (*u-Moshe*), 'the wilderness' (*ha-midbar*), 'God' (*ha-Elohim*) and 'to Horeb' (*Horevah*), expressions that point already to significant themes in the narrative of the Exodus, the revelation at Sinai – here called Horeb – and the 40-year wandering in the desert, no other word has more than two syllables, as though these words sound out the steady but lonely pace of the shepherd's footsteps into the wilderness. My nephew chants the first word – *u'Moshe* – with its melodic cantillation of descending notes in a minor key, and it is clear that Moses is alone, leading the flock *akhar ha-midbar*. We remark on the unusual use of the word *akhar*, a preposition both of time and place meaning 'after' or 'behind'. The plain meaning conveys a sense of distance; Moses leads the flock to the farthest end of the wilderness and we could leave it at that. But learning the text of the Bible requires us not only to examine its vocabulary but to enter the imagination of the Hebrew writers and read the interpretations of generations of commentators. 'We live theologically; we live with images from our tradition every day; what does that mean?' asks American Professor of Jewish Studies Michael Fishbane. 'What is the status of language in the Scriptures? Is it an allegorical, figural cloak to deal with what is impossible to say, or should the words be read simply off the page?'[6] The phrase's unusual form compels an interpretation.

We must be attentive to where it is used elsewhere in the Hebrew Bible, to its 'organic narrative connection'. And so, before we turn to the commentators, we find passages elsewhere in the Hebrew Bible in which the word, as a kind of *Leitwort*, can be found.[7] The word *akhar* has a common enough root but is charged with the resonance of other narratives both before and after this moment: the opening words of the *Akedah*: *Va-y'hi* akhar *ha-d'varim ha-eleh* – 'And it came to pass *after* these things',[8] and in the same chapter: *v'hineh ayil* akhar *ne-ekhaz ba-s'vach b'karnav* – 'and behold *behind* him a ram caught in the thicket by his horns',[9] among many others. The word *akhar*, then, suggests not only the distance traversed by Moses into the farthest reaches of the desert, but a passage of time. This is the way the Torah conveys the timelessness of religious experience and encounter, how the linear progression of hours and minutes will cease and there is a momentary suspension from the narrative. Like Abraham before him, whose son is rescued from death by a heavenly voice and a ram caught in a bush, Moses, too, is summoned by God's revelation from a bush that burns and a voice that commands him to rescue the Israelite people from slavery. Later on, after the Exodus from Egypt and standing in the very same place on the mountain of God, Moses asks to see God's 'Presence'.[10] God replies that no one can see his face and live, but that Moses will see *et-akhorai* – God's back.¹¹ The repetition or echo of the root *akhar* here in this bold anthropomorphism, *achorai*, establishes a connection between the texts; it serves to intensify the experience of Moses, who not only sees the bush burning, but feels an almost visceral brush with the Divine Presence, God's 'back'. Time – past, present and future – is folded, corrugated into that single moment of revelation and encounter.

From this internal biblical, midrashic intertextuality, we turn to the medieval commentaries to see if they can shed some further light on the meaning of the phrase *akhar ha-midbar*. Rashi, whose commentary is printed next to the biblical text in traditional printed editions, explains according to the *p'shat*, the plain meaning,¹² that Moses removes himself to the farthest reaches of the desert, but embellishes his commentary with an explanation of Moses' ethical character: 'so that the flocks are prevented from pasturing in the fields of others and Moses, the shepherd, cannot be accused of robbery'.¹³ Sforno,¹⁴ on the other hand, contemplates the language in a more mystical way: the text anticipates the encounter with God, or, rather, Moses – perhaps unconsciously – prepares himself for God's call: 'He [Moses] came alone, in order to be by himself and to pray on the way to Hebron.'¹⁵ Why is he going to Hebron, asks my nephew, skipping over the references to solitude and prayer. Hebron is the location of the Cave of Makhpelah, the burial place of the patriarchs and matriarchs, the place towards which Moses is heading in order to stand in the proximity of the spirit of his ancestors and deliver his prayers to God. Sforno has theologized the text, purified it, prepared us for the awakening of Moses' religious consciousness and God's words to Moses, 'I am the God of your father, the God of Abraham, the God of Isaac, and the God of Jacob,'¹⁶ as though implying that his journey to Hebron is an unconscious preparation for the redemptive narrative of Jewish history.

וַיֵּרָא מַלְאַךְ יְהֹוָה אֵלָיו בְּלַבַּת־אֵשׁ מִתּוֹךְ הַסְּנֶה וַיַּרְא וְהִנֵּה הַסְּנֶה
בֹּעֵר בָּאֵשׁ וְהַסְּנֶה אֵינֶנּוּ אֻכָּל:

An angel of the Lord appeared to him in a blazing fire out of a bush. He gazed, and there was a bush all aflame, yet the bush was not consumed.¹⁷

Another Shabbat – as we draw closer to my nephew's Bar Mitzvah. He has mastered the Hebrew and cantillation, one aspect of the legacy of the Hebrew Scriptures. But there is more; for he is struggling with the images of God that present themselves in this story – the angel, the blazing bush that is not consumed and the urgent call of God from the bush: 'Moses! Moses!'[18] Paradoxically, the closer he comes to the text, the greater is the risk of the unravelling of his childlike faith in a personal God; the image is in danger of becoming an absurdity while, at the same time, it has the potential to guide him heuristically[19] towards something else. We note the verb in verse 2 – *va-yera* – 'An angel of the Lord *appeared*.' Does the appearance of an angel in the Torah mean its assured existence? Or is this a literary device – the use of the verbal Niphal (passive) form of the root *resh-aleph-heh*, 'to see', telling us that this is Moses' perception? Why does an angel appear to Moses, yet God speak to him from the bush? And what kind of angel is this being? For Maimonides, the expression *mal'akh* – 'angel' or, literally, 'messenger' – points to heavenly bodies that are incorporeal, Aristotelian 'Intelligences', the intermediate beings between 'the Prime Cause and existing things'. They effect the motion of the spheres on which the existence of all things depends. An angel is also the imaginative faculty of humanity, it can be a part of the prophetic vision, the means whereby divine communication is conveyed to the prophet.[20] Maimonides suggests that the words *b'labbat esh* – literally, 'in the flame of the fire' – are to be understood figuratively: from the depths of his imagination and understanding or, more plainly and simply, from God. He has a moment of illumination in which his own heart or will is aligned with the will of God.[21]

If, for Maimonides, the concern is to ensure the incorruptibility and purity of monotheism, for the much earlier authors of Rabbinic *midrashim*, the legacy of the text and specifically its images of God become vehicles for a variety of theological messages. *Exodus Rabbah* 2.5 is one example of the way some Rabbis expressed a theology for their own time from one single verse: 'An angel of the Lord appeared to him in a blazing fire out of a bush.'[22]

> It is written in Song of Songs 5.2: 'I sleep, but my heart is awake.' I am asleep as regards the commandments but my heart is awake to do them. 'Listen, my beloved knocks. Let me in, my dearest friend, my dove, my undefiled, *tamati*.'[23] *Tamati* because they attached themselves *nit-tam'mu*[24] to Me at Sinai and said: 'All that the Lord has spoken will we do, and obey' (Ex. 24.7). Rabbi Yannai said: Just as in the case of twins, *te'omim*, if one has a pain in his head the other feels it also, so God said, as it were: 'I will be with him in trouble' (Ps. 91.15) ... It says: 'In all their trouble He was troubled' (Isaiah 63.9). God said to Moses: 'Do you not realise that I live in trouble just as Israel live in trouble? Know from this place out of which I speak to you – from a thorn-bush – that I am, as it were, a partner in their trouble.'

Beginning with a verse from Song of Songs 5.2, seemingly unconnected to Exodus 3.2, the author forms a deft chain of allusive verses or 'intertextual correlations'[25] that will lead back to the original Torah verse. The Rabbis play on the ambiguity of the phrase in Exodus 3.2, *b'labbat esh* – 'a blazing fire'. Its literal meaning is derived from the word *lehavah* – 'flame' (the construct form here is *labbat*, a contraction of *lah'bat*), but here the Rabbis read *libbat-esh* – 'the heart of the fire' (which is also how Maimonides understands it) and hence the connection with the Song of Songs: 'I sleep, but my heart (*libbi*) wakes.' The lover, here understood as the Community of Israel, stands before God and says, 'I am asleep in the neglect of the performance of the commandments, but my heart is awake to do them.'

The opening of this passage is a contracted form of a longer midrash on Song of Songs 5.2,[26] which continues by drawing on the epithet the lover uses to call his beloved: *Kol dodi dofek, pit'khi-li akhoti, ra'yati, yonati, tamati* – 'Hark! My beloved knocks: "Let me in, my dearest friend, my dove, my undefiled, *tamati*." Why does Israel call God *tamati* – "my undefiled"? Because they attached themselves (*nit-tam'mu*) to God at Mount Sinai and said, "All that the Lord has spoken will we do, and obey" (Ex. 24.7).' The midrash creates its own paronomasia, or pun, hearing in the epithet for God – *tamati* – a play on the words *nit-tam'mu* and *te'omim* – 'twins'. This weaving of three distinct, yet aurally similar, words into one thread in an extraordinarily taut poetic phrase, injects the original verse from Exodus with an audacious theological implication. Just as in the case of twins, if one has a pain in his head the other feels it also, so God said, as it were: 'I will be with him in trouble.'[27] God appears to Moses as though in a dream; he sleeps, but his heart is awake to a God who is suffering with Israel in their slavery; who hears their cry in the midst of their oppression, who will listen to them as they stand on the shores of the Sea of Reeds, the chariots and horses of the Egyptians thundering towards them: 'In all their trouble He was troubled.'[28] As much as Israel suffers, so too I, the Eternal One, suffer with you and I speak to you from a thorn-bush, from the lowliest shrub in the desert, from a bush that is full of spines and thorns, because I am, as it were, 'a partner in [your] trouble'. This word *kiv'yakhol* ('as it were') comes as a Rabbinic word of caution ahead of a bold theological statement. Can one really say that God suffers as Israel suffers? Can one imply that the suffering of humanity is felt too by an incorporeal God?

The *Zohar*, a late thirteenth-century mystical commentary on the Pentateuch, lacks this Rabbinic diffidence in attributing to God anthropomorphisms. When Israel is in exile below, when everything is in disorder on earth, then the *Sh'khinah*, the Presence of God, conceived as the last of the ten emanations in the kabbalistic system, is in disorder above.[29] The *Sh'khinah* shares the tragedy of Israel's exile from the Land and the destruction of the Temple.

Israel's tragedy is its exile from the Land and the destruction of the Temple. How can God dwell among Israel when the dwelling place of God and the glory of its worship have been swept away? The feminine principle of God is loosened from God himself, accompanying Israel into exile. The *Zohar* understands the Burning Bush not as part of the mythic-historic narrative of Israel in Egypt, but as a powerful theological image expressing God's suffering, and likens God to a king whose son has died, who dismantles his bed in mourning, places thorns and thistles into the mattress and then lies on it. This is God grieving for his children who have been cast out of the Land. His grief is a metaphysical expression, mirroring the grief of Israel in exile, and yet even while she is in exile, the *Sh'khinah* appears to her from amid the thorns of the bush, the husks of evil that exist in the world.[30]

I have concentrated on these opening verses from Exodus not only because of their apparent narrative simplicity and rhythm, but because I wanted to show that the legacy of the Hebrew Scriptures for Jews does not only lie in the text of the Bible alone, but in the many layers of interpretation that have shaped the thought and theology of God and Israel in the world. These, as much as the texts themselves, form an iconographic and sometimes iconoclastic legacy of our Scriptures.[31]

'In a strange house' – reading together St Paul's Letter to the Corinthians

Over nearly a year, I was privileged to share periods of study with Professor Ford in preparation for writing this chapter. Our study was always focused on a text, either from the Hebrew or Christian Bible, in Hebrew, Greek and English. In this shared endeavour, I had to remember that my study partner was bringing not only an appreciation of the Hebrew text and its narrative, but a different faith, a different set of theological constructs. And that the Hebrew text that we read together was not only my sacred text but also from his Bible. I had to, as it were, step back from occupying an exclusive sense of ownership of the text.

We did not have to agree on our understanding and interpretation but listen to each other, to try and understand what the other was bringing to the text. So, for example, some elements of the text we were studying, which may have had less importance for Jewish commentators, may well have different connotations or resonance for Christians. When Moses is told to remove his shoes from his feet before approaching the Burning Bush, Jewish interpretation does not hear the allusion to John 1.27 and John's testimony, 'I am not worthy to untie the thong of his [Jesus'] sandal.'[32] In the act of Moses taking off his shoes – retold in Acts 7.33 – the Christian may see the promise of the coming of Jesus: 'Let it be known to you therefore, my brothers, that through this man forgiveness of sins is proclaimed to you; by this Jesus everyone who believes is set free from all those sins from which you could not be freed by the law of Moses.'[33] The simple act of untying a shoe, a symbol of humility and awe, is transformed through a Christian reading to become a symbol of untying oneself, freeing oneself from sin. Jewish reading of the Christian Scriptures has often reacted in a hostile and suspicious way to the integrity of Christian interpretation of the Hebrew Bible, preventing shared readings and remaining cautious and fearful of losing the theological boundary between Judaism and other religions.

Shared reading of Scripture between Jews and Christians challenges the notion of an exclusive covenantal relationship between Israel and God for Jews on the one hand and, on the other, between Christians and God. Jews carry the memory of mutual hostility between the faiths and yet, in a new era, are challenged to reconfigure that memory and see themselves, in David's words, as part of a project orientated towards a future for Judaism and Christianity and how they relate to each other. What promises do we live by, asks David, and what is God's promise to us? In our conversation, he described the bush as a 'radical surprise' to Moses and sees it as a metaphor for the shared moral and religious endeavour of Jews and Christians; if we are involved in a history together for the sake of future generations, then we require a 'radical openness to God doing new things'. Jews have to find a contemporary way of being with Christians that is not hurtful or offensive, while Christians ask themselves what is a way of being Christian with Jews; can we retune our relationship while having proper respect for the truth, and in what ways can Scripture help us?

The disclosure of God's name in Exodus 3.14 allowed us to explore not only the Jewish legacy of interpretation and various translations, including, of course, the Septuagint, but also for David to share a Christian reading and understanding of a text that lay at the heart of his own faith. He pointed to John 1.18: 'No one has ever seen God. It is God the only Son, who is close to the Father's heart, who has made him known.' A Jewish response to this verse may well question its exclusive claim – for did not Jacob see God *panim el panim*, face to face,[34] and did not God speak to Moses 'face to face' as one man speaks to another?[35] Yet in this new shared endeavour of reading together, it wasn't our task to diminish the truth and integrity of the other's faith and texts, but to hold ourselves open to the 'occasionalism'[36] of religious encounter – whether Moses' on Horeb or John's witness to 'the Word [which] became flesh and lived among us'.[37]

> For a Christian, Jesus is one who looks on the world with eyes of compassion. Right at the heart of the suffering of Jesus is one who became fragile, vulnerable, and to see the world through his eyes, to be his disciple is to follow his gaze in the world and to act in his experience.[38]

How is the Jew to hear and comprehend these words of David? Can we learn from the Christian hermeneutic as much as from the interpretations of Rabbinic *midrashim* or mystical insights of our texts? For we are not only speaking about coexistence but about the possibility of a new theological relationship. If the future matters, if both religions are committed to a redemptive future in partnership with God, then how can we frame this shared reading of Scripture? Are Jews able to acknowledge that Christianity is 'the extension of the Jewish covenant at Sinai'?[39] If the purpose of the Jewish covenant is to teach the world about God and his moral law, can it not be argued that Christians have helped to achieve that mission by helping to spread the knowledge of God throughout the world?[40]

Neither Christians nor Jews possess an overview of God in their respective faiths. When David says that 'Jesus is the face of God' and that he lives 'before the face, in the name of Christ', he signifies that he lives before the face of one who is identified:

> ... through the gospel stories – the one who did this, did that, who was crucified. One lives before the face of someone who has been dead and raised and breathes his spirit into you and invites you to follow him in the world; who, through his spirit constantly leads you to pray, study, relate everything to him because he is at the right hand of God/is at one with God.[41]

The christological language is difficult. I find my own frame of references through the Torah and its interpretations and have no need to justify a rationale for study because these are the texts that are part of the Jewish story, they flow into my own identity as a Jew and are part of the weekly liturgy. Whereas the encounter with David, and specifically with a christological hermeneutic, forces me to create a rationale not only for studying the Christian Scriptures, but for listening and apprehending something fundamental about his own Christian faith.

Over a century has elapsed since the scholar and founder of Liberal Judaism in the United Kingdom, Claude Montefiore, required Jews to read the Christian Scriptures and see the figure of Jesus with a detachment of mind and impartiality. He asked:

> What is the right Jewish attitude towards the New Testament? What are we to think about the Gospels and the Gospels' hero? I cannot believe that the best and final answers will be purely negative. They will not be formed along the familiar lines that what is new in the Gospels is not true, and what is true is not new.[42]

Montefiore pushes against the barriers of exclusivism to challenge the idea that Judaism has nothing to learn from the New Testament. There are teachings, he wrote, that 'supplement and carry forward some essential teachings in the Old Testament'. We need both – and here he remains caught by the accusation that the Old Testament is preoccupied with righteousness and the New Testament with love – 'we need both the severity of justice and the tenderness of love. As regards the latter pair of apparent opposites they are both present in both Testaments, but in different ways.'[43]

There is something courageous and generous in Montefiore's embrace of both Testaments and his admiration for Jesus as teacher, preacher and prophet. Yet at the same time, there is a hint of Jewish – if not supersessionism – then pride in the primary and fundamental role of the Hebrew Bible, to which, he implies, New Testament authors owe their achievements. It is far more difficult to lay the foundations of monotheism and prophetic ethics, he says, and much easier to develop the message of religion and morality.[44] To be fair, Montefiore was refuting the claims of generations of Christian theologians charting the progress of religion from the God of vengeance and justice in the Hebrew Scriptures to the God of love, worshipped in spirit and truth in the New Testament.

The last conversation with David began with a reading of 1 Corinthians 13 and with the following questions: can a Jew be a 'witness' to a New Testament text? What significance does this text have for Christians? And can it have significance for me as a Jew?

The verses were almost as evocative to me as the words of Exodus 3. I was educated in a Church of England school from the age of seven until seventeen. The Head Mistress, a classicist and Christian, regularly read 1 Corinthians 13 as part of our morning assemblies and I remember her reading from Paul's Letter to the Corinthians days after her husband had been killed in a plane crash in Paris in 1974.

It was with the rhythm of Paul's rhetoric in the back of my mind that I now listened in on David's reflections on Paul's letter:

How can you be utterly God-centred and Jesus-centred at the same time? Paul is almost identifying Jesus with God, but not simply. Paul is deeply Jewish and monotheist. For him Jesus Christ is utterly intrinsic to God, but he is not simply God. He uses the divine title of Lord for him. He has not worked it all out conceptually, but the challenge of a different sort of monotheism is there. Above all Jesus embodies the love of God.[45]

I found Paul's rhetoric moving, brilliant – the convert writing to a new church in Corinth: 'Now you are the body of Christ and individually members of it ...'[46] What better way to involve the members of this church and to help them understand the most important message of this new faith: Jesus' love for them? One may speak in the 'tongues of mortals', one may have 'prophetic powers, and understand all mysteries and all knowledge', one can give away all one's possessions, but if there is no love (*agape*) 'I gain nothing.' [47] What is the nature of love, how does it express itself within the body of the Church? For 'God has so arranged the body, giving the greater honour to the inferior member, that there may be no dissension within the body, but the members may have the same care for one another. If one member suffers, all suffer together with it; if one member is honoured, all rejoice together with it.'[48] For Paul, Jesus is the embodiment of this love: patient, kind, neither envious nor boastful nor arrogant; not rejoicing in wrongdoing, but rejoicing in the truth. 'It bears all things, believes all things, hopes all things, endures all things.'[49]

> What is it that one sees when one looks at this faith? One wants to be the servant of all; you see his (Jesus') gaze on other people and that gaze directs you to other people ... You are before the mystery of the face who commands you and opens up what it is like being in a world where this person looks on all with compassion and love. It is utterly embracing, a non-negotiable thing, the secret of things. The only fundamental appeal is to love.[50]

These words from David in our conversations were not attempts to abstract a systematic theology from Paul, but to be part of Paul's journey – he called them 'journeys of intensification'. 'You can't go on two journeys simultaneously in interfaith encounters; other people are doing their journeys of intensification, you listen to them, there is no overview.'[51]

Paul's image of looking in a mirror 'dimly', the enigma and puzzling reflections that prevent us from seeing God face to face, held a different kind of symbolism for me as a Jew listening in to the reflections of a

Christian on his Scriptures. I listen to the poetic and lyrical language of Paul's Letter to the Corinthians, I am struck by its beauty and rhythm, by the simplicity but depth of his message – 'And now faith, hope, and love abide, these three; and the greatest of these is love,'[52] but I am still the outsider to his 'Father's house'. I can gaze and listen and be in awe, I can hear the resonances of my own Scriptures in these words about love: 'Love the Eternal One your God with all your heart and soul and might';[53] 'Love your neighbour as yourself';[54] 'And now, Israel, what does the Lord your God require of you, but to fear the Lord your God, to walk in all his ways and to love him';[55] 'Love the stranger, for you were strangers in the land of Egypt';[56] 'I drew them with gentle cords, with bands of love';[57] 'For the Lord is righteous, he loves righteousness, his face gazes on the upright'.[58]

In the preparation I enjoyed with both my nephews, I wanted them to deepen their own faith and identity through a Jewish understanding of the Scriptures. I wanted them to know about midrash and Maimonides and to help them see that the decisions they make about their own lives could be informed by the teachings of generations of Jewish scholars and sages. As they progressed further in their religious education, participating in their Kabbalat Torah,[59] the emphasis widened. Just as the child moves beyond the boundaries of their home and family life as a teenager and young adult, so too the young Jewish person must explore what lies beyond the security of their own faith and identity and learn how to reconstruct and deepen that identity and faith with generosity, grace and love in relation to others who are not of their faith.

What is the legacy of our Scriptures for Jews and Christians in an era of friendship, desire for conversation and dialogue? Perhaps conversation and, more importantly, listening help us to acknowledge the hurt and offence on both sides and to be more diffident, more gracious in our reading of the other's Scriptures. Faith is intimate, private, subjective, mysterious, surprising; but our religions and the richness of texts in both our faiths could allow us to explore ways in which we can come closer to each other, to see in the face of the other humanity's radical responsibility to place others before themselves and to plough a furrow that will lead to justice and compassion in the world.

Notes

1 Babylonian Talmud, Tractate *Ta'anit* 27b: 'Resh Lakish said: Man is given an additional soul on Friday, but at the termination of the Sabbath it is taken away from him, as it is said, *He ceased from work and rested, shavat va-yinafash* (Exodus 31.17), that is to say, Once the rest had ceased, woe! that soul is gone', pointing the word *va-yinafash* as *oy* and *nefesh* to mean 'Woe!' and 'soul'.

2 Ruth Langer, 2013, 'Jewish Liturgical Memory and the Non-Jew: Past Realities and Future Possibilities', in Alon Goshen-Gottstein and Eugene Korn (eds.), *Jewish Theology and World Religions*, London: Littman Library of Jewish Civilization, p. 168. While Langer deals here with traditional forms of the liturgy, viz. texts that constitute self-perceptions of Jewish identity and portrayals of the Other which can be less than complimentary, she does acknowledge in a footnote the substantial theological and liturgical changes made by Progressive Jewish liturgists, particularly in relation to non-Jews. So, for example, in the British Liberal prayer book, *Siddur Lev Chadash*, ed. John D. Rayner and Chaim Stern, 1995, the Havdalah blessing omits the distinction made between 'Israel and the Nations' and the implicit comparison of 'the Nations' with that which is 'not-holy', darkness and six days of work.

3 This and subsequent quotations are what was said by David to me in the course of our dialogue. I subsequently wrote it down and it has been confirmed by David.

4 David Ford, 2012, *The Shape of Living*, Norwich: Canterbury Press, 2012, p. 22.

5 Exodus 3.1. Translations from the Pentateuch are from the *JPS Torah Commentary*, 1991, Philadelphia, PA: The Jewish Publication Society.

6 From a lecture entitled 'Images of God in Jewish Thought', given on 10 March 2013 at a seminar organized by the Oxford Centre for Hebrew and Jewish Studies in conjunction with Friends of www.LouisJacobs.org.

7 Martin Buber discusses the significance and meaning of *Leitwort* style in his essay '*Leitwort* Style in Pentateuchal Narrative' (first published 1936 in Germany, in *Die Schrift und ihre Verdeutschung*), in Lawrence Rosenwald with Everett Fox (trans.), 1994, *Scripture and Translation, Martin Buber and Franz Rosenzweig*, Bloomington, IN: Indiana University Press: 'By Leitwort I understand a word or word root that is meaningfully repeated within a text or sequence of texts or complex of texts; those who attend to these repetitions will find a meaning of the text revealed or clarified, or at any rate made more emphatic' (p. 114).

8 Genesis 22.1.

9 Genesis 22.13.

10 Exodus 33.18.

11 Exodus 33.22–23.

12 There is not the space here to explicate the fourfold method of scriptural interpretation, employed by Jews and Christians from the Middle Ages. Jews called it *PaRDeS*, an acronym for *P'shat* – the literal meaning; *Remez* – the allegorical meaning; *D'rash* – the moral or figurative meaning as expressed in aggadah; and *Sod* – the mystical meaning. See Gershom Scholem, 1996, *On the Kabbalah and Its Symbolism*, New York: Schocken Books, p. 57, and Michael Fishbane, 1989, *The Garments of Torah*, Bloomington, IN: Indiana University Press, pp. 112–20.

13 Rashi, Exodus 3.1. Rashi's comment is based on *Exodus Rabbah* 2.3 where Moses is compared to David; both are tested for leadership by this way with sheep: 'Similarly in the case of Moses it says: "And he led the flock to the farthest end of the wilderness – in order to keep them from despoiling [the fields of others]." God took him to tend Israel, as it is said: "You led your people like a flock in the care of Moses and Aaron."' (Psalm 77.21).

14 Rabbi Obadiah ben Ya'akov Sforno, Italian rabbi, Bible commentator and philosopher, *c.* 1470–1550, Italy.

15 Sforno, Exodus 3.1.
16 Exodus 3.6.
17 Exodus 3.2.
18 Exodus 3.4.
19 I am using this technical term to convey that my nephew's experience of the text had the potential to lead him through his own discovery to something not absurd but profound and meaningful.
20 Maimonides, *Guide of the Perplexed* II.6 and 41 and III.45: 'It is clear that the belief in the existence of angels is connected with the belief in the Existence of God; and the belief in God and angels leads to the belief in Prophecy and in the truth of the Torah. In order to firmly establish this creed, God commanded [the Israelites] to make over the ark the form of two angels. The belief in the existence of angels is thus inculcated into the minds of the people, and this belief is in importance next to the belief in God's Existence; it leads us to believe in Prophecy and in the Torah, and opposes idolatry.'
21 *Guide* I.39. Maimonides does not appear to distinguish between the word *lehavah*, flame and *lev*, heart, connecting the phrase with Deuteronomy 4.11: *ud lev ha-shamayim*, to the heart of heaven.
22 Exodus 3.2.
23 *Tamati* and *nit-tam'mu* are both derived from the root *taf-mem-mem* meaning completeness, soundness, integrity.
24 A rare, post-biblical form meaning to attach oneself to.
25 Michael Fishbane, 2000, 'Types of Biblical Intertextuality', *Supplements to Vetus Testamentum* 80, p. 43.
26 See *Song of Songs Rabbah* 5.2:

> 'I am asleep, but my heart is awake.' Said the Community of Israel before the Holy One, blessed be He: 'Sovereign of the Universe! I am asleep in the neglect of religious observance, but my heart is awake for the performance of charity. I am asleep in respect of righteous deeds, but my heart is awake [in the desire] to do them. I am asleep in respect of the sacrifices, but my heart is awake for the recital of the Sh'ma and Prayer. I am asleep in respect of the Temple, but my heart is awake for synagogues and houses of study. I am asleep in respect of the end, but my heart is awake for the redemption. I am asleep in respect of the redemption, but the heart of the Holy One, blessed be He, is awake to redeem me.'

The midrash portrays a stunned and somnolent Israel in the aftermath of the destruction of the Temple, attempting to make sense of the loss of Jerusalem, the cult and its sacrifices, but awakening to the hope of something else – charity, prayer, community, study and future redemption. The midrash is a stunning expression of the ways in which Rabbinic Judaism sought to come to terms with the loss of each major institution of antiquity: the Temple in Jerusalem, the Land, the sacrificial cult and the active priesthood, and establish new practices.

27 Psalm 91.15.
28 Isaiah 63.9.
29 For a definition of the *Sh'khinah*, its meaning in Rabbinic Judaism as opposed to its significance in Kabbalistic literature, see Scholem, *On the Kabbalah*, pp. 104–05:

> In Talmudic literature and non-Kabbalistic Rabbinical Judaism, the *Sh'khinah* – literally in-dwelling, namely of God in the world – is taken to mean simply

God himself in His omnipresence and activity in the world and especially in Israel. God's presence, what in the Bible is called His 'face,' is in Rabbinical usage His *Sh'khinah*. Nowhere in the older literature is a distinction made between God himself and His *Shekhinah*; the *Shekhinah* is not a special hypostasis distinguished from God as a whole. It is very different in the usage of the Kabbalah ... Here the *Shekhinah* becomes an aspect of God, a quasi-independent feminine element within Him.

The *Sh'khinah* in Kabbalistic literature is seen as a 'providential guide of Creation'; in addition it is identified with the mystical 'Ecclesia' of Israel and with the soul, or with the dwelling place of the soul. The idea of the exile of the *Sh'khinah* goes back to the Talmud, but in the Kabbalah the concept of God going into exile with Israel is transformed to mean that 'a part of God Himself is exiled from God' – a separation of the masculine and feminine principles of God (pp. 107–08).

30 *Zohar* I.159b–160a, quoted in Isaiah Tishby, 1989, *The Wisdom of the Zohar*, trans. David Goldstein, London: Littman Library of Jewish Civilization, vol 1, p. 413.

31 See Fishbane, *The Garments of Torah*: 'Scripture – even its blank spaces – is a kind of icon of divinity for the purpose of envisaging God. But it is also an icon to be broken so that one may spiritually ascend into the imageless life of God' (p. 43).

32 See also Matthew 3.11; Mark 1.7; Luke 3.16; Acts 13.25.

33 Acts 13.38–39.

34 Genesis 32.31.

35 Exodus 33.11.

36 Professor Ford describes his use of the term 'occasionalism' as 'an understanding of God as having an infinitely particular form of agency, relating both freely and faithfully to each moment, occasion, person, etc. ... God is relating to all creation in this way, and while the general constancy of its statistical laws testifies to God's faithfulness, God is also free to spring surprises, such as Exodus 3.'

37 John 1.14.

38 See note 3 above.

39 Eugene Korn, 2016 (reprinted edition),'Rethinking Christianity', *Jewish Theology and World Religions*, Oxford: Littman Library of Jewish Civilization, p. 210.

40 Korn, 'Rethinking Christianity', p. 211.

41 See note 3 above.

42 Claude Montefiore, 1910, *The Synoptic Gospels*, London: Macmillan, vol. 1, pp. cxxxvi–cxxxviii.

43 Montefiore, *Synoptic Gospels*.

44 Montefiore, 1918, *Liberal Judaism and Hellenism*, London: Macmillan, p. 128.

45 See note 3 above.

46 1 Corinthians 12.27.

47 1 Corinthians 13.2–3.

48 1 Corinthians 12.24–26.

49 1 Corinthians 13.7.

50 See note 3 above.

51 See note 3 above.

52 1 Corinthians 13.13.

53 Deuteronomy 6.5.

54 Leviticus 19.18.

55 Deuteronomy 10.12.
56 Deuteronomy 10.19.
57 Hosea 11.4.
58 Psalm 11.7.
59 Kabbalat Torah ('Receiving Torah') is the term used since the 1970s to describe Jewish confirmation, held most often in a young person's fifteenth or sixteenth year. The new Hebrew term was taken from the writings of the philosopher Rabbi Abraham Joshua Heschel.

Reading Together: Receiving the Legacies of Our Scriptures Today

DAVID F. FORD

*Your word is a lamp to my feet
and a light to my path.* (Psalm 119.105)

Both Jews and Christians have found that our Scriptures have illuminated our paths century after century, and continue to do so. The legacies of our Scriptures have been immensely rich and complex – in commentary and community life, thought and prayer, ethics and politics. Their sheer superabundance of meaning is overwhelming, and no one person can ever take in more than a fraction of either tradition. They have also been very different, including much conflict. One obvious difference is that by 'Scriptures' Jews mean the Tanakh,[1] received in the context of one set of traditions of interpretation and worship, and Christians mean the Old and New Testaments,[2] received in the context of a very different set. As we receive these legacies today, it is not only the Scriptures and associated traditions that are diverse: there is also the distinctiveness of our time at the beginning of the twenty-first century.

The best use for a legacy is to provide for the continuation of life in ways that contribute to flourishing. How might Jews and Christians draw on our scriptural legacies today to enable a better future? Each has had its own path lit up by 'the word of the Lord' as it has been read within its own community; what light might come from reading together? It is one of the distinctive features of our period that such reading together is happening more than at any other time in history. Often in the past the reading that happened was in the interests of attack or defence, and rarely in settings of trust where both Jews and Christians could read together face to face and feel equally at home. Now deep sharing together around our texts is becoming more common – the Council of Christians and Jews Theology Project has been an encouraging example of this. Major questions for the future are how more Jews and Christians might participate in such reading together and what are the wisest ways to go about it.

Reading *lishmah*

When faced with the task of tackling the topic of our Scriptures Rabbi Alexandra Wright and I decided to read some of them together, and we spent many hours doing so. But we did not, in the first instance, study together in order to produce our chapters or even in order to open up a better future for relations between Jews and Christians – desirable though that is. It was not primarily a functional exercise. We agreed that for each of us the fundamental motivation for our study was summed up in the Hebrew phrase *lishmah*. It means literally 'for the name (of it)', and can be interpreted in many ways. For us it meant that we saw ourselves reading together in the presence of God, and doing this for the sake of God and God's purposes. Of course, each of our understandings of God and God's purposes has been shaped in our different traditions, so our agreement included some profound disagreement. The naming of God has been one of the most fundamental issues between Jews and Christians. In taking Exodus 3.1–15 as one of our main passages for study we were going to the roots of this, and I take this further below.

Alex has written of her engagement with this text as inspired by our reading together and also by many layers of experience (not least in exploring it with her nephew as part of his Bar Mitzvah preparation), by the detail of the Hebrew words, by resonances with other biblical texts, by commentators through the centuries (from early Rabbis who contributed to the Talmud, through medieval philosophical and mystical teachers, up to Martin Buber and Michael Fishbane in the twentieth and twenty-first centuries), and by worship through a liturgy pervaded by the chanting of Scripture. It is a reading immersed in the life of a community and its tradition, and it is at once theological, literary, historical, philosophical, ethical, political and liturgical, yet able to improvise in new circumstances and in response to the questions of a new generation. Hers is a 'journey of intensification'[3] that makes one realize how such a path carries with it a complex ecology of elements and niches in interplay. It brings home to me afresh something that the richest experiences of other religious traditions have increasingly impressed upon me: I cannot have an overview of them, any more than I can live two or more lives at the same time. They are shaped by pervasive traditions and habits of mind, heart, imagination and physical observance in communal settings and long-term relationships across generations; I can at best learn something of them and share something of my own analogous formation through being a Christian; and together we can seek to go on understanding each other better, living together in mutual hospitality and, if possible, collaboration and friendship. It is an ethos which gives priority to interreligious learning that is conducted face to face over many years between those who are committed within religious communities.[4] Without such long-term learning the interreligious ecosystem is impoverished and more vulnerable to shallow interpretations, inadequate responses, and all sorts of prejudice, discrimination and hatred.

My understanding of Exodus 3 has been affected permanently by reading it with Alex and many further insights have been generated by it. My notes from our hours of study include other reflections on the way seeing and hearing are in interplay throughout, on the many meanings that have been given to the Burning Bush itself, from Israel and the Church to the Virgin Birth and the Bible, on the ways God interrupts ordinary life, on the cries of suffering in our world, and on the ways Exodus 3 in the Septuagint[5] opens up new angles of interpretation – especially in relation to the New Testament and Christian tradition. Out of the abundance of possible further explorations, however, I want to pursue two, both sparked off by remarks of Alex.

Audacious theology: naming God in Exodus 3 and the Gospel of John

The first relates to reading *lishmah*: the question of the naming of God. It is far too vast to treat adequately here, so I will do it through just one Christian text – the Gospel of John, as it relates to Exodus 3 – and even this not at all exhaustively. I will especially have in mind a discussion of Exodus 3.14 by the French philosopher Paul Ricoeur,[6] and an essay on divine names by the American Methodist theologian Kendall Soulen,[7] both of which also summarize and engage critically with a range of interpretations over the centuries.

I take as a point of departure Alex's description of how a Rabbinic midrash 'injects the original verse from Exodus with an audacious theological implication'.[8] The idea of audacious midrashic theological interpretation is, I think, helpful in understanding how the Gospel of John reads Exodus 3.14–15.[9] John's *midrashim* are Jewish Christian, rereading his Scriptures through the lens of the life, death and resurrection of Jesus Christ and the coming of the Holy Spirit. The two distinctively novel Christian claims in the New Testament are that Jesus is the Messiah and that the Holy Spirit has been given through him. The first chapter of the Gospel of John draws especially on Genesis, Exodus, Isaiah and the Wisdom literature to identify Jesus as the Messiah who baptizes with the Holy Spirit. Through its midrash on Genesis 1.1 it also identifies Jesus as divine: 'In the beginning was the Word, and the Word was with God, and the Word was God …'[10] The emphatic negative statements of John the Baptist – 'I am not the Messiah …'[11] – then open up the space for the positive 'I am' statements by Jesus through the rest of the Gospel, especially the radical 'stand-alone' ones without predicates,[12] recalling above all Exodus 3.14. Yet it is also clear that the intention is to be completely faithful to the confession of one God. How might this be understood as conceivably in line with Exodus 3?

'I am who I am' or 'I will be who I will be' – both are possible translations – can be understood as the statement of a God who is free to be God in God's own ways, including new and surprising ways. In addition to being 'the God of Abraham, the God of Isaac, and the God of Jacob', God can also be the God of Moses understood through the new event of the Exodus. And Christians in addition testify to the freedom of God's self-identification in Jesus through the events of his life, death, resurrection and the giving of the Holy Spirit. So God can be proclaimed by Christians as the God of Abraham, Isaac, Jacob, Moses and Jesus. A critical issue is the meaning of that last addition; the Gospel of John articulates what has become the classic Christian interpretation: that the 'I am' of God has become present in human life uniquely in this person. It is the task of another pair of essays in this volume to consider further the question of Christology. Here the important point is to note that a central element in how Jesus, as represented by John, affirms his identity is by audacious, midrashic-theological interpretation of his Jewish Scriptures. Such practices of interpretation are intrinsic to both Judaism and Christianity and to appreciate this through reading together is to deepen our mutual understanding even when it also clarifies the depth of our disagreements.

Disagreement about the person of Jesus in relation to God is one of the enduring issues between most Christians and most Jews, but on the Christian side it has often been accompanied by forms of 'replacement theology' or supersessionism, in which the Church has replaced Israel, and God's covenant with Jews has been regarded as abrogated. The critique and reinterpretation of this tradition since the Holocaust has been important in helping many churches to face and repent of terrible elements in the history of their relations with Jews. A key New Testament text in rejecting supersessionism has been Paul's wrestling with the question in Romans 9—11, leading to his affirmation of God's mercy on all. His culminating cry (Romans 11.33–36) affirms in the language of Isaiah and other Scriptures the mystery of God's wisdom, knowledge, unsearchable judgements and inscrutable ways, concluding: '"For who has known the mind of the Lord? Or who has been his counsellor?" … For from him and through him and to him are all things. To him be the glory for ever.

Amen.' The repeated 'all' of those verses, together with the trust in a God who continues to surprise, opens up for Christians ways of radically revising many of their traditional approaches to Jews.

This Paul-inspired, God-centred liberation from supersessionism needs to be accompanied by fresh, critical reception of the Gospel of John and its resources for repairing the appalling history of anti-Judaism for which it has been partly responsible. I am at present trying to write a theological commentary on the Gospel of John, motivated in part by considering it the single most important Christian theological text, but also in part by nearly two decades of regularly reading the New Testament, alongside the Tanakh and the Qur'an, with Jews and Muslims. I have become convinced of several things: that John is not only an audacious reader of Scripture but also expects his readers to be comparably daring – not least in going beyond what he wrote and engaging in midrashic interpretation for today;[13] that in John, as in Paul, the 'all' of God's love and compassion allows for fresh surprises, not least in how Christians might relate to Jews; that Rabbinic ways of dealing with difficult and even offensive texts have much to teach Christians; that Christians should seek to read all their texts with Jews; and that Christians should be open to some radical surprises in their relations with Jews on precisely the subject of greatest contention, the person of Jesus. The Synoptic and the Johannine Jesus indicates that believers' expectations of him might well be drastically revised in the event of his 'return'. Many Jewish hopes of the Messiah sound a similar note of expecting the unexpected. If all are likely to be surprised, it is unwise of any to be too confident that their particular hope will be fulfilled just in the way they expect. A combination of humble agnosticism, honest sharing of differences about messianic expectations and trust that God has good surprises in store may be the best way for both Jews and Christians to approach the future.

The reasons for Christians to read their Scriptures with Jews may be very different from those motivating Jews to read with Christians. One of the many fascinating aspects of reading with Alex has been to converse with her as she worked out her approach to reading the New Testament – and responded to my interpretations of it – as described in her chapter. Perhaps the most important factor helping us to read respectfully and hospitably together, while at the same time keeping us strongly aware of our differences, was that both were continuing to pray and worship in traditions where the Scriptures are above all read for God's sake, *lishmah*. There are so many ways of instrumentalizing our Scriptures, whether for personal, communal, political, polemical, academic or other uses, that we need to be constantly vigilant in sustaining the holiness, the God-centredness, of our reading and living. That not only relativizes everything else, it also reminds us to be humble before God in our interpretations and applications, aware that we do not have a God's-eye perspective on Scripture or the rest of reality and therefore can be open to light coming through the readings of others and through divine surprises. In all our reading of Scripture, the question of our deepest motivation, whether or not we are reading for the sake of God, cries out to be repeatedly addressed. Audacious theology is one fruit of that liberating motivation.

Rereading in the aftermath of destruction

The second seminal statement of Alex is her endnote comment on *Song of Songs Rabbah* 5.2:

> The midrash portrays a stunned and somnolent Israel in the aftermath of the destruction of the Temple, attempting to make sense of the loss of Jerusalem, the cult and its sacrifices, but awakening to the hope of something else – charity, prayer, community, study and future redemption. The midrash is a stunning expression of the ways in which Rabbinic Judaism sought to come to terms with the loss of each major institution of antiquity: the Temple in Jerusalem, the Land, the sacrificial cult and the active priesthood, and establish new practices.[14]

The suffering of the Eternal One as a partner in Israel's trouble, speaking from a bush full of spines and thorns, or even as a king whose son has died and lies in mourning on a bed of thorns and thistles: these themes for a Christian inevitably resonate also with Jesus and his crucifixion. From whatever angle, some of the most difficult theological issues that face Jews, Christians, or anyone else who trusts in God, are opened up.

For me the vital connection between traumatic human suffering and the reading of Scripture in our time was brought home vividly with consequences that are still continuing by encountering a group of Jewish text scholars and philosophers called Textual Reasoning in the early 1990s.[15] They were a fringe meeting of the American Academy of Religion and I used to sit on its fringe with my father-in-law, Professor Daniel W. Hardy.[16] We were utterly gripped by the intensity of the conversation, argument and humour – and by the range and richness of the learning and thinking. On the one hand, they engaged with Tanakh and Talmud, on the other with Hermann Cohen,[17] Franz Rosenzweig,[18] Emmanuel Levinas and other modern Jewish thinkers, but also pervaded by references to western philosophy since Plato and diverse disciplines of the contemporary academy. At one level it was philosophers and text scholars overcoming their isolation from each other; but it was also a group of Jews working out how to be Jewish in the aftermath of the Holocaust/Shoah. As I later analysed it, they were combining three dynamics, each of which they saw as essential to healthy contemporary Jewish life and thought.

First, there was a rereading of their classic texts of Tanakh and Talmud. They were convinced that, just as the Babylonian exile had been the stimulus for Ezra, Nehemiah, Jeremiah and much of Isaiah, generating a renewal of faith and practice, and just as the destruction of the Second Temple by the Romans in 70 CE had been responded to by the development of Rabbinic Judaism and the Talmud, so the Shoah could be a generative trauma too. As in the Babylonian exile and with the early Rabbinic sages, the previous ways of interpreting the tradition and its texts had to be rethought, and ways of living in new circumstances had to be discerned anew.

Second, one of the distinctive things in the post-Shoah situation is the pervasive influence of western modernity, a set of interrelated, transformative understandings, sciences, technologies and ways of living that was also complexly involved with the Shoah. How to come to new terms with all of that? The answer was: by rereading the classic texts while at the same time engaging with modern philosophies and other attempts to understand the developments of the past few centuries.

There was a third dynamic too: any Jewish attempt to reread their classic texts and come to terms with the traumas and achievements of modernity might be helped by conversing with others who were involved in analogous projects. This was where we Christians on the fringe came in, and soon some of us joined with some from Textual Reasoning (including Peter Ochs, Laurie Zoloth, Steven Kepnes, Robert Gibbs, Aryeh Cohen and Shaul Magid) to form Scriptural Reasoning.[19]

Muslims, beginning with Basit Koshul,[20] joined Scriptural Reasoning soon afterwards, and it has developed in diverse ways since then – both in many academic settings and in schools, prisons, hospitals, leadership courses, local synagogues, churches and mosques, and elsewhere. But I want now to reflect on that short period when it was bilateral – between Jews and Christians. Studying with Alex and taking part in the discussions of this CCJ Theology Project has been a renewal of that time. It has underlined something that has been confirmed in many ways in the years I have been concerned with interfaith engagements. It is that the 'ecology' of types of engagement needs many sorts of group. There is a role for multilateral groups (covering many religions – there are awkward issues about which bodies come under that heading, and often a good deal of political correctness when so many are involved); the Abrahamic religions need trilaterals – I have been struck by how helpful it is for each of the pairs, Jewish/Christian, Muslim/Jewish, Christian/Muslim, to be able to bring in the third, and how good the dynamic of mutual hospitality around the three Scriptures can be; but bilaterals are also essential, and through them there can often be greater specificity, depth and intensity. The Jewish–Christian bilateral is perhaps the most challenging of all because of the ways these traditions have been intertwined since the beginning of Christianity. Among the issues between them none is more vital or difficult than the Shoah and its aftermath.

In this aftermath Christians too have to reread their texts and traditions and consider their relationship to modernity. They need to do so both among themselves and in engagement with Jews – if Jews are willing. And always the questions of how God relates to evil, suffering and death recur. The sort of wrestling with these questions that Alex's discussion of Exodus 3 introduces is perhaps the main criterion for authenticity in both of our traditions. To find a group of Jews who were, and are, committed to such engagement has been one of the most important events for my theology (and more than theology). I am by no means alone in this, but the actual practice of Jews and Christians regularly reading their Scriptures together is still quite rare. I have a vision of both traditions beginning to work out ways of making study of our Scriptures together part of normal life for more Jews and Christians.

Reading our Scriptures together: an ethos inspired by 1 Corinthians 13

Paul's hymn to love in 1 Corinthians 13 is worth considering as a possible guide to the ethos of such reading together. It can certainly give guidance to Christians and the extent to which it also rings true for Jews is a further question. Alex's reflections on it, arising out of our joint study, attend carefully to some of the distinctively Christian comments that I made on it and then, as she writes, she can 'hear the resonances of my own Scriptures in these words about love'.[21] It is clear that each of us can have a different rationale for our joint reading, one Christian and one Jewish, and that the two can also learn from each other. I want to interpret 1 Corinthians 13 as suggesting elements for a Christian approach to joint reading.

The first thing to note is that Paul is writing to a church plagued by serious problems and divisions. He is proposing a wisdom of love as the way to reconciliation and healing, so it would not be surprising if what he writes is relevant to the coming together of Jews and Christians in the face of a history of deep division and estrangement:

> 1 If I speak in the tongues of mortals and of angels, but do not have love, I am a noisy gong or a clanging cymbal. 2 And if I have prophetic powers, and understand all mysteries and all knowledge, and if I have all faith, so as to remove mountains, but do not have love, I am nothing. 3 If I give away all my possessions, and if I hand over my body so that I may boast, but do not have love, I gain nothing.

From those first three verses I gather that the one utterly essential thing to bring to my joint reading is love. I might have superb linguistic competence and articulateness, extraordinary insight, wisdom, theological learning, faith and self-sacrifice, but all that will be of no long-term benefit to the relationship if love is lacking. And, conversely, I might be linguistically, theologically and academically inadequate in many ways, but if I come in love there will be the possibility of permanent fruitfulness:

> 4 Love is patient; love is kind; love is not envious or boastful or arrogant 5 or rude. It does not insist on its own way; it is not irritable or resentful; 6 it does not rejoice in wrongdoing, but rejoices in the truth.

The NRSV translation[22] does not quite catch the extent to which these verses are packed with active verbs. Anthony Thiselton, in his excellent commentary, translates:

> Love waits patiently; love shows kindness. Love does not burn with envy; does not brag – is not inflated with its own importance. It does not behave with ill-mannered impropriety; is not preoccupied with the interests of the self; does not become exasperated into pique; does not keep a reckoning up of evil. Love does not take pleasure at wrongdoing, but joyfully celebrates the truth.[23]

These can be seen as instructions for how to read together, questions to have in the back of my mind: Am I spending long enough patiently trying to understand this text and its interpretation – why not spend another hour on this verse? Am I being kind and generous enough in how I hear alternative readings to mine? Am I placing alternative readings unnecessarily in competition with each other? Am I pushing my own reading too insistently? Can I put up with being shown to be wrong? What is the best etiquette to observe in this setting, what sorts of courtesy and good manners, including appreciating the practices of the fellow readers' interpretative traditions?[24] With texts that have been used polemically, oppressively or to assert superiority is it possible for me to start afresh and reread them in love, forgiveness and truth? And when moments of truthful insight happen can I savour and celebrate them with my fellow readers? (The Greek for the second 'rejoice' in verse 6 is *sugchairei*, 'rejoice with'.)

Thiselton's comment on love joyfully celebrating the truth is:

> Genuine love ... alone *decentres* the power interests of the self and of its peer group, and in recentring them in the Other (primarily in God, but also in the other person) disengages from self-interest. Only now can truth emerge as disengaged from a power agenda. True disinterested integrity is free to seek truth, without anxiety about what it helps or hinders in one's personal agenda. Love ... is honest and open, not defensive, for it has placed the good of the other above the good of the self.[25]

Such words spring from a lifetime grappling with power-centred worldviews and with the 'hermeneutics of suspicion' of Feuerbach, Marx, Nietzsche, Freud or Foucault that have often shaped both popular and academic approaches to religion:

> 7 It bears all things, believes all things, hopes all things, endures all things.

Here Thiselton translates: 'It never tires of support, never loses faith, never exhausts hope, never gives up.' That rightly puts the emphasis on the absence of limits and on perseverance rather than on any totalitarian embrace or triumphalist mastery. Joint reading of difficult, disputed texts requires that sort of unlimited commitment: I will not give up this practice whatever the problems and whatever the temptation to withdraw or have other priorities, I will always trust that God has a way through, that there is a better future together whatever our current disagreements, and that understanding together what we receive as sacred Scriptures will be part of that. The culmination is the final word, *hupomenei*, literally 'abiding underneath', with associations of staying in difficult places, refusing to despair, hoping against hope, taking as long as it takes. It even echoes the literal meaning of understanding/standing under:

> 8 Love never ends. But as for prophecies, they will come to an end; as for tongues, they will cease; as for knowledge, it will come to an end. 9 For we know only in part, and we prophesy only in part; 10 but when

the complete comes, the partial will come to an end. 11 When I was a child, I spoke like a child, I thought like a child, I reasoned like a child; when I became an adult, I put an end to childish ways. 12 For now we see in a mirror, dimly, but then we will see face to face. Now I know only in part; then I will know fully, even as I have been fully known. 13 And now faith, hope, and love abide, these three; and the greatest of these is love.

Here is the essential eschatological perspective: love never ends, does not fall apart, is eternal, permanent and utterly reliable in the long term, because love is of God and what God wills for all. We cannot ultimately go wrong if we read together in love. It relativizes everything else. It is God's future for us and also the way towards that future with its many surprises. To read 'the word of the Lord' together now in love is to taste something of that future, including frequent surprises. It is to mature in the only way that really matters: by growing in love. It is to glimpse a little the ultimate 'face to face' with God and other people in mutual knowledge, trust, hope, peace, joy and love.

Alex's final question is: 'What is the legacy of our Scriptures for Jews and Christians in an era of friendship, desire for conversation and dialogue?' Her answer above all emphasizes the quality of listening that helps us 'to acknowledge the hurt and offence on both sides and to be more diffident, more gracious in our reading of the other's Scriptures',[26] enabling us through faith ('intimate, private, subjective, mysterious, surprising') to:

> explore ways in which we can come closer to each other, to see in the face of the other humanity's radical responsibility to place others before themselves and to plough a furrow that will lead to justice and compassion in the world.[27]

Such responsible listening and reading before God, each other and the cries of our world can be a light for the path ahead in the twenty-first century.

Feasting to keep our promise of never again

I conclude with the poem 'Never' by Micheal O'Siadhail, and some comments on it. 'Never' is from the final part of O'Siadhail's *The Gossamer Wall: Poems in Witness to the Holocaust*,[28] written out of immersion over many years in the literature of the Holocaust and meetings with survivors. It has sections on the historical roots of the Holocaust; the way the Nazis took power in one German town, Northeim; the story of one unit, Batallion 101, that killed Jews in the wake of the German army's advance eastwards; a central suite of sonnets on the extermination camps; stories of Jewish resistance, and of Le Chambon, the French village that saved many Jews; and the aftermath of the Holocaust. The latter concluding section is called 'Prisoners of Hope' (a phrase from Judah Halevi) and wrestles with the possibilities for life after such trauma: 'Out of this eruption, can we prepare another climate?'[29]

The 14 poems open up one fundamental question after another.[30] 'Never' is especially relevant to the theme of meaning, texts and the conversations around them:

> That any poem after Auschwitz is obscene?
> Covenants of silence so broken between us
> Can we still promise or trust what we mean?
> Even in the dark of earth seeds will swell.
> All the interweavings and fullness of being,
> Nothing less may insure against our hell.
> A black sun only shines out of a vacuum.
> Cold narrowings and idols of blood and soil.
> And all the more now, we can't sing dumb!
> A conversation so rich it knows it never arrives
> Or forecloses; in a buzz and cross-ruff of polity
> The restless subversive ragtime of what thrives.
> Endless dialogues. The criss-cross of flourishings.
> Again and over again our complex yes.
> A raucous glory and the whole jazz of things.
> The sudden riffs of surprise beyond our ken;
> Out of control, a music's brimming let-go.
> We feast to keep our promise of never again.

There the seeds of hope are found in 'All the interweavings and fullness of being', in the richness of open-ended 'conversation', in 'dialogues', 'flourishings', affirmations of life, the improvisatory surprises of jazz, and feasting. The response to the 'black sun' (a phrase of Paul Celan, the Jewish Romanian-French poet of the Shoah), 'vacuum' and 'Cold narrowings' of evil and its culture of hatred and death is the intensity of meaning that is explored endlessly together, and the celebration of an overflowing, uncontainable, unpredictable superabundance of life: 'A raucous glory and the whole jazz of things'. If that is anything like the fullness of life that God invites us into, then the Tanakh and the Bible surely have a role to play not only in feeding 'A conversation so rich it knows it never arrives/Or forecloses' but also in inspiring us to say 'Again and over again our complex yes' to God, to each other and to each one in the image of God, and even to 'feast to keep our promise of never again'.

Notes

1 Tanakh is the term used by Jews for the Jewish Bible or Hebrew Scriptures, composed of the initial Hebrew letters of its three parts: Torah, Prophets and Writings.

2 Different Christian traditions have somewhat different canons, some Protestants not acknowledging or giving a lower status to the Apocrypha.

3 *Supra* p. 147.

4 Cf. http://www.interfaith.cam.ac.uk/en/resources/papers/cadbury, and Michael Barnes, 2011, *Interreligious Learning*, Cambridge: Cambridge University Press.

5 The first translation of the Hebrew Scriptures, made into Greek by Jews in Alexandria, which became the Sacred Scripture of most writers of the New Testament.

6 Paul Ricoeur, 'Exodus 3:14. From Interpretation to Translation', in André LaCocque and Paul Ricoeur, 1998, *Thinking Biblically: Exegetical and Hermeneutical Studies*, Chicago, IL, and London: University of Chicago Press. Vital for my suggestion are three points of Ricoeur: first, his insistence that a reading of 3.14 'can legitimately oscillate between a minimizing and an amplifying reading of this chain of '*ehyeh*'s culminating in the Tetragrammaton' (p. 336) – both the Jewish and the Christian traditions of interpretation are 'amplifying' in his sense, though in different ways; second, his positive answer to the question 'whether the Johannine proclamation that "God is love" leads to thought unless we make a detour through Exodus 3.14' (p. 358); and, third, his argument that 'the declaration of John's Gospel unfolds, through the resources of metaphor, dialectic and narrativization, the proclamation of Exodus and Deuteronomy' (p. 359).

7 R. Kendall Soulen, 2011, *The Divine Name(s) and the Holy Trinity*, vol. 1, *Distinguishing the Voices*, Louisville, KY: Westminster John Knox Press. One of his most fruitful suggestions is that the pattern he discerns in the New Testament and later trinitarian teaching is also present in the Old Testament/Tanakh, and especially in Exodus 3. This is the combination of God's uniqueness ('The Lord, the God of your ancestors ...', v. 16), presence ('has appeared to me, saying: "... I declare that I will bring you up out of the misery of Egypt ..."', vv. 16–17) and blessing ('to ... a land flowing with milk and honey', v. 17). He is perceptive on the importance of the Tetragrammaton for Christianity as well as for Judaism, and gives a non-supersessionist account of Christian trinitarianism – how the christological pattern of naming God as Father, Son and Holy Spirit and the pneumatological (Holy Spirit-centred) pattern of an open-ended multiplicity of divine names can complement without contradicting the theological pattern of oblique reference to the Tetragrammaton.

8 *Supra* p. 142.

9 Likewise her opening reflections on Ruth Langer's remark that the religious or political Other of the Hebrew Bible 'is almost universally negative' can be applied to the Gospel of John's controversial treatment of 'the Jews'. This is taken up elsewhere in this volume; and cf. below on John's 'anti-Judaism'.

10 John 1.1.
11 John 1.20–21.
12 John: 4.25–26; 6.20; 8.24; 8.28; 8.58; 13.19; 18.4–8.
13 On this, see David F. Ford, 2013, 'Meeting Nicodemus: A Case Study in Daring Theological Interpretation', *Scottish Journal of Theology* 66.1, pp. 1–17.
14 *Supra* note 26, p. 00.
15 Peter Ochs and Nancy Levene (eds.), 2002, *Textual Reasonings: Jewish Philosophy and Text Study at the End of the Twentieth Century*, London: SCM Press.
16 1930–2007.
17 German Jewish philosopher, 1842–1918.
18 German Jewish philosopher, 1886–1929.
19 On Scriptural Reasoning, see www.scripturalreasoning.org; the websites of the Cambridge Inter-faith Programme, www.interfaith.cam.ac.uk; the international Society for Scriptural Reasoning, www.scripturalreasoning.org; and the Journal of Scriptural Reasoning, http://jsr.shanti.virginia.edu. Note that there are other websites bearing similar names which are not affiliated to the Scriptural Reasoning movement referred to in this chapter. The sites listed here offer the best online resources for learning more about it. For Jewish, Christian and Muslim essays on Scriptural Reasoning, see David F. Ford and Chad C. Pecknold, 2006, *The Promise of Scriptural Reasoning*, Oxford: Wiley Blackwell; for a superb Christian (Anglican and Quaker) account of it, see Mike Higton and Rachel Muers, 2012, *The Text in Play: Experiments in Reading Scripture*, Eugene, OR: Cascade Books; for a wide-ranging set of discussions and account of developments, see David F. Ford and Frances Clemson (eds.), 2013, *Interreligious Reading after Vatican II: Scriptural Reasoning, Comparative Theology and Receptive Ecumenism*, Oxford: Wiley Blackwell.
20 Professor in the Humanities Department at Lahore University of Management Sciences and co-author, 2007, of *Scripture, Reason and the Contemporary Islam–West Encounter*, London: Palgrave Macmillan.
21 *Supra* p. 148.
22 The New Oxford annotated Bible: New Revised Standard Version, 4th edn, 2010, Oxford: Oxford University Press.
23 Anthony C. Thiselton, 2000, *The First Epistle to the Corinthians: A Commentary on the Greek Text*, Grand Rapids, MI: Eerdmans; Carlisle: Paternoster Press, p. 1026.
24 See www.scripturalreasoning.org for one set of guidelines for interfaith reading.
25 Thiselton, *First Epistle to the Corinthians*, pp. 1055–6.
26 *Supra* p. 148.
27 *Supra* p. 148.
28 Micheal O'Siadhail, 2002, *The Gossamer Wall: Poems in Witness to the Holocaust*, Tarset: Bloodaxe Books, p. 120.
29 O'Siadhail, *Gossamer Wall*, 'Dust-veil', p. 112.
30 For further reflection on these poems, see David F. Ford, 2007, *Christian Wisdom: Desiring God and Learning in Love*, Cambridge: Cambridge University Press, ch. 4.

Further Reflections

TONY BAYFIELD

No pair of essays could be more clearly illustrative of our methodology. This is a book of dialogue, written in a process of dialogue, and Rabbi Alexandra Wright and Professor David Ford demonstrate the dialogical – in almost every line of their essays. They make considerable use of Scriptural Reasoning, an approach strongly identified with David. What could be more encouraging for Jews than the Regius Professor of Divinity at Cambridge employing Scriptural Reasoning to such profound and loving effect and stressing the significance and challenge of the bilateral relationship between Christianity and Judaism?

But let me begin with Alex, who approached our process with considerable trepidation. Though a Liberal Jew herself, she brought with her community-wide Jewish fears and inhibitions. The New Testament has been used as a vehicle for anti-Judaism and an instrument of assault for the preponderance of time that the two siblings, Rabbinic Judaism and Christianity, have unsuccessfully coexisted. The very term 'New Testament' proclaims a covenant replacing the covenant at Sinai and epitomizes supersessionism. Jews have an understandable reluctance to go where love has been proclaimed but seldom expressed towards them. Or to explore the intense feelings of rejection experienced by their fellow Jews who found/find revelation in Jesus Christ. It would be fair to add that studying the New Testament text with one of the country's foremost Christian academics was also daunting.

The essay Alex has produced is a testament to her commitment, courage and openness of mind. It's transformatory. First, she shows how helpful the Rabbinic approach to the text of the Torah can be in illuminating present, shared theological questions. What's unsurprising but important to witness is how powerfully past experiences of destruction and suffering resonate for us today. Second, all the rich resources of classical Rabbinic Judaism and its exegetical method can be deployed in a way that is authentic for all the Jews in the Group whatever their denomination.

THE LEGACY OF OUR SCRIPTURES

The midrash Alex selects from *Song of Songs Rabbah*[1] addresses twenty-first-century Jews and Christians alike. She ends with two questions at the sharpest edge of contemporary theology: 'Can one really say that God suffers as Israel suffers? Can one imply that the suffering of humanity is felt too by an incorporeal God?'[2] Both in the Jewish present and in the Jewish past this is a sea of reeds from which some will instinctively pull back and some wish to go forward.

Let's go back to the second century CE. While the response from Rabbi Ishmael[3] and his school is 'no', his equally great contemporary Rabbi Akiva[4] and his school answer 'yes', God does suffer and does feel the suffering of humanity. A vital theological tradition emerges in the shadow of the destruction and expulsion of the first and second centuries in which God is passible – has emotions – and vulnerable. I remember a day, 30 years ago, when Berlin-born theologian Rabbi Dr Albert Friedlander *z"l* introduced the Revd Dr Richard Harries, who was about to become Bishop of Oxford, to that stream of Jewish tradition, intellectually and emotionally uniting the two men. Both Abrahamic traditions, born in the same place at the same time, address the fundamental issue of God and human suffering. The light each sheds is complementary and penetrating. Jacob and Esau embraced. As Alex and David demonstrate, we must never again go our separate ways,[5] but grapple with this most troubling of mysteries together.

Alex not only illustrates the dialogical power of Scriptural Reasoning, but also shows how the approach transcends issues concerning the Torah text and its origins which have plagued the Jewish world for 150 years. In the nineteenth century, Samson Raphael Hirsch took a fateful stand against the historicity of the Torah, affirming it as *Torah min HaShamayim*, Torah from Heaven, and standing against the tide of modern historical criticism.[6] That stance was confirmed by Rabbi Lord Sacks in a long and powerful essay[7] – the Torah is extra-historical, resistant to modern critical methods. When, more than 50 years ago, Rabbi Dr Louis Jacobs reasserted the historicity of the Torah, it further 'denominationalized' the British Jewish community. Alex refers to 'the biblical authors' and there's no doubt as to where she stands on that debate. Yet, remarkably, the issue well-nigh vanishes. By adopting the age-old methodology of Rabbinic enquiry and interrogation of the text, she demonstrates that the voice of God is 'amplified' (to use the word employed by David Ford) for all the Jewish denominations sitting round our dialogue table – Liberal, Masorti, Orthodox and Reform. Isn't it remarkable that what rarely happens elsewhere took place in the context of Jewish–Christian dialogue? Is it possible that it could *only* have happened among those who have the courage (and confidence) to take part in interfaith dialogue? God works in truly mysterious ways!

David puts a loving arm round Alex's shoulder and welcomes her as a respected guest at his Scriptural Reasoning table. The person she meets there is a leading Christian figure who renounces supersessionism unequivocally. The respect that he has long demonstrated for Jews and Judaism is not superficial. He welcomes Alex as a sibling, as an equal, entitled to her own theological space. There's no 'overview' – supersessionist or of any other kind. We sit together, we study each other's Scriptures, we express our difficulties, we listen. We don't expect always to understand but – and this is, for me, the most important part of a most important paper – we recognize that God is an endless source of surprise.[8]

For me, the differences between Judaism and Christianity over Messianism have never been an insuperable obstacle. The more I study, the more I realize that it's a family disagreement which became the *broiges*[9] par excellence but needn't remain so. In Rabbinic tradition, debates over which no agreement can be reached – and there are very many of them, Louis Jacobs identifies 319 in the Babylonian Talmud alone[10] – are deferred to the time of the coming of the Messiah with the word *teyku*. The word is a shortening of *teykum*, let the matter stand, move the next item on the agenda. However, tradition has read it as an acrostic for 'Elijah the Tishbite will resolve the issue'. In Jewish tradition Elijah will return to herald the coming of the Messiah. What precisely that will mean could well be yet another surprise from our shared and endlessly surprising God – as David so tellingly points out.

David, like Alex, doesn't explore the nature of the text of the New Testament. I personally find that sitting at the Scriptural Reasoning table is made more comfortable by another of my Christian heroes, Professor Mary Boys,[11] who writes, 'If Jesus was crucified as seditious by the power of the Roman Empire, why do the Gospels shift blame to Jews?', and insists that 'precisely because of the terrible consequences for Jews … the complexity of the passion narratives become a pastoral priority for the church'. If some Christians can say 'The New Testament's polemic against Jews should be classified as a rhetorical strategy of the Hellenistic world that does not have authority for Christians of our time,'[12] I feel compelled to respond with equal humility and generosity.

I go further. For me the Torah text is, in itself, interpretation – of a metaphystorical[13] event witnessed but individually and only partially comprehended, discussed, told and retold and only finally, respectfully but with the limitation of human beings, written down. Is such an understanding of Scripture possible for the adherents of other Scriptures? It's my hope and preference but I emerge from reading the Wright–Ford dialogue far less bothered than I might have been before we started.

David – and Alex's response – does provide a difference of *perspective*, highlighted by David's passionate reading of Corinthians on love. As the American scholar Max Kadushin in *The Rabbinic Mind* demonstrates,[14] struggling with the balance between justice and compassion is more characteristic than emphasizing love alone.[15] But importantly, the climax of David's essay took me back to an earlier reference to God and surprises. He concludes: 'A combination of humble agnosticism, honest sharing of differences about messianic expectations, and trust that God has good surprises in store may be the best way for both Jews and Christians to approach the future.'[16]

Who could fail to find that the shared way forward? Nevertheless, I – and some other Jews – find the 'good' in 'good surprises' difficult to access because of the many 'bad' surprises of the twenty-first century. I don't travel the same road as David when it comes to anticipating surprises will be good and experiencing the overwhelming sense of God's love. I wonder just how many Jews stand closer to my place than his? Does that matter? Not at all – as long as we acknowledge the right of our siblings to their feelings, understand the journey history has taken them on and learn by trying to retrace their particular steps. That's so evident from these two essays and why they're a triumph of humanity as well as theology – and of love.

Notes

1 Difficult to date but containing much early material, *Song of Songs Rabbah* is part of one of the greatest collections of *midrashim*. A classic example of Rabbinic Judaism and early Christianity grappling with the same questions, and it's not clear where the balance of influence lies.

2 *Supra* p. 142.

3 A towering and defining figure of Rabbinic Judaism from the first half of the second century CE.

4 Akiva was a contemporary of Ishmael, one of the five Rabbis remembered in the *Hagaddah* as spending the entire first night of Passover discussing the relationship between the liberation from Egypt and its implications for action under Hadrianic persecution. For a profound insight into Akiva (and the different approach of Rabbi Ishmael), see Abraham Joshua Heschel, 2005, *Heavenly Torah As Refracted through the Generations*, New York: Continuum International.

5 Genesis 33.17.

6 The text of Hirsch's stand is quoted by Jonathan Sacks, 1992, *Crisis and Covenant: Jewish Thought after the Holocaust*, Manchester: Manchester University Press, p. 189.

7 *Le'ela* 40, September 1995. It's an amalgamation of chapters 7 and 8 from *Crisis and Covenant*, representing a rare foray into the minefield of theology after Rabbi Lord Sacks became Chief Rabbi.

8 *Supra* p. 157.

9 A highly personalized row.

10 Louis Jacobs, 1981, *Teyku: The Unsolved Problem in the Babylonian Talmud*, London: A Leo Baeck College Publication, Cornwall Books.

11 Mary C. Boys is Professor of Practical Theology at Union Theological Seminary, New York City, USA.

12 Quotations from Philip A. Cunningham *et al.* (eds.), 2011, *Christ Jesus and the Jewish People Today: New Explorations of Theological Interrelationships*, Grand Rapids, MI, Eerdmans, and Gregorian & Biblical Press, pp. 60–2.

13 A word I coined a few years ago to explain my understanding of revelation as a moment when God and history touch – whether it be at Sinai or Golgotha – out of which emerges the narrative of a particular people and faith.

14 Max Kadushin, 1972, *The Rabbinic Mind*, 3rd edn, New York: Bloch Publishing Company.

15 The Rabbis ask whether God prays. In the Babylonian Talmud, *B'rakhot* 7a we find the following: R. Zutra bar Tuvia said in the name of Rav [that God prays]: 'May it be My will that My mercy conquers My anger, My mercy is revealed in My attributes, I treat My children with the attribute of compassion, and, for them, I go beyond the bounds of strict justice.'

16 *Supra* p. 157.

5
Religious Absolutism

Rethinking Revelation, Exclusivity, Dialogue and Mission

ALAN RACE

The rightness of our religion is among the most intransigent and incorrigible of our cherished convictions; so much so that anyone who believes, thinks and acts differently is wrong. As a result, the experience of religious difference can evoke discomforting anxiety, if not full-blown fear.[1]

Religious difference, it seems, is not something that can be lived with easily. If American Professor of Religion James Wiggins is correct that religious difference produces anxiety and fear then we are obliged to enquire into the origins of such strong emotional reactions. Further, given that religious conviction can never be confined simply to a supposed private sphere in the human personality, when religious difference is expressed through social and political power, anxiety and fear easily lead to defensiveness and even violence within and between religions. Modern calls for toleration or respect might signal a definite improvement in interreligious relations, but it must be admitted that they seldom get to the theological heart of what is at stake. 'I want to know what you think of my religion' is the query lurking within every interreligious encounter and it takes us beyond toleration and respect. What is it about the religious other that generates feelings of anxiety and fear? Is it to do with religious poaching, having adherents stolen from 'my' group through proselytization, which would eventually undermine 'my' group's very existence? Or is it to do with a perception that others are the ones who pollute our minds and morals, who entangle us in their deceits? Historically, this motive has often lurked behind religious violence, with its need to eliminate anything which threatens our eternal safety.

Whatever the surface motive, at root is the theological issue of religious absolutism. By absolutism I mean the conviction that the divine guarantee of one's own identity has invariably entailed assigning other communities either, at best, to second-class status in the divine economy or, at worst, to rejection altogether. The logical puzzle seems to be this: if God establishes one community on secure foundations, how can it be that God also establishes other communities on different foundations? But this is not only an issue of logical concern; it affects our whole sense of religious belonging in community. For how can God communicate with more than one accent, a proposition which would surely be tantamount to contradiction? And if God contradicts Godself, what assurance can there be that 'my' rightness is on the right track?

Responding theologically to one another entails facing together the difficult issues of religious absolutism, and these involve questions of identity, the nature of religious truth and the meanings of our particular religious commitments in the light of our different histories. In these areas Christian responses to Judaism have undergone some searching questions during the last 50 years or so, mainly in the light of critical historical studies of biblical origins, accusations of the 'teaching of contempt' in the doctrine of supersessionism, and, most of all, the impact of the Shoah. So explorations in the critical study of the New Testament, for example, have made us aware of how fluid and 'unformed' the place of an emerging Gentile Christian faith was in relation to its Jewish heritage. Most of all, the doctrine of supersessionism has been the target of relentless criticism, both academically and doctrinally, as a result of both critical study and the impact of the Shoah. This has brought obvious gains for Jewish–Christian relations.

And yet. Even 50 years since the ground-breaking document *Nostra Aetate* at Vatican II, which called for a new pastoral and theological platform for Jewish–Christian relations, the supersessionist doctrine has not been completely abandoned. Commenting on the last 50 years of Jewish–Christian relations, the veteran Catholic theologian of dialogue John Pawlikowski has asked whether *Nostra Aetate* (as a symbol of a general shift in approach towards a new relationship) has lived up to its promise. His observation is: 'The answer to that question within the Christian churches, and within the Jewish community as well, is "not quite".'[2]

A similar response has also been voiced by Mary Boys, another veteran Catholic theologian of Jewish–Christian encounter.[3] Both writers point to a stepping back from full recognition of Judaism and Christianity as inspiring sources of *different yet equally valid* religious insight.

As an illustration of this dilemma let me draw your attention to the resourceful book *John Paul II and Interreligious Dialogue*,[4] edited by two Jewish scholars, Byron Sherwin and Harold Kasimow. In this book the editors collected many speeches and addresses made by the strong advocate of interreligious cooperation, Pope John Paul II, to audiences of Jews, Buddhists and Muslims. They then invited various scholars from these traditions to reflect on their experience of encounter with the former pontiff. Overwhelmingly, the scholars from all three religions praised the Pope for extolling common humanity, universal human rights, shared values and the need for dialogue in order to face together the many problems besetting the world. Yet when the Pope returned to his study to write his theology of religions, they observed that none of that lifting up of mutuality was allowed to influence what he thought theologically of the other three religions. We were thrust back, they complained, into second-class religious status – as preparations for the gospel or as lacking some key ingredient for a truly fulfilled spiritual life. It was as though the powers of Christian empathy were subsumed by the need to retain a sense of superiority in the global competition of religions. The strangenesses between traditions were allowed to downgrade the evident resonances between people of compassionate religious spirit. What was granted with one hand seemed withdrawn by the other. One Jewish scholar in this book says that what we could do with is a little more epistemological modesty – that is, with less certitude or obviousness in what we know and how we know it, in the ways we write our theologies.

This brings us to the nub of the issue in relations between the religions: what to do with our absolutisms? What to do with them in the light of the insights we are learning through dialogue and the appreciation of different spiritualities, in response to critical thinking with regard to our Scriptures, belief systems and practices, and in the face of new learning in every sphere from the sciences to the humanities? Epistemological modesty ought to help us to adjust to these challenges from the modern/ postmodern age. But the religions have mostly been far from modest about their claims and proposals.

Before I turn to exploring afresh the notion of religious absolutism, it is instructive to note in advance how the journey of my colleague Rabbi Debbie Young-Somers resonates with the theological changes which I suggest are necessary if we are to make sense of religious commitment in our pluralistic world. Her journey into Judaism has always involved her in interreligious dialogue and, indeed, has often deepened as a result of such dialogue. It is a journey from experience to belief, one which has learned to appreciate the full impact of the assumptions and fruits of dialogue. Naturally she seeks out those aspects of the rich tapestry of Judaism which help her to make sense of what experience has unearthed. This leads her to adopt a narrative style which vividly highlights how she has learned the value of other commitments at the same time as learning the value of her Judaism. My own account here takes the opposite route and asks how Christian tradition might adapt to reflect the new realities facing all traditions – realities of plurality, mutuality and appreciation of differences. But the results are largely convergent with Debbie's own conclusions.

Let me now explore the notion of absolutism under four headings: revelation, exclusivity, dialogue and mission.[5] These represent a cluster of religious dimensions which bear on the subject of the absolute in religion from their varied angles. They touch on the nerve centre of religious identity. But without this examination the impasse in Jewish–Christian theological relations, illustrated by both Vatican II's partial success and theological ambiguity over supersessionism, will remain.

What follows does not represent every Christian position – how could it? Moreover, its strong call for the reinterpretation of Christian tradition in the light of critical study and interreligious encounter is unlikely to be convincing for many traditional voices. But it does assume that without a radical reinterpretation of tradition, interreligious relations – and in particular Jewish–Christian relations – will remain in unresolved and unproductive tension.

Revelation

'God transcends even the mind,' said Augustine of Hippo. If that is so – and there is nothing unusual about affirming that within the philosophical traditions of Christianity – then the question of how we come to know God presents an acute challenge. Traditionally, the appeal is made to some concept of 'revelation', which signals an initiative in communicating the knowledge of God: God imparts something of God's character – such as God's will, goodness, holiness, demands – to human beings. The Abrahamic religions, for example, have portrayed this through their scriptural accounts: God speaking to Moses from out of the Burning Bush; God conferring an anointing sonship on Jesus at his baptism; or God whispering Qur'anic words into Prophet Muhammad's ear through the angel Jibrail – all pictures portraying communication through words. Are these accounts to be taken literally, in the sense that this is how God does actually communicate? If so, their differences become an almost insuperable problem for those who accept the virtues and fruits of dialogue, for how might we imagine the consistency of God if the revelation of God is offered and received in such diverse literal manners? Might an alternative approach – one which renders accounts of revelation in terms more akin to parables or metaphors, that is, word-pictures with a message and a meaning – be more plausible in a critically minded world, in so far as it seeks to interpret the notion of revelation more indirectly?

RETHINKING REVELATION, EXCLUSIVITY, DIALOGUE, MISSION

In Christian thought, the idea of revelation has been moving steadily in the direction of parable and metaphor, at least since the rise of scriptural criticism.[6] This fits with the ways in which human beings come to know about the world more generally. 'How we know' (epistemology) is a complex enquiry but most would agree that we come to know as a matter of interpreting experience rather than through divine implantation. The role of the mind in organizing sense data, established in cognitive psychology and the sociology of knowledge, is well known. In this way we have come to echo the ninth-century Muslim thinker Junayd of Baghdad who averred that 'The colour of the water is the same as that of its container.'[7] God speaking through Moses, Jesus and Muhammad says as much about the container as the water, as much about cultural embeddedness as about the content of the mind of God.

Religious knowing, then, is more indirect than we had once assumed. The absoluteness of God is glimpsed in frail vessels and is therefore humanly limited, materially constrained, linguistically formed and historically shaped. Moreover, there is more of a voluntary sense about it, appropriate to its subject matter, than with other forms of knowing. As the Australian philosopher of religion, Max Charlesworth, has put it: 'authentic religion is the gratuitous human response to a gratuitous revelation of the divine'.[8] Nothing is forced; revelation is a relationship of gratuitousness on both sides of the human–divine divide.

Debbie resonates with this sense of how a concept of revelation might make its impact when she speculates that the diversity of human openness is matched by a notion of God 'who appears to each individual in a form they are able to receive, expressed in a way that speaks to them, where they are, with their limited yet unique and necessary individual mix of experiences and approaches'.[9] There is a hint of Hindu insight in this comment, but it is also no less Jewish, as Debbie makes clear through her observation of Jewish commentary and interpretation.

Perhaps we can think of religious knowing through revelation occurring at one end of a spectrum of how we know things more generally. So, at the hard end of human awareness, the material world, investigated through scientific ways of knowing and interpreting, presses itself upon us in ways which compel our attention and which require interpretation according to the categories that have developed within the scientific disciplines. At the other, softer, end, interpreting life religiously involves us in a greater sense of cognitive freedom in relation to the ambiguity of experience: God does not compel God's presence or claim upon us. What Christians call 'faith' is the interpretive element in our human awareness of the divine environment in which we live. It is the faculty for responsiveness to the uncompelled divine presence which is 'revelation' – what

Canadian Professor of Comparative Religion Wilfred Cantwell Smith[10] has called our 'capacity to live at more than a mundane level; to see, to act in terms of, a transcendent dimension'.[11] In this sense 'faith' is shared by anyone who is orientated on life religiously, irrespective of whether or not the term itself is part of a tradition's lexicon. It describes Jews as well as Christians.

Emphasizing the subjective dimension of ways of knowing, and observing that this is maximal in religious knowing, opens up the door for 'revelation' in Jewish and Christian traditions to be non-absolute. Nothing is compelled either by our human interpretive faculties or by any divine intention to make divine-self known. 'God' – as ultimate, transcendent, absolute, infinite – is capable of interpretation through more than one lens. Which leads us straight to the next section.

Exclusivity

'Unique – final – decisive – distinct – particular' is a cluster of terms which have long featured in discussions analysing the relationship of Christianity to other religions. Phenomenologically, they simply differentiate Christianity – or any religious tradition – from other religions. They indicate difference as a function of history and cultural development. However, when employed theologically they signify the traditional sense of Christian faith's superiority over others – not superiority as a matter of historical observation, which would be hard to demonstrate, but as a matter of claimed divine intention. The strong form of that divine will intends Christian faith to 'supplant' all others, while the soft form 'fulfils' others. Jewish–Christian relations have often been shaped by these alternatives.

In so far as the idea and reality of revelation is interpreted in interventionist ways it has been hard to ignore the conclusion that the absoluteness of God necessarily involves the exclusivity of the Christian message, the one-way religion outstripping all others. Even some sophisticated theologians, who are dialogically inclined and hold to a positive role for the religions of the world, nevertheless retain the conviction that at death all will be confronted by the 'decisiveness' of Jesus Christ.[12]

The roots of such exclusivity lie essentially in the notion of 'eschatological finality' which runs through the New Testament witness, and which then became embodied in the theological language of incarnation of later classical tradition. Let the following from a celebrated, moderately orthodox Anglican theologian of a previous generation, John Macquarrie,[13] explain the New Testament root:

> When Christianity was born in the first century, people supposed the earth to be at the centre of things, so that terrestrial history was cosmic history. Moreover this had been a short history, or at least short enough for people to know what had happened from 'the beginning' down to their own day, and it was all going to end soon. Thus it was natural enough to suppose that there might be one exclusive or at any rate immeasurably superior revelation in the course of this short history.[14]

What can 'finality' mean now in an era vastly different from the first century, with an utterly different cosmology and changed sense of history?

The grounding of Christianity's superiority encoded in the language of incarnation is possibly harder to dislodge, for it has been core to Christian understanding since the early centuries of the Christian era. However, there have been significant alternatives proposed in recent times which speak, in Christian terms, more of Jesus as a parable, symbol or metaphor of how God is with the world. These moves, while being in the minority in the Christian theological world, interpret the presence and incarnational impact of God in Jesus more in tune with modern critical historical, cultural and cosmological insights.[15] The implication in the context of dialogue is that they point away from the need to defend the absoluteness of belief in terms of propositional Greek philosophy, and more in the direction of that 'epistemological modesty' which was demanded by the theologians of other traditions in dialogue with Pope John Paul II outlined earlier.

It may be that a choice will need to be made by Christian theologians (as well as Jews and others from other traditions) between these approaches in the context of interfaith dialogue. What can absoluteness mean in the light of critical understanding and the facts of sheer cultural change?

One answer to that rhetorical question has been offered by the Christian feminist theologian Rosemary Radford Ruether, who notes how the main world religions, as these have developed over time, have come to embody differences which are significant but not necessarily incommensurable. She writes:

> Although there is true relationship to the divine, authentic spirituality, and viable morality in all religious systems, this does not mean that they are all just different words for the same thing. Each religion, like each culture, is a unique configuration of symbolic expressions that has been shaped by the total experience of peoples, their particular histories, and ecological settings. Although there is much overlap among religions, they also represent a broad spectrum of possible ways of experiencing the divine. Some may focus on the historical struggle for justice, some

on the renewal of natural processes, and some on mystical ecstasy. Each has incarnated its way of symbolizing life and its relationship to the higher powers in unique ways that make it impossible simply to translate one religion to the other, or to create some abstraction of them all into a universal, ethical faith.[16]

What, then, is the solution to plurality? It lies in accepting that religious differences can coexist, where the limitations of each represent 'an adequate way of experiencing the whole for a particular people at a particular time'.[17] The infinite richness of the Eternal One is refracted through the diverse spectrum of the world religions.

Some may think that a slippery move has been made here from acknowledging difference phenomenologically to asserting theological plurality normatively. However, for me, without some such move we remain rooted in exclusivity which then masquerades as a universality, and it is this which is being questioned in our time. Furthermore, I should add that the affirmation of pluralism does not mean that 'anything goes', as the accusation of relativism often puts it. Affirming the authenticity of many traditions as vehicles of transcendent awareness and practical living remains subject to critical thinking, which entails accountability at ethical levels as well as in relation to the best of human knowing discerned through the sciences and sociological insight at any one time.

My colleague Debbie raises the spectre of Jewish exclusivity from a related but not incompatible angle. Although Judaism, she says, has ample theological resources for affirming the authenticity of other traditions, Jews have nevertheless veered towards separation from other nations, which is its own form of exclusivity. There may, of course, be many reasons for this, and not all of them religious. Rather than explore this more fully she points out that there is also both a myth about Jewish exclusivity through history and an unrealistic expectation when it comes to sustaining it in the future. Experiences of encounter and dialogue draw Jews and Christians (and others) willy-nilly into interdependent relationships. At this level, therefore, experience renders exclusivity null and void. It is experience which creates change, or at least opens up the possibility for new interpretations from tradition appropriate for a culturally interdependent world.

Interfaith dialogue

For some, dialogue describes mainly a process of encounter, where listening and respect are accorded paramount value; for others it coincides with a whole shift in what it means to be religious in the contemporary world. The Catholic historian and theologian Leonard Swidler, for example, has written about the de-absolutizing of religious truth in the following way:

> [I]f my perception and description of the world are true only in a limited sense – that is, only as seen from my place in the world – if I wish to expand my grasp of reality, I need to learn from others what they know of reality that they can perceive from their place in the world, which I cannot see from mine. That, however, can happen only through dialogue.[18]

If Swidler is correct here, then dialogue cannot remain an optional extra for those who like that kind of thing, but it assumes a more central place in evolving religious identity and practice.

Dialogue, we might say, exists in the space between 'we're all different' and 'we're all the same'. If there was no difference or only difference, dialogue would be a pointless pursuit. At the very least, beyond correcting stereotypes and historical misrepresentation, dialogue harbours an expectation that something can be learned from engagement with the other, that an expansion of religious consciousness is possible.

There have been many gains in Christian–Jewish relations in the period since the Shoah and the beginnings of an expansion of consciousness in the modern dialogical sense. In terms of scholarship, historical perspectives regarding the 'parting of the ways', textual exploration in relation to hermeneutics and experience, shared reflections on the Shoah and attempts to fathom the depths of evil, have all played their part. Jewish contributions to historical Jesus research and Christian contributions to the history of biblical Hebrew research have made their marks too. Christian supersessionism has itself largely been superseded in all major denominations (the reservations noted above notwithstanding), with the recognition that 'God does not give up on God's own promises'. The old 'Law' versus 'Grace' as a frame for dialogue is a dead letter. None of these gains, carefully and often agonizingly won, should be underestimated. Over against them, however, I sometimes wonder whether there remains an unspoken Jewish assumption that Christian faith was really founded on a category mistake (incarnation) and an unspoken Christian assumption that Judaism is incapable of breaking out of a certain inward-lookingness (chosenness), such that its intended spiritual universality seems always to be pulled back into preoccupations with Jewish peoplehood.

Has the time come when the Jewish–Christian relationship should now see itself as part of the larger Abrahamic interfaith endeavour, and beyond that, of the wider interfaith movement? That at least would be one trajectory for energizing a dialogue, which sometimes seems stuck on issues such as supersessionism and barren debates about whether God has arranged one or two covenants in the divine redemptive purpose.

As I have already noted, dialogue for Debbie has been a major factor in her own evolving identity as a Jew in the modern world. She seems quintessentially to exemplify the Swidler motto that dialogue is the new way of being religious and is key to greater perceptions of reality than isolated traditions thus far have managed! She speaks wisely about balancing appreciation for common ground with the celebration of differences.

There is a tension between dialogue as an exercise in encounter, with few assumptions about the status of the dialogue partner, and that between participants who are valued as being in some sense equal. It is the latter which Debbie advocates and which concurs with my own understanding. Both of us would be happy to embrace the German-born Jewish theologian Martin Buber in the bid to accept the other as being in 'rough parity' with oneself.

Mission

The Christian theology of mission has undergone considerable development during the last 100 years. In 1910, delegates to the Edinburgh Missionary Conference (a global gathering of Christian missionaries from all continents and involving most denominations) gathered under the banner of the evangelization of the world in this generation. However, by 1993 the World Council of Churches had redefined the goal of mission to mean a renewed and reconciled creation, under the theological category of *missio Dei*, the mission of God to and for the world. A renewed and reconciled creation is universal in scope, is not focused primarily on church expansion or saving souls, is critical of empire ideology, is embracing of partnerships for justice around the world and includes the way of dialogue between religions as part of what it means to be in mission. As it is, a good case can be made for saying that the Christian *raison d'être* for dialogue springs from the experience of Christian missionaries around the world. They discovered that God had been there before their arrival! This is not to say, of course, that all Christian missionaries have absorbed the new theological outlook.

Still, the theological expansion of the concept of mission has not generally entailed letting go of that sense of absolutism which had fired the missionary imagination in previous centuries. But it has generally meant a softening of the rhetoric of Christian expansion as being the one true faith which others need for the good and true life. There is still mission, but now it is couched in the language of 'telling the story' or 'witnessing to the hope that has been handed down in tradition' or 'sharing the existential meaning of the good news'. In other words, less saving from damnation and more an invitation to view life according to a certain faith-light.

Christian mission in relation to the Jewish people has undergone the most significant volte-face over the last 60 years. The impact of the Shoah, revisions in scriptural interpretations, and the near-ending of supersessionary doctrine have made an impact which effectively moves towards undermining a good deal of the old Christian outlook, even if not completely. One might say that mission is giving way to dialogue and work together for the common good.

Of course, the agenda for dialogue is ongoing and it is inevitably sometimes contentious, especially in the need continually to clarify the heritage of the past. But if this can be done without the suspicions stemming from old missionary motives seeking the conversion of individual Jews to Christian faith, the advantage for furthering Jewish–Christian relations will be obvious. Both traditions will still have their stories to tell and their theological and spiritual accounts to give, but it will be a mission of receiving as well as giving, of learning as well as teaching.

Past relationships cannot be ignored, but neither should they entrap us for all time. Both Judaism and Christianity need reminding that they are religions not simply of the past: God 'speaks' from the future too and that generates a sense of hope which the world needs. I have long been fond of the following words from Wilfred Cantwell Smith:

> The future of the Christian mission turns on our learning to see God's mission in the Church as one part of his whole mission to mankind; not as his whole mission to one part of mankind (fallacy of indifference); nor as his sole mission to all mankind (the fallacy of arrogance).[19]

On this view, religious communities missionize each other as well as the world; it is mutual mission. Christians might pursue this on the grounds of the notion of the 'Kingdom of God', first proclaimed by the Jesus figure over against the prevailing tyrannical 'Kingdom of Caesar' of his own times, and which is capable of being reinvented at any time throughout history. A dialogue on our shared this-worldly future could empower mutuality between Christians and Jews fruitfully and help rescue both communities from their preoccupations with the past alone.

Jews often say that they are a non-proselytizing religion, but they welcome converts who declare an interest in Judaism. When they occur, however, conversions are accompanied by a period of instruction before acceptance into the community can take place. But mission in terms of seeking conversions has always been part of Jewish consciousness in the past, though political circumstances may often have been unfavourable towards it. Although Debbie believes that there might also be theological kudos in excluding mission, in terms of seeking converts, from the Jewish agenda, nevertheless there is much in her which resonates with the emerging Christian reinterpretation of mission in terms of seeking mutual understanding and shared practical endeavours towards creating a better world. Even more than that, dialogue itself comes to be seen as the new meaning of mission for our times.

Final remarks

My argument has been that in our modern, democratic, critical-minded and plurally conscious world, clinging to religious absolutism seems unsustainable. This is not to say that there are not those who perpetrate it still. But the cultural paradigm shift which has been underway for 150 years, at least in those parts of the world which have been shaped by modern perceptions of reality, now places the *onus probandi* on those who wish to defend absolutism rather than those who now find it an outmoded category for pursuing the spiritual life. From a Christian viewpoint, changes in the notions of revelation, exclusivity, dialogue and mission all witness to the prevailing impact and power of the shift itself.

Yet there is resistance in many quarters to the shift. For some, the resistance is religious-intellectual: they simply remain unconvinced that religious conviction can survive the jettisoning of absolutism. They willingly embrace the dialogical mood of the times but are reluctant to be drawn into dialogue's ramifications. The American Catholic theologian of dialogue Paul Knitter has outlined various strategies of resistance which he believes are essentially tantamount to theological avoidance. As he says of the resisters:

> Their calls for greater interreligious conversation are loud and clear, the theological follow-up, or warm-up, is missing. You might say that, when it comes to engaging the pressing and messy reality of religious diversity and plurality, there has been a widespread *theological avoidance*.[20]

I agree with Knitter's assessment but link that avoidance with issues of absolutism. The resisters continue to harbour that corner of the mind which holds on to the conviction of the eventual superiority of 'my' tradition.

On the other hand, the re-evaluation of absolutism increases the potential for human empathy. Empathy entails a sharing among human beings at existential levels of emotion – joy, fear, anxiety, wonder; a desire to be known, loved and valued as we know, love and value – and a mutual interest in discerning what constitutes a 'good and fulfilling life'. These associations of empathy draw us into a common humanity and an ability to see the world as others see it. That 'seeing', moreover, is bound to be a case of both strangeness and resonance. The question of religious identity then becomes a negotiation between these two poles of an emerging new relationship.

Theologically, the Christian approach should no longer perpetuate the splitting off of Christianity from 'Old Testament' and Rabbinic Judaism as a division between 'impersonal law' and 'personal grace', between 'preparation' and 'fulfilment', and so on. In the present globalizing context, this is nothing other than an ideological bid for continued superiority.

For some the new relationship is akin to a new friendship. Best cultivate friendship, they aver, and the stand-offs between Jewish and Christian versions of religious truth will take care of themselves. Friendship cuts through the religious posing and the theological treacle. It opens the whole self to another and transports us to the human heart of our respective commitments where we can confront the great questions of human existence. But like respect and toleration, friendship is not a substitute for theological thinking; indeed, it leads us directly into it. Dialogue is about friendship *and* theology. At a basic level, it is about *learning*, so that change may happen.

There remains, finally, the definite need to distinguish between good and bad, adequate and inadequate, true and false religion. The call to a new learning is that we do this together. In this regard, Jewish–Christian dialogue will have its own specific issues to deal with, but in so dealing it may also thereby make its contribution to wider interfaith tasks and pursuits. For the ending of absolutism suggests that our theologies and spiritualities are but windows on to a transcendent reality which is more all-embracing than we once imagined.

Notes

1 Jim Wiggins, formerly Chair of the American Academy of Religion, personal correspondence.

2 John Pawlikowski, 2014, 'Fifty Years of Christian–Jewish Dialogue – What Has Changed?', *Journal of Ecumenical Studies* 49:1, Celebrating Fifty Years of Ecumenism and Interreligious Dialogue, pp. 99ff.

3 Mary C. Boys, 2014, 'Doing Justice to Judaism: The Challenge to Christianity', in *Journal of Ecumenical Studies* 49:1, Celebrating Fifty Years of Ecumenism and Interreligious Dialogue, pp. 107–10.

4 Byron Sherwin and Harold Kasimow (eds.), 1999, *John Paul II and Interreligious Dialogue*, Maryknoll, NY: Orbis Books.

5 When we as a Group first discussed our assignments and what was required, it became clear both to Debbie and me that it was these four dimensions which, in varying extents, troubled our Group.

6 For an example of how this applies even to whole Gospels, see John Dominic Crossan's, 2012, remarkable *The Power of Parable: How Fiction by Jesus Became Fiction about Jesus*, New York: HarperCollins. The Gospels become revelatory through what they evoke rather than impart.

7 Cited in R. A. Nicholson, 1963, *The Mystics of Islam*, London and Boston, MA: Routledge & Kegan Paul, p. 88. Al-Junaid (830–910 CE), known as Junayd of Baghdad, was an early Persian Muslim mystic and highly significant in the development of Sufi thought.

8 Max Charlesworth, 1997, *Religious Inventions: Four Essays*, Cambridge: Cambridge University Press, p. 10.

9 *Infra* p. 00.

10 1916–2000.

11 Wilfred Cantwell Smith, 1980, *Towards a World Theology*, London: Macmillan, pp. 113f.

12 E.g. Joseph A. DiNoia OP, 1992, *The Diversity of Religions*, Washington, DC: The Catholic University of America Press.

13 1919–2007.

14 John Macquarrie, 1977, *Principles of Christian Theology*, 2nd edn, London: SCM Press and Charles Scribner, p. 172.

15 See my own account of this in 'The Value of the Symbolic Jesus for Christian Involvement in Interfaith Dialogue', in Sharada Sugirtharajah (ed.), 2012, *Religious Pluralism and the Modern World: An Ongoing Engagement with John Hick*, Basingstoke: Palgrave Macmillan, pp. 83–94.

16 'Feminism and Jewish–Christian Dialogue: Particularism and Universalism in the Search for Religious Truth', in John Hick and Paul F. Knitter (eds.), 1987, *The Myth of Christian Uniqueness: Toward a Pluralistic Theology of Religions*, Maryknoll, NY: Orbis Books, pp. 141f.

17 Hick and Knitter (eds.), *Myth of Christian Uniqueness*.

18 Leonard Swidler, 2012, 'Humankind from the Age of Monologue to the Age of Dialogue', *Journal of Ecumenical Studies* 47:3, Summer, p. 470.

19 Wilfred Cantwell Smith, 1988, 'Mission, Dialogue, and God's Will For Us', *International Review of Mission* 78:307, p. 367.

20 Paul Knitter, 2014, 'Can We Put Our Theological Money Where Our Dialogical Mouth Is? Looking Back Over the Past Fifty Years', *Journal of Ecumenical Studies* 49:1, Celebrating Fifty Years of Ecumenism and Interreligious Dialogue, pp. 166f.

A Jewish Theology Embracing Difference

DEBBIE YOUNG-SOMERS

In dialogue I always encourage participants to speak from the 'I' not the 'we' or 'they'. We cannot represent anything other than ourselves, our faiths being diverse from within, and our lived experience unique to us. Our lenses and experiences are shaped by our faith, and we speak from within it, but not for its entirety. Theologically, I am designed to balk at absolute truths when it comes to faith and my own spiritual journey has shaped that response. When my Rabbi – Alex Wright, the co-author of the previous chapter – suggested to me, aged 16, that I consider becoming a rabbi, I rejected the idea completely. I did not believe it was possible for God and the Shoah to coexist and, as Holocaust revision wasn't really my thing, I rejected God, assuming that belief was an important prerequisite for the rabbinate!

After various interfaith encounters, which resulted in a significant deepening of my own Jewish engagement but not faith, I had what I would describe as a spiritual experience. It occurred in the Oranienburger Strasse Synagogue in Berlin, in the midst of a lively, multi-generational, prayerful German Jewish community. I left that encounter with a very strong sense that God is far beyond my comprehension. I am very small and my brain is limited; God is not. It felt that God had communicated to me that it was absolutely fine not to understand God. Indeed, anything I try to use to frame or express an understanding of God seemed merely to limit God and fell short of what was needed. But God, for me, was nevertheless real. I left the synagogue knowing that my intended path was the rabbinate. Interestingly, the community, the sense of peoplehood I experienced in Berlin, still dominated the encounter with God in directing my journey.

It is entirely possible for me to explain away my experience psychologically. Furthermore, it offers no connection to God for anyone except me. Crucially though, at the core of the peace I found, was the understanding that I do not understand, I do not know and cannot grasp everything. If I do not have a full hold on that single, ultimate Truth and am moderated in my expression of it by my experience, language and so on, then from the core of my religious experience there is also a huge amount of space for others' expressions of belief.

We should be driven to hear from others the core motivations for and of their faith, the truths from within their tradition that make them whole. There is a need for us to stand together in exploring our truths, for to do so in dialogue with the other is part of the journey to encountering each other as real – in curiosity and openness, rather than in opposition, fear and violence. Understanding that my experience was mediated by who I am has created an approach to encounter, framed by my sense that each person's attempt at expressing anything about their concept of the Divine is inevitably distinctive, deeply informed by who they are. This recognizes the fact that they may well express some piece of learning or truth which was not part of my encounter and can add to my own limited insight. Learning with those from outside my Jewish world-view has allowed me to grow and learn in relationship to my own tradition as well as gaining insight and understanding into that of my partner in dialogue. Through such a dialogue we learn of the many things we share and are able to grow from and celebrate that which is different.

With these as my personal lenses, I have naturally been drawn towards working with texts and models within Judaism that express a similar core. Finding these expressions has helped me to formulate a Jewish theology that creates space for the other and, coming from within the Jewish textual tradition, this has been for me an authentic way of expressing faith. I freely acknowledge that it is possible to use religious texts to justify multiple, contradictory things – both opposition to and justification for equal marriage opportunities, for example. Who you are and what you have experienced determine the lenses through which you see and therefore the texts you gravitate towards or, indeed, away from. So I choose to prioritize texts within Judaism that, for me, express an openness to multiple viewpoints, to embracing difference, and a pluralism that emerges naturally from an avoidance of theological absolutes.

This could create a dialogical model of how Judaism might function internally and, to the extent that it doesn't already, function externally. This is, of course, one Jewish approach not *the* Jewish approach to texts that can take us on a journey which allows for others' truths to exist yet not negate our own, nor be negated by a spurious need for absolutes. This is born out for me in the reality that Jewish life – and Christian life too – has never been homogenous. Even before the emergence in the nineteenth century of denominations, both interpretation and practice was diverse and varied from country to country. Different communities have relied on different rabbinic authorities and rulings to determine their particular path. Even before Judaism was Judaism, the Israelite encampment

A JEWISH THEOLOGY EMBRACING DIFFERENCE

allowed each of the 12 tribes to embrace their own flag and identity, demonstrating from the outset that unity does not have to mean uniformity.

Both Alan and I explore our approach to religious absolutism by unpacking four areas: revelation, exclusivity, mission and dialogue.

Revelation

One's approach to Scripture and revelation is a key element in how one coexists with others' truths – so this is my starting point, as it is for many intra-Jewish and dialogical conversations. In Exodus 33.18–20, Moses asks God to reveal God's full glory to him:

[18] וַיֹּאמַר הַרְאֵנִי נָא אֶת־כְּבֹדֶךָ:

[18] He [Moses] said: 'Show me, I implore You, Your glory.'[1]

[19] וַיֹּאמֶר אֲנִי אַעֲבִיר כָּל־טוּבִי עַל־פָּנֶיךָ וְקָרָאתִי בְשֵׁם יְהוָה לְפָנֶיךָ וְחַנֹּתִי אֶת־אֲשֶׁר אָחֹן וְרִחַמְתִּי אֶת־אֲשֶׁר אֲרַחֵם:

[19] God said: 'I will make all My goodness pass before you, and will proclaim the Name Eternal before you; I will be gracious to whom I will be gracious, and show mercy to whom I will show mercy.'

[20] וַיֹּאמֶר לֹא תוּכַל לִרְאֹת אֶת־פָּנָי כִּי לֹא־יִרְאַנִי הָאָדָם וָחָי:

[20] [God] said: 'But you cannot see My face, for a human being may not see Me and live.'

How revelation is understood is crucial to any absolutist position. But so it is for me, as a pluralist. This text from the Torah encapsulates a universal truth embedded in the story of Jewish revelation – whether you understand Sinai literally or metaphorically; it couldn't point more clearly to the human inability to embrace the fullness of the Truth that is the Divine.

Even Moses, the receiver of Torah, is not granted the honour of seeing the fullness of God – he sees only God's back. The Torah he receives is couched in language and imagery specific to people, time and place. Moses, in Jewish tradition, is the greatest of all prophets but if even he can only see where God has been and experiences revelation in language specific to him and his people, how can anyone else be expected to grasp more? Indeed, isn't that the lesson from Sinai? Moses was a great leader but nonetheless human, limited – how much more so am I limited – by the events and surroundings that formed him and, therefore, experienced revelation through his remarkable but particular lenses. So even with the revelation at Sinai, the giving of truth to the Jewish people, the Truth is limited to truths. No one person – or group of people – can grasp divine fullness or lay claim to a monopoly on the Truth of God. There is infinite space for more. There is infinite room for the other.

This theme is beautifully expressed in the collection of classical Rabbinic *midrashim* known as *Pesikta de Rav Kahana*, or the *Sections of Rav Kahana*, 12.25.[2] The passage conveys the understanding of a God who appears for each person, and differently for different people, and yet who is still Whole and One:

אָנֹכִי יְיָ אֱלֹהֶיךָ (שמות כ ב): אָמַר רַבִּי חֲנִינָא בָּר פָּפָּא נִרְאָה
לָהֶם הַקָּדוֹשׁ בָּרוּךְ הוּא פָּנִים זְעוּפוֹת, פָּנִים בֵּינוֹנִית, פָּנִים
מַסְבִּירוֹת, פָּנִים שׂוֹחֲקוֹת.
פָּנִים זוֹעֲמוֹת לַמִּקְרָא, כְּשֶׁאָדָם מְלַמֵּד אֶת בְּנוֹ תּוֹרָה צָרִיךְ
לְלַמְּדוֹ בְּאֵימָה. פָּנִים בֵּינוֹנִית לַמִּשְׁנָה. פָּנִים מַסְבִּירוֹת לַתַּלְמוּד.
פָּנִים שׂוֹחֲקוֹת לָאַגָּדָה.
אָמַר רַבִּי לֵוִי: נִרְאָה לָהֶם הַקָּדוֹשׁ בָּרוּךְ הוּא כְּאִיקוּנִין הַזוֹ שֶׁיֵּשׁ
לָהּ פָּנִים מִכָּל מָקוֹם, אֶלֶף בְּנֵי אָדָם מַבִּיטִין בָּהּ וְהִיא מַבֶּטֶת
בְּכֻלָּם.

'I am Adonai thy [in the singular] God' (Ex. 20.2). Rabbi Hanina Bar Papa said: the Holy Blessed One was revealed to them with a severe face, moderate face, friendly face and a joyful face.

A severe face for the reading [of scripture]. When a person teaches their child the Torah, they must teach them with awe. A moderate face for the memorising of the teaching – Mishnah. A friendly face for the scholarly learning of the teaching – Talmud. A joyful face for the process of elaboration on the scripture – Aggadah.

The Holy Blessed One said to them: 'Even though you see [me in] all these [different] images, yet [I am still] "Adonai thy [in the singular] God."'

R. Levi said: The Holy Blessed One appeared to them like a statue with a face looking at every side. A thousand people might be looking at [this statue], but it still [appears to be] looking at each one of them.

As so often in Rabbinic literature, there are several layers here. The midrash asserts the possibility of each individual entering into relationship with God as an individual. It also conceives of God as appearing to

A JEWISH THEOLOGY EMBRACING DIFFERENCE

each individual in a way they are able to grasp, expressed in a manner that speaks to them, where they are, with their limited yet unique and necessary individual mix of experiences and preconceptions. In this midrash God is 'seen' in many different ways. In *Exodus Rabbah* 5.9, God spoke, the author insists, in a way appropriate to each individual. God's voice was heard and understood because the voice spoke to each individual according to that person's particular ability to hear and understand – to the elderly in keeping with their ability, to the young in keeping with their ability, to the little ones in keeping with their ability, and so on.[3]

These Jewish insights into revelation give expression to what one might call a postmodern sense that we each experience and see things differently, yet God is able to work within these human limitations to be in relationship to us. I therefore come to dialogue keen to hear and understand what God has revealed to those around the table, wanting to share with them what is true in my religious life. We can see a little more of the whole together than alone.

Diversity, then, is at the heart of the matter. We are created, I would argue, to inhabit that diversity. As the Babylonian Talmud says in Tractate *B'rakhot* 58a:

תָּנוּ רַבָּנָן: הָרוֹאֶה אוּכְלוּסֵי יִשְׂרָאֵל אוֹמֵר בָּרוּךְ חֲכַם הָרָזִים,
שֶׁאֵין דַּעְתָּם דּוֹמָה זֶה לָזֶה, וְאֵין פַּרְצוּפֵיהֶן דּוֹמִים זֶה לָזֶה.

Our Rabbis taught: If one sees a crowd of Israelites, one says, Blessed is the One who discerns secrets, for the mind of each is different from that of the other, just as the face of each is different from that of the other.

If we are diverse and yet all in the image of God, it may well be that it is our infinite diversity and difference that is integral to the image of the All-Encompassing.

But it is not just in the Torah and in the *midrashim*, which explore its meaning, that I discover Judaism is a faith with space for pluralism and multiplicity. The Talmud, that vast compendium of Rabbinic debate – and disagreement – is a further, shining demonstration of this. Each page is constructed as a conversation and the text contains redacted discussions from sages who lived generations apart. Each page contains a core paragraph, sometimes of Mishnah and always of G'mara (commentary on the Mishnah). The material in the Mishnah dates from the first two centuries of the Common Era and the G'mara is composed of voices from the third, fourth and fifth centuries. In columns to either side of this are the later commentaries of Rashi (eleventh century) and the Tosafot (medieval commentators following on from, and sometimes disagreeing with, Rashi). The page continues to work outwards with later and later commentaries and glosses. In all of these conversations, one voice does not necessarily agree with the other voice, but tries to understand the application of the rule or value in its own time. In the G'mara, importantly, conclusions are not always drawn, and minority opinions are fastidiously recorded, in case a later generation should need them. It is a model where the discussion is as important – if not more so – than the conclusion. Each page encourages us to add our own voice, for our generation. Rather than a simple rule book, it demonstrates that grasping what is demanded of us by God – and who God is – is far from easy to establish. The 'Truth' appears and sounds as different 'truths'– depending on who is reading the text, when and in what circumstances.

But let me reiterate. I will be selective in the texts, discussions and claims that I choose – those which support my liberal, pluralist instincts. Not all Talmudic texts – and that is the intrinsic challenge of all religious traditions – support such an approach. It is open to another reader to select passages which appear to justify xenophobia, anti-Christianity and misogyny, appealing equally to the text of the Torah itself. As with Christianity and Islam, the Jewish reality as lived is not always one of openness to difference and respect for the other.[4]

In preparing these papers, Alan asked me if it was becoming the norm for Progressive Rabbis to engage much more with classical Rabbinic texts than they had in the past. I cannot speak for the past and, though my colleagues of all generations have certainly used many Rabbinic sources in study and prayer, it can certainly be argued that earlier reformers struggled with the authority of such texts in the light of modernity. Yet I can say that Rabbinic texts have always been a rich and exciting source for me, not least because they embrace this sense of discussion and diversity, allowing disagreement and the recording of the conversation as much as – if not more than – the majority view or final conclusion.

This becomes even more exciting when we reflect on *midrashim* that express contradictory perceptions, found nestling among each other in the wings, waiting for us to find a role for one or the other – or both. That seems to me to model a Judaism that, once more, encourages debate and development through the generations and so remains at the heart of my Judaism.

A JEWISH THEOLOGY EMBRACING DIFFERENCE

Exclusivity

It has been suggested that Christians feel themselves theologically superior but that, in practical terms, they value friendship and are open and welcoming to the outsider. By contrast, the argument goes, Jews are theologically pluralist but practically exclusivist.

Even as far back as the Torah itself, we see this derogatory view of Jews. In Numbers 23.9, Balaam – who has been sent to curse Israel – says of the Israelite encampment:

הֶן־עָם לְבָדָד יִשְׁכֹּן וּבַגּוֹיִם לֹא יִתְחַשָּׁב: There is a people living alone and not reckoning itself among the nations.

In his essay, Michael Hilton demolishes the myth.[5] Jews and Christians have seldom lived in isolation – and where they have it has always been an enforced 'aloneness'. We have always cross-fertilized each other and, of course, others among whom we have lived. This is even more today's reality. Where a people wishes to retain its identity, maintain a distinctive culture and communal life, however integrated they are, they evoke ambiguous feelings in the wider community. They can evoke suspicion, envy and even make the majority feel outsiders. That can then spark feelings of exclusion and lead to hostility. The hostility, in turn, causes the group, anxious to preserve its own identity, to 'close ranks'. We can see that occurring in Britain's relationships with its newer immigrant communities today. Hence the importance of dialogue, which allows these various identities to be celebrated and maintained, while remaining open to the importance of shared experience and living – and disagreeing – well together.

It is in this context that I want to look at the concept of 'the chosen people', so often used by non-Jews as a stick with which to beat Jews and often a growing source of discomfort to Progressive Jews in recent decades. It is significant that the phrase 'chosen people' has no Hebrew equivalent, classical or otherwise. It is rooted in a sense, from the Torah onwards, that Jews have been singled out to receive a particular revelation and to live according to the demands – primarily ethical – of that tradition. Only very rarely has it been understood to carry with it notions of superiority. Judaism has never suggested that Jewish ethical teachings are exclusively Jewish and that all truth is to be found in Judaism. Many frame it today as one of many chosen-nesses – being chosen for Torah, while others are chosen for other revelations and tasks. It has frequently been understood as a yoke, voluntarily taken upon us – and, particularly in the twentieth century, as a crushing burden. The Lithuanian-born poet

Kadya Molodowsky, who fled to New York in 1935, wrote ten years later:

> O God of Mercy
> For the time being
> Choose another people.
> We are tired of death, tired of corpses,
> We have no more prayers.
> For the time being
> Choose another people.
> We have run out of blood.[6]

Dialogue disabuses others of false perceptions. But even more, it has the potential to help Jews out of spiritual and intellectual ghettoes which persist long after the physical ghettoes have been dismantled. I personally have never been an isolationist. I was, however, very aware of accusations of Jewish exclusivity and have only become more confident in my Judaism as a result of conversations with others. This has clarified for me that we are different entities, not just with different histories but with different configurations. We don't have to be identical or even to understand faith in the same terms to respect each other's individuality or space. Indeed, dialogue has helped me to articulate my Judaism and, ironically, made me more observant and more engaged with it. In having to find answers that satisfied my questioners – who ask questions that another Jew would never ask – I discovered a Jewish voice that is mine and fell in love with practice and belief that otherwise might have been dismissed.

When others shared/share their truths with me, I grew/grow and learned/learn, whether or not it was/is a truth that spoke/speaks to my own and helped/helps to nurture it. If dialogue helped shape my Judaism founded on a theology of humility, what I do not understand in the other must also remain authentic. There is an unconditional need for the other in Judaism, not just to allow us clarification through differentiation but to allow us to grow in understanding of that which is greater than any particular faith. As Leonard Swidler says: 'Dialogue is ever more clearly the way of the future in religious and ideological reflection on the ultimate meaning of life and how to live accordingly.'[7]

We need each other not just so that we can glimpse more parts of the whole, but also to test boundaries and explore our limits. Fifty years ago, Polish-born American rabbi and theologian Abraham Joshua Heschel[8] wrote: 'We are all involved with one another. Spiritual betrayal on the part of one of us affects the faith of all of us.'[9] This is even truer

A JEWISH THEOLOGY EMBRACING DIFFERENCE

today than when Heschel wrote it – not the least because of the rise and rise of social media. The various forms of instant contact leave many who use them with a false sense of continuous communication and interconnectedness with others both near and far. The result is that true conversation and interpersonal communication – dialogue – is actually becoming rarer. The manipulation of social media may also mean we are frequently exposed to only that which we agree with and have to deal far less with difference – a dangerous trend for dialogue, for social cohesion, and for our fundamental ability to engage in conversations in which all the participants do not agree.

Mission

Mission creates a good deal of nervousness among many Jews. It has been a damaging element within the history of our dysfunctional coexistence as Jews and Christians and, post-Shoah, was of particular concern when the community saw itself decimated and many members were keen to hide rather than proclaim their Judaism with pride. Yet, instead of worrying about being missionized by Christians – or anyone else! – we should, as Jews, be focused on creating confident members who can deal with challenges of difference to their identity and who can articulate a meaningful Judaism.

Jews have often prided themselves – whether this is real or not – on the exclusion of mission from mainstream theology. Being Jewish has rarely been considered the only or the best way – I hesitate to say never because there are exceptions certainly to 'the best', even, sadly, today. Indeed the Rabbinic 'Noahide laws' are often touted as proof of this. Their origins are not in the biblical story of Noah, but in the Talmud:

תָּנוּ רַבָּנָן: שֶׁבַע מִצְווֹת נִצְטַווּ בְּנֵי נֹחַ - דִּינִין, וּבִרְכַּת הַשֵּׁם, עֲבוֹדָה זָרָה, גִּלּוּי עֲרָיוֹת, וּשְׁפִיכוּת דָּמִים, וְגֶזֶל, וְאֵבֶר מִן הַחַי.

> Our Rabbis taught; Seven commandments were commanded of the children of Noah: [to establish] laws, and [to prohibit] cursing God, idolatry, illicit sexual relations, bloodshed, robbery, and eating flesh from a living animal.[10]

This has been understood to mean that non-Jews who stay within the boundaries of these seven laws have an equal place in the world to come – they have no need to observe the 613 commandments said to be binding on Jews. The latter flow from the covenant made with the Jewish people at Sinai whereas the Noahide laws flow from the covenant made with Noah in Genesis 9.8–17 – the pre-existing covenant with all humanity. We Jews and Christians have our own particular stories which are part of the story of all humanity – of which we are equal parts. In fact, it is the huge leap in obligations – from 7 to 613 – that has, sadly, led some Jewish groups today to discourage conversion; it would be cruel to obligate a person to so many things when so few would allow them to secure their place in the afterlife anyway. It is this type of discouragement that may continue to foster the feeling that Jews may be theologically pluralist, but are practically exclusivist.

Dialogue

If I do not possess all the truth – and neither do you – together we may come to understand something closer to the Truth. Whether literally or metaphorically, many eyes and ears received revelation at Sinai; no one will have seen exactly the same thing or heard the same words. So only when they recount the experience together can the narration come closer to the reality. What a wonderful metaphor of human experience and human faith! The reality of dialogue means that through encounter we become less able to dismiss the truth of the other. We are encouraged to live with this multiplicity of positions and be at ease with dichotomous views, rather than resort to anger and violence in the face of disagreement about things that, nevertheless, really matter.

I would emphasize the importance of this need to hear many voices – in order to gain the fullest picture. Dialogue is a part of this hearing. Our experience of God is diverse and so are expressions of faith. Often, in dialogue, it is necessary for us to be conscious of the pitfalls of common language and, at times, we need to embrace the ability to accept that what you have said isn't necessarily what I heard. This is particularly true in conversations between Jews and Christians, when the same words – such as 'Israel', 'mission', 'forgiveness', 'redeemer' – can mean different things to the speaker and to the listener. This is made still more difficult by the layers of history on which today's relationship rests. As Heschel writes:

> We are heirs to a long history of mutual contempt among religions and religious denominations, strife and persecutions. Even in periods of peace, the relationship that obtains between representatives of different religions is not just reciprocity of ignorance; it is an abyss, a source of detraction and distrust, casting suspicion and undoing efforts of many an honest and noble expression of good will.[11]

There is still much to be done!

The way forward is undoubtedly in relationship, grappling with our histories with honesty but, above all, also grappling with areas of difference. We are now obligated to hear those truths that are essential for the other. We can learn from them, even if they do not compel us or speak to us in a way that our own narrative does. Finding common ground is only part of the journey; being comfortable – or, perhaps, uncomfortable – with difference is the greater step forward.

It is certainly a challenge to acknowledge that the truth of the other may contain what you regard as flaws or be completely unconvincing to you – and yet see that it is still truth for the other and may yet be one part of the larger truth. Of course, it is not essential to see truth in every aspect of the other's position and I would argue that all our truths must yield to ethical scrutiny. Even if they pass that test they are limited, but the potential for growth through dialogue demands that one enters the conversation without certainty in one's own grasp of the whole Truth.

This is particularly stark in dialogue between Jews and Christians. We have jointly inherited the Hebrew Scriptures but read them in different ways. We share common parents and deep roots but have come to some very different theological conclusions. Let me repeat: entering these conversations, neither of us holds the whole picture – the other holds truth, error and, above all, the glimpse, the partial, the provisional, the 'best-I-can-manage at the moment'; the same must be true of me. I do not know it all – and neither do you. That's why we can learn from one another. As Alan, my writing partner, has said elsewhere, we need 'humility in the face of the Divine Mystery'.[12] We do not enter dialogue convinced of the other's errors, arrogantly expecting the other to realize their 'mistake'. We do not need to agree. We are not the same. In embracing our human diversity, we better honour that which we all share; being made in the image of God – an image which embraces our differences.

While we may not agree in dialogue, there is, argues Martin Buber, a need to see the other as an equal in order to interact authentically. As American Reform teacher Rabbi Rami Shapiro summarizes: 'When people interact authentically, when they move beyond themselves to encounter the other person as an equal, they discover a basic reality, a "sphere of between" that links humanity in some greater wholeness.'[13]

Absolutist positions leave very little space for the other to exist as an equal and so, inevitably, will not produce the same quality of dialogue. Indeed, it seems likely that our attempts to frame our dialogue with each other in the Jewish–Christian world have been limited by this – very natural – need to frame the other within our own narrative, rather than seeking to understand theirs. Then again, that is not to say that we must always be changed by dialogue – but we must always be authentic in dialogue, and in so doing allow the other to embrace their own selves too. Ironically, of course, it is probably those with the most extreme absolutist positions who stand to gain the most in interfaith encounter and should not be excluded from the conversation. But, how one holds a conversation with someone who inherently sees you as wrong is a challenge; finding the space where we can enjoy a certain quality of disagreement is a noble goal.

I am aware that Alan's fundamental assumptions may not reflect the mainstream Christian position. It is interesting for me as a Jew to put his paper beside Patrick Morrow's paper[14] and see both common ground and different perspectives. But, then, my assumptions are far from being the driving force for many Jews that they are for me. In some ways, Alan and I share more when it comes to the assumptions we bring to dialogue than some of our co-religionists round the dialogue table out of which this book has emerged. Our views have – and have had – the potential for arousing strong feelings among even those committed to dialogue.

Nevertheless, even Alan and I see through different lenses and adopt different perspectives. Alan's approach has an integrity I deeply appreciate. I hope others will too – and extend that appreciation of integrity to my contribution as well. We both seek to be responsive to critical thought and the experience of dialogue. Religious perceptions and interpretations have changed over time, something which is no less true for Judaism than for Christianity, and Alan wishes to maximize the impact of historical change. Moreover, there is no reason why his more overt wrestling with Christian doctrine need contradict my own more experiential approach. Both are required and the scope for convergence in terms of the questioning of absolutism is strongly present within each. We hope both will be useful to different practitioners at different times, whether they affirm your own thoughts, challenge them or are at odds with them. No doubt we all bring our own absolutes to the conversation and know that they will meet absolutes that contradict our own. Yet behind all this pluralism, lies the unity of God. I, of course, have my own absolutes and firmly held beliefs, one of which is that I must not greet those whose absolutes differ from mine with violence or hatred.

We say of the Torah that she has 70 faces, meaning that there are plural ways of reading each word.[15] Similarly, each one of us is a changing, growing creature. As we Jews read the Torah in an annual cycle we will always and inevitably find a new face each year – after all, we are different and are seeing and seeking different things as we come to the text year after year. The Torah, as a symbol of Truth, encompasses this constant ability of the world and humanity to shift and change, with

A JEWISH THEOLOGY EMBRACING DIFFERENCE

things which were once firmly held turned upside down by the next generation. Each one of us embodies a lifetime of pluralities and has the possibility of meeting truths along the way that will help to guide the next stage, either in a positive joining or a negative rejection of what we have encountered. We have journeyed a long way with Jewish and Christian truths. May we, as Micah asks of us, continue to walk humbly together for, I trust, that will be the road God requires us to tread.

Notes

1 'Presence' is an interesting alternative translation used by the Canadian rabbi and Torah commentator Gunther Plaut.

2 A collection of Aggadic midrash which has proved difficult to date but is generally estimated as being from between the fifth and the seventh century, although probably continuing to change until published by S. Buber in 1868. You may also like to consult the English edition by William G. (Gershon Zev) Braude and Israel J. Kapstein (translators from Hebrew and Aramaic), 1975, *Pesikta De-Rab Kahana: R. Kahana's Compilation of Discourse for Sabbaths and Festal Days*, London: Littman Library of Jewish Civilization, and London: Routledge & Kegan Paul, Piska 12.25, p. 249.

3 Piska 12.25 in *Pesikta de Rav Kahana* continues in a very similar manner; *Exodus Rabbah* 5.9 may be earlier. You may consult *The Midrash Rabbah*, 1989, London: Sonchino Press, vol. 3, p. 87. This is my paraphrase.

4 Just read the Talmud text a line or two above my quotation from *B'rakhot* 58a!

5 *Supra* p. 93. See also Tony Bayfield, p. 6.

6 Kadya Molodowsky, 1999, *Paper Bridges: Selected Poems*, Detroit, MI: Wayne State University Press, pp. 353–4.

7 Leonard Swidler, 1990, *After the Absolute*, Minneapolis, MN: Augsburg Fortress, p. xi.

8 B. 1907, Poland, d. 1972, New York.

9 Abraham Joshua Heschel, 1991, *No Religion Is an Island*, p. 6. This originally appeared in *Union Theological Seminary Quarterly Review* 21:2, January 1966.

10 Babylon Talmud *Sanhedrin* 56a.

11 Heschel, *No Religion Is an Island*, p. 7.

12 Alan Race, 2001, *Interfaith Encounter: The Twin Tracks of Theology and Dialogue*, London: SCM Press, p. 92.

13 Rami Shapiro, 1989, 'Moving the Fence: One Rabbi's View of Interreligious Dialogue' in M. Darroll Bryant and Frank K. Flynn (eds.), *Interreligious Dialogue: Voices from a New Frontier*, New York: Paragon House, p. 33.

14 *Infra* pp. 243–63.

15 *B'midbar Rabbah* Xlll.15.

Further Reflections

TONY BAYFIELD

Historian Tom Holland managed to upset Jews, Christians and Muslims alike with his book on the origins of the three Abrahamic faiths, *In The Shadow of the Sword*.[1] Although the book perpetuates stereotypes of all three groups, it is nevertheless helpful for the purpose of this discussion.

Holland portrays the Jews of Babylon in the third, fourth and fifth centuries as 'a people that dwells alone',[2] driven by notions of superiority,[3] wanting only to concentrate on a bizarre[4] project – the Talmud. That portrait is, at best, born of misinformation, but it does serve as an important starting point for appreciating Rabbi Debbie Young-Somers delightfully personal and humble approach. Jews have seldom regarded themselves as superior. There are traces in the thought of Judah Halevi[5] – uncharacteristic but understandable in the face of unremitting Christian and Muslim hostility. The same is true of aspects of the writing of Shneur Zalman of Liady, the nineteenth-century founder of Habad Hasidism.[6] It's rare – by no means mainstream – for Judaism to claim to be the one true faith. The besetting sin of Judaism, if I may put it like this, is to conduct its love affair with God in technicolour to such an extent that everyone else appears in dull monochrome. In periods when acknowledgement of even the monochrome was not to be expected, there are still exceptions. I particularly enjoy that of the eighteenth-century German Jewish Talmudist and polemicist Jacob Emden who wrote:

> The founder of Christianity conferred a double blessing upon the world. On the one hand he strengthened the Torah of Moses, and emphasised its eternal obligatoriness. On the other hand he conferred favour upon the heathen in removing idolatry from them, imposing upon them stricter moral obligations than are contained in the Torah of Moses. There are many Christians of high qualities and excellent morals. Would that all Christians would live in conformity with their precepts! They are not enjoined, like the Israelites, to observe the laws of Moses, nor do they sin if they associate other beings with God in worshipping a triune God. They will receive a reward from God for

having propagated a belief in Him among nations that never heard His name: for He looks into the heart.[7]

You will doubtless recognize the line that always makes me smile! Despite the dysfunctionality of the Abrahamic family and its painful implications for Jews, we do not claim a monopoly on monotheism or the knowledge of God.

So Debbie comes to the dialogue table with that taken as read and something even more significant. She lives within a postmodern world in which we wrestle with uncertainty. Such uncertainty is a potentially life-enhancing antidote both to the 'certainties' of the past and to that which still, sadly, characterizes much of the present, even Postmodernism itself. But it's a position that can feel insecure and lonely. She has experiences of God which she doubts but which drive her journey and are integral to her rabbinic formation and passion for dialogue. It feels fragile and exposed in the light of public articulation. I reassured Debbie that not only isn't she alone with this complex and uncertain faith but it's been formed within the context of the Jewish peoplehood and tradition she's inherited and carries forward with such fidelity. Not every Jew comes to the dialogue table with her reassuring uncertainty, rich complexity and touching humility, but it's faithful to Judaism and hers is an authentic voice.

We need to return to Tom Holland to understand the extent to which the Christian sibling comes from a radically different context. As we've already noted in understanding where Steve Williams is coming from,[8] Holland highlights the imperial embrace and the role of the Emperor Justinian, seeing in the building of the Church of Hagia Sophia that 'The empire of the Roman people, once and for all, had been brought to Christ.'[9] Holland goes further and looks beyond the limits of the Empire:

> Barbarians who had always stood proof against the might of the legions might certainly be brought to Christ. There was nothing, after all, to stop the Gospel from being preached to the outermost limits of the world. Then, that once achieved, the dome of the heavens would serve to make of the entire earth one immense and universal Hagia Sophia. That, at any rate – in the court of Justinian – was the hope.[10]

Elsewhere, Holland plays the game of obtuse stereotypes, ridiculing the ascetic and monastic tradition evolving in the Syrian desert in the centuries leading up to Justinian. But here, perhaps uncritically, he highlights the absolutist claims of a faith newly wedded to Empire. Alan Race dismantles all theological imperialisms which deny siblings their independent theological space and make a dialogue of respect and mutual learning impossible.

Alan is characteristically lucid and logical, building the case against the claims, 'we're right and therefore you're wrong; we alone act in God's name; our religion is better than yours', as not only pernicious but absurd, not only misguided but the ultimate source of the violence which defaces all three Abrahamic faiths and threatens to undermine religion itself. I mentioned in the first chapter that Elli's paper provoked a storm when first delivered. Alan caused an equal storm, which rumbled on even longer. It seemed to me to have been touched off by his rejection of the literal and advocacy of an approach 'which renders accounts of revelation in terms more akin to parables or metaphors, that is, word-pictures with a message and a meaning'.[11] He then invoked the controversial Canadian historian of religion Wilfred Cantwell Smith and later on refers to 'the Jesus figure'.

I've reflected for some time on what might have been going on, recalling from my early days in dialogue being told quite firmly that the parallel to Torah was not the New Testament but Jesus. Perhaps something akin to the discussion of the nature of Torah which has fragmented the Jewish world over the last 150 years is at stake here – '*mere* metaphor?' I wonder whether Alan would have been on safer ground had he instead referred to the limited power of the human being to grasp God and conceptualize God. Christ is wholly human but also wholly God and therefore as resistant to naming and possession as Moses' God.[12] But that may cause both sides of what I see as an argument over 'metaphor or more than metaphor' to turn on the outsider, so I think I'd be wise to move swiftly on!

Not the least because, for me, that debate isn't central to the challenge to absolutism which Alan pursues with such broad shoulders and clarity – 'I'm right and you're wrong or my faith is better than your faith' is disrespectful (see the next chapter), provocative, hubristic and absurd. It's a major source of antagonism and violence in the world and the ultimate barrier to at-depth dialogue, wholehearted collaboration and religious progress. But note that Alan doesn't equate absolutism solely with the extremism of fundamentalism which we witness daily and dismiss as an aberration 'out there'. Absolutism and fundamentalism are not the same thing.

American scholar Martin Marty identifies five characteristics of fundamentalism.[13] First, it exhibits a very strong reaction against the culture and values of the modern – and postmodern – western world. Modernity is not just seen as threatening but as evil – not to be engaged with but fought against. Second, modernity is experienced as questioning the 'old truths and certainties', shaking the very foundations of both faith and religion. This threat is met by a reassertion of the old truths in a 'born-again', literalist way. Fundamentalism since 1960 has not so much been about verbal as ideological literalism and an unreasoned restatement of long-held theological positions challenged by modernity. The third characteristic goes beyond a reassertion of old truths and claims that the old truths are absolutes – inerrant. 'What we have is the Truth, the whole Truth and nothing but the Truth.' The understanding that the human grasp of truth is provisional,[14] developing, fragmentary is rejected in favour of a return to the absolutisms of the past. Fourth, fundamentalists often seek to return to or reconstruct a past world – a world that never quite existed but is an ideologically driven re-creation of what they would like it to have been. Finally, fundamentalists are not content to assert the authority of their interpretation of tradition for themselves. They seek political power which will enable them to impose their views, by force if necessary, on those who don't share them.

We all abhor fundamentalism, though Christians and Muslims particularly often make the mistake of dismissing it as an aberration – they aren't Christians and Muslims because real Christians and Muslims don't behave like that – rather than a poisonous expression of our respective faiths. Alan focuses on just one aspect – the absolutism reasserted in Marty's third characteristic and reformulated for the world today. Courageously – and in the dialogical context of the three Abrahamic faiths – Alan wrote recently:

> Having to deal with religiously motivated violence could be thought to be, at one level, a distraction from the real business of interreligious dialogue. But once enquiry uncovers some of the religious factors at work within such violence it is far from a distraction. *The real culprit is that sense of religious superiority over the 'ownership' of salvation* ... which is generally thought to be intrinsic to religious identity and absolutism ... A politics which upholds pluralism requires a dialogue built not simply on respect or hospitality but on an acceptance which affirms separate identities even as it might not approve of everything those belonging to any particular tradition want to promote. (My italics.)[15]

What, above all else, unites Alan and Debbie are two rhetorical questions: isn't it sheer hubris to suppose that any human being or group could grasp the whole of God's Truth? Isn't it absurd to suppose that God would entrust to any one group of people at any one time more than a fragment of the knowledge and experience of the One who cannot be captured and owned and who never ceases to surprise us? Such a challenge isn't thrown down to the fanatics and deranged 'out there'; it's thrown down to us all.

Notes

1 Tom Holland, 2012, *In the Shadow of the Sword: The Battle for Global Empire and the End of the Ancient World*, London: Little, Brown.
2 The view of Balaam, sent to curse the Israelites in Numbers 23.9.
3 Holland, *Shadow of the Sword*, p. 112.
4 He goes to great lengths to describe the halakhic enterprise as ridiculous and obsessive by characterizing it as about the copulation of geese and the size of Rabbinic penises.
5 In the *Kuzari*, Judah Halevi (d. 1141) argues Jews have a special religious faculty, a unique soul and are beneficiaries of special providence.
6 Louis Jacobs suggests Shneur Zalman was basing himself on the sixteenth-century kabbalist Hayyim Vital in suggesting, 'There is a divine spark deep in the recesses of the Jewish, and only the Jewish, psyche.' Louis Jacobs, 1995, *The Jewish Religion*, Oxford: Oxford University Press, p. 78.
7 Quoted by Louis Jacobs, 1973, *A Jewish Theology*, London: Darton, Longman & Todd, pp. 286–7.
8 *Supra* p. 85.
9 Holland, *Shadow of the Sword*, p. 194.
10 Holland, *Shadow of the Sword*, p. 194.
11 *Supra* p. 178.
12 When Moses, in Exodus 3.13, asks God God's name so that he can invoke God in the presence of the Children of Israel, God replies: 'I am Who I am.' I take this to mean: 'I'm not the kind of God who can be summoned by rubbing a magic lamp or pronouncing an unguessable name. I cannot be controlled, possessed or owned. That's not Who God Is.'
13 See Martin E. Marty, 1992, 'What is Fundamentalism? Theological Perspectives' in Hans Küng and Jürgen Moltmann (eds.), *Fundamentalism as an Ecumenical Challenge*, London: SCM Press. Marty's work expanded into a five-volume Fundamentalism Project published between 1991 and 1995. Alan Race reminds us the term 'fundamentalism' emerged in the first decade of the twentieth century in the United States as a reaction against historical criticism. This gives a particular nuance to Christian fundamentalism and we must recognize Jewish and Islamic fundamentalisms are not identical.
14 Science has taught us all knowledge is provisional: we rely on the best hypothesis available but recognize that sooner or later a better one will come along. The same is true of religious knowledge, but fundamentalism rejects the humility of recognizing human limitations and the never-ending quest for knowledge and understanding.
15 Alan Race, 2012, 'Religious Absolutism, Violence and the Public Square' in Tony Bayfield, Alan Race and Ataullah Siddiqui (eds.), *Beyond the Dysfunctional Family: Jews, Christians and Muslims in Dialogue with Each Other and with Britain*, London: Manor House, pp. 193–4.

6

What Does Respect between People of Faith Mean?

The Heart of How Things Ought to Be

WENDY FIDLER

Isn't it nice to think that tomorrow is a new day with no mistakes in it yet?

L. M. Montgomery, *Anne of Green Gables*

Let me set the scene with a personal memory from my childhood. I was born during the war and brought up in Manchester in the 1940s and 50s, surrounded by non-Jewish neighbours. In our house, wash day always followed Shabbat; every Sunday we all had to change the sheets on our own beds. However, even on rare rainless Manchester days and before tumble dryers, my mother would never hang out the washing in the garden on a Sunday. When questioned about this, her invariable response was to say that we must live with our Christian next-door neighbours; we must always be considerate to them and to the faith of the majority among whom we live. To hang out the washing on a Sunday would not, she was clear, show respect to the faith around us, and their faith is of equal validity, worth and importance to ours.

Initially, I thought my dialogue partner Joy and I had been allocated one of the less controversial subjects but, as I began to think about the precise meaning of the word 'respect', I realized it was not quite the straightforward assignment I had imagined. As a Jew, I instinctively start with biblical and Rabbinic sources. There is no single equivalent classical Hebrew term for 'respect' and the words that I began to examine show an evolution and development in meaning over time. Context is important and I also noticed that the later the text, the more frequently the translator would use a more contemporary word. In some ways, there is more common ground between Judaism and Christianity over ethical values than the distinctive theological issues which appear to divide us. I have also been selective because the issues relating to respect are many and could lead in directions well beyond the scope of this chapter. Let me take as my starting point the Torah scroll itself and the respect shown to it by Jews.

Synagogues have relatively few defining features but what all share is a 'cupboard', the *Aron HaKodesh*, the Holy Ark, in which the *Sefer Torah*, the handwritten Hebrew scroll containing the Five Books of Moses, is kept. Reading from the Torah forms the pivotal part of all synagogue services on Shabbat, Mondays and Thursdays[1] and on festivals. The scrolls themselves, whatever the Jewish denomination, are protected by embroidered covers and then dressed with silverware. Ceremony surrounds taking them out of the Ark and putting them back during the services. When they are carried in procession round the synagogue, the community stands and watches them as they go round, never turning their backs. In many synagogues the congregation will bow and there is a widespread custom of touching the fringes of *tallitot* (prayer shawls) to the Torah mantle, and then kissing the fringe where it touched the mantle. This constitutes a living ritual of respect – but what the gestures mean to each individual, what each person means by having respect for the Torah, is left to them.

What I would like to consider now is what the Torah itself has to say about respect.

Words for respect in Torah

There is no single word in the Five Books of Moses that unequivocally demands to be translated as 'respect', but several offer important insights.

Kavod comes from the three root letters *khaf-vet-dalet* which appear in the imperative form at the beginning of the Fifth Commandment: honour your father and mother.[2] The Hebrew root of *kavod* derives from 'weight' and is used in biblical Hebrew to mean being heavy, weighty, honoured. The sense is of a scale on which the respect due to a person weighs down one side of the scale which then needs to be offset by respectful action on the other side of the scale in order for it to balance. In the Fifth Commandment, 'honour' or 'respect' equally illustrate the meaning. There is a Talmudic text which considers this the hardest of all commands, so great is the debt owed to parents.[3] To return to what the specific example of the word *kavod* in the Fifth Commandment tells us about the meaning of the word: it's about the weight of honour that accompanies the individual in our relationships with them and the balancing weight of respect that we are obliged to give them. Giving *kavod* is no light matter.

This was well understood in classical Rabbinic literature. In the Talmudic Tractate known as *Pirkei Avot*, *Chapters of the Fathers*, Ben Zoma, an important second-century figure, says that the person who should be respected is the one who respects all humanity.[4] A few verses later, Rabbi Elazar ben Shammua says:

The respect you give to your students should be as dear to you as the respect you give to your colleagues; the respect you give your colleagues should be like the fear/awe in which you hold your teachers; and the fear/awe for your teachers should be like the fear/awe of Heaven.[5]

The same root *khaf-vet-dalet* occurs in a text in the famous midrashic collection *Exodus Rabbah* where the context is rather different. The midrash[6] instructs that a person should be like God when giving instructions on materials for the construction of the Temple and refrain from using wood from a fruit-bearing tree to build their house. Here the respect is for the economic and ecological.

Elazar ben Shammua equated respect with the fear of heaven. I offered awe as an alternative for fear – '*Mah nora hamakom hazeh*, How awesome is this place,' says Jacob when he wakes from his dream.[7] That same awed sense of recognition is conveyed by the Hebrew root *ayin-resh-tsadeh*, trembling in dread/awe. It can be used in the sense of respect/awe of God and of a person. It also introduces a sense of *admiration* and is used in this way particularly by Isaiah.[8] We also find the root *nun-khaf-resh* used in Deuteronomy, Job and Daniel to denote respect as meaning recognition of worth – a significant insight not the least in interfaith dialogue.[9]

Respect and human equality

I want now to turn to a term which became particularly familiar in the nineteenth century in connection with the famous German Orthodox Rabbi Samson Raphael Hirsch. The phrase *Torah im derekh eretz* is first found in the Mishnah in *Pirkei Avot* II.2: 'Beautiful is the study of Torah with *derekh eretz* as involvement with both makes one forget sin.' The term *derekh eretz*, literally 'the way of the land', is inherently ambiguous, with a range of meanings in Rabbinic literature, referring both to behaving appropriately among others and also to the advisability of earning a livelihood. There is even a minor tractate in the Babylonian Talmud entitled *Derekh Eretz Rabbah* in which we are told that we should neither rejoice among people who are weeping nor weep among people who are rejoicing – we should be sensitive to the feelings of others and care for our own reputations as well.[10] This adds further dimensions to the meaning of respect. First, respect includes a sensitivity to the feelings of others. Second, it says something about respect for oneself and one's own reputation – not being concerned about fame but valuing one's own good name. There is a distinctive Jewish theology behind this understanding of *derekh eretz* – namely, that every human being is equally precious in the eyes of God, so fundamental to attitudes to others that it can be taken as read. After all, Jewish ethics cannot be severed from Jewish theology. Above all else, *derekh eretz* teaches that, at the heart of how things ought to be, lies *respect for the value of every human being*.

In the earliest sources, *derekh eretz* is linked to having an occupation. In the Mishnah's book of wise aphorisms, *Pirkei Avot*, we've already read that Torah is good '*im derekh eretz*, along with a worldly occupation', because engaging in both pursuits keeps a person away from sin.[11] In *Leviticus Rabbah* we find the idea taken further in the dictum that 'the duty of *derekh eretz* preceded the Torah by twenty-six generations'.[12] This underlies its most famous modern usage by Samson Raphael Hirsch who called his approach '*Torah im* [with] *derekh eretz*', using the traditional term to convey the idea that one's learning should engage with both traditional Judaism and the secular world. What this strongly implies is respect for both traditional Jewish teaching and modern thought, for both our own community and those around us – not the least when we are drying our washing on a rare sunny Sunday in Manchester.

I want to underline the theology that lies behind the ethic of respect. There is a remarkable passage in Mishnah *Sanhedrin*.[13] We have been given a prosaic but meticulous record of how the Sanhedrin, the Supreme Court – abolished more than half a century earlier – had operated. Suddenly, in the midst of instructions on how to caution witnesses in capital cases, the Mishnah moves into a series of eye-opening theological statements, not only telling us that all humanity is equal in being descended from the first couple, Adam and Eve, but explaining that when an earthly king stamps coins they all come out the same; when God stamps human beings, we each come out differently, yet of the same incalculable value. If we are all descended from the same couple 'so that no one should be able to say that my family is greater than yours', all stamped by the same God and all of equal value – it could not be clearer that the ethic of respect flows from an unequivocal theology of equality and respect.

Being a person of our times, I feel it essential to acknowledge that there are verses in the Torah which are open to interpretations that are less than respectful. I do not need to detail the texts which are open to anti-feminist, misogynist and homophobic understandings. Some also appear to condone violence against others and not merely judicial punishments. By and large, Rabbinic interpretation has understood them in a more respectful manner, but the very process of interpretation and reinterpretation which is central to Judaism underlines the need for constant re-evaluation and reconsideration. It seems clear that, from its beginnings, Judaism placed a very high value on respect, meaning giving great weight to the honour due to one's fellow human beings who are our equals in their humanity. Now to end where I began this section: understanding now what the obligation to respect others asks of us demands more than considerations of etymology. It is a continuing crucial debate for each generation.

Forgiveness

One of the great benefits of writing a book through the dialogue process is having the time to think and engage with the other chapters of the book and their authors. Everyone taking part acknowledges the full extent of the dysfunctionality of our family, the children of Abraham and Sarah. No one evaded the history of Christian anti-Semitism and anti-Judaism. Bishop Gillett's quiet, patient work in Norwich is a very moving and helpful model. This made me realize that the concept of forgiveness was relevant to respect.

Jews and Christians tend to view forgiveness differently. Judaism sees it as a process whereby the perpetrator of the offence is expected to acknowledge her or his wrongdoing, repent and make restitution. Forgiveness comes at the end of that process. In Christianity, as I understand, forgiveness is more an act of aspiring to be like God. God is loving and forgiving and therefore we are obliged to forgive, regardless of repentance. Nevertheless, it seemed to me that, despite the difference, forgiveness is often a component of respect. The Emeritus Chief Rabbi, Lord Sacks, shortly before his retirement, addressed exactly this issue in one of his weekly communications, 'Covenant and Conversation'. His starting point is the reconciliation of Joseph and his brothers: 'Interpersonal forgiveness begins when Joseph forgives his brothers for selling him into slavery. Divine forgiveness starts with the institution of Yom Kippur as the supreme day of Divine pardon following the sin of the Golden Calf.'[14]

I understand Rabbi Lord Sacks to be saying that personal forgiveness comes chronologically before Divine forgiveness, illustrating the significance of respect between people. In this context the first step is respect. How we understand 'forgiveness', what it can mean in terms of the historical relationship between Jews and Christians and whether it is possible, is a matter that cannot even enter discussion until a relationship of respect between those not personally responsible has been established.

That having been said, the subject of forgiveness long ago became part of the problem and the denigration of Judaism which goes back to the early Church Fathers. King's College, London philosopher Simon May writes:

WHAT DOES RESPECT BETWEEN PEOPLE OF FAITH MEAN?

The widespread belief that the Hebrew Bible is all about vengeance and 'an eye for an eye,' while the Gospels invent love as an unconditional and universal value, must therefore count as one of the most extraordinary misunderstandings in all of Western history. For the Hebrew Bible is the source not just of the two love commandments but of a larger moral vision inspired by wonder for love's power.[15]

As May says, the polemic of Jews as vengeful, demanding their pound of flesh, unforgiving, as contrasted with Christians rising above such base motivation and being loving and forgiving, is just what it is – a polemic. Surely we have every right to demand of our Christian sisters and brothers that they renounce such slurs or, at the very least, ensure they are placed in context. They, equally, have a right to demand respect from us for an appropriate response, even if we have different theologies of forgiveness.

Intrafaith: Jews and Jews

Everything that I've written so far affirms respect and demands respect between Jews and Christians. This I firmly believe in, but I also believe that all people – including Christians and Jews – should practise what they preach in all, rather than in selected, contexts. I therefore need to consider respect and intrafaith, which, in my case, is respect between Jew and Jew; the Christians in our group must address respect between Christian and Christian.

When Jews entered the modern world at the beginning of the nineteenth century, one of the things that we acquired from Christianity was denominations. For the best part of 200 years we have lived with Ultra-Orthodox, Orthodox, Modern-Orthodox, Masorti, Reform and Liberal/Progressive Jews. Although that list has been written from left to right, it should be thought of as non-judgemental but complex rather than a descending list of authenticity and fidelity. We tend to categorize by levels of 'traditional observance' rather than theology or ethics. We are often guilty of the sin of regarding anyone more observant than us as being obsessive and anyone less observant as being scarcely Jewish at all. It is not a very attractive attribute. In a small community like the British Jewish community, it is wasteful and destructive. It is often about issues of power, authority and perceived 'rightness', the same attributes which poison interfaith relationships.

The situation has become worse not better since the rise of global fundamentalism in the 1960s, polarizing Jews by difference rather than bringing them together through common ground. The situation in Israel is, if anything, even more damaging. All over the world, Jewish leadership is modelling disrespect. I reject this completely, not the least out of my own personal experience.

The political in-fighting has got worse during my lifetime, particularly among older people lamenting the demise of 'their' world. Perhaps this is inevitable, as some older people find difficulty in seeing any change as progress, whereas I find some changes vibrant and exciting. New attitudes towards women are enlightening, freeing, liberating and most definitely respectful. I am delighted I have not missed the opportunities now available for me to do *kri'at Hatorah*, read from the Torah during a synagogue service, and to lead a congregation in prayer. I find it an emotionally fulfilling experience to witness young women taking leading roles. After all, they will be the future mothers of our children who will then be able to bring up their children with a knowledge, appreciation and respect for the Judaism into which they have been born. My mother, the same woman who wouldn't hang her washing outside on a Sunday, had her first *aliyah*, being called to stand and hold the Torah while a section is read, at the age of 85. Her comment was that she was very happy she had had that experience as she had never been so close to the Torah or even seen the text before. At 85, it had been a physical strain and she did not want to do it again but she was extremely relieved that women and young girls were progressing and playing a meaningful part within Judaism. She was clear that they deserve only our respect for all they are fighting for and achieving. As I wrote earlier, there are Torah texts capable of disrespectful as well as respectful interpretations. What is wonderful is that we can all find respectful interpretations if we want to.

The Oxford Jewish Congregation

Let me tell you about one group which has done just that. I am an active and committed member of the Oxford Jewish Congregation (OJC). Today, the OJC is a unique community yet a microcosm of British Jewry and a potential model. In Oxford there is a single Jewish Centre which welcomes all Jews regardless of denomination. The synagogue is open to all forms of Jewish worship and observance, under one roof. In practice, this means that Orthodox, Masorti and Progressive groups frequently hold services at the same time in different parts of the building, the system functioning because the OJC has enjoyed and cultivated a sense of unity and common Jewish identity, based on mutual respect for and collaboration between the different strands of Judaism. In short, the OJC operates as a single 'umbrella' organization to which Jews of any denomination can belong, while permitting and, indeed, encouraging and funding subgroups of members to organize different services.

The OJC in its present form emerged from the small and diverse nature of the local community and the need to serve its many transient visitors, the majority of whom are visiting Jewish academics from across the globe. Membership of the congregation is open to 'all persons of the Jewish faith', albeit with the crucial rider that any individual's access to religious rites (such as Bar/Bat Mitzvah, marriage, burial) depends on his or her halakhic status. Both men and women are counted as full members with any non-Jewish spouses/partners offered non-voting associate status. Significantly, the community does not have a rabbi or other formal spiritual leader except on High Holydays, when outside assistance is obtained for the Orthodox and, more recently, for the Progressive services. There are, however, rabbis who are members of the community.

Each group is entitled to and expected to maintain the integrity of its form of service; each group also understands and accepts that it is part of a wider, unified community. Activities are coordinated by the Synagogue Council. There are no 'block' interests on Council and no formal representation on Council for the non-Orthodox groups. The convener of the Orthodox religious services committee is an ex-officio member of Council and all elected Council members are encouraged to regard themselves as representatives of the whole community.

An example of the value of respect shown to this community ethos shone out over Rosh Hashanah, 5774/2013, when the address to the Orthodox community was given by Miriam Shire, a member of the Progressive group. She opened her sermon by saying how honoured she was to be speaking on the Second Day of Rosh Hashanah.[16] She then continued:

> We all know this is a unique synagogue where the different denominations of Judaism trust each other enough to share space, time and especially a good kiddush together! There are of course differences between the movements within this synagogue that we continually have to discuss and work out; it has not always been stress-free. But when members of a community value and respect each other as fellow Jews over and above denominational doctrine then trust and respect resides.

I fully appreciate that this model is not right for every Jew. It is surely a case, though, of ensuring respect for all those whose expression of Judaism enables them to be part of the 'mosaic' of Judaism. As the demography of the Jewish community leads to a shift towards the major Jewish centres, the smaller communities are literally marginalized, finding the older, exclusive and clearly delineated denominational models more difficult to maintain as separate entities. The Oxford *minhag* (custom or practice) should be considered seriously by other small communities not just as a means of keeping provincial Judaism alive but as a powerful way of modelling respect – which should be borne in mind even by those who are not being dragooned by demographic realities.

The giving of respect

Since all humanity is made in the image of God, should respect be given equally to all human beings, and should that respect be given unconditionally and non-judgementally? Can there even be respect if it has attached conditions? Am I obliged to respect everyone and everything they do? For example, respect a man who is so drunk on bad faith that he hijacks a passenger plane and flies it into a skyscraper or, at the other end of the scale, a mother whose child grows up into adulthood and takes decisions that engender parental disapproval, for example the choice of partner or occupation, acts that can be considered undesirable within the family? One might say, in the words of the late eleventh-/early twelfth-century Spanish Jewish philosopher Moses ibn Ezra: 'No sin is so light that it may be overlooked. No sin is too heavy that it may not be repented.'[17]

Let's take the first instance – acts of barbaric terrorism which so scar today's world and are often performed in the name of religion. We are all agreed that what they do is inexcusable and appalling. Am I obliged to love the terrorists? As a Jew, it isn't my language but I am obliged to respect them, though not their deeds, as equal human beings like myself, stamped in the image of God and infinitely precious. My respect at least means that I wouldn't want them treated with the same guiltless barbarity as they treat us.

What of the mother? My experience tells me that a mother's love is unconditional and if one of my children were to do something inexplicable, my love for them would (I hope) remain unconditional. My respect for my children's beliefs and views means that I don't have to *like* and accept all their beliefs and choices, but does mean that I respect their right to those beliefs and choices regardless of whether I share them. Parent-child relationships need to be based upon mutual trust and respect.

There is an interesting Rabbinic aphorism which I think is relevant. When are we God's children? When we act like God's children. When we don't act like God's children we are, as it were, not God's children.[18] That, I believe, focuses us on the act, the sin. The 'as it were' reminds us that we cannot erase the fact of our creation in the image of God completely; God, as it were, respects our free will even though God dislikes the choice we make.

Respect in the interfaith context

Finally, let me return to respect in the context of interfaith work, particularly between Judaism and Christianity. Until the second half of the twentieth century there was little or no formalized interaction and dialogue between our two faiths in Britain. The Council of Christians and Jews (CCJ) which, as the UK's oldest national interfaith organization, was established during the dark days of the Second World War, took the first steps on the tortuous road to establishing respect between Christianity and Judaism. There is no doubt that the foundation of CCJ was prompted by the growing recognition of the Jewish catastrophe in Europe but that should in no way detract from the courage and vision of the then Archbishop of Canterbury, William Temple, and Chief Rabbi Joseph Hertz.

The circumstances in which CCJ was founded influenced its terms of reference and an agenda that has persisted for many years. Jews wanted to call the Church to account for its anti-Judaism and its consequences and to enlist the help of its sibling in ensuring that the horrendous events of the Shoah are never repeated. Christians, like the Revd Dr James Parkes[19] and Methodist Minister W. W. Simpson, wanted to expose the anti-Judaism and anti-Semitism endemic in the Church and cleanse it. Yet even such an 'untheological' agenda was a 'risk activity'. Any attempt at reconciliation exposed Jews to Christian mission and to the danger – as well as disrespect – that posed. Joy, my Christian partner in this project, though involved in interfaith relations for more than 30 years, has not witnessed such activity. However, many Jews, including me, have been approached by extreme right-wing evangelical Christians whose aim is to bring non-Christians to 'the Christian God'. Though increasingly rare, Christian mission is still perceived by Jews as a threat and, even more, as grossly disrespectful. I am particularly grateful to Debbie Young-Somers and Alan Race for their discussion of mission.[20]

From its inception CCJ chose to be involved in dialogue. Much has been written about the construction and rules of dialogue,[21] but for an interfaith organization founded in Europe during the Shoah – whatever the forms and rules – dialogue was and is essential. Decade after decade of hard, underfunded work proved its worth and recognized the importance of respect as defined by the biblical terms cited at the beginning of this essay. As a recent symposium in CCJ's journal *Common Ground* indicates, the work underlined the fact that centuries of living next door to each other did qualify those who wanted to engage to know how to interact.[22]

Some have thought that responding to 20 centuries of Christian anti-Judaism and the catastrophes of the twentieth century should have been accomplished by now. But, as so much of this book suggests, the roots of estrangement and the pain of the past are so deep that they will take far longer and far wider engagement than anyone could have envisaged. The situation has, sadly, been greatly exacerbated by events in the Middle East, particularly since 1967. Whatever view one takes of the policies of particular Israeli governments, the situation is alarming. There is a growing refusal of many within the Christian world to accept Land as part of Jewish theology – as well as a pragmatic necessity – and a growing questioning of the legality of the Jewish State even though it was established, along with a Palestinian State that has never come into existence, by the United Nations. The subject is addressed elsewhere in this book but I want to underline the lack of respect implicit in assuming that Judaism must be Christianity's identical twin and in not allowing it to be different and theologically attached to the Land in a way that it has always chosen to be.

American Jewish psychologist Mark Braverman, in his book *Fatal Embrace*,[23] has shown how the Jewish quest for safety and empowerment and the Christian endeavour to atone for centuries of anti-Semitism have united to suppress the conversations needed to bring peace in the Middle East. Nevertheless, those conversations, now surfacing, have scarcely been conversations but rather monologues between those whose hearing is severely challenged.

Walter Brueggemann, the Protestant theologian, in his work *The Prophetic Imagination*,[24] writes about the prophetic call to grieve and to mourn as the only way we can hope to move to a better reality. Though there is absolutely no moral equivalence whatsoever, we need to accept the wrongs committed against the Palestinians in Israel, just as Christians needed to accept complicity in the Holocaust. We Jews need to acknowledge our wrongs as a prerequisite for reinstating respect for the 'other'.

To engage in Jewish–Christian dialogue today is to engage in a paradigm shift with regards to content. In a recent symposium on dialogue in the CCJ Journal *Common Ground*, both the Revd Peter Colwell[25] and Rabbi Lord Sacks[26] argue that dialogue evolves. It does not remain static, and the previous focus on 'existential phenomena' needs to move to embrace both political and religious realities, uncomfortable as these may be. It is at this nexus of discomfort that respect is risked. This is why, in his article, Rabbi Sacks emphasizes perseverance in efforts to sustain dialogue. Perseverance is needed because personal respect is at risk both of the other and by the other. This risk is seen most prominently in Colwell's challenge that our dialogue needs to encompass interdependence. His call is for a mutual respect and he used two Hebrew terms: *l'ha'arikh*, implying behaviour that *leads to* showing admiration for the other, and *hakarah*, which conveys the need to *recognize* the other's worth. This sentiment is also present in Dr Stephen Innes' article, which reflects on Jewish philosopher Emmanuel Levinas's work.[27] Here, respect as in *heh-khaf-resh* is moved to a deeper if not intimate level:

> Levinas's notion of ethics implies that for Christians and Jews to begin to have [this] new 'maturity and patience' which he caught sight of in the *Amitié Judéo-Chrétienne* dialogues, each must be invited to enter into the world of the Other, and in turn each must have the desire to truly see the face of the Other.

There is one final – and very important – point. We have seen how Jewish–Christian dialogue, made possible by CCJ, began as a response to the catastrophe born of the most dysfunctional relationship imaginable. It has embraced the ethics of respect which I have placed in the context of the supreme, contemporary Jewish ethicist Emmanuel Levinas. I've acknowledged Peter Colwell's insistence that dialogue moves on to embrace contemporary political and religious realities. But what CCJ has not done up to now is to move into the theological. This is undoubtedly because it's the most risky and difficult area of all. One should acknowledge understandable Jewish caution as expressed by the great American Jewish philosopher and thinker Rabbi Joseph Soloveitchik. In this respect, Christians have led the way but this book represents a wholehearted Jewish response and is remarkable for bringing together rabbis from the Liberal, Reform, Masorti and Orthodox communities.

What does it mean to respect not just the right to exist and the person of the other but for a Jew to respect the faith of a Christian and for a Christian to respect the faith of a Jew? What do a mutually respectful Christianity and Judaism look like? Thankfully, it is my colleagues and friends in this book who have to begin to offer some answers!

Notes

1 Possibly because these were market days when people came in from the surrounding countryside. The Talmud speaks of not allowing more than three days to pass without reading Torah. In any event, Monday and Thursday readings are now the preserve of Orthodox communities.

2 Exodus 20.12; Deuteronomy 5.16.

THE HEART OF HOW THINGS OUGHT TO BE

3 Palestinian Talmud, *Peah* 1.1.
4 *Pirkei Avot* IV. 1.
5 *Pirkei Avot* IV.15.
6 *Exodus Rabbah* 35.2.
7 Genesis 28.17.
8 Isaiah 8.12, 13,
9 For the root *nun-khaf-resh* as respect in the sense of a recognition, see Deuteronomy 33.9, and of worth, see Job, 34.19 and Daniel 11.39.
10 Babylonian Talmud *Derekh Eretz Rabbah* 2.1.3.
11 *Pirkei Avot* II.2.
12 *Leviticus Rabbah* 9.3. Because it came with Adam, the first human, while the Torah came with Moses, 26 generations later.
13 Mishnah *Sanhedrin* 4.5.
14 Jonathan Sacks, 2009, 'Covenant and Conversation', *Vayigash*, 26 December.
15 Simon May, 2011, *Love: A History*, New Haven: Yale University Press, pp. 19–20.
16 Because Liberal Jews only celebrate one day of Rosh Hashanah instead of two, as celebrated by Orthodox Jews in the Diaspora, this day was not in fact Rosh Hashanah for the speaker. However, she showed respect for Orthodox practice by introducing this occasion as the 'Second Day of Rosh Hashanah'. This was later recognized and acknowledged when the speaker was thanked by an Orthodox member for her address.
17 Moses ibn Ezra was both a poet and a philosopher, renowned for his analysis of metaphor in the Torah where he is frequently at odds with Maimonides. A further claim to fame rests with his aphorisms such as the one quoted.
18 See the discussion in Babylonian Talmud *Kiddushin* 36a.
19 1896–1981.
20 *Supra* pp. 184–6 and 197–8.
21 J. K. Aitken and E. Kessler (eds.), 2006, *Challenges in Jewish–Christian Relations*, New York: Paulist Press; H. Fry (ed.), 1996, *Jewish–Christian Dialogue*, Exeter: University of Exeter Press.
22 Emmanuel Levinas, 1999, *Alterity and Transcendence*, New York: Columbia University Press, p. 79. Levinas describes the ten points of Seelisberg, approved in July 1947, as formulating resolutions on the way Christians should speak of Jews. This text does not tell Jews what they should think about Christians. Levinas believes that the centuries in which Jews lived next to Christians well qualified them to know how to interact.
23 Mark Braverman, 2010, *Fatal Embrace*, New York: Beaufort Books.
24 Walter Brueggemann, 2001, *The Prophetic Imagination*, Minneapolis, MN: Augsburg Fortress.
25 Peter Colwell, 2013, 'Jews and Christians: Is There Any Point in Continuing the Dialogue?', *Common Ground*, Summer, pp. 3–4.
26 Jonathan Sacks, 2013, 'Is Christian–Jewish Encounter Still Important?', *Common Ground*, Summer, p. 5.
27 Stephen Innes, 2013, 'Towards a New Paradigm for Jewish–Christian Dialogue: Facilitating a Movement "Beyond Dialogue"', *Common Ground*, Summer, pp. 8–9.

Negotiating the Complexities of You and Me

JOY BARROW

I write as a Christian who has been engaged in interfaith relations since 1980 when I began teaching in a London secondary school. Subsequently, I was Inter Faith Relations Officer for the Methodist Church in Britain from 2008 to 2013.

Part 1: Five principles of respectful relations

The first school at which I taught was in a predominantly Asian area. I was the only Religious Education teacher, my academic qualifications being a degree in theology and a PGCE in Religious Education. There was neither a school RE syllabus nor any resources. Immediately, I set about writing a syllabus, with one-term courses on each of the five world religions then examined at GCE O Level – Christianity, Islam, Judaism, Hinduism and Sikhism. I had no knowledge of three of them and my knowledge of Judaism was derived from 'Old Testament studies'. So much for my theology degree and PGCE! My solution was to visit local places of worship, asking officials and members of the communities for information and guidance. They were incredibly helpful and relationships of trust and respect developed. I also attended evening sessions at the (then) National RE Centre at the nearby West London Institute of Higher Education. It was there I encountered living Judaism through, among others, Rabbi Tony Bayfield, then a rabbi in north-west Surrey. Membership of a local interfaith group further supported my understanding of religions as living faiths. This illustrates the foundations of any respectful encounter; it is relational and needs to be continually developed through personal contact and listening to, hearing and understanding people's narratives. Each person's narrative is different and, as both my Jewish dialogue partner Wendy and I discuss, there is a wide variety of beliefs and practices within – as well as between – religions.

NEGOTIATING THE COMPLEXITIES OF YOU AND ME

A major aspect of any interfaith relationship is the willingness for the encounter to change you. Among some people there is a concern that any contact with a member of a different religion may challenge a person's existing faith beliefs and could lead to converting to another religion. Wendy refers to Jewish fears in this regard but that, understandably, relates to a Christian conversion agenda. If we consider any personal encounter experienced in our daily lives, it has the potential to change us. This may be temporary, for example a brief encounter with a person that may encourage, frustrate or annoy us. But relationships of respect and trust, where we allow ourselves to explore the core of our beliefs together with members of the same religion or a different one – and where we are prepared to be open to change – have the potential to go beyond an academic understanding of religions into the depths of our spirituality. I have been greatly enriched by such encounters.

This is, in part, because, in such encounters, one is obliged to explain one's beliefs in words accessible to those with whom one is speaking. This necessitates a process of thinking through one's own beliefs and being able to articulate them without using terms that are exclusive to one's own faith. So the first principle of interfaith dialogue is that it depends upon the use of accessible language – in the context of a respectful relationship in which one is open to change.

Second, you need to ensure that your words are understood by your interlocutrix with the theological understanding you are using. It is important to recognize the same word or phrase may be used in many different ways. An example is the phrase 'Christian Zionism', which is one of the more problematic phrases in Christian–Jewish dialogue. In 2012, the Network for Inter Faith Concerns of the Anglican Communion published *Land of Promise? An Anglican Exploration of Christian Attitudes to the Holy Land with Special Reference to Christian Zionism*. Chapter 2 is devoted to a discussion of the various usages of the term 'Christian Zionism', including 12 different definitions and nuances the writers drew from sources available on the Internet.[1] How often does misunderstanding take place because a word or phrase is lost in theological translation, the hearer attaching a meaning very different from that intended by the speaker? As will be noted in Part 3 of this essay, there are also occasions when a word or phrase is used which is understood as disrespectful and gives pain to members of the Jewish faith, although that was not the intention of the interlocutrix.

Third, in any discussion of the meaning of sacred texts, it is preferable if those engaged have knowledge of the sacred languages of the religions being discussed. As will be noted in Part 2 of this essay, when sacred Scripture is translated, the nuance and subtlety of the original text is lost

– which may lead to misunderstandings. At the very least, a recognition that one is working with a translation is essential.

Fourth, it is absolutely essential that all encounters be based on trust and confidentiality. Both are crucial to ensure that those present have the freedom to think through their beliefs, articulating and testing them with others present, especially but not exclusively with those from their own religion, without being concerned that their comments will be repeated to others outside the group.

The fifth principle in any such dialogue is theological integrity. In any dialogue it is necessary to articulate what you believe in an open and honest manner. For many years I was engaged in textual studies in a small group where those present had a basic knowledge or better of the sacred language of both religions. Our conversations led to deep friendships that remain to this day. Our discussions were 'energetic' and some lasted late into the evening. We were challenged to think through our own beliefs and also gained an in-depth understanding of the other religion. As the group progressed and familiarity and trust developed, so too did our ability to be open and honest with each other – and ourselves!

As I have said, it is essential to explain clearly and concisely the theological terms being used, as people may understand them very differently. It is also necessary, where there are differences of belief and practice, for these to be acknowledged and respected. It must also be recognized that there will be differences of belief between members of the same religion, and such differences must be recognized and acknowledged. Consequently we have to be aware that a statement made by one or more members of a religion is the belief of the person, denomination or group concerned and should not be understood to be representative of that religion as a whole.

Within each religion there is a variety of attitudes towards developing respectful relations with people of different religions. Alan Race, in his *Christians and Religious Pluralism*, examines the theological approaches to different religions by what is known as the threefold paradigm of exclusivism, inclusivism and pluralism.[2] The first, in my view, rules out meaningful dialogue; the second makes a bid for ownership of all that is tolerable and recognizable in other traditions; while the third permits an encounter between respectful equals. The threefold paradigm does, however, make several presumptions. First, that members of different religions have a mature theological understanding of the relationship between, for example, Christianity and Judaism. In reality, for many people it is their personal relationship to God which is their primary focus. This they express in the way they behave towards other people as individuals, such as their neighbours and co-workers. Second, the threefold paradigm may not reflect the reality of the complexities of interfaith relationships, which may be influenced by, for example, historical or personal experience, or how such positive interaction would be understood by family or community members overseas. But these are matters we must be alert to and take into account; they do not discredit the threefold paradigm and underline the importance of dialogue to communal relations.

Let me stress how important it is to understand and respect the personal circumstances of other faith groups when we approach them in dialogue. For many years I was a member of a local Methodist church that had a thriving Pakistani-Christian community. Because they came from a background of persecution, any thought of respectful engagement with members of different religions, especially Muslims, was deeply painful and totally unacceptable. In other churches, for example, where there are strong Palestinian-Christian influences – whether through the presence of members of that community, family members who are Palestinian or political activists – developing positive relations with members of the Jewish faith will likewise be problematic.

This doesn't mean that respectful relations with other religions shouldn't be our goal but, especially in the former case – where there are co-religionists who have suffered persecution, whose families continue to do so, and who would be deeply distressed by any dialogue with members of a religion perceived to be their persecutors – great sensitivity is required.[3] While I never concealed the positive relations I had with members of different religions, I did not discuss them in the presence of members of the Pakistani-Christian community because, first, I knew it would distress them and, second, I did not want to damage the respectful relationships I had with them. I realize that some people may consider I should have challenged their position and encouraged them to meet with local members of the Muslim community in order to develop relations of respect with them. However, one can't ignore the impact of globalization – regular travel between countries, the use of electronic communications and satellite television. What one person does here will become known by family and co-religionists abroad. It is easy to be critical without understanding their situation; interfaith dialogue is essential, but between appropriate groups at the appropriate time.

I am aware there are Christians – many elderly – who feel powerless. They were born in the town in which they are living but are overwhelmed by the changes that have taken place during their lifetimes. They don't understand the beliefs and practices of the members of the different religions who have moved into the area. They see new places of worship being built and large numbers attending, while recalling the numbers who formerly attended services in their churches but where now the majority of seats are empty. Some have been supportive of my interfaith engagement, others extremely critical. Of the latter group, the most common criticism was that I had had the privilege of five years' theological education and that I should be using it positively in the Church, not spending my time studying different religions, attending their places of worship and developing friendships with their members. However, my understanding of Christian theology and my study of the Christian Scriptures taught me that in all his interactions with people, Jesus met them in the place, physically and spiritually, where they were and recognized their need.

Part 2: The concept of respect in the Christian Scriptures

In this section of my essay, I want to comment on a number of scriptural passages. My purpose is not to provide traditional exegesis but to explain how my understanding of them – how they spoke/speak to me – encouraged me on my journey of engagement with, and respect for, members of different religions.

In an essay 'Common Errors Made about Early Judaism', American Professor of New Testament Studies Amy-Jill Levine contends that to describe Jesus as focusing his ministry on 'outcasts' and 'marginals' is flawed.[4] Levine considers that to describe groups ranging from the sick and the poor, women, and Gentiles such as centurions, as marginal is 'historically inaccurate'. She writes that sinners and tax collectors are not 'cast out'; rather they are people who violate the welfare of the community and have deliberately removed themselves from the common good. She argues that they are not as such 'cast out' of anything, citing for example Luke 18.10–14, where a tax collector and a sinner are located in the Temple, and Luke 7.1–10 which reports that a Roman centurion – a Gentile – built a synagogue in Capernaum and describes how the Jewish leaders interceded on his behalf with Jesus. In summary, Levine argues that Judaism of this period was not an egalitarian or universalist utopia but nor was it a system that 'cast out' women and Gentiles, the poor and sick, and so on. Levine concludes that it is therefore important that pastors and teachers be more cautious when they use terms like 'marginal' and 'outcast'.

I am aware that during my undergraduate theological studies we had no lectures on first-century Judaism – or, indeed, Judaism today – although there were compulsory exams in New Testament Greek in the first two years. Many theological degree courses – including those training church ministers – still do not include courses that enable graduates to understand what was going on in first-century Judea when Rabbinic Judaism and Christianity were first emerging. This has led, through sheer lack of knowledge, to errors in the understanding of passages in the Christian Scriptures, resulting in great distress to members of the Jewish community.

The Christian Scriptures clearly record the respectful way in which Jesus behaved towards various kinds of people. In Luke 7.36–50 Jesus is reported as eating at the home of a Pharisee when 'a woman in the city who was a sinner' interrupted the meal; Jesus accepted her devotion. In John 3.1–21 there is an account of the Pharisee Nicodemus visiting Jesus in order to discuss his teachings about God.

The account of Jewish religious leaders approaching Jesus on behalf of a Roman centurion, recorded in Luke 7.1–10 and referred to above, provides an example of the way in which those concerned were respectful of the other people involved. Although an officer in the occupying army and someone who would have worshipped the Emperor as a god, the centurion had shown respect to the Jewish religion by providing the necessary finance for them to build a synagogue in Capernaum. While Jesus was en route to his house, the centurion sent a message telling Jesus that he was not worthy for Jesus to enter his house but, if Jesus uttered the word, his servant would be healed. In response to the centurion's message Jesus praised him, saying (v. 9) that 'not even in Israel have I found such faith'.

The Christian Scriptures record episodes in the life of the early Church where being respectful to others is stressed. Three examples are Peter's vision at the house of Cornelius; the Council of Jerusalem recorded in Acts 10 and 15; and Paul's teaching regarding the eating of meat offered to idols recorded in 1 Corinthians 8. While the last two can be understood as intrareligious issues, both are examples of how respect should be shown to people and of the acceptance of diversity of belief and practice within a religion.

As I have already pointed out, Acts records a controversy in the early Church which provides an understanding of how people should behave respectfully when there are differences of belief with co-religionists – for example whether the gospel of Jesus was restricted to members of the Jewish faith or if it included Gentiles. A related controversy was the extent to which Gentile Christians had to conform to Jewish practice – particularly with respect to circumcision – and obey the stipulations of early Rabbinic Judaism. There was a sharp division of opinion between Peter and Paul, the former's understanding being changed after he received a divine vision while staying at the home of Simon the Tanner in Joppa.

Acts 10 records Peter praying at noon and, as he did so, falling into a trance. He saw something like a large sheet being lowered to the ground from heaven by its four corners containing a variety of animals, reptiles and birds that were not *kasher*, permitted as food. When a voice, which he understood to be of divine origin, told Peter to 'kill and eat', he immediately responded that he had never eaten food that was profane or forbidden. In response the voice told Peter: 'What God has made clean, you must not call profane.' While the language used reflects that found in Leviticus with reference to Temple sacrifice, Peter's response relates to the foods that *he* was forbidden to eat as specified in Leviticus 11. However, the purpose of the vision was not to abrogate the dietary laws in the Torah.

Shortly after the vision, messengers sent from Roman centurion Cornelius arrived at the house of Simon, requesting that Peter come to Cornelius' house in Caesarea. Although a Gentile, Cornelius is described as a devout person who feared God, gave alms and prayed to God. Arriving at Cornelius' home Peter explained that, prior to his vision, he would not have entered his house.[5] The reason given in English translations such as NRSV is 'that it is unlawful for a Jew to associate with or visit a Gentile'.[6] However, this would appear to contradict accounts, both in the Christian Scriptures – for example Luke 7, referred to above – and secular literature relating to Gentile patrons of synagogues.[7]

Regardless of the customs and norms of the day, Peter entered Cornelius' house and recounted his vision, concluding that God shows no partiality but in every nation anyone who fears him and does what is right is acceptable to him.[8] While the immediate context of those words was that the gospel should no longer be restricted to Jews, it is my belief that God speaks to people in a variety of ways and through the beliefs and practices of different religious traditions. My experience has been of encountering God while participating in worship in different religions.

Acts 15 relates to Gentiles who became Christians. Some Christians believed that they should still observe the teachings of Torah. At the Church Council in Jerusalem, Paul – together with his companion Barnabas – reported on the numbers of Gentiles who had become Christians and the ways in which God had blessed them, exemplified by their receipt of the Holy Spirit. Peter also witnessed to God's blessing of Gentiles and challenged James, the leader of the church in Jerusalem, and other members of the Council not to impose additional restrictions on Christians. Peter's contention was that salvation was through God's grace; James' decision was that Gentiles should show respect for the beliefs and practices of the Jews among whom they were living and not behave in a way that would cause offence, that is, that they should avoid eating meat that had not been slaughtered in accordance with Jewish tradition. James' guidance echoes Leviticus 17 and 18, which sets out the behaviour required of the sojourner who lived in the Land with the Children of Israel.

Although he makes no reference to the decision of the Council of Jerusalem, the principle of showing respect for others is also found in Paul's first Epistle to the church in Corinth. The church was profoundly dysfunctional, although its members had little if any realization of the fact. It was riven with rivalries and disputes. In Corinthians, Paul addresses the issue of food which he describes as 'offered to idols'.[9] This was food offered for sale that had, in whole or part, passed through sacred rites in heathen religious establishments. Such food was prohibited to Jews, first, because it was tainted by idolatry, second, because it could not be assumed that tithes had been paid on it, third, if it was meat it would not have been slaughtered according to Jewish practice. In Corinth, there were undoubtedly travelling Jews who considered that Christians should observe the same prohibitions as Jews regarding the eating of food offered to idols, whereas there were also Christian Gnostics who claimed to possess spiritual knowledge and, because of it, had a freedom and authority to behave in accordance with this knowledge. Within a church that had endemic rivalries and divisions, it was necessary for Paul to provide clear guidance.

The issue was additionally complex because it was necessary for Paul to distinguish between the eating of such food and eating it in a specific context, which gave the act the significance of idolatry. Second, Paul had to balance the freedom of the individual Christian with the obligation to practise Christian love, which may on occasion lead to a person choosing to limit their own freedom, reasoning he develops in the following chapter. Paul concludes: 'Therefore, if food is a cause of [a Christian] falling, I will never eat meat, so that I may not cause one of them to [spiritually] fall',[10] thereby emphasizing that showing love and respect for another is more important than exercising one's own freedom of choice.[11]

Part 3: The present landscape

In her essay, Wendy raises the important issue of whether it is always possible or even desirable to show respect for those whose actions and opinions are extreme. In this part of my paper, I will provide a brief explanation of the theological context of the *Kairos Palestine* and *Kairos UK* documents, the World Council of Churches' Ecumenical Accompaniment Programme (EAPPI) and the recent decisions of the Churches in Britain, especially the Methodist Church, relating to Israel. What follows is the opposite of an apologetic. In no way would I seek to give support to actions and words which are distressing and hurtful to members of the Jewish community. While I believe there are times when it is necessary to be a 'critical friend', it is essential this comes out of a pre-existing relationship of respect and trust. Any guidance or advice must be offered with sensitivity, reflecting the complexities of the situation and acknowledging the different viewpoints that will be involved.

Wendy refers to Peter Colwell's paper, 'Jews and Christians: Is There Any Point in Continuing the Dialogue?'[12] In it he argues that one of the most significant changes within the churches in Britain over the last 50 years has been a shift from an at-best Euro-centric Christianity to an acknowledgement that the churches are part of a globalized faith. While church attendance in Britain is diminishing, in the Global South it is expanding exponentially. Two strands of development may be seen arising from this change of dynamic.

First was the emergence of liberation theology, which developed as a consequence of a change of emphasis at the Second Vatican Council of the Roman Catholic Church in 1965. At that council, the Church redefined its role from one of being a 'people of God' to becoming a body actively involved with the struggles of the poor. The Council rejected the position whereby the Church had aligned itself with powerful elites and, instead, affirmed the importance of challenging them and working for a more just world. When the bishops from Latin America returned home, the discussions at the Council provided the impetus for them to become more engaged in responding to the needs of the poor and oppressed in their own diocese. Consequently, a theological response, expressed in social action in support of the oppressed and the poor, developed. This became known as liberation theology. It arose from an understanding of the ways in which God had acted throughout the Hebrew Bible to liberate the Children of Israel from every form of oppression in order to create a more just society.[13] In addition to the account of God's salvation and loving-kindness for Israel in saving them from slavery in Egypt, liberation theologians also looked to passages such as Isaiah 61.1–4, the first two verses of which were read by Jesus in the synagogue in Nazareth.[14]

The cogent emphasis on Christianity as promoting liberation from the injustice and oppression that had developed in Latin America gave inspiration to Christians in South Africa opposed to the apartheid policies of the government. It provided the theological foundation for the *Kairos South Africa* document, first published in 1985. Christians in Palestine published a *Kairos Palestine* in 2009, which was followed by a response, *Kairos UK: A Time for Action*, which appeared in 2012.

We need to look at a radical shift in context. In Latin America, liberation theology was all about the churches themselves. It was active self-criticism often expressed by establishing new, reformed ecclesial communities. In South Africa, the signatories of *Kairos South Africa* were challenging apartheid policies held by the Dutch Reformed Church, the majority denomination in the country. Once again, the Church was urged to be consistent with its own teaching.[15]

The situation in regard to Palestine is fundamentally different. In 1990, the Sabeel Ecumenical Liberation Theology Center was established in Jerusalem. Sabeel is an ecumenical, grassroots liberation theology movement among Palestinian Christians. Inspired by the life and teaching of Jesus Christ, this liberation theology seeks to deepen the faith of Palestinian Christians, to promote unity among them toward social action. Fine in theory so far but the practice has had little to do with self-criticism. The NGO Monitor[16] has criticized Sabeel for its belief that 'Israel is solely culpable for the origin and continuation of the Israeli–Palestinian conflict', and for using 'anti-Semitic deicide imagery against Israel, and of disparaging Judaism as tribal, primitive, and exclusionary, in contrast to Christianity's universalism and inclusiveness'.[17]

In 2009, some Christian leaders in Palestine issued *Kairos Palestine: A Moment of Truth*. This they modelled on the *Kairos South Africa* document – but with a crucial distinction. It was not critical of Christianity but of Judaism as expressed by the State of Israel. It claimed that the Israeli occupation of Palestine was a 'sin against God' and against humanity and called on churches and Christians all over the world to consider it and adopt it and to call for the boycott of Israel. In section 7, *Kairos Palestine* calls for 'the beginning of a system of economic sanctions and boycott to be applied against Israel', arguing that isolation of Israel will cause pressure on Israel to abolish all of what it labels as 'apartheid laws' that discriminate against Palestinians and non-Jews. While the apartheid laws in South Africa categorized all people according to their perceived ethnic origin and imposed social, economic and political restrictions on those categorized as 'coloured' and 'black', the Constitution of Israel enshrines respect for members of all religions.

That fateful 2009 document gave impetus to a series of responses by Christians in the UK, for example the *Justice for Israel and Palestine* paper issued by the Methodist Church in 2010 and the publication of *Kairos UK: A Time for Action*.

The second development that Colwell identifies in his paper is that the Churches in the Global North realized that they needed to develop a greater emphasis on the needs of the Churches in the Global South in order to show support for the position of their co-religionists living in situations of poverty and oppression. One response was the World Council of Churches' (WCC) Ecumenical Accompaniment Programme for Israel and Palestine (EAPPI), launched in 2002, originally as part of the WCC 'Ecumenical Campaign to End the Illegal Occupation of Palestine:

WHAT DOES RESPECT BETWEEN PEOPLE OF FAITH MEAN?

Support a Just Peace in the Middle East'. The WCC delegated responsibility for the programme in the UK to Churches Together in Britain and Ireland. However, it is – significantly – administered by the Society of Friends (Quakers). The Quakers have an established and highly respected reputation for their work in care for the environment and pacifism which arises from their doctrine of realized eschatology.[18]

Both Christians and Jews understand the importance of having living witnesses – people who can testify with objectivity – to events. Both appreciate an unstinting quest for peace. EAPPI, however, is premised on the understanding that the 'occupation' by Israel is both illegal and harmful. It describes the aim as 'bringing internationals to the West Bank to experience life under occupation' and to 'provide protective presence to vulnerable communities, monitor and report human rights abuses and support Palestinians and Israelis working together for peace'.[19] The NGO Monitor states that 'often these activities instigate confrontation with Israeli settlers and the Israeli army'.[20] EAPPI members, known as 'Accompaniers', are located in the five places which the Programme has identified as being the most vulnerable for Palestinians: Yanoun, Tulkarm, Bethlehem, Hebron and Jayyous. The Accompaniers are, therefore, witnesses to events that happen in the five most challenging and sensitive areas. EAPPI, says the NGO Monitor, indulges in pejorative language, for example EAPPI 'consistently demonises Israel', making accusations of 'apartheid', 'war crimes' and 'Bantustans', and calls the security barrier 'evil'. It also considers that EAPPI 'presents a one-sided Palestinian narrative participating in activities commemorating the *Nakba*[21] and promoting the right of return [for all Palestinians]'. EAPPI ignores terror attacks against Israelis, blames Israel for the conflict and engages in boycotts, disinvestment and sanctions.

When the Accompaniers return they have the responsibility of giving talks to church groups and others about what they have witnessed. The Accompaniers use their own photographs and write their own scripts. In the UK, these talks have created enormous distress among the Jewish community, concern among some Christians because of their emotive and unbalanced content, and severe damage to Christian–Jewish relations. At least some of the concerns and distress that these talks cause could be alleviated if the Quakers monitored them to ensure that the language is sensitive rather than emotive, reflects the complexity of the situation in Israel and Palestine and does not express a single, Palestinian narrative. But even that largely misses the point. It fails all the tests that I have put forward for effective dialogue. It is completely without respect.

It is thoroughly disrespectful not least because of the shift of attention away from issues found in countries where Christianity is the dominant religion but about which the Church is silent. Jesus' parable of the mote and the beam is relevant. Too often the Church is quick to criticize the mote in the other's eye and ignores the beam in its own. Liberation theology began as a major reassessment by the Churches in South America of their own role in society – the alliance of church power with state power, ignoring the poor and dispossessed. They did exactly what David Gillett advises the Church to do in this country – start in your own backyard.[22] As I've already said, there was an apparent shift in South Africa but, once again, the critique was self-criticism – one group of Christians challenging the Dutch Reformed Church. The shift to condemning Israel as a pariah state to be sanctioned is colossal.

All this is deeply distressing for me because I have devoted my life to interfaith relations and been a member of the Methodist Church for over 20 years. At its 2009 Conference there was a notice of motion requesting the establishment of a Methodist working group to bring to Conference 2010 'a statement of the Methodist Church's position on Israel/Palestine'. The motion continued, indicating the direction the Report would take, that the working group

> should take into account past resolutions of Conference and international law ... including the Gaza War and Israeli incursions; the deteriorating conditions of occupation under which Palestinians are forced to live and their request for Christians in the West to visit them and to speak out on their behalf.

The last part makes implicit reference to EAPPI and Kairos Palestine.[23] When produced, the resulting paper was neither reasoned nor balanced. Instead it was written solely from a Palestinian perspective and illustrated by emotive case studies quoting EAPPI Accompaniers. Furthermore, the resolutions attached to the Report, all of which were agreed by the Conference, included:

1 'A call for Methodists to support and engage with a boycott of Israeli goods emanating from illegal settlements.'
2 Support for 'the Just Peace for Palestine initiative of the Amos Trust', which robustly advances a single, Palestinian narrative.
3 A direction to the Methodist Church as a matter of urgency 'to consider and develop further ways in which the Methodist Church of Great Britain and its people ... can work for an end to the Occupation, an end to the blockade of Gaza, adherence to international law by all sides and a just peace for all in the region'.

While the final resolution 'commended all the peoples of the region to the loving care of Almighty God', the Report caused unprecedented distress within the Jewish community. The Board of Deputies of British Jews responded that, in view of the contents of the Report, there could no longer be 'business as usual' between the Board and the Methodist Church. That relations were restored only six months later was because the Inter-Faith Relations Officers of the Board and the Methodist Church had a pre-existing relationship of trust and respect. Since then work has continued and made some progress. But the authors of the Report have not changed their viewpoint.[24]

Part 4: Conclusion

In reflecting on respect, I am reminded of the book *Games People Play*, which is a classic of transactional analysis.[25] Canadian-born psychoanalyst Eric Berne explains that in a person's transactions they may adopt the attitude of a child, an adult or a parent. The healthy transaction – and one that would be described as a respectful one – is where everyone adopts 'adult' behaviour. Unhealthy behaviour is when one person adopts a parental attitude forcing the other person to respond instinctively by adopting childlike behaviour. Adopting a superior, parental attitude is both unhelpful and disrespectful at all times. For a dialogue to be respectful it is necessary to:

1 Treat the other as an equal – both in ethical standing and in theology.
2 Listen to what the other person is saying and endeavour to hear it.
3 Understand what they mean by what they say.
4 Recognize the context in which they are speaking.
5 Respond with sensitivity and respect, adopting an adult manner.

If these five points are observed then even where something is said or written that is distressing, one can quietly and calmly – adopting the adult attitude suggested in Berne's model of transactional analysis – explain the reasons why it is distressing. My experience is that people who observe these principles of dialogue will respond in a respectful way by listening and trying to understand what is being said, even if they may not necessarily agree.

Notes

1 *Land of Promise? An Anglican Exploration of Christian Attitudes to the Holy Land, with Special Reference to Christian Zionism*, 2012, Network for Inter-Faith Concerns of the Anglican Church, pp. 9–22.

2 Alan Race, 1983, *Christians and Religious Pluralism*, London: SCM Press.

3 The Archbishop of Canterbury, Justin Welby, when asked why the Church of England did not support gay marriage in Anglican Churches, stated in a radio interview: 'The impact of [supporting gay marriages] on Christians in countries far from here like South Sudan, Pakistan, Nigeria and other places, would be absolutely catastrophic and we have to love them as much as the people who are here,' *i Newspaper*, 5 April 2014. Although this is tangential, it highlights sensitivities which have to be recognized if we are to take people along with us on a journey of deepening mutual understanding and respect.

4 Amy-Jill Levine, 2011, 'Common Errors Made about Early Judaism', in Amy-Jill Levine and Marc Zvi Brettler (eds.), *The Jewish Annotated New Testament*, Oxford: Oxford University Press, p. 503.

5 Further discussion of this may be found in Daniel Boyarin, 2012, *The Jewish Gospels: The Story of the Jewish Christ*, New York: The New Press, pp. 112–17.

6 In Acts 10.28 the phrase 'associate with' is a Greek word *kollasthai* meaning 'be glued together' – a strong association. In the LXX it is typically used to mean 'to cleave to'. Consequently there is the strong argument that in Acts 10.28 *kollasthai* means a really significant encounter that, in this context, may well indicate a meal. The word translated as 'Gentile' is the Greek word *allophulo*, meaning 'of another nation or tribe'. This is the only occasion it occurs in the New Testament, however in the LXX it is used most frequently with reference to the Philistines. It is therefore possible that its use refers to Gentile opposers/enemies/oppressors – which even a 'god-fearing' Roman centurion would be – rather than 'all non-Jews'.

7 An explanation for the apparent contradiction may be found with reference to the Greek text. In Acts 10.28, *athemiton*, meaning unlawful, criminal, wicked is used, not *anomos*. In other words, Paul may be referring to a *minhag*, or established custom, not a mitzvah or divine commandment. However, I am also aware that there may have been a ban on table fellowship between Jews and Gentiles, even if all the food served by the Gentile host was *kasher*.

8 Acts 10.35.

9 1 Corinthians 8.4.

10 1 Corinthians 8.13.

11 See also Paul's Epistle to the Romans, particularly 14.1–4 and 15.1–6.

12 Peter Colwell, 2013, 'Jews and Christians: Is There Any Point in Continuing the Dialogue?', *Common Ground*, Summer, pp. 3–4.

13 Although a small minority of people advocated outward force, for example Gustavo Gutiérrez, liberation theology was predominantly a pacifist theology that understood care for the poor as an expression of their personal Bible-based spirituality. See Gustavo Gutiérrez, 2010, *Theology of Liberation*, London: SCM Classics.

14 Luke 4.18–19.

15 The Dutch Reformed Church subsequently repented of the ways in which their theology had been interpreted in order to justify the racist policies known as apartheid.

16 Based in Jerusalem. Non-governmental organization founded in 2002, producing critical analysis and reports on the work of both international and local NGO networks.

17 www.ngo-monitor.org.

18 Realized eschatology is the doctrine that eschatological passages in the New Testament do not refer to the future but to the ministry of Jesus and his legacy. Quakers have a biblical vision of *shalom* in the Hebrew Scriptures, for example Isaiah 2.4 and 11.6–7, and of *eirene* in the Christian Scriptures, for example Revelation 21.1–6, which is the renewal of all things in which God's realm comes to earth. However, Quakers see the vision of the realization of the new creation and the overlapping of heaven and earth as pointing to a non-violent process in which the spirit of evil was destroyed and God's *shalom* was established on earth.

19 www.eappi.org.

20 www.ngo-monitor.org.

21 *Nakba* or catastrophe is the Arabic term for the displacement of Palestinians during the 1948 war.

22 *Supra* p. 103.

23 The Notice of Motion also stated that the proposer and seconder must be members of the Working Party. Consequently the Revd Nicola Jones, who is a trustee of Sabeel, and Dr Stephen Leah, Chair of the York branch of the Palestinian Solidarity Campaign, were both members of the Working Party.

24 No notices of motion on Israel/Palestine have subsequently been passed by Methodist Conference. Significantly, the organization Methodist Friends of Judaism is independent of the Methodist Church in Britain. See www.methodist.org.uk/mission/public-issues/peacemaking/israel-palestine.

25 Eric Berne, 2010, *Games People Play: The Psychology of Human Relationships*, London: Penguin.

Further Reflections

TONY BAYFIELD

Back in the 1970s, I was a young, innocent congregational rabbi in north-west Surrey. It was a new community in an area unfamiliar with Jews. A considerable amount of my time was spent giving talks to schools and colleges, voluntary organizations and church groups, most often C of E – this was quintessentially middle-class England. On one occasion, looking for the local Mothers' Union, I got to within striking distance of my destination but needed further directions from a passer-by. She looked at me quizzically and asked, 'Are you the Rabbi?' I smiled encouragingly and said, 'Yes.' She stared at me, then uttered the words, 'Not what I expected, not what I expected at all,' and walked off, leaving me none the wiser as to the whereabouts of the Mothers' Union meeting.

Some years later I reflected that what I did for more than a decade was to act as the North-West Surrey Synagogue's image consultant. Most members were not much interested in getting to know about Christianity – they'd learned, they believed, all they needed to know in school RE lessons which, as Joy Barrow implies, were bereft of multicultural influence. But the congregation did have a strong vested interest in deploying me, a short but otherwise normal-looking university graduate, to confound Jewish stereotypes and their malign effects.

Gradually, I became bored with the superficiality of the work and wanted a deeper engagement with the people I was talking at. It was then that my interest in interfaith dialogue began. I was able to find some members of my small community prepared to meet and talk with local Christians – both Anglican and Catholic. By the time of leaving Weybridge to return to the North West London ghetto in 1983, I'd had some experience of what might legitimately be called dialogue. As I was later to write, what struck me was not so much what was said as what was left unsaid. I was clear that many of the Christians both 'professional' and 'lay' were thinking: You Jews are really interesting. You certainly know how to maintain Jewish life through family and community and there's no doubt about the quality of your chopped liver and chicken soup. It's just such a pity you're missing out on the Greatest Truth of all.

WHAT DOES RESPECT BETWEEN PEOPLE OF FAITH MEAN?

My congregants' thoughts were a mirror image: It's the faith of these Christians that's so remarkable, particularly in this day and age. They really do believe, pray and practise self-sacrificing love. But how can they believe such incredible stories, all based on a ridiculous misunderstanding of the life of a rather unremarkable Jew?

What struck me then and has motivated me ever since is how disrespectful both thought-portraits are. What prompted the project expressed by this book is the search for a theology that is able to accommodate the existential reality of the faith of both communities.[1] It's the need to expose what true respect means for the reconstruction of relationships between Jews and Christians that makes Wendy and Joy's contributions so important in this dialogue.

I love what Wendy has to say. She approaches the subject with all the necessary skills but seemingly unburdened by a surfeit of academic research papers which can lead – certainly in my case – to leaden thinking and diversionary issues. As her mother exemplified, respect should be instinctive not politely qualified by the unstated. Take the wonderful sentence early on in the essay – respect is 'about the weight of honour that accompanies the individual in our relationships with them and the balancing weight of respect that we are obliged to give them'.[2] Respect means honouring, giving weight to the other to the extent that it balances the honour due to us. There's no qualification. It isn't limited to Jews. It extends to our neighbour and all that's symbolized by their day of rest, their Sabbath, and is rooted in a *religious* understanding of the human being. We are not the currency of the State. We are not, as the Chicago School of economics would have it, capable of a valuation by reason of our economic productivity.[3] We are the currency of God, each different and equal in our inestimable value. That cuts through the labyrinth of doctrine and provides us with the place from which the reconstruction of our theology of 'our most significant other'[4] must start. We are all descended from the same parents; no one can say my lineage is superior to yours – we are all worthy of respect without reservation, expressed or hidden.

For me, however, what's most inspiring about Wendy Fidler's contribution is that, unlike most of the rest of us, she has the honesty and integrity to point out that Jews – and, though she's too kind to say so, Christians – can't manage to respect each other let alone the other in this dialogue. She reminded me that this book is – as for Joy – rooted in the intra-faith as well as the interfaith experience.

From my return to North West London in 1983 to my 'retirement' at the end of 2010 I became involved in intra-communal relations. My commitment was much influenced by my relationship with Jonathan

Sacks. We were undergraduates at Cambridge together[5] and formed a friendship, maintained – against the odds – throughout our professional careers. At the very least, we strove to introduce civility, eliminate public denigration and establish mechanisms for cross-communal collaboration. But I reached the same conclusion as Wendy and Joy: what can respect mean if it doesn't include an acceptance of the other for who they are, not deviant versions of ourselves but women and men to be valued like ourself, in the way that God values each individual person in God's creation?

Joy, though a 'professional', shares with Wendy a life devoted to working at the 'coalface'. Nothing is allowed to stand in the way of what experience has taught her – that other faiths are precisely that, other faiths, equally demanding respect. That respect requires knowledge – not knowledge that comes from theory or academic study alone but knowledge that comes from experience. That experience in turn teaches sensitivity and a recognition that we aren't all standing in the same place. We cannot always confront and challenge but we are obliged to support the journey of the other into and through this complex and challenging postmodern, multicultural society.

In many ways, Wendy and Joy's starting points are very different and that explains why they don't seem to have engaged with each other as closely as some other pairs. Joy, in particular, has an extraordinarily difficult road to walk – disclosed in the last part of her paper – which, in the last analysis, only she can walk.

When I heard Joy give the first version of her paper to the Group, there were sharp intakes of breath among her Christian colleagues at the way she deployed the texts which constitute the material for the middle section of her essay. 'That's not what the text means'; 'I'll point you in the direction of the latest scholarship.' It was very understandable and how I responded until I was reminded of the Jewish tradition of commentary, so powerfully embraced by Alex Wright. What Joy demonstrates triumphantly is that all texts are open to commentary, all can speak to the present and all can and should be read in a respectful manner – even texts which are usually understood as emerging from a fierce Jewish–Christian polemic, a struggle between the Christian and Jewish siblings.

The final section of Joy's essay brought tears to my eyes – tears of gratitude and recognition of her courage. Her own Methodist Church, to which she has devoted her life, has fallen into the terrible trap of rejecting its Jewish sibling by treating it as a deviant twin rather than a sibling with its own separate identity. That identity includes, in this instance, a commitment to Land which is justified pragmatically, morally, historically, legally and theologically.[6] To enter the political fray against one's sibling is a very different thing from defending the poor, the needy and the oppressed. Joy makes that distinction crystal clear. One can or, rather, one is obliged to respect one's sibling *as well as* respecting those whom the complexities of history and international politics marginalize and victimize.

If respect is to mean anything in interfaith dialogue, it has to encompass the *faith* of the other. Respect isn't a matter of etiquette but a requirement of theology – both Jewish and Christian theologies and the theology of dialogue. Not least, it follows from a rejection of absolutism and leads directly to our two final pairings.

Notes

1 While I rest my conviction on having worked with Christians whose faith, to quote American Jewish theologian Eugene B. Borowitz, 'I could palpably feel and share', the same conviction would appear to be present in early Rabbinic Judaism. A text in the Babylonian Talmud *B'rakhot* 58a demands the recitation of almost identical blessings on seeing the sages of Israel and non-Jewish sages: 'Blessed be the One who has given (a portion) of God's wisdom to those who fear God.'

2 *Supra* p. 210.

3 The founder of the Chicago School, who died in 2014, was the Nobel Laureate Gary Becker (as it happens, Jewish). Becker's ultra-rationalist approach attempts to calculate the value of human beings and human transactions in free-market terms. The purchase by a productive American of a kidney from a poor Brazilian from a Rio favela can be regarded as a justifiable transaction even at a price lower than that which would enable the Brazilian to buy the health care required by the increased risk of having only one kidney.

4 Archbishop Williams' description of Judaism, justifying the bilateral focus of CCJ, in a discussion at a meeting of CCJ Presidents at Lambeth Palace *c.* 2006.

5 Lord Sacks studied a Jewishly suspicious subject, Philosophy. I was the proper Jew, studying Law!

6 *Infra* p. 321.

7
Christian Particularity

Incarnation and Trinity

PATRICK MORROW

Prologue: What this chapter is not

One of the great privileges of my life has been to play some small but real part in Jewish–Christian rapprochement, often starting with its painful history. I need to explain that this essay is not an attempt to think of our interrelationship overall. It is not a primer on 'What Jews need to know about Christians and Christianity'. Still less, of course, is it an attempt to convert Jews to Jesus.

Even today what Jews most need to hear from Christians is that we are penitent, we have embraced and do embrace *t'shuvah*. We have looked at our history. We know something of the *Adversus Judaeos* tradition of the Church Fathers (spiritual writings 'Against the Jews'). We know of the belittling, discrimination, expulsions, lies, Crusades and pogroms that often seemed as natural as breathing to our own ancestors. We know how the Shoah took place in Christian Europe and that the anti-Judaism of the Church was one resource (not the only one) on which racial anti-Semitism drew. In our theology, we know of the traditions of supersessionism or replacement theology which treated the Jews as abandoned by God, as carnal, sinful 'Christ-killers', such that all the blessings of the Bible are transferred to the Church, while the curses remain for the Jews, now outside the covenant. There are other stories, of course, alongside this history, of Christian admiration for Jews – and not only as Hebrew teachers. There was some resistance to the dominant position. Furthermore, much repentance has been in evidence especially since the Shoah – but not enough and not universally.

Such things would need saying in any general-purpose introduction to Christian self-understanding. But all of that is for elsewhere (including other chapters in this collection, of course). My purpose has been much more limited and focused. It has been to reflect on Christian particularity – and on the hard case, rather than where revisionist theology has won the day. I am not dismissing the latter; liberal–liberal dialogue can yield much good fruit for us all. Nevertheless, I have taken my assignment to mean the full-blown creedal orthodox teaching on incarnation and Trinity, especially the former, as the latter flows from it. This represents my own journey, from (arguably!) a liberal Christian first to an utterly confused one who stopped going to church and went to synagogue for a year, then to one who describes himself as a small-o orthodox Christian (I am and remain an Anglican) – though I still go to synagogue when I can!

Setting the scene

> We believe ... in one Lord Jesus Christ, the only-begotten Son of God, begotten of the Father before all worlds, Light of Light, very God of very God, begotten not made, of one being/essence/substance with the Father, by whom all things were made, who, for us human beings and for our salvation, came down from heaven and was incarnate by the Holy Spirit of the Virgin Mary, and was made a human being ... And in the Holy Spirit, the Lord the Giver of Life, who proceeds from the Father, who with the Father and the Son together is worshipped and glorified, who spoke by the prophets.
>
> (From the Creed from the Council of Constantinople, 381 CE, based on the Creed of the Council of Nicaea, 325 CE)

> [Jesus Christ is] one and the same Son, the same perfect in Godhead, the same perfect in Humanity, truly God and truly a Human Being ... in two natures without confusion, without change, without division, without separation.
>
> (From the Definition of the Council of Chalcedon, 451 CE)

It is a commonplace, both within and without interfaith dialogue, to see these creedal claims as elaborate and unhelpful philosophical abstraction. But they are reflected in mainstream Christian liturgical worship, daily: 'Glory to the Father, and to the Son, and to the Holy Spirit'. And, while many a Christian–Jewish discussion begins with the historical Jesus of Nazareth, as a Pharisee or proto-Rabbi or Hasid, if it always stops there, there may come a point when Jews wonder if they are actually engaging with authentic Christianity.[1] This chapter will take the narrower way and equate Christian particularity with developed orthodoxy – fourth rather than first century.[2] Readers for whom this seems self-defeating for dialogical purposes are asked to treat it as an experiment in what an orthodox–orthodox encounter, within the wider dialogue, might be.[3]

Let us spell out what Christian orthodoxy (hereafter 'orthodoxy') means. Within this orthodoxy it is axiomatic that Jesus is 'Gd',[4] indeed wholly Gd (not a demi-god), but is not the whole of Gd. This is a distinction between *totus Deus* and *totum Dei*. The Son is not the Father, nor the Spirit. The three Persons are alike in all things, save their mutual relations. If, instead, they were held to have different roles, then the door would be open to modalism (Gd is one Person, with three different hats) or tritheism (Gd is a team of three). Both of these things the Fathers of the Councils were very clear they wished to avoid. So the 'Persons' (*hypostases/personae*) are not persons as we understand human persons to be, with distinguishable personalities, histories etc.; they are in 'perichoretic' unity, meaning mutual interpenetration, co-inherence or indwelling. In this way, it is maintained that Gd is One, the insistence being on the oneness of uniqueness,[5] not number.

The claims of orthodoxy are more audacious still. For it is held that these statements are, at heart, in spite of their linguistic and philosophical sophistication, consonant with the story of Jesus, as told in the canonical Gospels, and ultimately even in history. It is not that Jesus thought of things this way. The Gospels have little to say about Jesus' 'inner life'. Jesus, as a human being, like us in all things save sin, would have knowledge only as formed by his historical context. And how many human beings, however wise, can claim more than a morsel of true self-knowledge?

Nevertheless (so the claim goes) the creeds 'do justice' to Jesus. They allow to grow what is there in embryo in the New Testament. In other words, even if this is not often 'admitted', of the four Gospels, a special place is given to John. This Jews may regret, given how the text has functioned in history as spelled out in Michael Hilton's paper.[6] Nevertheless, John's 'high Christology' is determinative. It is through John that we have the two ancient ways of naming the Persons of the Trinity combined: (a) Father, Son, Spirit and (b) Gd (or *Arche*/Source), Word, Spirit.

How can such Christian orthodoxy be a resource, rather than an embarrassment, to Christians in dialogue with Jews? Only by locating it within its historical context, to see what it is reacting against. As well as emergent Rabbinic Judaism,[7] this was the religion or family of religions that come under the heading 'Hellenism'. My claim is that, while the creeds are often spoken of as 'the Hellenization of Christianity', they might instead be thought of as the 'Christianization of Hellenism'.[8] Inasmuch as that has validity, it follows that we can even speak of them as 'Hebraicization of Hellenism', transplanting Hebrew ideas into admittedly alien soil. In particular, this means that the irreducibly Personal nature of Gd gives sacred dignity to human beings as persons. But that is to rush ahead.

First, it is important to own that the claims of orthodoxy are not themselves revelation. Jesus Christ is (in his person) the revelation of

Gd, Christians believe. Orthodox doctrines emerged within contingent human history. 'What would have happened if Christianity had flourished principally east of the Holy Land?' people ask legitimately. The creeds are indeed bound up with particular controversies which might not have happened. Of course, that they are time-and-place-bound does not mean they can be dropped without loss. Contingent human history can be the means by which important context-transcending truths are brought to light.

Second, it is even more important to give a defence of orthodoxy to its cultured despisers, to those who would see any orthodoxy as necessarily absolutist, arrogant, arbitrary and wilfully blind to modern awareness of history and science. For this, it is necessary to expose as a false dichotomy language as 'literal' and 'factual' versus 'symbolic' and 'metaphorical'. On the one hand, all language is drenched in metaphor.[9] On the other, language which is only ever the interplay of linguistic symbols is not worth getting out of a (real) bed for!

Certainly, the Church Fathers did not think they were making 'literal' statements about Gd. On the contrary, they – perhaps supremely the fourth-century Cappadocian Fathers – are Christians' principal source of the apophatic or negative theological tradition, which says what Gd is not.[10] They would no doubt have embraced the *kiv'yakhol* of the Rabbis, 'as if such a thing were possible', well aware that positive language about Gd works, at best, analogically.[11] The 'we believe' (*pisteuomen*) of the creeds means more 'we place our trust in' and commit to behaving accordingly than 'we have worked out that'. Thus it is not wholly different from the Hebrew root *aleph-mem-nun*, which gives us *emunah*, faithfulness, as in Genesis 15.6, *he'emin b'Adonai*, Abram trusted in Gd.

However, in saying this, we have not said all that needs to be said. For orthodoxy does believe one can articulate some things about Gd which are authentic. They celebrate, though never capture, something about Gd and Gd's nature. Were this impossible – were every statement about Gd always only *kiv'yakhol* all the way down – then, indeed, we would be agnostics. Then everything called 'revelation' would actually relate wholly and exclusively to the community, would be ultimately indistinguishable from the community addressing its own needs, ideals and impulses, just partly in narrative form. There may be much edification in the message, but the Messenger has wholly disappeared from view,[12] is a blank X, about which nothing can be said. Such an X is not only philosophically but also existentially redundant. Now, this agnosticism is clearly a valid religious option but it has costs.

This is to distinguish between two meanings of 'agnosticism', which are mutually exclusive. On the one hand, there is *devout agnosticism* which, on theological grounds, recognizes that Gd's fullness is beyond language and experience. It will be so eternally: it is not a result of the current smallness of our brains; it is of the essence of Gd to be beyond. On the other hand, there is what I should call *ideological agnosticism*. This is the conviction – the word fits – that Gd-as-Gd cannot in any sense be known, met with, or speak. There is no reason to think that this latter agnosticism is more 'humble' than any other ideology.

All of this may play out quite differently within our two faiths. In our discussions, we have asked repeatedly: must a Jew believe anything?[13] The majority report has been that a Jew need not. It is belonging, and acting in ways consonant with belonging – variously understood – which count. But this distinction in turn must not be overplayed. For committed Jewish communities must be operating and reflecting on the rationale for their commitment at one level of consciousness and explicitness or another, and that rationale typically has something to do with Gd or at least the character known as 'Gd'. And the impression must not be given that Christianity is based on 'doctrine alone'. Many Christians, no less than Jews, relate to formal claims by believing, half-believing, wondering, trusting, hoping, questioning and despairing yet somehow still feeling connected. To be baffled yet still intrigued by the patterning of Christian faith has been the raw material of many saints.

However critical one might be of Christian creedal claims, they should not be presented as some dull gentrification or fossilization of the exciting message of the Nazarene or his immediate followers. They were forged in the furnace of passionate controversy, mutual anathemas and worse. Indeed, the life-and-death concern of the Fathers – and, yes, those who come to be labelled as 'heretics' – was: how can we know we are avoiding idolatry? For the Fathers, like the Rabbis, recognized that idolatry is not only worship of an alien god, but also worship of the true Gd in alien fashion.[14] I should like to honour the passion of the debate by presenting the development of orthodoxy as the clash of different characters.

Dramatis personae

Jesus of Nazareth

The discussions with my dialogue partners have brought home to me how Christians really do start with Jesus Christ. It is not that we have doctrines of Messiah-hood, the eschatological age, resurrection power, the transcendence or immanence of Gd, or the nature of Gd's unity, over against which we measure Jesus, finding him to fit. Rather, it is 'the Christ event' itself to which we return over and over, to seek out those patterns of thought and speech which rightly celebrate truth.[15]

We can be blunt about this: this is a radical difference between Judaism and Christianity. I have heard the claim made that there is an analogy with the rebbe of a Hasidic community, understood to be Gd's gift to the people, who speaks through the Holy Spirit. 'Surely some of Rebbe Nahman of Bratzlav's expressions about his own uniqueness can be said to have a family resemblance with some of Jesus' sayings in John.'[16] But while the rebbe is an authority figure who can comment on the revelation at Sinai, he is not one who, like Jesus for Christians, is revelation itself[17] and can at least in some ways de facto relativize the prior revelation at Sinai.

This is a foundational position, a necessarily circular argument: Jesus is revelation because revelation is Jesus. It does not, however, commit me to a narrow, exclusivist interpretation of biblical sayings such as, 'I am the way, and the truth, and the life. No one comes to the Father except through me.'[18] Nor need I portray Jesus as uniquely good, set against a backdrop of shabby imperfection. Jesus may *not* be – according to the logic of the case – the greatest wonder-worker, nor the first liberal, or liberator. The claim is only that in his person, and in the pattern of relationships he begins, he brings in the messianic 'difference' (however that is understood).

In the Gospel accounts, this 'difference' does have real content, which either is or includes Jesus' own 'resurrection'. Jesus is raised to newness of life. This is more like a new creation than a resuscitation. It is a mystery which can never be explained and which may well baffle Jews. It is the beginning of the messianic age, and the age to come, and the vindication of the character of the mortal Jesus.

What to make of this? First, the assertion that Jesus is the first fruits of the resurrection age[19] at least reminds us that both classical Rabbinic Judaism and Christianity believe in a general resurrection at the culmination of history.[20] Second, even cynical historians tend to recognize that soon after the shameful death of their founder, the disciples emerge as energized and confident, such that we might say that at least metaphorically they met with new life. Third, differently but still pertinently, Pinchas Lapide, the Israeli diplomat and historian,[21] goes so far as to say that Jesus might be among those who evade or transcend death, after the manner of Elijah and Enoch.[22] For him, this would not threaten his Orthodox Jewish convictions; it would simply be one of the surprising things Gd does, in this case for the Gentiles. For Christians, however, it is foundational. Again, no evidence can be brought to justify this; it is a properly circular argument on which faith is founded.

But, if Jesus' resurrection marks 'the Eighth Day' of creation (as has often been claimed),[23] unlike the first, it comes at great cost, the cost bearing the name 'cross'. Orthodoxy has never committed itself to one understanding of the meaning of the cross. A crude version of substitutionary atonement, whereby the Son had to die to avert the anger of the vengeful Father, cannot ultimately be held within orthodoxy. It seems to imagine the Persons of the Trinity as different personalities. My emphasis is on the cross as the locus of revelation of the human condition. This means we all – all persons – find ourselves within the narrative of the Passion, as deliberately treacherous or culpably negligent, treating other people as expendable, and so on. The message of resurrection is not that good people are rewarded with a second life but that Gd stays faithful to faithless humanity, no matter what, bearing the price for that faithlessness.

So the Christian story has an irreducible element of tragedy. What is wrong with us is not simply lack of willpower or knowledge; the distortion of the will runs all the way down. This, I should contend, is the core meaning of 'original sin'.[24] The distortion normally leads to violence in one form or another – whether to other, self, truth, imagination, etc. Hence the symbol of the cross fits. If, as is often claimed, Jews not only reject any notion of 'original sin' but see the *yetzer hara* as a drive which includes selfishness, but is also the necessary spur to survival and creativity,[25] then it seems to me here is a second radical difference between Christians and Jews. Aquinas is one Christian who insists that our problem is we are not selfish enough: we do not sufficiently will our own happiness but, more usually, act out of fear, habit, compulsion, spite etc.[26] The cross shows us this with perpetual force, never as sheer condemnation, but always as an invitation to repentance.

The Hebrew Scriptures

The second 'character' I bring is the Hebrew Bible itself and, in particular, its portrayal of Gd. For these purposes, the timing of the completion of the canon is not crucial, nor whether the Masoretic or the Septuagint is the more reliable. Rather, what matters is that there were honoured collections of texts, some time before Jesus, in which YHWH has a/the leading role.

Some things can and must be said about this YHWH, which may seem too obvious to mention, but which in fact bear great weight. The first is that Gd is Creator. Gd creates *ex nihilo*. Gd is not compelled to create but chooses to create. Gd creates out of sheer freedom, love and delight, not need. This is not wholly dependent on Genesis 1, where indeed *tohu vavohu* – whatever they are – may be pre-existent; it draws even more on passages from Isaiah, Psalms and Job.

Second, Gd as Creator is also free to interact within creation. However Gd is transcendent – and as free Creator of this and every possible universe, Gd must be transcendent – it is not the sort of transcendence which inhibits Gd from choosing to be an agent in the world, one who can 'speak' and 'act'. Bringing these together means we must think of Gd as Personal, as Person. More precisely, this is less wrong than treating Gd as impersonal. For Gd to be an agent within the world in any sense must involve some divine self-limiting, condescension or *kenosis* (self-emptying). I do not wish to rush to use Christian language, but do not see how it can be wholly avoided. This we see perhaps most clearly in Hosea, who considers it entirely appropriate – necessary even – to portray Gd as hurt, cuckolded husband.

Others saw – and see – things differently. Now, no less than then, the idea that Gd is intimate Creator and Friend and can speak and has indeed spoken at a historic moment (or moments) is counter-intuitive to many spiritually minded persons. Yet these things are the common sense of the Hebrew Scriptures[27] such that when they are absent (famously, in Esther), the absence is striking.

Second Temple Judaism

I treat Second Temple Judaism as a character in its own right, only to make a twofold denial. This Judaism is not (quite) that of the Hebrew Scriptures.[28] It is not (quite) that of the Rabbis. There is the broad point that as long as the Temple stood, the idea that transcendent Gd can be localized, by Gd's free choice, would have had intrinsic plausibility. But there is the yet more important point that of those days one might – and many scholars do – speak of Judaisms, plural, or Judaism at its most variegated.[29]

The American Jewish scholar Daniel Boyarin is but one among many who insist that in Jesus' day not a few Jews were waiting for a saviour figure to come down from heaven.[30] This is based on his reading of Daniel 7, where 'an Ancient One' gives 'one like a son of man ... dominion and glory and kingship, that all peoples, nations and languages should serve him'.[31] He notes:

> From the earliest layers of interpretation and right up to modern times, some interpreters have deemed the 'one like a son of man' a symbol of a collective, namely the faithful Israelites at the time of the Maccabean revolt ... Other interpreters have insisted that the '[one like a] son of man' is a second divine figure alongside the Ancient of Days.[32]

Boyarin presents the extra-biblical First Enoch and Fourth Ezra as offering supporting evidence.[33] In the former, Enoch has a vision of 'the son of man' whose identity resolves into being that of Enoch himself: 'This book provides us with our most explicit evidence that the Son of Man as a divine-human Redeemer arose by *Jesus' time* from reading the Book of Daniel.'[34] In these and in other ways, Boyarin seeks to back up his premise:

> I wish us to see that Christ too – the divine Messiah – is a Jew. Christology, or the early ideas about Christ, is also a Jewish discourse and not – until much later – an anti-Jewish discourse at all. Many Israelites at the time of Jesus were expecting a Messiah who would be divine and come to earth in the form of a human. Thus the basic underlying thoughts from which both the Trinity and the incarnation grew are there in the very world into which Jesus was born and in which he was first written about in the Gospels.[35]
>
> The great innovation of the Gospels is only this: to declare that the Son of Man is here already [as Jesus].[36]

I make no pretence to have made Boyarin's case for him; I have merely outlined it. But my purpose is correspondingly small, namely to insist that to reject all ideas of the descent and incarnation of a heavenly figure, in intimate relationship with a divine Father, as necessarily and wholly Gentile and pagan is problematic. I put it no more strongly than that. It is the case that Rabbinic Judaism comes over time to reject these ideas and insist that the Messiah is an exceptional political and religious man only, as Natan Levy will show, citing Maimonides.[37] Daniel has long been relegated to the Writings. Nevertheless, in the days when Jews were first making sense of Jesus, these patterns of thought were available. For all they were controversial, yet were they considered Jewish.

Rabbinic Judaism

The Judaism of the Rabbis is different again. Historians today are clearer than they were that Rabbinic Judaism was often in dialogue – virtual/threatened/promised and real – with emergent Christianity. The two faiths, over several centuries, come to define themselves over against each other,[38] which in turn means they continue to influence each other substantially.[39]

Through the dialogue I have learned more about the complex relationship between aggadah and halakhah, the stories from which teaching that might be called 'theology' is drawn, and the practical outworking of the given commandments. Bluntly, no account of the right relationship between *mitzvot* and story, praxis and theology would satisfy all Jewish dialogue partners (and why should it?). On the one hand, it is the case that contemporary British Orthodoxy defines itself by one cardinal belief, namely in *Torah min HaShamayim*, that Gd revealed the whole of Torah miraculously at Sinai. This may be thought to require secondary beliefs, for example, in the trustworthiness of the idea of divine–human communication. But this inference has been disputed and the insistence has been strong that, this notwithstanding, it is and remains the practice which is primary. There is no aggadah which an observant Jew must 'believe'.[40] The Mishnah does not begin with an eloquent account of Gd and creation, but with the question about the timing of the evening recital of the Sh'ma. I want to take this seriously.

For those who do want to attend to reflection on possible rationales for halakhah, there is a strong component within Rabbinic Judaism which takes seriously the principle of Gd's condescension – self-limiting – to be, as it were, with us. It takes two forms. First, the focus which begins with Rabbi Akiva and his School on the *Sh'khinah*, the Divine Presence who goes into exile with Israel and feels what Israel feels. This contrasts with the opposing School of Rabbi Ishmael for whom God is wholly disinterestedly transcendent.[41] Second, it is reflected in the Rabbinic interpretation of Deuteronomy 29.11–14 which arrogates to the Rabbis their right to interpret Torah, the interpretation being on their mouths and in their hearts. Jeremy has already quoted the text from the Talmud[42] where Rabbi Eliezer is in dispute with his peers about a point of halakhah. In spite of Eliezer being able to align his view with miracles, and even a Heavenly Voice confirming that he is right, his peers respond that the word is not in heaven and that the majority are right to decide. Gd, we are told, laughs and says: 'My children have beaten me.'

Again, my point is a modest, negative one: it is not the case within the classic Rabbinic frame that Gd's transcendence is incompatible with Gd's involvement with us, including Gd's self-limitation to the situations of the Jewish people. Gd (Creator) and humanity (creatures) are not in all ways opposites. To put it bluntly, reading the texts of classical Rabbinic Judaism reveals the closeness of Christianity and Rabbinic Judaism on this point better than reading Maimonides and his Aristotelian view of divinity.

Hellenism

The Gospels present the focus of Jesus' earthly ministry on his own people, Israel. Newer readings of Paul suggest compellingly that Paul envisioned a Church where Jewish believers in Jesus would still 'own' their Judaism in circumcision, dietary rules and Shabbat, while Gentiles would follow

INCARNATION AND TRINITY

a Christ-centred version of what came to be called the Noahide laws.[43] But this Pauline project failed. In the space of a couple of centuries a burning question within the Christian community was not: 'Must the Gentile believers keep the Torah?' but, 'Are Jewish believers permitted to keep Torah?'[44] This we can see as a tragedy. Indeed, it may be the single biggest failure of the Church. But Gd is capable of bringing good things out of failure, out of sin, and Gentile Christianity (strictly, Christianity which understands itself as Gentile) may be seen as Gd-blessed failure.

The Church as a growing, Gentile phenomenon was destined to engage with the dominant Gentile religious school, namely Hellenism. This had two complexly interwoven strands. One was a monism which looked back to Plato. According to this, the universe is a simple harmony and the cosmos has rules which are unchanging, derived ultimately from abstract and pure forms. There may be – are – gods of various descriptions but these gods themselves must obey the laws and will be pulled into line if they seek to rebel. It follows that Being Itself is impersonal and wills nothing. The art forms of this Hellenism, tellingly, are sculpture, where shapes may seem to be alive but are not, and the theatre, where humans, as masks (*personae*), may seem to be choosing courses of action but are, in fact, following a set plot where the final resolution is predetermined.[45]

The other strand is dualism. According to dualism, matter is a side-effect or error at best and evil at worst. What is most real and good is Spirit or Intelligence or nous, pure reason. Matter is either the result of some lesser being's error or the result of some emanation (dilution) upon emanation of Spirit. There is a necessary ontological gulf between Spirit and matter. The best creatures can hope for is the escape of the spiritual spark within us, out of the body of corruptible matter. Gnosticism is the major form of this dualism, positing a *gnosis* (knowledge) which sets out how some – the elite – may achieve such a release. Greek-born Eastern Orthodox Metropolitan Zizioulas summarizes:

> To answer the question about the being of God, during the patristic period, was not easy. The greatest difficulty stemmed from ancient Greek ontology which was fundamentally monistic: the being of the world and the being of God formed, for the ancient Greeks, an unbreakable unity ... while biblical faith proclaimed God to be absolutely free with regard to the world. The Platonic conception of the creator God did not satisfy the Fathers ... because the doctrine of creation from pre-existing matter limited divine freedom. So it was necessary to find an ontology that avoided the monistic Greek philosophy as much as the 'gulf' between God and the world taught by the gnostic systems – the other great danger of this period.[46]

The drama

All the characters are now in place. Christians in the emerging Church held:

1. To Jesus as both historically real and of cosmic importance, thus sanctifying human history as the site of divine encounter.
2. To the faith of the Hebrew Scriptures, according to which, Gd – Creator – is free, personal, and able and willing to be, as it were, an agent in the world. Gd speaks and acts.
3. To some interpretation of the more mystical elements of the Hebrew Scriptures, literature and trends of Second Temple Judaism, such that, staying within a broadly Jewish frame, it might be thinkable that Jesus is some sort of divine 'son of man'.
4. To a belief shared with the Jewish Sages in the dignity granted to all humankind as made in the image of Gd, such that Gd and humanity are not opposites in a binary system.

Christianity needed to secure these beliefs against Hellenism. This meant a conceptual and ecclesial battle. Hellenism, for its part, rejected all ideas of the Ultimate as immediately involved with human beings. It would offend the dignity of Transcendence to have directly to do with flesh/matter, which is subject to distinctly un-divine processes like circumstance, chance, decay and death.

My claim is that the way the Church found to ground its insistence on the closeness of Gd, which – let me stress – they had already determined could be identified with Jesus Christ,[47] was to insist that he himself *was* Gd, in one of his two natures. Anything else would be and was heard as saying he was 'like Gd', in a way which actually meant the opposite, stretching 'likeness' out of recognition. For it would mean that he, not being truly Gd, was ultimately 'unlike Gd', just a pale reflection, as pale as can be, as that is all that matter can bear. The most pervasively challenging version of this – Arianism – held that Jesus was the first creature, created outside of time who, being so much more glorious than us, nevertheless radiates divinity.[48] This was a neat solution, with plenty of biblical 'proof texts' in its favour. But it made Jesus neither Gd (as Gd is Gd) nor human (as humans are humans). As fourth-century Greek Church Father Gregory of Nazianzus famously countered: 'What is not assumed is not saved.' What is not embraced by divinity in Christ is not healed. We need a real meeting between true Gd and true humanity.

The genius of the Church Fathers is to take Hellenism, wherein 'Being Itself' is pure form/abstraction/Spirit, and transform it, by insisting that the most real Reality, Being of all being, is Personal. Being wills, loves, chooses, acts, delights, engages. When we meet with Gd within history, it is a result of Gd's free choice and it really is Gd, not some semblance. It is on this basis that I say that the Fathers of the Ecumenical Councils of the Church actually brought about the Christianization – and, yes, even the Hebraicization – of Hellenism.

A review

I may, after a fashion, have given a defence of the possibility of a localization of the genuinely Divine Presence which nevertheless also preserves divine transcendence. Further, it may be that Jews and Christians can simply, honestly and honourably differ as to whether this localization is – or is especially – in Jesus Christ or not. But many will nevertheless urge: why *incarnation* as such? Why the 'becoming-flesh' (*sarx*; *carnis*) of Gd in Jesus? Why could Jesus not simply speak authentically divine words, to have that point of contact, such that his human speech might have two natures (one divine, one human), but not his human flesh?

Different answers are possible. In the first place, it is vital to insist that this ('inverbation'?) would be no less miraculous and paradoxical than incarnation. Typically, one requires fleshly/material apparatus to think and speak. It demands – we must suppose – as much self-condescension on Gd's part to limit Gdself to the all-too-human phenomena of human language. The alternative is to suppose that Gd somehow thinks as we think. Beyond that, Christianity need have no a priori theory as to why Gd chose to be, as it were, 'maximally' among us, sharing 'even' our embodiedness. It is the archetypal example of 'found theology'; it is what we find in Jesus. Strictly, it is what over centuries proved the least misleading way of articulating what was found.

A different Jewish account of the impossibility of incarnation is that it is simply unnecessary. Gd has come as close as Gd needs to and wills to, to be with us, at Sinai – however understood – and its ongoing enactment in the People of Israel. Against this I have nothing to argue; I simply note that here is a demarcation between Christians and Jews, again, an honest and honourable one.

Inasmuch as this is true, the difference between us can be expressed thus: Christians intensify and in some ways limit the coming-to-us of Gd to Jesus. Does this proclaimed limitation mean that Christians think of themselves, as Jesus' followers, as superior or more loved by Gd than Jews and others, or of Christianity as the superior way? Should not the revelation at Sinai and that in Christ be understood as *equal*? These challenges have played a large part in our dialogue and deserve urgent attention.

I will be bold: nothing in this paper suggests Christians' superiority. Orthodoxy (lower case!) insists all are equally loved by Gd; all are indestructibly made in the image of Gd. This is so whatever they believe. After all, it is evident to all that within and without our two traditions people believe much that is nonsense and harmful. I might ask in turn – not facetiously – does Gd love a Scientologist less than us? We are all in the image of Gd as persons, and respect for persons is unconditional in a way that respect for world-views is not.[49] Moreover, I align myself to modern Catholic thinking after the Second Vatican Council, which is insistent that all – 'even' atheists – can be 'saved'. One is saved by following one's truest conscience, which is understood to be a response to Divine grace, however inchoate: 'we ought to believe that the Holy Spirit in a manner known only to God offers to every man the possibility of being associated with the [saving] paschal mystery.'[50]

This position is rightly associated with German Jesuit 'inclusivist' Karl Rahner,[51] who taught that people from faiths other than Christian might be thought of as, in differing ways, 'anonymous Christians'.[52] This is often misunderstood, as if Rahner merely encouraged people to look to agree with practices and teachings which resembled the Church's own. But such encouragement would need no articulation; it was the existing missionary common sense. Rahner's more radical position is that whenever persons acted well, in response to some intimation of the transcendent, however the action differed from what the Church considered good and proper, they were responding to grace. All grace (for Rahner) was in Christ, in Gd, in the Holy Trinity. That – and not some surface agreement with the Church – is what makes it logically necessary to see that person, and potentially all persons, as to some extent 'anonymous Christians'.

This 'inclusivism' can be criticized on many grounds. For our purposes, most pertinent is that Rahner never engaged with the idea that, for Christians, Judaism is different from the 'non-Christian' religions. Judaism – as the Catholic Church has come to make clear – is an outworking of biblical revelation, which is different from the Church and which has its own authentic integrity or charism. This complicates Rahner's system, to say the least.[53] But his 'inclusivism' does not entail a Christian claim to superiority. It is the frame for – and not the content of – inter-religious dialogue. In the real-life dialogue, the Christian should and can enter with humility, even expectant of greater holiness and wisdom in the other. This does indeed logically mean that Christians may be a small minority in heaven, especially when one remembers that Christians are more culpable for Christ's death than all others, since they, when sinning, cannot claim they know not what they do.[54]

For all practical purposes, our two revelations or covenants can be said to be equal. Both have led to religious civilizations in which people – as far as one can tell – have equivalent opportunities to grow spiritually or, to put it more cautiously, for which we have no working criteria for mutual assessment. In all practical senses, they are two different languages for things ineffable or two calendars to shape the year with two stories of hope-against-hope.

However, I cannot move from this joyful recognition of pragmatic equivalence to certainty that in every single respect the two revelations are 'equal'. The two are clearly not identical and I cannot judge a revelation on the basis of evident spiritual usefulness alone. Doesn't the urging to do so anyway prize agreement – or, strictly, refraining from disagreement – over a mutual fascination with radical difference? If the content of revelation at heart is intimacy with Gd's self, then the possibility must be left open that in one revelation there is something – though it might never be pinned down – which gives a fuller or a final account of the way things are. Reason does not judge revelation, but is judged, expanded and perfected – though never contradicted – by it. Naturally, it follows that I am not the least offended if a Jew agrees – and adds that the fuller revelation is that of Sinai.

Am I here desperately clinging to conservatism out of fear or nostalgia? I think not. Let us revisit the conviction that all human beings are equally loved by Gd and equally bear Gd's image. This is, I suggest, something that revelation teaches us. It is not self-evident. Prima facie, human worth and dignity are distributed unequally among human beings. People often find this right and proper, judging their own group superior. So when Debbie earlier took the doctrine of the image of Gd in humankind in all its diversity as the basis for dialogue, I am in profound agreement.[55] But this holds good only if it is a teaching understood to be authentically foundational. If, on the contrary, it is not to be privileged as 'truth', but is only one item in an ever-self-reinventing game, then it has no force to resist a counter claim. To note this – to value revelation in this way – is not to claim superiority, but to choose devout agnosticism over ideological agnosticism, for the sake of the image of Gd among us.

To press the point: logically, it might be that, far from Christians being 'superior' to others, we may be the most spiritually dull-witted. We are the ones who need everything spelling out repetitively, in detail, and with full clarity; others can reach the spiritual goal by evocation of things Divine alone. I am not, you understand, claiming to know that Christians are dull in this way, merely that this is as cogent a way of spelling out the dialectic of orthodoxy as a presumption of Christians' 'superiority'.[56]

No defence and articulation of Christian orthodoxy is complete without some discussion of trinitarianism. At heart, the doctrine of the Trinity is an outworking of the doctrine of the incarnation. Most obviously, it comes from the insistence that when Jesus prays to the Father, and promises the Spirit, he must be involved in real relationships and not acting solipsistically. Further, if this is so, the real relationships discerned here must be real both as Gd acts towards us – and as Gd is in Gdself. This is as bold a claim as can be made. It may sound like groundless speculation but it does not mean that Christians claim to have, as it were, an accurate map of Gd. Rather it is what must be the case, lest the door is once again flung wide to Hellenistic impersonalism. If Gd is Trinity only 'for us' and not 'in Gdself', then the Reality of the Most Real, in essence, outside of time and creation, may be impersonal after all. Then the Personal Gd and the priority of love, relationship and communication may be all just a ruse to supply some spiritual edification for us.

One Jewish response to some of this has been that there may be some merit in using the above strategies against the Hellenists, but it may amount to a 'local theology', proper to that place and time, and one that can now be set aside. One way of testing this claim is to ask whether Judaism might have, albeit only implicitly, a logical necessity for a similar kind of dialectic. Thus I ask: is there, as mystery and miracle, a real meeting between Gd and Israel at 'Sinai' (however understood)?

If there is, then indeed Judaism has – again, implicitly – a similar dialectic. Gd limits Gdself to be authentically known at a particular time and place (or times and places), and Gd also transcends all that. If there is not, then Judaism is perhaps a cultural variant of ideological agnosticism, and Gd-as-Gd-is remains utterly unknown. This may be untroubling to (some/many) Jews, but it is worthy of note. I myself am torn: I have passionate respect for the devout reticence of the Rabbis to speak of Gd in Gdself, or of Gd before and outside of Gd's dealings with creation, which Michael sets out. But I also understand that the Church Fathers faced a challenge that the Rabbis did not. They were *existentially* troubled by the idea that Gd is in *no* sense known.

So it is possible that Christianity's encounter with Hellenism was fortuitous if not providential. It forced Christians to give some account of how Gd 'speaks' and 'acts' in the world. The piety of Rabbinic Judaism had no need to give such an account, never doubting that Gd had spoken, because Gd is *Ehyeh*, YHWH who will be who YHWH will be.[57] For Christians, embedded in Hellenism, the doubt was real, wide and deep. But this led to Christian clarity about the necessary dialectic of any belief in biblical revelation that:

- Gd is somehow met with in a limited/localized way and that Gd as free Creator remains beyond any limit or locale

- this is so because Gd is never not Personal and is radically free
- this in turn gives dignity to us, for we are also free – contingently free, but still free
- we too are persons-in-relation, sharing in the image of Gd, because Gd wills it so.

I offer two conclusions. For Christian readers, I hope to have given an account of how 'even' orthodox, creedal Christianity bears a 'family resemblance' to Rabbinic Judaism, drawing as it does from the same biblical wells. For many Jewish readers, my hope may have to be more modest: that you might see that not all of creedal orthodoxy is entirely Greek/Gentile/pagan. Rather, what most fascinates and/or repels you about Christianity 'has to do' with our common heritage in complex and perhaps necessarily ultimately unclassifiable ways.[58]

Given my brief, I have presented Christian doctrine as being largely conceptual. But the Fathers always linked their claims to the life of the Church. *Pisteuomen* means 'we place our trust in', we remember. There is, it is true, no 'patristic halakhah', in the sense of a detailed pattern for all of human life. But there is most assuredly the insistence that right living is necessary to embrace right believing. Consider this introduction to the Nicaeo-Constantinopolitan creed itself, from the Orthodox liturgy:

Priest	Peace to you all.
People	And to your spirit.
Deacon	*Let us love one another, that with one mind* we may confess
People	Father, Son and Holy Spirit, Trinity consubstantial and undivided.[59]

These words are not decorative but close to the heart of what Christian orthodoxy intends.

Notes

1 Buber's famous quotation that he regarded Jesus as his 'great brother' is often cited as if it were the climax of his thought. In fact, Buber went on to say: 'That Christianity has regarded and does regard him as God and Saviour has always appeared to me a fact of the highest importance which, for his sake and my own, I must endeavour to understand.' Martin Buber, 1951, *Two Types of Faith*, London: Routledge & Kegan Paul, pp. 12ff.

2 'Narrower' in the sense of one subgroup within interfaith dialogue and – it has proved – harder but not in the sense of being the exclusive way to salvation (cf. Matthew 7.14).

3 Admittedly, whether there is such a thing as Jewish 'orthodoxy' ('right belief') even among the Orthodox is a question often contested in this dialogue. I am an

Anglican and, while the folkloric belief is that the Church of England believes in nothing more than the niceness of niceness, it is actually unambiguously aligned with the creedal statements of the undivided Church. It does not police dissent but dissent is still dissent. It must be noted that, among those identifying as 'Orthodox' Christian, the Oriental Orthodox reject the Council of Chalcedon, cited above (on Christ's two natures). The Western Church added centuries later that the Spirit proceeds from the Father 'and the Son'.

4 In employing this abbreviation for God I am heavily influenced by R. Kendall Soulen, 2011, *The Divine Name(s) and the Holy Trinity: Distinguishing the Voices. Volume One*, Louisville, KY: Westminster John Knox Press. Soulen presents a powerful case that Christianity has from earliest days practised, at least in one of its modes of speaking of the Divine, a reticence about naming, writing and speaking of God Godself which is analogous to (if not a version of) the Jewish reticence about speaking the Divine Name. In Christianity, this is found, inter alia, in Jesus' speaking of the Kingdom of Heaven (or the heavens) in Matthew, and in the later practice of writing *nomina sacra*, for example Theta-Sigma with a line on top (signifying an abbreviation) for *Theos*, God, Iota-Sigma, for *Iesous*, and so on. These abbreviations were not for practical purposes, but came from a theological understanding, Soulen insists. Greek translations of the Hebrew Bible employed different ways of circumscribing the Divine Name. But none attempted a pronunciation based on the Hebrew consonants. Thus I'd contend that Gd (with or without the line above it) is as much a Christian pious 'holding-back' as a Jewish one, though I do not pretend this will feel natural or right to many. As an innovation, it does not have all the connotations of the Jewish practice, in some quarters, of writing 'G-d'.

5 Jews have a similar understanding of 'one' at the end of the first line of the Sh'ma. God is not 'one' (as opposed to 'two' or 'three') but unique and whole.

6 *Supra* p. 95.

7 See, for instance, Daniel Boyarin, 2004, *Border Lines: The Partition of Judaeo-Christianity*, Philadelphia, PA: University of Pennsylvania Press, p. 130 and throughout.

8 In this and in much of the following I owe a debt especially to John D. Zizioulas, 2004, *Being as Communion*, 2nd edn, London: Darton, Longman & Todd.

9 From the 'selfish gene' to the 'charm' of modern physics.

10 The Cappadocian Fathers are Basil the Great, Gregory of Nyssa and Gregory of Nazianzus. 'The Cappadocians are regarded as exponents of the negative theology, and of the mystical tradition in Christianity. The supreme antinomy of the Triune God, unknowable and knowable, incommunicable and communicable, transcendent and immanent is the primary locus of their apophaticism. Moreover, the negative theology of the Cappadocians is balanced by their acute sense of the revelation of God ... Thus they are compelled to recognize an ineffable distinction between the essence (*ousia*) and energies (*energeiai*) within the uncreated God. The divine nature is eternally transcendent and beyond man's experience and comprehension.' Anita Strezova, 2010, *Knowledge and Vision of God in the Cappadocian Fathers*: www.thevoiceoforthodoxy.com/knowledge-and-vision-of-god-in-cappadocian-fathers/.

11 Cf. Aquinas, *Summa*, Part 1, Question 13, Article 5: descriptors 'are said of God and creatures in an analogous sense, i.e. according to proportion'. With regard to the negative theology, there are clear similarities with Maimonides; it is

interesting to compare and contrast Maimonides and Aquinas on the (im)possibility of speaking of Gd via analogy.

12 Not unlike *mitzvah* without *M'tsaveh*, commandment without an expressed Commander.

13 Menachem Kellner, 2006, *Must a Jew Believe Anything?*, 2nd edn, Oxford: Littman Library of Jewish Civilization.

14 Cf. Mishnah *Avodah Zarah*; differently, Colossians 3.5; Ephesians 5.5.

15 That this is the natural way for Christian theology to proceed is discussed in Ben Quash, 2013, *Found Theology: History, Imagination and the Holy Spirit*, London: T & T Clark.

16 B. 1772, Poland, d. 1811, Ukraine. 'The world needs me very much indeed. Without me, the world cannot exist at all.' 'You yourself know how much you need me. All the Tzaddikim also need me, because they too need to improve. Even the nations of the world need me. I could draw the gentiles to God and bring them closer to the faith of Israel … My mission is a secret. It is such a secret that even when I reveal the secret, it still remains a secret.' Abraham Greenbaum (trans.), 2006, *The Essential Rabbi Nachman*, Jerusalem: Azamra, pp. 11–13.

17 I am acknowledging Tony Bayfield's understanding that Torah and Jesus not Torah and New Testament are the Jewish–Christian equivalents.

18 John 14.6.

19 1 Corinthians 15.20.

20 While the argument remains strong – following Kellner – that a Jew is not bound to ascribe to any set of beliefs, it is worth noting that the Mishnah lists the one 'who says that there is no allusion in the Torah concerning resurrection' as among those of Israel who have no place in the world to come (Mishnah *Sanhedrin* 10.1).

21 1922–97.

22 Pinchas Lapide, 2002, *The Resurrection of Jesus: A Jewish Perspective*, Eugene, OR: Wipf and Stock.

23 For example St Cyprian of Carthage, third-century Latin Church Father, Letter LVIII.

24 A distortion which need not and does not wholly obscure the image of Gd; this is not to speak of 'utter depravity'.

25 See the famous midrash in *Genesis Rabbah* IX.7 and the less well-known Babylonian Talmud *Yoma* 69b in which even eggs vanish without the presence of the *yetzer hara*.

26 Timothy Radcliffe OP, 2005, *What Is the Point of Being a Christian?*, London: Burns & Oates, p. 51.

27 And of much classical Rabbinic literature, as Alex Wright makes clear.

28 Historically, this claim is fraught, of course. Which came first: lived Second Temple Judaism or Tanakh as we know it now, with the contents of the Writings as settled as those of Torah and the Prophets? Since my claim here is small – that Second Temple Judaism contained elements which had not or will not 'make it' into Tanakh, but which were *at the time* considered 'Jewish' – I contend that nothing for our purposes is at stake.

29 Cf. Wayne O. McCready and Adele Reinharz, 2008, *Common Judaism: Explorations in Second Temple Judaism*, Minneapolis, MN: Fortress Press.

30 Daniel Boyarin, 2012, *The Jewish Gospels: The Story of the Jewish Christ*, New York: The New Press.

31 Boyarin, *The Jewish Gospels*, p. 38; cf. Daniel 7.9–14.
32 Boyarin, *The Jewish Gospels*, p. 39.
33 Boyarin, *The Jewish Gospels*, ch. 2.
34 Boyarin, *The Jewish Gospels*, p. 76, my italics.
35 Boyarin, *The Jewish Gospels*, p. 6.
36 Boyarin, *The Jewish Gospels*, p. 101.
37 *Infra* pp. 271–2.
38 Boyarin, *Border Lines*; Adam Becker and Annette Yoshiko Reed, 2007, *The Ways that Never Parted: Jews and Christians in Late Antiquity and the Early Middle Ages*, Minneapolis, MN: Fortress Press.
39 Michael Hilton, 1994, *The Christian Effect on Jewish Life*, London: SCM Press.
40 Indeed, the question which so exercised Rashi and Nachmanides (from a later period), which Natan's paper brings, as to why Torah begins with the story of creation and not with the first commandment within Exodus, is 'unaskable' in Christianity. For the Rabbis, it was self-evident that Torah is 'about' the *commandments*; for the Fathers it was equally self-evident it was 'about' the *narrative* of Gd being with Gd's people, such that it is perfectly proper to start with the framing narrative of creation.
41 See Abraham Joshua Heschel, 2005, *Heavenly Torah as Reflected through Generations*, New York: Continuum, especially pp. 93–143.
42 Babylonian Talmud *Baba M'tzia* 59 a–b, *supra* p. 252. See also Jeremy Gordon's note 3 on p. 83.
43 Cf. Mark S. Kinzer, 2005, *Post-Missionary Messianic Judaism: Redefining Christian Engagement with the Jewish People*, Grand Rapids, MI: Brazos Press, pp. 122–42.
44 Cf. Kinzer, *Post-Missionary Messianic Judaism*, p. 194.
45 Zizioulas, *Being as Communion*, pp. 31–3.
46 Zizioulas, *Being as Communion*, p. 16.
47 By the fourth century no one claiming to be a Christian thought he was only a prophet; the debate was all about *how*, not *whether*, he was divine.
48 Rowan Williams, 2001, *Arius*, 2nd edn, London: SCM Press.
49 See Wendy Fidler's essay, *supra* p. 217.
50 *Gaudium et Spes*, section 22, having just spoken of 'all men of good will in whose hearts grace works in an unseen way' – however religious or irreligious.
51 B. 1904, Germany, d. 1983, Austria.
52 Karl Rahner, 1996, *Christianity and the Non-Christian Religions, Theological Investigations, Volume 5*, London: Darton, Longman & Todd, pp. 115–34.
53 On how, see Patrick Morrow, 2012, *Christian Understandings of the 'Other': An Unfashionable Defence of Karl Rahner's 'Anonymous Christians'*, at http://iccj.org/fileadmin/ICCJ/pdf-Dateien/Morrow.PDF (accessed 21 August 2014).
54 *Catechism of the Council of Trent*, citing Luke 23.24.
55 See Debbie Young-Somers' essay, *supra* pp. 189–201.
56 Cf. 1 Corinthians 1.26ff.
57 Exodus 3.13ff. See also Alex Wright's and David Ford's essays.
58 That Christians and Jews are set both to fascinate and repel each other is an insight I owe to Franz Rosenzweig, as discussed in Jeremy F. Worthen, 2009, *The Internal Foe: Judaism and Anti-Judaism in the Shaping of Christian Theology*, Newcastle: Cambridge Scholars. For example, p. xiii: 'As an "internal foe," Judaism

is both uniquely provocative and uniquely generative for Christianity. Anti-Judaism keeps the Church facing Judaism even as it seeks to push it away: "we are the louse in your fur," as Rosenzweig says in the same passage.' The inverse is not exactly the case, of course, but I suggest, drawing on the newer understanding of the hesitant parting of the ways, that Christianity plays something of this role to Judaism. Rosenzweig's language is to be understood as a colourful way of describing a holy rivalry rather than necessary antagonism, which latter the dialogue of recent decades has helped us to lose.

59 *The Divine Liturgy of Our Father among the Saints: John Chrysostom*, 1995, Oxford: Oxford University Press, p. 29, my italicizing.

Friendship and Respect in the Face of Impenetrable Doctrine

VIVIAN SILVERMAN

I read the final draft of Patrick Morrow's paper and was aware of just how much care and attention he had paid to the preceding discussions. His effort to explain orthodox Christianity and answer the questions from the Group is tireless and painstaking. I listened to the final discussion, humbled by the sincerity but unable to contribute.

I have worked as an Orthodox rabbi within the British Jewish community for many years. When it comes to relationships with others, be they other faiths or other sections of the Jewish community, I have never allowed what Christians would call doctrine to get in the way of good relationships. That is why I have worked happily with the Council of Christians and Jews – being on good terms with others, explaining ourselves to others and understanding others is very important. It's also how I came to meet Rabbi Elli Tikvah Sarah and built a respectful friendship. Indeed, it was Elli who introduced me to the Dialogue Group.

I've found my membership of the Group extremely interesting but also challenging. As I've said, I've always worked on the level of mutual understanding before, never engaged in what Rabbi Bayfield calls 'the theology of dialogue'. Over the last three years I have listened, learned and enjoyed the experience of being exposed to Christian and Jewish thinking about doctrine. However, when it came to responding to Patrick's paper on Christian doctrine, I found a world that is foreign to me and with which I cannot engage. That is why my friends and colleagues Natan Levy and Michael Hilton have joined me in adding their comments.

Gnosticism

When I say that I have never engaged in interfaith theology before, that does not mean I have not done any reading. When it comes to Jesus the Jew and the development of Christianity, I have read widely for the past 25 years. But I start – as an Orthodox rabbi – with an unshakeable premise: Jesus was not God, doctrines such as incarnation and Trinity are not Jewish doctrines – rather they come from Gnostic and Greek sources. That is why they are such difficult concepts for Jewish people even to grasp, let alone accept. I appreciate Patrick's valiant attempt to show that these doctrines are rooted in (Second Temple) Judaism as well as Hellenistic thought, but I am not convinced. That Jesus is the Second Person of the Trinity – Father, Son and Holy Spirit – is incomprehensible. How can God be both divine and human?

The Torah, God's teaching, is not an emanation of the divine but, rather, the blueprint from which the Almighty created the world and everything in it. Even the descent of the *Sh'khinah* – the Divine Presence – on Mount Sinai, or its appearance to Moses in the Tent of Meeting, was but God's means of communication with mankind. The distinction between God and man in Judaism is absolute. But it is not so in Christianity which understands Jesus to be both.

Why did this departure come about? For early Christianity, God himself coming down to earth in the form of his Son was in order to redeem this world from sin. It offered a way to express the fundamental teaching of Gnosticism which emphasized the escape of the self from the sinfulness of the flesh and its reunion with the pure realm of light. The early Church was much concerned with the arguments and erudition of Basilides, Valentinus and Marcion, who lived during the second century and were members of the Gnostic school of Christianity. The Church felt compelled to define the creed more precisely and, in the process, trinitarianism emerged. In other words, the Church was shaped by the Gnostic challenge and its rejection of the physical world as evil. It was Christ, the second Person of the Trinity, who took away the sin.

The conflict was no longer between those who followed the original teaching of the Ecclesia that Jesus was fully human and those who asserted that he was the Son of God. Now it was between those who upheld the incarnation and those who maintained that Jesus had not come in the flesh at all, but only *seemed* to have done so – if the flesh and sexual relations were sinful, how could Jesus have been flesh in reality? This latter position was known as Docetism: if Jesus was divine, then he could never have assumed human form because, by doing so, he could not have been without sin. We can see the impact of Gnosticism very clearly – it was repugnant to imagine that Jesus could have had bodily functions: eating, drinking, excretion and sex. So, he only *seemed* to be human. Consequently, he could not have suffered on the cross.

Quite early on the Church repudiated this view, but it left its mark in the form of the doctrine of the Immaculate Conception (Mary was free from sin from conception) and perpetual virginity (Mary had no sexual relations with Joseph). And so, Jesus' brothers and sisters (mentioned in the Gospels) must have been children of Joseph's previous marriage.

Judaism, Gnosticism and sin

Rabbinic Judaism took a very different route, rejected Gnosticism and never regarded this world as full of sin. Each baby born was pure. Upbringing, environment and friends as well as personal choice determined whether one did right or wrong. Furthermore, if a person sinned, he or she could pray directly to God for forgiveness and repent without an intercessor.

Philo and Christianity

Since mainstream Christianity held that the Hebrew Bible was sacred text and that the world was created through Jesus as the Logos (Platonic in origin) the only sure way to combat Gnostic views without abandoning the deity of Jesus Christ was to assert the unity of God in the Trinity.

Philo of Alexandria,[1] the Jewish philosopher much influenced by Greek thought, interpreted the visit of the three strangers to Abraham in Genesis 18 as divine messengers in human form. This could be seen as a form of incarnation but it applied solely to messengers of God, not to God himself.

Incarnation understood as the creative Word of God, manifesting its power in the world of matter, Logos, as cosmic force, gave Philo of Alexandria the means by which to construct his Jewish philosophy. His 'divine thought' finds echoes in the opening of John's Gospel: 'In the beginning was the Word, and the Word was with God, and the Word was God ... And the Word became flesh and lived among us.'[2]

But it's the Word – with a capital letter – being made flesh in the person of Jesus Christ that creates an unbridgeable gulf between Philo and John. The union of Father, Son and Holy Spirit – so foreign even to Hellenized Jews – is a fundamental part of Christian belief, alluded to in Paul's Second Letter to the Corinthians 13.13: 'The grace of the Lord Jesus Christ, the love of God, and the communion of the Holy Spirit be with all of you.'

Trinity

At the Council of Nicaea in 325 CE, Jesus was recognized as fully divine:

> We believe in one God, Father Almighty, maker of all things visible and invisible; and in one Lord Jesus Christ, the Son of God, begotten as only-begotten of the Father, that is: of the substance of the Father, God of God, Light of Light, true God from true God, begotten, not made, consubstantial with the Father.

Though the Ebionites, who regarded themselves as the authentic followers of the immediate circle of Jesus, protested against this deification of their Master, the Gentile Church accepted it. And they found a proof text in the threefold repetition of Isaiah 6.3: 'Holy, holy, holy is the Eternal of Hosts'.

Jewish polemics against this doctrine date from early in the rise of Gentile Christianity. A classic example can be found in Tractate *B'rakhot* 9.12 of *Y'rulshalmi* (the Palestinian Talmud): 'Rabbi Simlai declared that the three names – *El, Elohim, Adonai* – mean one and the same, as a person might say – King, Emperor, Augustus.'

Throughout the Middle Ages, whether God as One and God as Trinity – with one part of the Trinity being both human and divine – are compatible formed a major part of disputations between a representative of the Church – usually a learned, renegade Jew – and a rabbi. They were staged by the Church, often in the presence of the King. Disputations took place in Paris (1240) between Nicholas Donin and several distinguished French rabbis, notably Yehiel of Paris; and in Barcelona (1263) between Pablo Christiani and Rabbi Moses ben Nachman (Nachmanides). Jews were placed in the position of either rejecting Christian doctrine and confirming their stubborn sinfulness – or of accepting a teaching which is not just alien to Judaism but incomprehensible to us.

The historical Jesus and the Jesus of Christian theology

The Jesus of history and the Jesus of theology are two distinct concepts. The Gentile domination of the Church from the second century onwards altered the landscape of what had been Nazarene Judaism – the belief in Joshua/Jesus as the *Mashiakh*, Anointed One, who would redeem the Jewish people from under the yoke of the Roman oppressor. There began a gradual removal from history of Jesus' ever having been a fully practising and observant member of the House of Israel. However, sufficient New Testament passages remain which, despite causing embarrassment, could not be completely excised – because they contain Jesus' original teachings directly handed down:

> 'Go nowhere among the Gentiles, and enter no town of the Samaritans, but go rather to the lost sheep of the house of Israel. As you go, proclaim the good news, "The kingdom of heaven has come near."'[3]

> 'Do not think that I have come to abolish the law or the prophets; I have come not to abolish but to fulfil. For truly I tell you, until heaven and earth pass away, not one letter, not one stroke of a letter, will pass from the law until all is accomplished. Therefore, whoever breaks one of the least of these commandments, and teaches others to do the same, shall be called least in the kingdom of heaven; but whoever does them and teaches them will be called great in the kingdom of heaven.'[4]

Each of the four Gospels (eventually accepted out of many others) was originally composed for a particular community and for a set time and circumstance, whether Rome, Alexandria, Antioch or Ephesus. They were theological tracts written to give encouragement to late first-century or early second-century followers of 'the Way', who were being harassed and persecuted. Tragically for the Jewish people, these same Gospels became part of the New Testament writings and then became canonized as the word of God. Once sanctified, whatever was written about Jews had to be taken as 'gospel truth'. And so Jewry suffered down the long centuries because of the words of the Gospels.

Belief in the coming of the Messiah and the resurrection of the dead at the End of Days is as important to Rabbinic Judaism as the death and resurrection of Jesus Christ is for Christians. Indeed, one of the tests which distinguished the Pharisees – from whom Rabbinic Judaism is descended – from the Sadducees is whether or not belief in resurrection is a doctrine of the Torah itself.[5] It was for the Pharisees but not the Sadducees. In Mark 12, Jesus is asked sarcastically by a group of Sadducees about a woman who observed the biblical practice known as *yibum* of marrying her dead husband's brother (and did so seven times!) – whose wife would she be in heaven? Jesus, a Jew in the tradition of the Pharisees and Rabbinic Judaism, answers: 'Is not this the reason you are wrong, that you know neither the scriptures nor the power of God? For when they rise from the dead, they neither marry nor are given in marriage, but are like angels in heaven.'[6] The world to come will be a purely spiritual experience.

The second blessing of the Amidah, dating from the end of the first century, declares: 'You are mighty for ever, Eternal One, you revive the dead – and establish your faithfulness with those who sleep in the dust – the King who causes death and revives.'

Judaism, like Christianity, developed and retained a doctrine of resurrection. In Judaism it remained resurrection at the End of Days. In Christianity it took the very different direction of the resurrection of God incarnate, thus saving believers from the Gnostic world of sin.

Judaism and Christianity went separate ways and, in so doing, Christianity ceased to be a form of Judaism. Patrick says that Christianity is Hellenized Judaism – but it is so Hellenized as to cease to be compatible with Judaism or even understandable by Jews. However, we don't have to fully understand each other to be friends and collaborate in every way we can.

Notes

1 *c.* 25 BCE – *c.* 50 CE.
2 John 1.1 and 1.14.
3 Matthew 10.5–7.
4 Matthew 5.17–19.
5 See Mishnah *Sanhedrin* 10.1.
6 Mark 12.24–25.

Morrow, Maimonides and Torah in Translation

NATAN LEVY

In the space of a couple of centuries a burning question within the Christian community was not: 'Must the Gentile believers keep the Torah?' but, 'Are Jewish believers permitted to keep Torah?' This we can see as a tragedy. Indeed, it may be the single biggest failure of the Church. But Gd is capable of bringing good things out of failure, out of sin, and Gentile Christianity (strictly, Christianity which understands itself as Gentile) may be seen as Gd-blessed failure.[1]

In Patrick Morrow's far-reaching theological treatise on orthodox Christology, he briefly notes a tragedy within the formation of the early church doctrines. A failure, Patrick suggests, in the formative early Church to value Jewish legal histrionics, the halakhah, as a worthy vehicle of religious gravitas. Perhaps, he concludes, 'the single biggest failure of the Church'. A striking claim from an orthodox Christian theologian. And yet, Patrick claims that a certain grace or blessedness emerges from this failure to integrate a thread of halakhah into the foundational tapestry of creedal code.

As our dialogue in this Group has always been predicated on radical honesty, I would like to examine this fraught moment within Patrick's essay from a Jewish lens. Specifically, a text from Maimonides' *Mishneh Torah*[2] on the question of Christianity as historical and, thus, divine failure or success.

The text in question was long censored from most printings of the *Mishneh Torah*. The historical record of the origins of censorship of the *Mishneh Torah* provides a fascinating glimpse into the fraught dynamics of Jewish–Christian relations in medieval Europe. The Dominican friar and apostate Jew Pablo Christiani probably brought the text in question to the notice of the church authorities around the time of his involvement with the Barcelona Disputation in July 1263. Thereafter, King James I of Aragon ordered the confiscation and burning of the particular section of the *Mishneh Torah*, which contained the offensive lines. The persistence of vigilant censorship and prosecution of those who possessed copies of the Rambam's text continued for over a century. In 1389, the Dominican Inquisitorial Commissary Guillem de Tous of the monastery of Tarragon initiated proceedings against members of the Jewish community of Montblanc for the sin of possessing the blasphemous 'Talmud of Rabbi Moses of Egypt'.[3] The ubiquitous censoring of these difficult paragraphs in the *Mishneh Torah* in every extant printed copy in Christendom – without a single footnote to mark the lacuna – would indicate that, at some point, the text became so perilous to the community that housed it that even the memory of the censorship itself was wilfully forgotten. Within Europe at least, the Rambam had never spoken of Jesus.

However, the Arab world was a different matter. Manuscripts translated from the original Hebrew into early medieval Arabic were carefully preserved for generations by the Yemenite community. When they immigrated en masse to Israel in the early 1950s, one of its young leaders, Rabbi Yosef Kapach, carried these folios with him. Kapach published the uncensored version of the *Mishneh Torah*, translating the Arabic text back into Hebrew. Kapach's edition is widely considered the most authentic reproduction of Rambam's original work and most of his corrections, including the text in question, were included in the Hebrew Frankel edition of the *Mishneh Torah*. I have translated the relevant text into English.

Rambam, *Hilkhot M'lakhim* 15.4 begins:

> If there arise a king from the House of David who meditates on the Torah, occupies himself with the commandments, as did his ancestor David, observes the precepts prescribed in the written and the Oral Law, prevails upon Israel to walk in the way of the Torah and to repair its breaches, and fights the battles of the Lord, it may be assumed that he is the Messiah. If he does these things and succeeds, rebuilds the sanctuary on its site, and gathers the dispersed of Israel he is beyond all doubt the Messiah. He will prepare the whole world to serve the Lord with one accord.

Up until this point in our text, Rambam's codification of the prescribed signifiers of messianic fulfilment remained uncensored. Here the Rambam is compiling, integrating and evaluating various strands of messianic promise and fulfilment alluded to in the Babylonian Talmud, most notably in the Tractate *Sanhedrin*. It is worthy of note that while the Messiah's task is daunting – fighting and winning the 'battle of the Lord', building anew the Temple in Jerusalem and gathering the diasporic

Jewish community to Israel – none of these tasks are supernatural, nor demanding of a supra-human being. Let us note as well how little belief enters this scheme. If, and only if, the messiah fulfils these certain tangible results can he be considered as the true Messiah. Charismatic belief in such a being prior to his completed work plays no functional purpose.

This messianic formula for a very real human being who brings redemption with very tangible results is sharply distinct – if not a direct polemic against – a divinely embodied saviour from heaven. As Patrick notes in his brief survey of Daniel Boyarin's *The Jewish Gospels*, the Second Temple milieu in which Jesus lived, preached and died may have held out other possibilities for a Jewish Messiah beyond the human one posited by the later Talmudic establishment and codified in the Rambam's work. In one poignant quote, Boyarin notes:

> Many Israelites at the time of Jesus were expecting a Messiah who would be divine and come to earth in the form of a human. Thus the basic underlying thoughts from which both the Trinity and the incarnation grew are there in the very world into which Jesus was born and in which he was first written about in the Gospels of Mark and John.[4]

However, as Patrick concedes, while Boyarin's research holds scholarly interest for our two faiths seeking common ground, the intervening two millennia have literally wiped such a divine reading of the Messiah from the Jewish text and conversation. On a purely personal and first-hand observation, I have noted a number of encounters between Christian and Jewish living faith communities in which the Christian speakers, seeking a bridge towards deeper dialogue, presented some variant on Boyarin's careful research. The rabbis in every one of these encounters either ignored the reference or became threatened by its perceived overture of an un-anchoring of Judaism from its Rabbinic grounding towards some threatening syncretic end-design.

This is all to imply that when we speak to one another in these postmodern times, from the mainstream Jewish perspective, it is the Rambam – rather than Boyarin's diffuse rereading of the book of Daniel – which holds the real leverage in the encounter.

Now, the text becomes more historical in scope and critical of failed messiahs in design. Here is the censored portion of the text on messianic fulfilment:

> And if he does not succeed or is killed, then it be known that this is not the one whom the Torah has assured us, rather he is like all the kings of the house of David who were whole and fit but died. God has

established him in order to test the multitudes, as it is said, 'Some of the knowledgeable will fall, that they may be refined and purged and whitened until the time of the end, for an interval still remains until the appointed time.' (Daniel 11.35)

Even Jesus of Nazareth, who imagined that he would be the Messiah and was killed by the court, Daniel had already prophesied concerning him, as it is said, 'the lawless sons of your people will assert themselves to confirm the vision but they will fail.' (Daniel 11.14) Is there any greater failure than this? For all the prophets spoke that the Messiah will redeem Israel and save them and gather in their outcasts and strengthen their observance of the commandments but this one caused the destruction of Israel by the sword and the dispersal of their remnant and their downfall and the exchange of the Torah and the leading into error of most of the world, to worship a god other than the Lord.

One can well imagine why such a text was hidden or self-censored from medieval society. Here is the crux – in all meanings of that word – of what ails the Christian–Jewish encounter. Halakhic Judaism would consider Jesus as a failure, not merely because of the rise of the Trinity but, more importantly, as a Jewish messiah who did not complete the messianic mission that Judaism demands. Patrick speaks of the Christian doctrine of incarnation as a crucial component of 'found theology', in which Christology – if I understand his point correctly – narrows itself to the task of merely formulating a language about God that most closely corresponds to the experienced phenomena of the confessing community. We, as Jews, necessarily are pushed right to the margins in this venture because the very act of finding Jesus Christ in death and reincarnation is precisely the moment in which Jesus qua 'Messiah', once dead, is lost to the Jewish world. Here is the beginning of the schism which cuts to the core of what separates Jews and Christians. A schism of language, in which we use the same words, but our meanings are violently and harshly opposed to one another. Is this the end-goal of our honest conversations as Jews and Christians? Will we define our theology so clearly to each other, only to discover that, in the end, it is these very definitions that are our deepest divides?

The Rambam is not yet finished in his assessment of false messianic claims. And, as we shall witness, his concluding paragraph prefigures Patrick's claim that there can be such a creation as a failure blessed by God:

> But man does not have the capacity to comprehend the thoughts of God, for our ways are not his ways and our thoughts are not his thoughts, and all these matters of Jesus, and of that Ishmaelite who arose after

him are solely in order to pave the path for the King Messiah and to prepare the entire world to worship the Lord together ... How so? The world has already been entirely filled with the concept of the Messiah, and the concept of the Torah, and the concept of the commandments, and these concepts have spread to faraway continents and to many nations of uncircumcised hearts. And they discuss these concepts and commandments of the Torah, some saying that these commandments were true but have become nullified now and were not operative for ever, and some saying that there are hidden things in them and they are not be understood in their simple meaning, and the 'messiah' has already come and revealed their mystery. Thus, when the true Messiah will arise, and will be successful and will be exalted, they will all repent and know that they have inherited lies from their forefathers and that their prophets and ancestors led them astray.

Though Rambam is asserting the truth of halakhic-rabbinical Judaism over and against Christianity and Islam ('that Ishmaelite who arose after him ...'), there is a true vein of dialogical gold within the medieval rock of absolutism here. For God intended these (false) messiahs to live and teach in order to promulgate essentially intact teachings on the Jewish vision of divine covenant to a wider audience. It is a radical claim for a halakhic logician such as Rambam to state openly. According to the halakhic structure, messiahs who fail to complete the messianic tasks are simply of no further interest to the Jewish mind. Yet, despite all halakhic claims to the contrary, Jesus and Muhammad in their lives and teachings are implementing a divine will in history. Jesus and Muhammad are involved with the divine plan, conceived entirely within the Jewish frame of reference, as post-halakhic actors in history.

Though the end-point is radically different, perhaps this is what Patrick himself alludes to when he refers to a Christianity that, early on, divorced itself from the Jewish legal dialectic as a sort of failure blessed by God. A failure that works for the divine best ends.

According to Patrick, by stripping away the halakhic forms of Judaism, a core Jewish theology became capable of meeting and transforming the non-Jewish western world in the second century. Incarnation and Trinity become, in this thesis, the mechanism by which a personal God who lives in history, the God of intimate considerations, termed *hashgakhah pratis* in Talmudic terminology, bridges the Hellenistic schism between spirit and matter. The Trinity is simply the most effective means of translating the Jewish concepts of personal revelation and historical redemption for the non-Jewish ear. Patrick terms this compelling moment the 'Hebraicization' of Hellenism:

The genius of the Church Fathers is to take Hellenism, wherein 'Being Itself' is pure form/abstraction/Spirit, and transform it, by insisting that the most real Reality, Being of all being, is Personal. Being wills, loves, chooses, acts, delights, engages. When we meet with Gd within history, it is a result of Gd's free choice and it really is Gd, not some semblance. It is on this basis that I say that the Fathers of the Ecumenical Councils of the Church actually brought about the Christianization – and, yes, even the Hebraicization – of Hellenism.[5]

Though similar notions of Christianity as the Hebraicization of Hellenism have been proposed by such widely divergent modern thinkers as Nietzsche and Franz Rosenzweig, Patrick's move here feels unique. For he is writing specifically with dialogical intent. And thus, perhaps Patrick, echoing the Rambam up to a point, provides an answer to our original question. Is a Christianity that dismisses halakhic reference points a failure in Jewish eyes? Not according to the Rambam and, I think, not according to Patrick as well. Christianity is Torah in translation. And though the very first translation of the actual Torah into the Greek Septuagint is a black day in the Jewish calendar of history, marked by the early medieval Rabbis as a day of fasting and mourning, it also stands out as the most primary and earliest of dialogical bridges in Rabbinic Judaism. For, according to the Rabbinical ritual law code, if no *Sefer Torah* can be found in Hebrew, the Greek Septuagint can be read in the synagogue in its place. With this profound nod to both the threat and blessing of translation, the Rabbis pave a difficult path for Jewish–Christian engagement. What they do not do is turn aside from the encounter. And thus, even in our most orthodox garbs, neither should we.

Notes

1 Morrow, *supra* p. 253.

2 Among Jews, Maimonides is more usually referred to as Rambam – from the initial letters of Rabbi Moshe ben Maimon. *Mishneh Torah*, Repetition of Torah, was Maimonides' code of Jewish Law, compiled between 1170 and 1180. It comes in 14 volumes.

3 Paola Tartakoff, 2012, *Between Christian and Jew: Conversion and Inquisition in the Crown of Aragon, 1250–1391*, Philadelphia, PA: University of Pennsylvania Press, pp. 24f.

4 Daniel Boyarin, 2012, *The Jewish Gospels: The Story of the Jewish Christ*, New York: The New Press, p. 6.

5 Morrow, *supra* pp. 254–5.

Response to Patrick Morrow: We Are the Louse in Your Fur[1]

MICHAEL HILTON AND VICTOR SEEDMAN[*]

Patrick Morrow's contribution poses questions for his Jewish dialogue partners. His perspective is that of orthodox Christian belief and doctrine to which he assigns great value as the authentic roots of Christianity today. In consequence of this he argues that dialogue with Jews ought not to compromise the foundational beliefs of Christianity. Taking a different stance might make the enterprise of dialogue appear easier but then the orthodox would feel estranged or excluded and in their absence an authentic dialogue cannot be conducted. By the same token Patrick is not looking for Judaism to change in the process of dialogue with Christians, the assumption being that orthodox Judaism is, like Christianity, a belief system with core tenets. For him, even the most open-minded dialogue partner will always want to hold that their relationship contains the truth, however defined: this being, as Patrick puts it, 'something about Gd and Gd's nature'.[2] We appreciate Patrick's sincerity and clarity but need to indicate where we disagree with him, particularly his stress on the importance of doctrinal truth, while acknowledging that there is much to learn from his back-to-basics approach.

Patrick notes changing views in biblical and Rabbinic Judaism on the nature of God and contrasts these with the development of Christian doctrine. We wholeheartedly agree with him that Judaism has historically concerned itself with questions of God's nature, like Christianity, but would counter that it has been very different in the way it has approached them, as Vivian Silverman has cogently shown in his response to Patrick. Furthermore, we would want to add that theological speculation, though it exists, does not have the same status or importance in Judaism as in

---

[*] **Victor Seedman** is an independent scholar who came to interreligious dialogue via the Centre for Jewish–Christian Relations at Selly Oak Colleges, the International Council for Christians and Jews, JCM Europe and a Jewish–Christian dialogue group in Jerusalem. As a Jew who is familiar with Christian theology, he has been very pleased to accept the invitation to work with Michael Hilton on this response to Patrick Morrow.

Christianity. One might even go further and suggest that one Jewish response to the development of Christian doctrine was to remove dogma and doctrine from Judaism. That so much blood has been shed over doctrine does not make this an unreasonable assumption.

Orthodox as well as progressive thinkers should be concerned about state power officially sanctioning religion.[3] When Christianity became dominant, opponents were labelled 'Judaizers'. All other religions were excluded as false, with Judaism singled out for particular criticism as a true but wrong religion. Was the emergence of these struggled-for, passionately debated truths, 'forged in the furnace' as Patrick puts it,[4] sufficient justification for the suffering they entailed? Michael Hilton has shown earlier in this volume how John the Evangelist read back the disputes of his own day into the time of Jesus. For John, the term 'Jew' may have referred to those from a particular geographical area, Judea. As we move forward in time that sense of the word faded, and we find more and more a struggle between two opposed religions: that is, between Jews and Christians. It is certainly true, as Patrick states, that orthodox creedal Christianity bears a 'family resemblance' to Rabbinic Judaism. However, it is also true that the Council of Nicaea in 325 continued a process of distancing the Church from Jewish practice, the most well-known example being the calculation of the date of Easter. The fourth century became a time of increasing persecution of Jews after Christianity gained power in Rome, culminating in the vicious anti-Semitic writings of St Ambrose and the expulsion of the Jewish community of Alexandria in 415.[5]

The emergence of doctrine as a foundation for any faith has led to the exclusion of those deemed to be sectarians or heretics, even up to the present day.[6] Dialogue needs to be underpinned by an appreciation of the other's faith, not an avowal of the importance of doctrinal orthodoxy.[7] We do not need to compete either for hegemony, or (even worse) about which of us has been more victimized. In our view, we are better served by a common secular language of detached but interested enquiry than by a doctrinal one. We could do worse than follow the Slovenian psychoanalytic philosopher Slavoj Žižek in his claim that 'the only terrain of the divine is contact with other humans'.[8]

The written Torah does not enquire into God's existence. Even there, however, one can find speculation about the nature of God and warnings about going too far. Moses asks to see God's glory and God replies:

> You will not be able to see my face, for no human can see me and live ... I shall cover you with my hand until I have passed by. Then I shall remove my hand and you will see my back but my face may not be seen.[9]

The text suggests through this metaphor that no human can have a complete understanding of God but the most enlightened can reach a partial understanding. Any statement about the nature of God is therefore to be regarded as speculation, which may ask more questions than it provides answers.

Through ancient apocalyptic and mystical literature, through midrash and Talmud, through *Zohar* and medieval Bible commentaries, right through to modern Holocaust theology, such speculation on the nature of God has continued. There is no prohibition on doing this, but the Rabbinic literature does also contain warnings about it, as in this enigmatic story:

> Four entered the garden, Ben Azzai and Ben Zoma, Akher and Rabbi Akiva ... Ben Azzai looked and died ... Ben Zoma looked and was smitten ... Elisha looked and cut the shoots ... Akiva went in peace and came down in peace. To him the scriptural verse applies (Song of Songs, 1.4) 'Draw me, we will run after you: the King has brought me into his chambers.'[10]

Here 'the garden' pardes (paradise) is used to mean the world of mystical experience or the place to which the mystic is transported in his trance. Akher was a name used for Elisha ben Abuya, a teacher of Rabbi Meir, who lost his faith (cut the shoots). Only Rabbi Akiva had the strength of mind to survive the experience. Akiva was a great aficionado of the Song of Songs, opposing those who wished to exclude it from the Bible.[11] He viewed the book as an allegory of the love of God for the People of Israel, a method of interpretation which helped to frame a long tradition that speculation about the nature of God was best carried out in metaphorical language.[12] Following Akiva, then, we might say that Judaism presents theology in an apophatic way, a term we will now explain.

In his book, *A Jewish Theology*, Louis Jacobs enquired whether or not it is necessary or desirable to speak at all of the nature of God.[13] The attitude that God is completely unknowable is described in the history of religious thought as the *via negativa* or apophatic theology, though Jacobs explains that this is 'only a negation of religion for those limited in vision. The mystic bows before God in adoration not in spite of God's ineffability but because of it.'[14] Hence the suggestion of medievals such as Bachya ibn Pakuda[15] and Maimonides that to ascribe any positive aspects to God is a form of polytheism. Even ideas such as God's unity and eternity can only be understood in terms of what God is not.

Although Patrick clearly recognizes the importance in Christian tradition of the apophatic way,[16] which was so important to several of the

Greek Fathers, and the mystical tradition, which made more of what is called 'presencing', of being in the presence of God, than of the elaboration of doctrine, he does nevertheless suggest in his paper that it is 'axiomatic'[17] to accept certain ideas about God. Some might find this inconsistent with the assertion made almost immediate afterwards[18] that orthodox doctrine was invented through the debates of the Fathers of the Church Councils. Was this logic, or did church politics play a role? It is perhaps not surprising that Jewish thinkers were very reluctant to engage in such speculation. Moreover, in answer to Patrick's question, 'Must a Jew believe anything?'[19] the answer is no. Christianity is self-proclaimedly doctrinal, Judaism is not. Even so, and despite the existence of a variety of mystical and kabbalistic concepts, it would be hard to argue against there being a consensus in the Jewish religious tradition that God is to be understood as unique, single and invisible. In response to Patrick's question, we would like to suggest that something of this is owed to debates with Christians and with Muslims. Over the centuries, Jews in Europe have borrowed many aspects of Christian culture, though at the same time distancing themselves from Christian trinitarian theology.

The importance of metaphor, allegory and allusion in the Jewish tradition is consistent with Judaism being not so much a religion, clearly defined by doctrine, as a cultural complex. Originally branded by nascent Christianity as a religion and so given credence, initially Judaism did construct an orthodoxy,[20] in essence a religious Other for Christianity. However, already by the end of late antiquity Judaism had reverted to being, as it still is today, an identity: a given, not something to be achieved – or to be lost – through the recognition or denial of Truth. Judaism has no word for 'religion':[21] it is not separate from the complex of our history, civilization, culture, narrative, law and thought. Kabbalistic literature certainly distinguishes between the knowable and unknowable aspects of God, analogous to the distinction invoked by Patrick between *totus Deus* and *totum Dei*.[22] But the authors and readers of kabbalistic texts can only travel so far into this realm: 'Whereof one cannot speak, thereof one must be silent', to adopt Wittgenstein's dictum.

As with the development of Nicene Christianity, a process of heresy-hunting was involved in the establishment of Rabbinic Judaism in its formative years. It has recently been cogently argued by Daniel Boyarin, an illustrious scholar of early Rabbinic Judaism and Christianity, that some of the beliefs that were eventually suppressed by the Rabbis as heresy were those most in tune with the emerging Christian viewpoint, just as some Christian viewpoints were stigmatized around the same time as 'Judaizing heresy' in a process of the mutual construction of the two religions each in contradistinction from the other.[23] In consequence of this we would argue that the historical context is unpromising for an orthodox–orthodox dialogue in our time – especially so for those of us who see the Shoah as the inevitable culmination of centuries of invective against Jews. We admit the possibility that we may indeed need a new approach to dialogue because of a sense that we Jews are only too quick to focus blame on Christians: dialogue must surely be based on trust, which blame works constantly to undermine. Indeed, it is only in recent years that we have developed the ability through dialogue to build trust and constantly renew it.

Regrettable though it is that the beauty of each religion does not shine out adequately to the adherents of the other, it is not surprising: history militates against such optimism. However awe-inspiring in their detail the great edifices of Christian doctrine and of Jewish tradition, the Summae and Codes of Law, they do not find a ready audience beyond the faithful. Nor do they seek one. The Othering of the other faith, in suspicion, has been the norm for centuries, with honourable exceptions. One looks in vain for a theological suggestion that unconverted Jews were anything but damned, should be allowed to sojourn anywhere except under sufferance, or legitimately belonged anywhere. That Jews were entirely without power is an overstatement – Jewish history is not just a matter of being acted on – but Jewish life was almost everywhere subject to restriction and insecure. The contingency of history, then, which for Patrick is above all the vehicle through which (religious) truth breaks through into the world, is also an obstacle to the mutual recognition of Jewish and Christian tradition as equals, honouring our differences. Most would surely want to affirm, though, that in the years following the Second World War and the foundation of the CCJ it has also come to be seen as a ground for the emergence of reconciliation.

Let us consider the development of two separate faith traditions, Judaism and Christianity, as enabled by theology, a little further. The predominant rabbinic response to christological doctrine over the centuries has been silence, not proclamations about truth. Rulings that certain things not be said go back to the second or third century CE, if not earlier. Discussing the blessing in the Amidah (standing prayer) known as *modim* ('we give thanks'), said three times daily, the Mishnah teaches that if someone recites the word *modim* twice, he is to be silenced: the Talmud gives the reason, namely that it would sound like an acknowledgement of *sh'tei r'shuyot*, two powers in heaven. American Professor of the History of Religion Alan Segal, a brilliant scholar of the 'parting of the ways', points out that even when attacking binitarian rather than trinitarian doctrine, Rabbinic literature may well have Christianity in its line of fire. The concept of the Holy Spirit, *Ruakh HaKodesh*, was one that Rabbis understood and accepted, so it was essentially the doctrine of God the Father and God the Son that was subjected to such silencing.[24] For Daniel Boyarin, *sh'tei r'shuyot* applies not primarily to Christianity but to an ancient Jewish belief which the Rabbis named as a heresy and gave over to Christianity. At the same time, moreover, bishops of the Church were declaring 'one power in heaven' to be Monarchianism, a prominent heresy.[25]

In his book *Border Lines*, Boyarin shows the similarities between the two developing faiths as well as the ways they pulled apart. In his more recent and controversial book, *The Jewish Gospels*, a source Patrick Morrow uses,[26] Boyarin goes even further, arguing that crucial ideas taken up by Christianity reflect biblical ideas. In particular, he reads the vision in Daniel 7, with its two thrones, as an example of 'two powers in heaven'. In so doing, Boyarin forgets that had the early Rabbinic tradition so read the text, the book of Daniel would never have been accepted as part of the Tanakh. Indeed, such an interpretation is already condemned in the *Mekhilta*, an early midrash which, after quoting the 'two thrones' from Daniel 7.9, continues: 'Scripture therefore would not let the nations of the world have an excuse for saying there are two powers, but declares "I am Adonai your God" (Exodus 20.2).'[27]

Segal points out that this passage is an attack on those who saw the words 'Adonai' (the Tetragrammaton) and 'Elohim' (God) as denoting two different gods. Because that is an impossible interpretation in the context of Exodus 20, it must be impossible in other texts as well. Daniel 7, with its prophecy of the coming of the Son of Man, was a crucial passage for early Christianity but Jews could go no further than to see this as a messianic text – not as a vision of an incarnation of God – and even that was disputed.[28] In Jewish tradition, incarnation is not just unnecessary but impossible. Patrick's use of Boyarin to suggest that the Jewish tradition has intermediaries between humans and God is therefore misguided.

Patrick further asks, 'How can Christian orthodoxy be a resource, rather than an embarrassment, to Christians in dialogue with Jews?'[29] Indeed, we could pose the same question of Rabbinic Judaism, if one considers the small number of embarrassing stories about Jesus' parentage and behaviour recorded in the Babylonian Talmud. They have to be seen as making sense only within a polemical dialogical tradition, as Peter Schäfer has explained: because of the anti-Jewish bias especially in the Gospel of John, the Rabbis 'fought back with the means of parody, inversion, deliberate distortion, and not least with the proud proclamation that what their fellow Jews did to this Jesus was right ... and that those who follow his example ... will share his horrible fate'.[30] Happily now such polemic has become the exception rather than the norm. As regards Christian or Jewish orthodoxy being a 'resource' for dialogue, we certainly agree with Patrick on the importance of Jews knowing what Christians believe and practise and that the same applies for Christians knowing about Jews. However, as part of his call for orthodox–orthodox dialogue in our time, Patrick seems to be hoping to discover a commonly held concept about the nature of God in Judaism, equivalent somehow to what has emerged in Christianity. From our perspective, this is clearly impossible. Christ, to Christians, is a saviour (Greek *soter*), the Christian religion a soteriology. Normative Judaism, whether Orthodox or Reform, is not a soteriology so much as a way of living in the world, doing what God requires of us in covenant with God.

This distinction between the two faiths has enabled us to pursue separate but parallel paths through history, remaining connected in dialogue while not feeling the need to agree on the nature of God. It is, we might add, this which enables us as Jews to repudiate Karl Rahner's assertion, of which Patrick appears to approve, that all persons are potentially 'anonymous Christians'.[31] Judaism has no parallel teaching: instead, it is an important tenet of Judaism that the righteous of all nations have a place in the world to come. Judaism has the eschatological aim of the recognition of the one God by the whole world but that does not make other nations in any sense potential Jews.

Rahner's assertion that what non-Christians believe does not matter at all is not a basis for today's dialogue. Fortunately in citing Rahner, Patrick reinterprets him, to make the point how important it is to enter into dialogue in all humility. Nowhere in his paper is Patrick asserting the superiority of the Christian revelation. This is welcome – and there are Catholic theologians whose concept of truth is more nuanced than Rahner's.[32] Let us not forget the specific recognition of the importance of the Jewish people to the Church and the special nature of Jewish theology and purpose that has been recognized by the Catholic Church since the Second Vatican Council. Speaking in 2002, Cardinal Walter Kasper expressed the relationship like this:

> Because as Christians we know that God's covenant with Israel by God's faithfulness is not broken (Romans 11.29; cf. 3.4), mission understood as call to conversion from idolatry to the living and true God (1 Thessalonians 1.9) does not apply and cannot be applied to Jews ... This is not a merely abstract theological affirmation, but an affirmation that has concrete and tangible consequences; namely, that there is no organised Catholic missionary activity towards Jews as there is for all other non-Christian religions.[33]

This statement marks an important progressive development which fits with Patrick's statement that Judaism has its own authentic integrity or charism.[34]

We are entirely in agreement with Patrick's concluding statement that our two faiths have both attracted and repelled each other. Perhaps this was especially so at the time of the formation of Rabbinic Judaism and Patristic Christianity. Through a process of psychological splitting and Othering, each faith historically has projected and is still at risk of projecting its dark side onto the other,[35] Christianity its fears of not being saved and Judaism those of being insincere and violent: Christians as Esau and Edom.[36] We have found Patrick's approach a useful stimulus to us in discussing what dialogue should be about. We concur with him that more orthodox Jews could and should be encouraged to take part in dialogue with Christians. All of us, orthodox and liberal, Jew and Christian, must increase our efforts at understanding and appreciating the others with whom we are in dialogue; and through this, a deeper understanding of ourselves and our own faith so that we can live it better in the challenging times in which we live. Our two religions are not incommensurable. Let us therefore work hard to continue these efforts within and between them in order to make a *tikkun*, repair of and amends for the past, and walk together in productive peace in the future. The challenges are difficult: the reward may be great.

Notes

1 From Franz Rosenzweig, as quoted by Patrick in his note 59. The suggestion is that Christianity requires Judaism as a constant and necessary irritant.

2 *Supra* p. 246. He appears to be advancing the position that religions must be 'true' and we relativize at our peril.

3 Censorship played a decisive role in Natan's response. Whether the censorship was external or internal, it was a fearful response to oppression by the State in the person of the Church.

4 *Supra* p. 247.

5 Marcel Simon, 2009, *Verus Israel: A Study of the Relations between Christians and Jews in the Roman Empire* AD 135–425, new edition, Oxford: Littman Library of Jewish Civilization, especially ch. 8, 'Christian Anti-Semitism'.

6 In Judaism, there is the notion of *herem*, of which the best known example is Spinoza. It was his historical criticism which undermined the doctrine of the dual Torah on which Rabbinic Judaism was founded.

7 As shown by John Hick, 1973, *God and the Universe of Faiths*, Oxford: One-World Publications, and Norman Solomon, 1991, *Judaism and World Religion*, London: Macmillan.

8 Slavoj Žižek, 2004, 'On Divine Self-Limitation and Revolutionary Love', *Journal of Philosophy and Scripture*, Villanova University, 1 February.

9 Exodus 33.18–23.

10 *Tosefta Chagigah* 2.3–4, Babylonian Talmud, *Chagigah* 14b. Translation and commentary based on Hyam Maccoby, 1998, *Early Rabbinic Writings*, Cambridge: Cambridge University Press, pp. 136–8.
11 Mishnah *Yadayim* 3.5.
12 For a comparison of this with ancient Christian allegorical interpretation of Song of Songs, and likely dialogical encounters, see Reuven Kimelman, 1980, 'Rabbi Yohanan and Origen on the Song of Songs: A Third Century Jewish–Christian Disputation', *Harvard Theological Review* 73:2, pp. 576–95.
13 Louis Jacobs, 1973, *A Jewish Theology*, New York: Behrman House.
14 Jacobs, *A Jewish Theology*, p. 39.
15 Eleventh-century Spanish philosopher.
16 *Supra* p. 246.
17 *Supra* p. 244.
18 *Supra* pp. 244–6.
19 *Supra* p. 247.
20 Rowan Williams, 1989, 'Does It Make Sense to Speak of Pre-Nicene Orthodoxy?' in *The Making of Orthodoxy: Essays in Honour of Henry Chadwick*, ed. Rowan Williams, Cambridge: Cambridge University Press. Also, Daniel Boyarin, 2004, *Border Lines: The Partition of Judaeo-Christianity*, Philadelphia, PA: University of Pennsylvania Press, Introduction.
21 See Elli Tikvah Sarah, *supra* pp. 22–3.
22 *Supra* p. 245.
23 Boyarin, *Border Lines*, especially ch. 6. Boyarin there argues that the whole notion of a Jewish orthodoxy was a response to Christianity. However, he later modified his view, concluding that Jewish and Christian orthodoxy developed in parallel: see Daniel Boyarin, 2009, 'Rethinking Jewish Christianity: An Argument for Dismantling a Dubious Category (to which is Appended a Correction of my Border Lines)', *The Jewish Quarterly Review* 99:1, pp. 7–36.
24 Alan F. Segal, 1977, *Two Powers in Heaven: Early Rabbinic Reports about Christianity and Gnosticism*, Leiden: E. J. Brill. Also, Alan F. Segal, 1986, *Rebecca's Children: Judaism and Christianity in the Roman World*, Cambridge, MA: Harvard University Press.
25 Boyarin, *Border Lines*, p. 130.
26 *Supra* p. 250.
27 *Mekhilta de-Rabbi Ishmael, Bahodesh* 5.27, 1976 Lauterbach edn, Philadelphia, PA: JPSA, vol. 2, p. 231.
28 Babylonian Talmud, *Hagigah* 14a.
29 *Supra* p. 245.
30 Peter Schäfer, 2007, *Jesus in the Talmud*, Princeton, NJ: Princeton University Press, p. 129.
31 *Supra* p. 00, though Patrick adds a reservation as regards Jews.
32 For example Paul Knitter, 1985, *No Other Name?*, London: SCM Press, especially p. 219 on relational truth.
33 'Reflections by Cardinal Walter Kasper', Boston College, 6 November 2002, as quoted by Edward Idris Cassidy, 2005, *Ecumenism and Interreligious Dialogue: Unitatis Redintegratio, Nostra Aetate*, New York: Paulist Press, p. 261.
34 *Supra* p. 256.
35 Daniel Boyarin suggests this in *Border Lines*, p. 130.

36 Fears of the insincerity of Christianity are shown by Rabbinic interpretations of Genesis 33.4, where Esau and Jacob embrace. See the Introduction by Tony Bayfield to Tony Bayfield, Sidney Brichto and Eugene J. Fisher (eds.), 2001, *He Kissed Him and They Wept: Towards a Theology of Jewish–Catholic Partnership*, London: SCM Press. For the image of Edom as representing the Catholic Church, see Israel Yuval, 2006, *Two Nations in Your Womb: Perceptions of Jews and Christians in Late Antiquity and the Middle Ages*, Berkeley, CA: University of California Press, especially ch. 1.

Further Reflections

TONY BAYFIELD

Particularity proved a deeply disturbing challenge – far more so than any of us had anticipated. Over the course of our dialogue, acknowledging our unique family relationship as children of Abraham and Sarah had become more and more explicit. We were increasingly comfortable in recognizing Rabbinic Judaism and Christianity as born in the same place, at the same time, with a common inheritance apparent in both faiths. It was our particularity – that which makes us different and distinctive siblings rather than identical twins – that changed the tenor of our dialogue: not light but rather darkness was often visible! Interestingly, this was as often an intra-faith as an interfaith phenomenon.

Patrick, innocent of what was to come, had volunteered to go first. He recognized that for some the (to them) self-evident existential reality of the faith of our Christian sisters and brothers round the table – and of our commitment to respect as something more than a principle of etiquette – compels us to try to understand, value and learn from them. We – because I include myself in this group – accept that there will always be aspects, teachings which are different, puzzling, troubling, but they aren't mistakes or errors. Patrick's approach was not addressed primarily to us. He's an orthodox Christian and wanted to start with the orthodox *doctrines* on which his faith is founded and explain them in order to build bridges of shared understanding with his fellow Jews, particularly the orthodox whose starting position he imagined would be parallel to his own. With surprising results.

The first big surprise was that several of the liberal Jews found his presentation – especially when we'd penetrated the technical, doctrinal language (all Greek to us!) – genuinely helpful. Unlike my colleagues Natan Levy and Michael Hilton, I've always fought shy of the patristic period and those remote Councils held so long ago in the shadow of Constantinople. Patrick's thesis that we should understand them as a 'Hebraicizing of Hellenism'[1] was new to me: I've never enjoyed Franz Rosenzweig's[2] writings on Christianity, finding them the least appealing aspect of his theology. In any event, to use the terminology of TV singing

FURTHER REFLECTIONS

contests, Patrick sang that song and made it his own. What I found most enlightening was his affirmation of the personal, passible (loving, compassionate, just) God of the Hebrew Bible and the extent to which Jesus, the Christ figure, was a fundamental embodiment of that experience and understanding of God.

The second surprise – which shouldn't have been a surprise at all – was Vivian Silverman's response: he was only able to see the Hellenization of Christianity which made it incompatible with his Jewish beliefs and, at its incarnational heart, incomprehensible. That response to incarnation was shared by every Jew round the table. It nailed the key 'particularity' of Christianity which Jews not only find difficult to understand but instinctively react against with every fibre of their Jewish being as contrary to our understanding of the nature of God.[3] As often, David Ford came to our rescue by saying that it may be of the very nature of the Christian revelation that it is those who experience fulfilment in the revelation at Sinai who find it most difficult to understand. For me, not understanding and wrong are not the same.

Previously unplanned, we turned to Natan Levy who, though orthodox, comes from a background where engagement goes further than even Vivian's lifelong friendship and collaboration. Natan builds his response on that of Maimonides (Rambam) and refuses to dismiss Christianity as a failure in Jewish eyes. 'Christianity', says Natan, is 'Torah in translation' and 'the Rabbis pave a difficult path for Jewish–Christian engagement. What they do not do is turn aside from the encounter.'[4] Those last two sentences are, quite simply, game-changing.

I'm in no way diminishing the value of Natan's reasoning and conclusion if I point out two things. First, it's significant that Natan founds his argument on Maimonides. While Maimonides' authority is unimpeachable, his understanding of God was very different from that of God in much Rabbinic aggadah and in particular to the Akiva tradition of a God who is with us in our suffering and suffers with us.[5] Second, Natan refers to the 'halakhic – rabbinic tradition' and in so doing doesn't acknowledge aggadah. Some of us take a different view and follow the Polish-American Jewish scholar Abraham Joshua Heschel,[6] who wrote:

> *Halakhah* represents the strength to shape one's life according to a fixed pattern: it is a form-giving force. *Aggadah* is the expression of man's ceaseless striving, which often defies all limitations. *Halakhah* is the rationalisation and schematisation of living; it defines, specifies, sets measure and limit, placing life into an exact system. *Aggadah* deals with man's ineffable relations to God, to other men, and to the world ... The interrelationship of *halakhah* and *aggadah* is the very heart of Judaism.[7]

CHRISTIAN PARTICULARITY

We also called on Michael Hilton for assistance. Michael is, as you will know from his essay, a historian so he in turn sought help outside the Group from a specialist in the field, Victor Seedman. They make two vital observations. First, they contest Patrick's enthusiasm for demonstrating that the Christian concept of Messiah as God incarnate is already present in the literature of the second and first centuries BCE, for instance in the book of Daniel.[8] Trying too hard to make the incarnation and resurrection part of our shared heritage and therefore more approachable/palatable is probably not historically sustainable and it's certainly not the best of dialogical tactics to tell Jews that a doctrine is present in their tradition when Christianity has been so critical over so many centuries of this particular doctrinal absence in Judaism!

Even more important, Hilton and Seedman point out that doctrine plays a much more fundamental part in Christianity than Judaism. We're back to the two adjacent and connected gardens differently configured and with different plantings.[9] Jews have a particular concept of peoplehood[10] and have placed a much greater stress on practice in everyday living – Natan's 'halakhic-rabbinic' character – in order to create a portable way of life[11] which a minority community could live out wherever and whenever they were. It's easy to forget that the framework of practice both expressed and contained the aggadic, the ethical and theological. Modernity has loosened the containing framework for the majority of Jews and, today, identity comes first. One can be a Jew whatever one's attitude to Judaism.[12]

In addition, it isn't true to say that Judaism contains no doctrine. Ever since the abolition of the Sanhedrin by the Romans there have been no defining, authoritative bodies to agree doctrine, no equivalents of the Christian Councils. But Maimonides' Thirteen Principles of the Jewish Faith[13] look decidedly doctrinal, notwithstanding the extent to which they were contested.[14] The history of Judaism over the last 150 years underlines the importance of the doctrine of the Dual Torah[15] to Rabbinic Judaism and Orthodoxy defends it against other streams of Judaism with fierce intensity. Just over a quarter of a century ago it seemed as though Orthodoxy was not only intent on denying the term Judaism to the non-Orthodox world but writing non-Orthodox Jews out of it as well. That's why Rabbi Lord Sacks wrote his first major book, *One People?*,[16] to ensure doctrinal disputes didn't fracture the unity of peoplehood. I found his supporting argument not to my taste[17] – just as I'm troubled by the notion of Christianity as Torah in translation[18] – but the objective here is more important than the argument deployed, which needs to be tailored to a particular constituency.

Patrick's venture teased out a great deal and challenged the liberals both Christian and Jewish. If you've moved on in some way from the fourth-century creeds or outside the Maimonidean principles of the Jewish faith, what is it that gives authority to your Christianity/Judaism and stamps it as authentic? It became clear that almost all the other Christians in the Group wanted to explain Trinity, incarnation and resurrection differently from Patrick but the range of responses was as great as that evinced by the Jews when discussing the nature of Torah. We also had some confused/confusing discussions of metaphor. For me Christ as God incarnate can be approached as a metaphor for the Divine response to human suffering. As I've already pointed out,[19] a major stream in Rabbinic thought follows Rabbi Akiva in teaching that God is deeply affected by our suffering. For some in our Group the inference took them beyond a line they couldn't cross; for others it (re-)introduced a concept of God as passible which they don't share. But it seems to me that a doctrine which so deeply divides us also obscures a profound and essential shared understanding.

Judaism and Christianity are branches from the same trunk. But Christianity's embrace of Rome and encounter with Hellenism gave it a numinous particularity. Incarnation and – if it's a dependent concept – resurrection[20] are the two aspects most likely to prove challenging in Jewish–Christian dialogue in the coming decades. However, to follow Natan, that does not permit us to 'turn aside from the encounter'. After all, God God's self is at stake. It's long been my belief that God, necessarily, has many faces – the God of Abraham, Isaac and Jacob, Sarah, Rebekah, Rachel and Leah; Christ; Allah – yet what we sense beyond, *Ein Sof*,[21] God God's self is what we share. Only now do I realize that we never got to test that supposition. How much more work there is to do and how potentially exciting and enriching is the journey stretching ahead.

Notes

1 *Supra* p. 245. Morrow, correctly, distinguishes between the Judaism of the Bible and Rabbinic Judaism. Since Christianity, like Judaism, emerged during the inter-testamental period, it wasn't Judaism as Rabbinic Judaism which early Christianity took with it into the Greco-Roman world. Hence Hebraicization rather than Judaization.

2 Rosenzweig, I now understand, used a similar argument.

3 As Vivian wrote on all our behalves: 'How can God be a human being?'

4 *Supra* p. 275.

5 But much closer to Akiva's contemporary Rabbi Ishmael.

6 Abraham Joshua Heschel, b. Warsaw, 1907, d. New York, 1972.

7 Abraham Joshua Heschel, 1997, *Between God and Man*, New York: Free Press, p. 175.

8 *Supra* pp. 280–1.
9 *Supra* p. 9.
10 A Jew is someone either born a Jew according to rules concerning parentage or who chooses to become a Jew and conforms to rules concerning conversion. All Jews – by birth or by choice – form links in a chain which stretches back to Sinai.
11 Essential to survival after the expulsion from the Land by the Romans.
12 Many Jews reject Judaism partially or completely. What this means for the long-term survival of Jews and Judaism is a question exercising rabbis of every denomination.
13 Found in his commentary on the Mishnah, compiled between 1170 and 1180.
14 Despite being contested, time and widespread acceptance hallowed Maimonides' Principles. Louis Jacobs' great theological work is called *Principles of the Jewish Faith* – of which there are 13!
15 The doctrine that Moses received not only the written Torah but an oral, interpretive Torah passed from Sinai to the founders of Rabbinic Judaism. See *Pirkei Avot* I.1.
16 Jonathan Sacks, 1993, *One People? Tradition, Modernity and Jewish Unity*, London: Littman Library of Jewish Civilization.
17 He uses the Talmudic principle that a child – i.e. the non-orthodox – brought up by non-Jews (in the postmodern world) is not responsible for imbibing what they have been wrongly taught. See Sacks, *One People?*, especially pp. 33–4.
18 What was astonishing, open and generous in the twelfth century feels very different today.
19 The Christian doctrine of the resurrection is inseparable from the doctrine of incarnation. Certainly in Patrick's paper and not disputed by his colleagues in the Group.
20 See p. 287.
21 'Without End', the term used in the Jewish mystical tradition.

8
Jewish Particularism

Spying on Israel: Morality of a Promised Land

NATAN LEVY

There is a classic question the Rabbinical commentators, consummate legalists, ask about the entire book of Genesis. What is the purpose of such a collection of stories in a Scripture devoted to teaching, practical ethics and ritual? What is the purpose of long and intricate narratives in a Scripture by which each mitzvah is so perfectly parsed that 39 must be derived from a single word.[1] Should not the Torah begin with the book of Exodus, specifically at the moment when God invests Israel with its first command of counting the months: 'This month shall be unto you the beginning of months'?[2]

The eleventh-century French biblical commentator Rashi offers an answer sourced from midrashic literature:

> In the eschatological future, the Nations of the Earth will exclaim: 'Israel, you are nothing but rogues! You have stolen the Land of Israel from its rightful owners!' Then the Children of Israel will answer: 'Have you not read, in the book of Genesis, that God is the creator of heaven and earth. He can take and give the Land to whomsoever He pleases.'[3]

Israel the Land belongs to Israel the Nation by divine fiat alone. And that notion is warrant enough for the entire book of Genesis.

However, the Spanish commentator Nachmanides, struck by the same burning question almost a century later, is not entirely convinced by Rashi's answer. While many elements of the book of Genesis do seem extraneous for Nachmanides, surely its first verses play a fundamental role in the religious gestalt:

> And one can question [Rashi's answer], because there is great need to begin the Torah with 'In the beginning God created' for it is the root of faith; and one who doesn't believe this and believes that the world is primordial, he is an apostate and has no Torah whatsoever.[4]

However, the book of Genesis as a whole still cries out for an explanation. Why include such a book in the Torah? According to Nachmanides, the stories of Genesis are the weaving together of a separate motif, a clarion call of sorts that reverberates from the beginning to the end of the book:

> The Torah began with 'In the beginning God created' and the story of the whole topic of creation until the creation of Adam, and made him ruler of the work of His hands and all that was given over beneath his feet, and the Garden of Eden – which is the best of all the places created in this world – became established for his dwelling, until their [Adam's and Eve's] sin drove them from there. And the people of the generation of the Deluge, by their sin were driven from the entire world, and the righteous one among them [Noah] alone was spared, him and his sons. And Noah's descendants, their sin [of the Tower of Babel] caused them to be scattered in places and planted in lands, and they captured for themselves the places according to their families among their peoples, as the opportunities arose to them. If so, it is appropriate that, when a people continues to sin, it will be destroyed from its place and another people will inherit his land, for this is the law of God in the land from always. And all the more so with what is told in the text that Canaan is cursed and was sold as an eternal slave, and it is not appropriate that he inherits the choicest places of settlement, but it will be inherited by the slaves of God, the seed of he who loved Him, like the issues which is written (Psalm 105.44–45): 'And He gave them the lands of nations and the labour of peoples they shall inherit so that they shall keep His laws and guard His instructions.' That is to say, He chased out those who rebelled against Him, and settled His servants there, so that they would know that by serving Him they will possess it – and if they sin against Him, the Land will vomit them up just as it vomited up the Nation before them.[5]

In Rashi's interpretation, the Land of Israel is Promised Land, heteronomously given and unconditionally acquired. God can give and take what he chooses, and he chose the Jews as the inhabitants of Israel. But Nachmanides remains wary of such a reading. Israel is Permitted – rather than Promised – Land. The entire book of Genesis builds each story into a crescendo of meaning to pass on only this: every land is given over to its inhabitants as utterly conditional. Genesis is that primordial reminder that the very maws of exile extend below every home and country, with only the thinnest gossamer net of morality and ethics to keep us from that descent.

SPYING ON ISRAEL: MORALITY OF A PROMISED LAND

Do we, Jews, inherit a Promised Land or a Permitted Land? That is the dilemma – and the title[6] – of a short essay by the postmodern French philosopher and Talmudist Emmanuel Levinas.[7] It is an essay of such honest dignity on the moral questions of the State of Israel that I feel it would be best if I were simply to paste Levinas's entire article into these pages and leave you – the reader – and Levinas in direct and unmitigated dialogue. I would have fulfilled my obligation, inasmuch as a matchmaker refrains from following the couple she has arranged into the private chamber. But, as an essayist has far less shame than any matchmaker, I will enter with Levinas into the dialectic.

Levinas delivered his essay in a colloquium dedicated to Israel, held in 1965. Let us keep the date in mind throughout as it fell in the pensive shadow of a nearly daily media diatribe of threatened violence from the Arab neighbours of Israel that would eventually coalesce into the Six Day War in two years hence. However, while Levinas will spar briefly with politics, his task – on the surface – is simply to engage his audience with two pages of Talmudic dialogue taken from the Babylonian Talmud Tractate *Sotah* (34b–35a) and devoted almost exclusively to the aggadah – the ethical and philosophical component of the Talmud couched in the genre of slight stories or fables.

The sages on this page of the Talmud are transfixed by the crisis that occurred at the end of the first year of the Israelites' journeying in the desert, a crisis described in Numbers 13:

¹ וַיְדַבֵּר יְהוָה אֶל־מֹשֶׁה לֵּאמֹר:	¹ The Eternal spoke to Moses, saying:
² שְׁלַח־לְךָ אֲנָשִׁים וְיָתֻרוּ אֶת־אֶרֶץ כְּנַעַן אֲשֶׁר־אֲנִי נֹתֵן לִבְנֵי יִשְׂרָאֵל אִישׁ אֶחָד אִישׁ אֶחָד לְמַטֵּה אֲבֹתָיו תִּשְׁלָחוּ כֹּל נָשִׂיא בָהֶם:	² 'Send men, that they may spy out the land of Canaan, which I give to the children of Israel; of every tribe of their fathers you shall send a man, every one a prince among them.'
³ וַיִּשְׁלַח אֹתָם מֹשֶׁה מִמִּדְבַּר פָּארָן עַל־פִּי יְהוָה כֻּלָּם אֲנָשִׁים רָאשֵׁי בְנֵי־יִשְׂרָאֵל הֵמָּה:	³ Moses sent them from the wilderness of Paran according to the commandment of the Eternal; all of them men who were heads of the children of Israel.
⁴ וְאֵלֶּה שְׁמוֹתָם לְמַטֵּה רְאוּבֵן שַׁמּוּעַ בֶּן־זַכּוּר:	⁴ These were their names: of the tribe of Reuben, Shammua the son of Zaccur.

לְמַטֵּה שִׁמְעוֹן שָׁפָט בֶּן־חוֹרִי:	⁵ Of the tribe of Simeon, Shaphat the son of Hori.
⁶לְמַטֵּה יְהוּדָה כָּלֵב בֶּן־יְפֻנֶּה:	⁶ Of the tribe of Judah, Caleb the son of Jephunneh.
⁷לְמַטֵּה יִשָּׂשכָר יִגְאָל בֶּן־יוֹסֵף:	⁷ Of the tribe of Issachar, Igal the son of Joseph.
⁸לְמַטֵּה אֶפְרַיִם הוֹשֵׁעַ בִּן־נוּן:	⁸ Of the tribe of Ephraim, Hoshea the son of Nun.
⁹לְמַטֵּה בִנְיָמִן פַּלְטִי בֶּן־רָפוּא:	⁹ Of the tribe of Benjamin, Palti the son of Raphu.
¹⁰לְמַטֵּה זְבוּלֻן גַּדִּיאֵל בֶּן־סוֹדִי:	¹⁰ Of the tribe of Zebulun, Gaddiel the son of Sodi.
¹¹לְמַטֵּה יוֹסֵף לְמַטֵּה מְנַשֶּׁה גַּדִּי בֶּן־סוּסִי:	¹¹ Of the tribe of Joseph, namely, of the tribe of Manasseh, Gaddi the son of Susi.
¹²לְמַטֵּה דָן עַמִּיאֵל בֶּן־גְּמַלִּי:	¹² Of the tribe of Dan, Ammiel the son of Gemalli.
¹³לְמַטֵּה אָשֵׁר סְתוּר בֶּן־מִיכָאֵל:	¹³ Of the tribe of Asher, Sethur the son of Michael.
¹⁴לְמַטֵּה נַפְתָּלִי נַחְבִּי בֶּן־וָפְסִי:	¹⁴ Of the tribe of Naphtali, Nahbi the son of Vophsi.
¹⁵לְמַטֵּה גָד גְּאוּאֵל בֶּן־מָכִי:	¹⁵ Of the tribe of Gad, Geuel the son of Machi.
¹⁶אֵלֶּה שְׁמוֹת הָאֲנָשִׁים אֲשֶׁר־שָׁלַח מֹשֶׁה לָתוּר אֶת־הָאָרֶץ וַיִּקְרָא מֹשֶׁה לְהוֹשֵׁעַ בִּן־נוּן יְהוֹשֻׁעַ:	¹⁶ These are the names of the men that Moses sent to spy out the land. Moses called Hoshea the son of Nun, Joshua.
¹⁷וַיִּשְׁלַח אֹתָם מֹשֶׁה לָתוּר אֶת־אֶרֶץ כְּנָעַן וַיֹּאמֶר אֲלֵהֶם עֲלוּ זֶה בַּנֶּגֶב וַעֲלִיתֶם אֶת־הָהָר:	¹⁷ Moses sent them to spy out the land of Canaan, and said to them: 'Arise here into the South, and go up into the mountains;

SPYING ON ISRAEL: MORALITY OF A PROMISED LAND

¹⁸ וּרְאִיתֶ֥ם אֶת־הָאָ֖רֶץ מַה־הִ֑וא וְאֶת־הָעָם֙ הַיֹּשֵׁ֣ב עָלֶ֔יהָ הֶחָזָ֥ק הוּא֙ הֲרָפֶ֔ה הַמְעַ֥ט ה֖וּא אִם־רָֽב׃

¹⁹ וּמָ֣ה הָאָ֗רֶץ אֲשֶׁר־הוּא֙ יֹשֵׁ֣ב בָּ֔הּ הֲטוֹבָ֥ה הִ֖וא אִם־רָעָ֑ה וּמָ֣ה הֶֽעָרִ֗ים אֲשֶׁר־הוּא֙ יוֹשֵׁ֣ב בָּהֵ֔נָּה הַבְּמַֽחֲנִ֖ים אִ֥ם בְּמִבְצָרִֽים׃

²⁰ וּמָ֣ה הָ֠אָרֶץ הַשְּׁמֵנָ֨ה הִ֜וא אִם־רָזָ֗ה הֲיֵֽשׁ־בָּ֥הּ עֵץ֙ אִם־אַ֔יִן וְהִ֨תְחַזַּקְתֶּ֔ם וּלְקַחְתֶּ֖ם מִפְּרִ֣י הָאָ֑רֶץ וְהַ֨יָּמִ֔ים יְמֵ֖י בִּכּוּרֵ֥י עֲנָבִֽים׃

²¹ וַֽיַּעֲל֖וּ וַיָּתֻ֣רוּ אֶת־הָאָ֑רֶץ מִמִּדְבַּר־צִ֥ן עַד־רְחֹ֖ב לְבֹ֥א חֲמָֽת׃

²² וַיַּעֲל֣וּ בַנֶּגֶב֮ וַיָּבֹ֣א עַד־חֶבְרוֹן֒ וְשָׁ֤ם אֲחִימָן֙ שֵׁשַׁ֣י וְתַלְמַ֔י יְלִידֵ֖י הָעֲנָ֑ק וְחֶבְר֗וֹן שֶׁ֤בַע שָׁנִים֙ נִבְנְתָ֔ה לִפְנֵ֖י צֹ֥עַן מִצְרָֽיִם׃

²³ וַיָּבֹ֜אוּ עַד־נַ֣חַל אֶשְׁכֹּ֗ל וַיִּכְרְת֨וּ מִשָּׁ֤ם זְמוֹרָה֙ וְאֶשְׁכּ֤וֹל עֲנָבִים֙ אֶחָ֔ד וַיִּשָּׂאֻ֥הוּ בַמּ֖וֹט בִּשְׁנָ֑יִם וּמִן־הָרִמֹּנִ֖ים וּמִן־הַתְּאֵנִֽים׃

²⁴ לַמָּק֣וֹם הַה֔וּא קָרָ֖א נַ֣חַל אֶשְׁכּ֑וֹל עַ֚ל אֹד֣וֹת הָֽאֶשְׁכּ֔וֹל אֲשֶׁר־כָּרְת֥וּ מִשָּׁ֖ם בְּנֵ֥י יִשְׂרָאֵֽל׃

¹⁸ and see the land, what it is; and the people that dwell there, whether they are strong or weak, whether they are few or many;

¹⁹ and what the land is that they live in, whether it is good or bad; and what cities there are that they dwell in, whether in camps, or in strongholds;

²⁰ and what the land is, whether it is fat or lean, whether there is wood there, or not. Be courageous, and bring back the fruit of the land.' It was the time of the first-ripe grapes.

²¹ So they went up, and spied out the land from the wilderness of Zin up to Rehob, at the entrance to Hamath.

²² They went up into the South, and came to Hebron; and Ahiman, Sheshai, and Talmai, the children of Anak, were there. Now Hebron was built seven years before Zoan in Egypt.

²³ And they came into the valley of Eshcol, and cut down a branch with one cluster of grapes, and they carried it on a pole between two; they also took pomegranates, and figs.

²⁴ That place was called the valley of Eshcol, because of the cluster which the children of Israel cut down there.

²⁵ וַיָּשֻׁבוּ מִתּוּר הָאָרֶץ מִקֵּץ אַרְבָּעִים יוֹם:

²⁶ וַיֵּלְכוּ וַיָּבֹאוּ אֶל־מֹשֶׁה וְאֶל־אַהֲרֹן וְאֶל־כָּל־עֲדַת בְּנֵי־יִשְׂרָאֵל אֶל־מִדְבַּר פָּארָן קָדֵשָׁה וַיָּשִׁיבוּ אוֹתָם דָּבָר וְאֶת־כָּל־הָעֵדָה וַיַּרְאוּם אֶת־פְּרִי הָאָרֶץ:

²⁷ וַיְסַפְּרוּ־לוֹ וַיֹּאמְרוּ בָּאנוּ אֶל־הָאָרֶץ אֲשֶׁר שְׁלַחְתָּנוּ וְגַם זָבַת חָלָב וּדְבַשׁ הִוא וְזֶה־פִּרְיָהּ:

²⁸ אֶפֶס כִּי־עַז הָעָם הַיֹּשֵׁב בָּאָרֶץ וְהֶעָרִים בְּצֻרוֹת גְּדֹלֹת מְאֹד וְגַם־יְלִדֵי הָעֲנָק רָאִינוּ שָׁם:

²⁹ עֲמָלֵק יוֹשֵׁב בְּאֶרֶץ הַנֶּגֶב וְהַחִתִּי וְהַיְבוּסִי וְהָאֱמֹרִי יוֹשֵׁב בָּהָר וְהַכְּנַעֲנִי יֹשֵׁב עַל־הַיָּם וְעַל יַד הַיַּרְדֵּן:

³⁰ וַיַּהַס כָּלֵב אֶת־הָעָם אֶל־מֹשֶׁה וַיֹּאמֶר עָלֹה נַעֲלֶה וְיָרַשְׁנוּ אֹתָהּ כִּי־יָכוֹל נוּכַל לָהּ:

³¹ וְהָאֲנָשִׁים אֲשֶׁר־עָלוּ עִמּוֹ אָמְרוּ לֹא נוּכַל לַעֲלוֹת אֶל־הָעָם כִּי־חָזָק הוּא מִמֶּנּוּ:

JEWISH PARTICULARISM

²⁵ They returned from spying out the land at the end of forty days.

²⁶ They went and came to Moses, and to Aaron, and to all the congregation of the children of Israel, into the wilderness of Paran, to Kadesh; and brought back word to them, and to all the congregation, and showed them the fruit of the land.

²⁷ They told him, and said: 'We came to the land you sent us to, and it flows with milk and honey; and this is the fruit from there.

²⁸ But the people that dwell in the land are fierce, and the cities are fortified, and very great; and we also saw the children of Anak there.

²⁹ Amalek lives in the land of the South; and the Hittite, and the Jebusite, and the Amorite, dwell in the mountains; and the Canaanite dwells by the sea, and along by the side of the Jordan.'

³⁰ Caleb stilled the people toward Moses, and said: 'We should go up at once, and possess it; for we are well able to overcome it.'

³¹ But the men that went up with him said: 'We are not able to go up against the people; for they are stronger than us.'

SPYING ON ISRAEL: MORALITY OF A PROMISED LAND

³² וַיּוֹצִיאוּ דִּבַּת הָאָרֶץ אֲשֶׁר תָּרוּ אֹתָהּ אֶל־בְּנֵי יִשְׂרָאֵל לֵאמֹר הָאָרֶץ אֲשֶׁר עָבַרְנוּ בָהּ לָתוּר אֹתָהּ אֶרֶץ אֹכֶלֶת יוֹשְׁבֶיהָ הִוא וְכָל־הָעָם אֲשֶׁר־רָאִינוּ בְתוֹכָהּ אַנְשֵׁי מִדּוֹת:

³³ וְשָׁם רָאִינוּ אֶת־הַנְּפִילִים בְּנֵי עֲנָק מִן־הַנְּפִלִים וַנְּהִי בְעֵינֵינוּ כַּחֲגָבִים וְכֵן הָיִינוּ בְּעֵינֵיהֶם:

³² They spread an evil report of the land that they had spied out to the children of Israel, saying: 'The land, through which we have passed to spy on it, it is a land that eats up the inhabitants there; and all the people that we saw in it are men of great stature. ³³ There we saw the Nephilim, the sons of Anak, who come from the Nephilim; and we seemed to ourselves as grasshoppers, and so we were in their sight.'

I have taken the liberty of quoting from the biblical text at length for two reasons. First, because the Talmudic sages themselves will pull from the innocuous and most banal moments herein worlds of new meaning. Second, because in seeing the story unfold, we cannot really miss the monstrous project that the newly released slaves of Egypt must now embark upon. Promised Land for Israel? What of the native people who already call this place home? Moses' directive to the spies is underpinned with violence. 'Are the people weak or strong ... Are the cities open camps or strongholds?' That is to say, how clinically can we displace – dare we say it, massacre – the populace before eating from their fields and living in their houses?

In Levinas's commentary on the Talmudic discussion, the sages experienced the moral problem at the core of this text. For Levinas, these spies – or 'explorers', as he will label them – are afraid. But it is not a primitive fear of the weaker party before entrenched giants but a trembling awareness before the monstrosity of the project that God has demanded within the covenantal relationship. The Lord of Heaven and Earth has called his chosen people to embark on a divine land grab. Levinas writes:

> What seems so simple in the Biblical text, the fear which seizes the Children of Israel when they are about to reach their goal, will become problematic in the Talmudic text we are reading. In the great fear of the explorers, we may discover anxieties more familiar to us ... that in the course of history, Jewish thought, like Jewish conscience, has known every scruple, every remorse, even when it comes to the most sacred rights of the people troubled by this thought.[8]

JEWISH PARTICULARISM

The Talmudic rationale behind the betrayal of the explorers – their refusal to enter the Land – has almost nothing to do with their trepidation before a giant race of human beings and is, instead, the ethical unease about conquering already inhabited land.

Let us now turn to the Talmudic discussion directly:

> Rav Hiyya bar Abba said: The explorers sought only the shame of the Land, for about this it has been said 'That they may explore (*v'yakhp'ru*) the Land.' (Deut. 1.22) And elsewhere it has been said (Isaiah 24.23): 'The moon will be ashamed (*v'khaf'ra*) and the sun will be confounded.'⁹

In the Levinasian exegesis of the Talmud, the Rabbinical mind will always seek more out of a proof text than the mere lines offered on the page. It is the entire context of the newly introduced material, its undergirding story, which the Rabbis were seeking to intermingle into the original discussion, and the few quoted verses are the most delicate of bridges, connecting these two textual worlds. Thus, in the verse from Isaiah, the Prophet foretells of an anguished sun and moon, shamed by the triumph of the Eternal One. And the commentators on that passage from Isaiah infer that the shaming of the sun and the moon can refer to the shaming of those who worship the sun and the moon. God's truth shames the idol-worshippers of celestial bodies. From this understanding of the Isaiah text, the intention of the explorers is manifest. From the onset, the explorers' express purpose was to bring shame to the Land and – akin to Isaiah – to bring shame upon those who would worship the Land, by confronting such worship with a higher moral truth. 'They have decided,' Levinas writes, 'in the name of truth, to confound the Zionists.'¹⁰ All this from one passing reference to Isaiah! Yet, isn't the Jewish covetousness over a particular piece of real estate in the midst of such a proud ethical monotheism shameful enough that perhaps only a passing comment is all that is required to stir those real misgivings?

Let us continue with Levinas and go further into the Talmudic dialectic. We move quickly from lofty moral dilemmas to a dissection of names:

> Here are their names: 'For the tribe of Reuben, Shammua son of Zaccur'. (Num 13.4). Rav Isaac said: 'We have a tradition according to which the explorers are named after their actions but only one has survived with us, S'tur, son of Mi'kha-el. S'tur because he has given the lie to (*satur*) the words of the Holy One, Blessed be He. Mi'kha-el because he has weakened Him (*mak*).'¹¹

It's a very forced reading of rather beautiful biblical names! No parent reads into Michael a name of Divine weakening. Michael is a prayer: 'Mi ka-el, Who is like God?' Yet the explorers are destined by their very names and the names of their fathers for this betrayal. Their lies are only natural, it is in the DNA itself to weaken God's plan regarding the Land of Israel. For to believe in the Land of Israel is to transcend the order of things and grasp hold of a sacred history that is never transduced to the relationships of cause and effect. The names indicate the trajectory of the explorers. Levinas comments:

> The first concern of the explorers would therefore consist in giving the lie to the legend about the acts accomplished by the Holy One, by contesting, demystifying, sacred history; all that was done, the coming out of Egypt and the miracles and the promises, all that is not true. Or at least it is possible not to talk about it. Sacred history can be passed over in silence ... Jewish history is like any other history.[12]

Once the Jewish State becomes like any other state (Herzl's own lofty vision),[13] then the settlers in Hebron are simply weird, then the rights of *aliyah* are simply an anachronistic holdover from the Shoah, then the claims to particular land are colonial at best. And then, too, the Kirk can title a report on Israel *The Inheritance of Abraham?* concluding with that hurtful question mark like a slap; the Director of Greenbelt[14] can stand up in a tent of over 1,000 listeners and call Israel 'the Land once called Holy'[15] (as if sacred history may once have been tangible, but was subsequently pushed aside by some other, more sacred form); and the Methodist Church can release a report on boycotting the Jewish State of Israel, and only mention God once, in the final perfunctory line. God is weak, sacred history lies, this is the crisis of the explorers, carved into the flesh of their very names.

The argument of the explorers and their ilk can be restated at this point succinctly. No human can legitimately claim the land of another as the Divine will of things, without calling into question the legitimacy of their prophetic project overall. The plagues, leaving Egypt, the miracle of the sea split, none can justify a colonial end-game in Canaan. This is a strong argument, an argument of identity and, thus, names. Now the Talmud will go even further, first strengthening the case for the explorers, before calling them to dreadful account.

The Talmudic text continues with a play on the elusive quality of biblical pronouns:

But the men who had gone with him said: 'We shall not be able to ...' (Num 13.31). Rabbi Hanina bar Papa said: 'The explorers uttered a great thing at that moment: "He (i.e. the Canaanite Nation) is stronger than we are."' (Num 13.31). Do not read: 'than we are'; read 'than Him.' Even the master of the house cannot remove his tools from there.[16]

A mysterious notion, indeed. What is this 'great thing' the Rabbis speak of in the mouth of these diminishers of the Holy? Levinas expounds:

> ... the native inhabitant of Canaan is stronger than God. At least two interpretations are possible: against the strength of this indigenous population, nothing moral can hold its own. He is moral reality; they are historical reality. According to this first lesson, the great thing expressed by the explorers would be human despair before the failure of ideas, which are always crushed by history, the universal vanquished by the local.[17]

No justification, no matter how lucid, can stand before an old man holding his key to the garden gate he left behind in Jaffa! However, let us bear in mind always that the words of the explorers, despite, or perhaps because of, their greatness are ultimately a seduction towards failure; to follow the truth of the explorers will lead directly to the curse of wandering overlong in the desert, to a dying out of a generation too pure to act.

Levinas continues with a second reading of this 'great thing':

> But this text can be read differently and the explorers will reveal themselves to be yet purer than we imagine: he (the Canaanites) are stronger than Him. The right of the native population to live is stronger than the moral right of the universal God. Even the master of the house cannot retrieve the tools entrusted to them; as long as the tools correspond to their needs, there would be no right on earth that could deprive them of them; one cannot take away from them the land on which they live, even if they are immoral, violent and unworthy, and even if this land were meant for a better destiny ... even an absolutely moral people would have no right to conquest.[18]

Let us remind each other that Levinas was interned in a work camp by the Nazis; that his theological writings are alive to the narrative of *Hatikvah*[19] – the Hope – for return to Israel. Yet, does an Auschwitz ever justify a West Bank? The explorers raise their objections and the Rabbis, while never agreeing, are attuned to their argument.

What then is stronger than the 'great thing' before which even God cannot act? What is wrong with the protest of the explorers? The Talmudic sages now open us to the other side of the dialectic. The two explorers who did not join with the rest, Caleb and Joshua, remain steadfastly committed to the Land:

> 'Caleb calmed the people about Moses' (Num 13:30). Rabbah said: 'He seduced with words'. When Joshua began to address them, they cried out: 'That lopped-off head [Rashi: a slur given to one who has no children] seeks to speak!?' Then Caleb thought: If I admonish them, they will answer me in the same way and will reduce me to silence. So he said: 'Has the son of Amram done nothing but this?' They then thought he was going to attack Moses and became quiet. He then continued: 'He brought us out of Egypt, split the sea for us and fed us manna. Shouldn't we listen to him, even if he were to tell us to build ladders and ascend to heaven?' 'We shall go up and gain possession of it.' (Num 13.30).[20]

In the retelling of the biblical narrative in the Talmud, Joshua is easily dismissed. A Zionist without children is not to be trusted; a Zionism that simply exists as an answer to the lachrymose nature of the past fails before it can even be fully articulated. It is lopped off, it is dead. But Caleb – and this is of vital import, insists Levinas – speaks to a movement of ascending ladders to heaven:

> What meaning do Caleb's words have? Is he simply following the cult of personality, defending Moses' policies, come what may? Or is he aware of the disproportion that exists between messianic politics and all other politics? Is our history an ordinary history then? ... If Moses brought us out of Egypt, split the sea, and fed us manna, do you think, then, that under his leadership we are going to conquer a country the way one conquers a colony? Do you think that our act of conquest can be an imperialistic act? Do you think that we will appropriate a plot of land for ourselves so that we can use and abuse it? We are going – and here the text is extraordinarily explicit – we are going toward this Land in order to experience celestial life.[21]

Lest we think that Levinas is engaged in some sort of dispensationalist agenda with his notion of 'celestial life', he will clarify – in the voice of Caleb – what is implied by this vision:

> We will not possess the Land as it is usually possessed; we will found a just community in this Land. I am telling you all this in a very flat way,

but that is what it means to sacralise the earth ... You will say that everyone can imagine that he is founding a just society and that he is sacralising the earth, and will that encourage conquerors and colonialists? But here one must answer: to accept the Torah is to accept the norms of a universal justice. The first teaching of Judaism is the following: a moral teaching exists and certain things are more just than others ... And it is in the name of this universal justice and not in the name of some national justice or other that the Israelites lay claim to the Land of Israel.[22]

Now the Talmud turns in a new direction. For once it comes to the support of the explorers:

'And we were grasshoppers in our own sight, and so we were in theirs.' (Num 13.33) Rav M'sharsheya said: 'The explorers were lying! They could be grasshoppers in their own eyes, but how could they know that they were so in the eyes of others?' That is not an objection. The latter – the inhabitants – were eating their meal under the cedars. When the former – the Israelite explorers – saw them, they climbed the trees, they sat in them. They would then hear the ones below exclaim: 'We see men like grasshoppers in the trees!'[23]

Here is the retelling by the explorers of the first interaction between native inhabitants and usurpers. It is a pithy insight into the crux of violence that so often accompanies contact with otherness. Levinas now links the Talmudic passage to the very real events of 1965:

And that is how they knew they had been taken for grasshoppers by the Canaanites. It is a situation as strange as it is natural. Didn't someone say recently: 'We are one hundred million strong to crush you.' When Israel arms itself against its neighbors, pacifists ask: How did you know that your neighbors do not want to make peace with you? Did they say so? Yes, they did say so; they told us we were like grasshoppers. It is a remarkable contemporary passage. That way of taking human faces for grasshoppers! Or that way of taking the historical act of Return for a movement of grasshoppers.[24]

An interjection from a recent trip to Northern Ireland. In East Belfast, an art teacher I met there has developed a project of drawing with 11- and 12-year-olds from both sides of the conflict. Before they will meet and sketch together, she asks the children in their own separate groups to draw a picture of the other. 'What does a Protestant child look like?' she will ask the Catholic students, and vice versa for the Protestant ones. She shows me a few examples from these first pictures, and they are striking. Exacting detail and colour is devoted to the uniforms and clothing of the other but, more often than not, the faces are either entirely lacking or sketchy. 'Even when I ask them to draw just the faces, there is always something crucial missing,' the teacher tells me. 'No eyes or no mouth, usually.' In Rwanda, in the weeks before the genocide, the Hutu-backed radio station, *Radio Television Libre des Mille Collines*, replayed again and again the injunction to 'kill the cockroaches'. The listeners knew who the cockroaches were.

So much of my work at the Board of Deputies is committed to protecting Israel. And yet my very sanity, I think, is tied up with the struggle to see faces, eyes and a mouth at the very source of the attack upon my precious homeland. I did not interject this personal comment in order to stir the pity of our Dialogue Group. In my eyes, if conversations on Israel are to have any worth, they will depend on each participant striving to see faces where once there were only grasshoppers.

The sages now alert us to the significant response of the community upon hearing the explorers' report:

> 'Then the whole community broke into loud cries and the people wept that night.' (Num 14.1) Raba said in the name of Rabbi Johanan: 'It was the ninth of Av and the Holy One, Blessed be He, said: "They cried without cause. I will change this day into a permanent day of lamentation."'[25]

The Ninth of Av is the most infamous day in Jewish history when – tradition records – both the First and Second Temples were destroyed, and when *c.* 135 CE the Bar Kochba revolt – the last flicker of Jewish sovereignty before our modern age – was crushed by the might of Rome. The Ninth of Av is already set in motion as the Children of Israel wander the desert – a remarkable twist to history. Levinas notes:

> The date of their exile is fixed before that of their conquest. They do not know their crisis is the source of their right, for there is no right that cannot be revoked. They assume a responsibility without indulgence and are summoned to pay for their own injustice with their exile. Only those who are always ready to accept the consequences of their actions and to accept exile when they are no longer worthy of a homeland have the right to enter this homeland.[26]

And what of our own modern Israel, West Bank and all – is it worthy enough? In the face of that question – freighted and pensive as it sits between us – I will conclude with a remarkable statement I heard recently, by the Ambassador of Israel to Great Britain, HE Daniel Taub. It was Ambassador Taub who alerted me to the true dynamics of the dispute between Rashi and Ramban on the conditional quality of Promised Land. But he went further, offering a far greater personal intensity:

> In my role as Ambassador for Israel [he concluded], I figuratively, keep the commentary of Rashi in one pocket and that of Ramban in the other. When those who would deny the Jewish people a home after our long wanderings, who speak of boycotts of my home, I look to Rashi. This Land is the Land of my forefathers, as was promised by God. This brings me comfort and strength. But [Ambassador Taub continued], when I am confronted by the injustice carried out in the name of my Israel, I turn to Ramban to grate against my platitudes and comfort. This Land is only our Land so long as we act with moral exactitude towards stranger and citizen alike.

Postscript

In the context of our Jewish–Christian dialogue encounter, a fundamental critique can be raised against this short essay, namely that it fails to grapple with Christian ideologies of Holy Land. What good is the face-to-face dialectic with the Christian 'other', if one then turns exclusively towards Jewish sources to inform one's essay? It is a valid challenge to which I can offer only the following in response. This essay has emerged out of three wonderful and challenging conversations with Sister Teresa and, though it may not be obvious, the impetus to write about complex and difficult texts rather than sound a single note of Zionistic fervour owes much to the honesty and trust that runs in the current of that dialogue. As Ralph Waldo Emerson once wrote: 'A foolish consistency is the hobgoblin of little minds, adored by little statesmen and philosophers and divines.' My *chavruta*, study partner, Teresa has taught me that to speak of Israel is to wrestle with hobgoblins.

Notes

1 Babylonian Talmud *Shabbat* 49b.
2 Exodus 12.2.
3 Rashi to Genesis 1.1.
4 Ramban to Genesis 1.1.
5 Ramban to Genesis 1.1.
6 Emmanuel Levinas (trans. Annette Aronowicz), 1990, 'Promised Land or Permitted Land', in *Nine Talmudic Readings*, Bloomington, IN: Indiana University Press.

7 Emmanuel Levinas, b. Kovno (Kaunas), Lithuania, 1906, d. Paris 1995.
8 Levinas, 'Promised Land or Permitted Land', p. 54.
9 Babylonian Talmud *Sotah* 34b.
10 Levinas, 'Promised Land or Permitted Land', p. 56.
11 Babylonian Talmud *Sotah* 34b.
12 Levinas, 'Promised Land or Permitted Land', p. 57.
13 Theodor Herzl, 1988, *The Jewish State*, New York: Dover Publications, p. 147. 'We shall therefore prevent any theocratic tendencies from coming to the fore on the part of our priesthood. We shall keep our priests within the confines of their temples in the same way as we shall keep our professional army within the confines of their barracks.' Tellingly, Herzl also fails to mention the indigenous Arab population in the entirety of this utopian treatise on Israel: 'As soon as we have secured the land, we shall send over a ship, having on board the representatives of the Society, of the Company, and of the local groups, who will enter into possession at once. These men will have three tasks to perform: (1) An accurate, scientific investigation of all natural resources of the country; (2) the organization of a strictly centralized administration; (3) the distribution of land' (p. 141).
14 A festival of arts, faith and justice, energized by a Progressive Christian worldview, http://www.greenbelt.org.uk
15 Paul Northup, 2011, press release.
16 Babylonian Talmud *Sotah* 35a.
17 Levinas, 'Promised Land or Permitted Land', p. 66.
18 Levinas, 'Promised Land or Permitted Land', p. 67.
19 Israel's national anthem.
20 Babylonian Talmud *Sotah* 35a.
21 Levinas, 'Promised Land or Permitted Land', pp. 65–6.
22 Levinas, 'Promised Land or Permitted Land', p. 66.
23 Babylonian Talmud *Sotah* 35a.
24 Levinas, 'Promised Land or Permitted Land', p. 68.
25 Babylonian Talmud *Sotah* 35a.
26 Levinas, 'Promised Land or Permitted Land', pp. 68–9.

Christians, Jews and the Land

TERESA BRITTAIN

The challenge of change to Christians

We Christians are living through a remarkable historical period, challenging ourselves to re-examine our interpretation of our story and beliefs in the light of the multi-faith, multicultural world of which we are increasingly part. I feel privileged to be living at a time in which we are able to enter into dialogue and share stories in a way that was imaginable but never dreamed possible in the past.

Within the Christian dialogue with Judaism, the area that now engages us more and more is the reality of the existence of the country and State of Israel. What this means to the Jewish people – and how Christians can come to understand and respect the significance Israel holds both for the Jewish people and for the world – has become an increasing challenge.

In giving talks and working with groups, no matter what topic within the Christian–Jewish dialogue I have been invited to address, I find that the question of the Land of Israel is raised – usually with much heated emotion and little reasoned understanding. The hospitality that dialogue offers to the other can easily disappear in the mire of the zero-sum mentality which places one against the other without attempting to listen. I often witness this among deeply committed faith-filled people who are aware of one narrative and exclude the other narrative from their comprehension. This is an area with which Christians need to grapple and see if we can throw some light – not the least for ourselves. It is one of the greatest challenges facing our relationships as Jews and Christians today.

Where do we begin? How can we approach this? A journey starts with the first step and, hopefully, I can offer some tentative first steps from history and personal experience.

People

For the purposes of the evolving understanding of peoplehood I want to use an image that American Catholic theologian Mary Boys offers – 'parables' which 'catch a ray of the ultimate and glint it in our lives'. She says she uses parables 'to evoke insight leading to action'.[1]

I belong to a Roman Catholic Congregation, the Congregation of Our Lady of Sion. As our name indicates, ever since our foundation we have had a specific link with the Jewish people. We were founded in the 1840s by two Jewish brothers who converted to Catholicism and became priests. They always held their love for their people within their hearts but the way they expressed it then is no longer appropriate. The story of the Sisters of Sion can shed light on searching for ways of approaching the questions of People and Land from the Christian perspective. In my lifetime we have changed our theology from a 'Conversionist Stance to a Dialogical Way of Life'.[2]

Mary Boys chose to conduct an in-depth study of the Congregation as a 'parable' to illustrate the way that the new relationship with the Jewish people is being lived within the Roman Catholic Church since the promulgation of *Nostra Aetate* 50 years ago. Her précis describes the following:

> This essay traces the dynamics of the dramatic changes in the Sisters of Sion, a Roman Catholic religious congregation originally founded for the conversion of Jews that now exists for the promotion of understanding between Christians and Jews. Sion's foundational years reflect significant aspects of the longstanding tradition of *Adversus Judaeos*. However, beginning in the late 1950s, the rethinking of their mission anticipated and then implemented to a remarkable degree the work of Vatican II. *The sorts of attitudes and questions evident among the sisters of Sion today serve as a model for Christians who consider a faithful portrait of Judaism and the Jewish people to be essential to Christian identity.*[3] (My italicization.)

In the essay, she traces the development and shifts that have happened within the congregation in the last 60 years. These changes have required not simply an exterior change in the way we dress but, much more deeply and painfully, a complete change in the way we perceive our specific call within the Church and the world. This has been a deep, searching and agonizing process which has challenged us to move out from secure traditional positions and approach the other in genuine dialogue. Above all we have been challenged to allow the other, the face of the other, to influence and change us and the way we interpret our own identity as Christians.

The promulgation of *Nostra Aetate* was a springboard for further explorations and understandings which are continuing today. We have, like Abraham and Sarah, begun a journey. On this journey we are unsure of the end but the first step has been taken and we have now reached a place on the journey where we cannot turn back. The call to change became an urgent summons which grew stronger because of the Shoah. Nevertheless, this is about authentic Christian identity even more than guilt.

For many of the sisters, the opportunity to converse with and accompany Jewish people instead of simply praying for them brought about radical changes in perceptions. Mary Boys uses Sion's story as an interpretative frame for *Nostra Aetate* by showing:

1 How deeply internalized the *Adversus Judaeos* tradition had become.
2 What the struggle entailed in repudiating this tradition.
3 The impact of interreligious dialogue on Christian identity.

There is neither the space nor the time here to go into further detail about our particular story but I want to use what I've already said to show that the change in relationship, brought about by engagement and dialogue, is not something simple. It continually challenges us and will continually challenge us as Christians to re-examine our identity in the light of the face of the other. The 'face-to-face' relationship transforms us.

The Church Documents, the Notes and Guidelines,[4] which were issued in the years following *Nostra Aetate*, guided the first stage and the dialogue began changing Christians from a deep place within their own identity. The official Church continued the journey with Pope John Paul II, his famous visit to the Rome Synagogue in 1986 and the 2000 Papal visit to Israel. A further landmark was the publication in 2002 of *The Jewish People and Their Sacred Scriptures in the Christian Bible*.[5]

In 1993, the Vatican recognized Israel's Statehood and launched full diplomatic relations. The present Pope Francis has a personal friendship with Buenos Aires Rabbi Abraham Skorka and together they have written a book.[6] The personal friendship and relationship changes many things: we move from 'The Jews', 'The ancient people of Israel' to Jewish people, to conversation and to understanding gained from acknowledging the point of view of the other.

Is the change that I have been describing real? Yes it is, because it is built upon a solid foundation. It's not simply a whim or another conversionist stance in disguise but a genuine attempt to relate to our

Jewish sibling as siblings should relate, to understand what People and Land mean to Judaism in order to bring about healing, reconciliation and cooperation for the future. This radically new perspective of genuine openness and unqualified respect demands an authenticity which can only come from sifting out all that is untrue in the heart of our belief and practice. It involves nothing less than seeking a new way of understanding our Christian narrative.

In the 1870s our founders purchased property in Israel. A hundred and forty years later we continue our presence in the Land but in a new way, challenged to live with the other people of the Land. We see ourselves as 'healers and reconcilers'; feel keenly the tensions in this troubled area of the world – but the healing and reconciliation is *of us as well*, not exclusively of others.

I glimpsed something of Sion's profound commitment to Israel during our international theological reflection week in England in January 1991, on the brink of the outbreak of the Persian Gulf War. As the conference proceeded, the delegates became increasingly preoccupied with the steady movement towards war. People listened to conference papers with one ear and to the BBC with another. One evening, the members of the General Council invited all the Sisters of Sion at the conference and in the local community in Ammerdown near Bath – the venue of the meeting – to gather together in order to discern what should be done, to ensure both Sion's commitment to Israel and the safety of the sisters there. They graciously extended an invitation to me to join them.

I have no notes from that evening but certain comments and the overall tone are indelibly embedded in my memory. The first to respond, one of two delegates from Jerusalem, said with great simplicity: 'I have made Israel my home for many years. I have no right to be among the people I love if I am not willing to suffer with them. Now, above all, Sion must be a presence.' So, Sion remained during the Persian Gulf War, and our desire to be reconcilers can, in part, be seen in how we offered hospitality during this crisis. Our convent and hostel in the Muslim quarter of Jerusalem, Ecce Homo, served as a refuge for Palestinians. Not many miles away, in the western suburb of Ein Karem, our convent housed Jews fleeing Scud missiles exploding in Tel Aviv.[7]

Where does this commitment come from? In the most obvious way, it comes from our understanding of the new relationship with the Jewish people, yet in a mysterious way it has been there from the beginning, from the founding vision of the Ratisbonne brothers who purchased the properties in Israel in the last century. As a footnote, in 2014 Israel became a hub for the Congregation in that we have opened an international house for the formation of our younger sisters and brothers in Ein Karem.

Continually the new Christian identity found in dialogue is deepening the 'given' tradition. Christians find newness in the interpretation of given tradition for this time. Just as our Scriptures are continually both given and rediscovered and find newness within interpretation for the present day, so the Christian tradition, through dialogue, is both given and also continually rediscovered and new.

This new identity becomes possible only with the prerequisites for dialogue:

- Openness to hearing multiple narratives.
- Awareness of unconscious biases.
- Promoting understanding and reconciliation.

Dialogue requires that we have the capacity to be self-critical and to change our own hearts because we listen to the heart of the other and we 'engage in the reckoning of our soul'. In our dialogue I realized that the words 'promoting understanding and reconciliation' had been heard as a role in a peace-making within the political situation in Israel. This was not intended. For me the reconciliation refers to the way Jews and Judaism have been treated through centuries in the supersessionist interpretation of Christianity. This could lead to volumes of books in itself! The new Christian identity requires an honest appraisal of this and a reorientation towards a more authentic identity.

This new identity is slowly emerging within Christianity and our 'parable' is one instance of change brought about in one particular group. The Jewish people are being understood and valued in a way previously unknown within our tradition. It is as if, suddenly, our eyes are opened to something that has been there all the time but we did not see it. This is an ongoing process and we are as yet just making the first tentative steps into the unknown.

Land

> A thorough intermingling of history and legend, this tale has inspired Jews living some 3,000 years later to return to our never-forgotten land and to reassert Jewish rule over it. But the relationship between the Jewish claim to the land, the notion of divine promise, the special conditions of living in this land, and the very notion of what we mean by 'holy land' all need clarification.[8]

There is no doubting the importance of the issue – or the challenge it presents. People who have never been to Israel, who know nothing of the history, have strong feelings and emotions which lead to immediate polarization and an entry into the 'zero-sum' game of for or against and entrench their positions there. This 'Holy Land', as we Christians call it, now stands alongside the Shoah, overshadowing Christian–Jewish relations.

There has been a Jewish presence and the yearning to return has been expressed over nearly two millennia of Jewish prayers and rites. Since the time of Muhammad, the Land has been sacred to Islam. For Christianity the Land is Holy because it is the land of Jesus, where he was born, lived and died. Multiple claims and apparently incompatible narratives create an impossibly difficult situation.

There are also many groups within Israel and in other places working for understanding, for reconciliation, for justice.[9] Listening and structured dialogue are among the few things that can help towards reconciliation – the articulation of and real hearing of the many and varied narratives of this torn country. It's not my role to enter into the political issues and I need to sidestep the quagmire of polarization. I need to offer a way of moving forward to an understanding of how we can approach this question in a way which, hopefully, could be constructive. It flows from the work of the Dialogue Group which has produced this book.

Last year, I was speaking to a friend who – at the time – was working in interreligious relations in the Roman Catholic Diocese of Hexham and Newcastle. I grew up in Newcastle and, as a child, we would go every year on pilgrimage to a little ruined pre-Reformation Chapel called Our Lady of Jesmond. Veronica Whitty told me that she had been on an interfaith pilgrimage there with Christian and Muslim women. I was impressed that this place that had meant so much to me as a child was experiencing a new interfaith life in our time. This pilgrimage has happened every year for five years. There are readings from sacred texts and shared prayer.[10] It made me recognize how healing it can be when places that are precious to one faith can be respectfully shared with people of other faiths and none.

I have just come back from following the Passion Art Trail here in Manchester, which has been prepared for Holy Week and covers six major venues in Manchester city centre comprising more than 60 art works by 20 artists and ending with the Football Museum! The booklet prepared for the exhibition says:

> Come and explore your own personal journey in relation to the Easter Passion Story, reflecting on universal themes of grief and loss, love and kindness and our longing for hope, using traditional and contemporary art sited in the gallery, museum and sacred spaces … The human condition describes that part of our humanity which is universally shared despite race, gender or class.[11]

What could it mean if the places in the 'Holy Land' were now to be used as places where we journey together? What if we were to share the narrative of place and its preciousness to us and open a space in what has long been regarded as exclusively Christian or Jewish or Muslim? Would it not be a way forward to begin a process of respectfully sharing narratives of place with each other? Can places become shared places with shared narratives respected by each sibling? In the developments since the Second Vatican Council and *Nostra Aetate*, Catholics are beginning to discover a new identity which is 'given and found' for our times in our changed world. Perhaps we could also do this with place – we could rediscover place within the interfaith context. It would build friendship, mutual understanding and respect and provide a way of turning the places which currently serve to highlight our struggles and disagreements into places of healing and understanding.

Almost every meeting of our Dialogue Group, over a period of almost three years, has included a session – led by David Ford and Alex Wright – of 'Scriptural Reasoning'. We have studied together both Christian and Jewish scriptural passages in carefully planned, imaginative ways. We have been encouraged to be together, visit often problematic texts, and encouraged to share our different readings. Both the process and the outcomes have been enlightening and reconciling. I wonder whether we could apply the same process to places – both here and, because it is the particular focus of my Order, in the Holy Land/Land of Israel. Is there a way in which the principles of Scriptural Reasoning – now well established and immensely powerful – could be applied to place? Is there a way of re-seeing the Holy Places through sharing, much in the same way as scriptural texts are shared and seen anew? There may well be many people who would find the narrative of place more graphic even than the narrative conveyed by text. It would certainly open up many new possibilities and make it more likely that the multiple narratives are heard, respected and allowed to transform.

Ben Quash, Professor of Christianity and the Arts at King's College, London, has written about his experience of Scriptural Reasoning.[12] He draws a parallel with the novelist Walker Percy, who contrasts the experience of the first European seeing the Grand Canyon with that of the modern sightseer who brings more than a century of preconceptions. These make it almost impossible to see the Grand Canyon as it really is. The modern sightseer, says Ben Quash, 'measures his satisfaction by the degree in which the canyon conforms to the preformed complex'. Applying this to Scriptural Reasoning, Quash writes:

To build on Walker Percy's example, it introduces people who think they know what the Bible says ('what the Grand Canyon *should* look like') to people who are seeing it for the first time. The introduction of an 'other' (or more than one 'other') to the activity of studying scripture within a particular tradition can have radical and helpful effects, many of which are precisely a deepening of the relation of a particular tradition's scripture readers to their own scriptures, without this implying any kind of syncretism or watering down of commitment or devotion in the name of multi-faith synthesis.[13]

He continues:

A person whose texts are being studied at any particular point *ought* to be adopting an interrogative attitude towards them in the same way as a visitor to the Grand Canyon ought to be trying to look beyond her 'preformed complex'. Often the questions of the other religionists can help her do this, as she will always have an answer to their questions, and this will get her questioning hard herself.[14]

He goes on to describe the moment that often happens during Scriptural Reasoning where the text appears to 'collapse' or 'explode' and underlines how this can be a very creative re-engagement with the text and can also lead to personal change in the individual. I am convinced that the same is possible with place. And if place and text were combined, we might have a vehicle powerful enough to respond to the enormity of the challenge posed by the Holy Land to Jews, Christians and Muslims alike.

Varanasi

Varanasi is one of seven cities in India sacred to Hindus and Jains and significant in Buddhism. It inspired the following poem:

Early in the morning we crossed the ghat,
Where fires were still smouldering,
And gazed, with our Western minds, into the Ganges.
A woman was standing in the river up to her waist;
She was lifting handfuls of water and spilling it
Over her body, slowly and many times,
As if until there came some moment
Of inner satisfaction between her own life and the river's.
Then she dipped a vessel she had brought with her

And carried it filled with water back across the ghat,
No doubt to refresh some shrine near where she lives,
For this is the holy city of Shiva, maker
Of the world, and this is his river.
I can't say much more, except that it all happened
In silence and peaceful simplicity, and something that felt
Like the bliss of a certainty and a life lived
In accordance with that certainty.
I must remember this, I thought, as we fly back
To America.
Pray God I remember this.[15]

There is something of the depth of a place that can appeal to what is human within us, cut through the confines of our individual culture to our common humanity and shape how we live anew.

The Jewish existentialist philosopher Martin Buber[16] writes that relationships can be built in three different spheres, life with nature, life with humans and life with spiritual beings:

> In every sphere in its own way, through each process of becoming that is present to us we look out toward the fringe of the eternal *Thou*; in each we are aware of a breath from the eternal *Thou*; in each *Thou* we address the eternal *Thou*.[17]

The same is possible through the sharing – in friendship and respect – of significant places. Pope Francis said in a recent address in the Vatican:

> An attitude of openness in truth and love must characterise the dialogue with the followers of non-Christian religions, in spite of various obstacles and difficulties, especially forms of fundamentalism on both sides. In fact, contexts are not lacking in the world in which co-existence is difficult: often political and economic motives superimpose themselves on cultural and religious differences, also fuelling misunderstandings and mistakes of the past: all this risks generating diffidence and fear. There is only one way to overcome this fear, and it is that of dialogue, of encounter marked by friendship and respect.[18]

Covenant and Land

Christians speak of 'the Holy Land' and sometimes call the Land the 'Fifth Gospel'. We must also hear and appreciate the other sacred narratives of the Land, so it becomes 'Our (yours and mine) Land' instead of simply 'My Land'.

Within Christianity, we have many challenges when respecting the covenantal tradition within Judaism. Welsh Congregationalist theologian W. D. Davies[19] concludes:

> The New Testament leaves us with a two-fold witness regarding the land tradition. On the one hand there is a sense in which faith in Christ takes the believer beyond the land, Jerusalem and the Temple; yet on the other hand its history and theology cannot escape concern about these realities. In the New Testament, holy space exists wherever Christ is or has been. The Christ event has universalised the land tradition in a significant way, but it has not eliminated its centrality.[20]

Today, we stand in danger of universalizing the tradition of the covenantal connection with the Land in such a way that we lose the specificity of it. Renowned American theologian of interfaith dialogue John Pawlikowski demonstrates that the covenantal tradition within Judaism has aided the confrontation of a traditional weak spot in Christian faith expression:

> In much of Christian liturgy we have lost almost all consciousness of the need to proclaim the glory of creation. Our liturgical cycle is virtually bereft of festivals which highlight God's continuing presence in nonhuman creation. Such sensitivity must be resurrected by Christians if Churches are to assume a leadership role, in collaboration with Jews and others, in protecting our ecological heritage.[21]

This approach to 'place', a challenge to see place with new eyes, may seem to gloss over the bite of the problems, but actually offers us a different approach and changes our perspective.

Finally, I would like to draw together the points expressed here. I began by looking at the People and saying that the way Christians regard the Jewish People is changing: we are beginning to see with new eyes. This is demonstrated by the 'parable' of the Sisters of Sion who have a special relationship to Jews, Judaism and the Land. Because of the challenge of this new Christian identity we have to go where others might feel unable to go. During the years since the promulgation of *Nostra Aetate* we have had to step out from a traditional place of religious safety and go on a journey which has involved profound change without any certainty of where we are going. We follow one step after another and trust we will be led.

The journey we are involved in means we walk alongside Jews – as siblings, as children of the Good Parent who has no favourites. Ours must be a relationship that acknowledges that Jews, Christians (and Muslims) are siblings – not identical twins, one right and the other wrong.

The world situation means that we are continually challenged to try to live this faithfully and honestly. Here in England it is difficult but it is infinitely more difficult in the Land of Israel. I have suggested that we can approach some of this difficulty by applying the technique of Scriptural Reasoning to place. This could afford a way forward and could also attract different dialogue partners who may be more comfortable in sharing the experience of place rather than scriptural texts alone.

Christians need to explore further the concept of Land within our tradition. We express this in spiritual terms and can universalize the Land and neglect the specificity. As Pawlikowski suggests, we can also highlight more fully God's continuing presence in non-human creation and resurrect this sensitivity along with people of other faith traditions. Together we can grow from 'My Holy Land' to 'Our (yours and mine) Holy Land'. It is an important statement both theologically and in terms of interpersonal understanding – it is not a political statement. This, with the guidance of God, can lead us to deeper respect and understanding for each other and our traditions.

Notes

1 Mary C. Boys, 2000, *Has God Only One Blessing? Judaism as a Source of Christian Self-Understanding*, Stimulus Books, p. 15.

2 Mary C. Boys, 1994, 'The Sisters of Sion: From a Conversionist Stance to a Dialogical Way of Life', *Journal of Ecumenical Studies* 31:1–2, Winter–Spring.

3 Boys, 'The Sisters of Sion', Introduction.

4 Different Steps have been put in place now in the Roman Catholic Church:
- 1974: New Vatican Commission – renamed as the Holy See's Commission for Religious Relations with the Jews.
- 1 December 1974: 'Guidelines and Suggestions for Implementing the Conciliar Declaration Nostra Aetate (no. 4). Vatican Commission for Religious Relations with the Jews', in 1988, *Fifteen Years of Catholic–Jewish Dialogue 1970–1985*, Vatican City: Libreria Editrice Vaticana. In particular this document encourages Christians to 'acquire a better knowledge of the basic components of the religious tradition of Judaism and to learn by what essential traits the Jews define themselves in light of their own religious experience'.
- 1980: Pope John Paul II, 'A Covenant Never Revoked' – addressing the Jewish community in Mainz.
- *Notes on the Correct Way to Present Jews and Judaism in Preaching and Catechesis in the Roman Catholic Church*, 1985, Vatican City: Commission for Religious Relations with the Jews, Libreria Editrice Vaticana.

5 *The Jewish People and Their Sacred Scriptures in the Christian Bible*, 2002, Vatican City: The Pontifical Biblical Commission, Libreria Editrice Vaticana, is a thorough study of the relationship between the New Testament and the Hebrew

Scriptures. The document notes that Christians have much to learn from Jewish interpretation of the Bible and confronts the problem of anti-Jewish passages in the New Testament.

6 Jorge Mario Bergoglio and Abraham Skorka, 2013, *On Heaven and Earth: Pope Francis on Faith, Family and the Church in the Twenty-First Century*, New York: Image.

7 Mary Boys refers to this – see note 2 above.

8 Arthur Green, 2013, *These Are the Words: A Vocabulary of Jewish Spiritual Life*, Woodstock, VT: Jewish Lights Publishing, p. 219.

9 There are too many for a comprehensive list. However I personally have found the following helpful: www.oasisofpeaceuk.org; www.FamiliesForum.co.uk; Neve Shalom; see Wikipedia entry. There is a list of Resources for Peace in Michael Lerner, 2007, *Healing Israel/Palestine*, New York: HarperOne, pp. 185ff.

10 For details and photos, see the website of the Roman Catholic Diocese of Hexham and Newcastle Interreligious relations.

11 Cf. www.passionarttrail.co.uk.

12 Ben Quash, 2012, *Abiding*, London: Bloomsbury, pp. 59ff.

13 Quash, *Abiding*, p. 60.

14 Quash, *Abiding*, p. 62.

15 'Varanasi', from Mary Oliver, 2013, *A Thousand Mornings: Poems*, New York: Penguin.

16 B. Vienna, 1878, d. Jerusalem, 1965.

17 Martin Buber, 1937, *I and Thou*, Edinburgh: T & T Clark, p. 6.

18 Pope's address to Plenary Assembly of the Pontifical Council for Interreligious Dialogue, Vatican City, 28 November 2013, from https://Zenit.org.

19 B. Carmarthenshire, 1911, d. N. Carolina, 2001.

20 W. D. Davies, 1974, *Gospel and the Land*, Oakland, CA: University of California Press.

21 John Pawlikowski, 1989, 'The Re-Judaization of Christianity', in M. Lowe (ed.), *People, Land and State of Israel: Jewish and Christian Perspectives*, Jerusalem: Ecumenical Theological Research Fraternity in Israel.

Further Reflections

TONY BAYFIELD

In some ways, Natan Levy's essay is the mirror image of Patrick Morrow's. Both give an account of particularity from an orthodox perspective. What leaps out from the page is that, whereas Christian particularity expresses itself through doctrines at the heart of the revelation in Christ, Jewish particularity appears to be embodied solely in attachment to Land. What of Peoplehood,[1] or the 613 mitzvot and panoply of distinctive practices,[2] or lack of missionary zeal?[3] Israel isn't, of course, the whole story but it is – as Sister Teresa points out – all that many Christians see today.[4] Leaving until last the place of Israel as Land in Jewish theology could have been a high-risk strategy, ending this book on an angry and discordant note. That the reverse is true is entirely due to the clarity of Natan's ethically grounded exposition and Teresa's remarkable and courageous response.

The vast majority of Jews both in Israel and the Diaspora are deeply disturbed by politics – the politics of the international community in relationship to the Middle East and the internal politics of the State of Israel. It is a function both of the complexity of the situation and of widespread disillusionment with politics throughout the modern western world. My personal position was expressed by the author of *My Promised Land*, Ari Shavit.[5] If you want a searingly honest perspective on Israel, its history and place in the politics of the Middle East, this is the book to read. Shavit is a member of the Editorial Board of the daily newspaper *Ha'aretz*. On the anniversary of 9/11 in 2014, he wrote the following:

> You want the truth? We've had it. We've had it with the delusional nationalists who are leading Israel to destruction, and we've had it with the visionary leftists who are stoning Israel. We've had it with the skullcap-wearing post-Zionists who are burying Zionism in the hills, and we've had it with the bespectacled post-Zionists who are depicting Zionism as a series of crimes. We've had it with the messianic believers in the entire Land of Israel, who don't understand that without dividing the land, there will be no state, and we've had it with the messianic

believers in a perfect peace, who don't understand Hamas and Islamic State and don't know where they are living ...

You want the truth? It has to be stopped. The nationalist right has been acting for years in an anti-national fashion, weakening the Jewish nation-state and endangering the Zionist enterprise. The universalist left has been acting for years in a non-universal fashion, adopting a particularistic approach that blames Israel (for everything) and forgives the Palestinians (for everything) ...

The time has come for the silent 70 percent of Israelis in the centre to rise up against the extremists from both right and left and free themselves of their stranglehold. The time has come for a broad-based, angry Israeli rebellion that will return Israel to reality, morality and sanity. We mustn't give up this one country of ours without a fight. Our duty now is to repossess it, redefine it and put it back on track.

For most British Jews, the case for Israel's right to exist is pragmatically,[6] morally,[7] historically[8] and legally[9] irrefutable. We cannot begin to understand why faithful Christians should question it and are deeply suspicious of the motivation behind Israel denial. But many Jews themselves are hazy about Israel's place in non-fundamentalist theology. What Natan does is to provide a response from within the Orthodox community of formidable learning and clarity. His exegesis is a compelling example of how orthodox Judaism tackles difficult questions – by paying close, penetrating and creative attention to the Torah text. What Natan offers, in addition, is the insight of the remarkable Lithuanian-born French Jewish philosopher, Emmanuel Levinas – a thinker whose ethical primacy and intensity has inspired a number of contributors to this book, Christians as well as Jews.

At the end of his dazzling exposition, Natan quotes the present Ambassador of Israel to Britain, Daniel Taub – how pleasing that the Ambassador can not only tell his Rashi from his Ramban but is familiar with Simcha Bunam of Pzhysha[10] as well! Israel – and all Jews – must live with a paradox: 'This Land is the Land of my forefathers, as was promised by God.' Yet: 'This Land is only our Land, so long as we act with moral exactitude towards stranger and citizen alike.'[11] Rejecting the simplistic platitudes of contemporary fundamentalism unites Orthodox, Progressive, Masorti, and liberal secularists like Ari Shavit. God continues to be with Israel the People on its journey through Israel the Land, but does not sanction the unethical. The God of Israel will never give up on the demand, 'Justice, justice, shall you pursue.'[12]

Sister Teresa's faith has such honesty and integrity that, as far as I'm concerned, any doctrinal objections to accepting it should simply dissolve.

When I heard the first draft of her paper, however, I reacted as so many Jews do to Christian talk about Israel: you invented the term Holy Land. You placed it at the centre of maps. You sent armies there, murdered and pillaged and, less than 100 years ago, conquered it yet again. Britain and France divvied the area up, drew ridiculous lines on maps, moved rulers around and, only after you'd botched the job yet again, got out. Now that you've decided that Land has no place in theology, you still feel confident about giving advice and opinions. I even said to Teresa that I wanted her to be my Sister not my Mother Superior! It turned out to be a classic demonstration of my not listening.

Sister Teresa begins by acknowledging that Israel now colours all Christian–Jewish discourse. She even says explicitly that it's displaced the Shoah as the issue dominating meetings whatever the planned agenda. She offers no explanation but the observation lies there, at the end of this book, for contemplation and reflection. Why has the Jewish commitment to Land – despite its pragmatic, moral, historic, legal as well as theological underpinning – become the primary reason or excuse for conflict between the two siblings? It's no criticism of Teresa that she recognizes this profoundly distressing fact but then moves on – in a way that leaves me both humbled and admiring.

First, she acknowledges failures in the Christian response to Jews with unqualified candour. We looked but did not see, she says. We regarded Jews as objects for conversion, not our sisters and brothers. As a Sister of Sion, she embraces change: crediting the leadership provided by the pioneering American Catholic, Professor Mary Boys.[13] Teresa writes of radical change in her own order going far deeper than the superficiality of dress and demanding 'a complete change in the way we perceive our specific call within the Church and the world'. The Sisters of Sion must 'move out from secure traditional positions and approach the other in genuine dialogue ... to allow the other, the face of the other, to influence and change us and the way we interpret our own identity as Christians'.[14] That's breathtaking. Sisters of Sion have ceased to pray for and talk about Jews from a place of dogmatic safety. They now walk alongside us as partners on a journey into the unknown.

Teresa has been inspired both by Professor Mary Boys and by our Group's experience of Scriptural Reasoning.[15] What if, she asks, we were to apply the principles of Scriptural Reasoning to place, exploring each other's sacred places in Israel together in the same way that we explore text? Might we even combine the two – standing alongside each other in the Holy Land's holy places, sharing a religious (rather than political) agenda? 'There is something of the depth of a place that can appeal to what is human within us, cut through the confines of our individual culture to our common humanity and shape how we live anew.'[16]

She refers to the work of Professor Ben Quash of King's College, London, and the 'collapse' or 'explosion' of the text during Scriptural Reasoning and the personal change it can lead to. Teresa concludes, 'I am convinced that the same is possible with place.' Combining the two could provide a vehicle, 'powerful enough to respond to the enormity of the challenge posed by the Holy Land to Jews, Christians and Muslims alike'.[17]

Change is essential, says Teresa. We must walk side by side, using what we have learned from Scriptural Reasoning as our guide. But, as if this were not enough, Teresa also responds to Jewish hostility to Christian interference and clarifies the Christian role. We also have a commitment to Land, which should not be obscured or denied, she writes. It was the place where Jesus – the Jew – was born, lived and died. As Christians we have a vocation to healing and conciliation. But that doesn't mean we should set about healing and reconciling Jews and Muslims in the Holy Land. It's us who need it and that can only take place in the context of the three Abrahamic faiths – particularly by walking alongside the Jewish people, Christians' most significant other.

Teresa, you are truly our Sister and worthy of being Mother Superior!

Notes

1 Certain questions used to pepper dialogue regularly. Are Jews a race, ethnic group or faith community? How can a Jew be a passionate Jew while rejecting the metaphysical? Is Judaism a religion like Christianity and Islam or civilization/culture? What is meant by claiming to be the 'chosen people'?

2 How central to Judaism is distinctive dress or distinctive practices such as the dietary laws? Are these intended to keep Jews apart? To what extent is Judaism a religion of deed and Christianity a religion of creed?

3 Conversion is welcomed but there is no need to be Jewish to be 'saved'. Is Judaism, unlike Christianity or Islam, pre-imperial?

4 I don't want to end this book on too challenging a note. But there is a real need for Jews and Christians to discuss what it is about the otherness of the other that so disturbs. Jews currently express 'it' in terms of their discomfort at the doctrines accompanying the revelation in Christ. Christians express 'it' in hostility to Israel as Land. But what, in truth, is 'it'?

5 Ari Shavit, 2014, *My Promised Land: The Triumph and Tragedy of Israel*, Melbourne: Scribe Publications.

6 The pragmatic argument runs that, having been thrown out of or persecuted in much of Europe, treated as second-class citizens at best in the Islamic world, what alternative was there?

7 The moral argument is that, after countless centuries of being denied by those who had claimed the right to a land themselves, Jews have the right to be a free, self-governing people in their own land, just like everyone else.

8 The historical argument is that Jews lived in Israel/Judah/Judea for more than a thousand years, were expelled against their will and yet maintained an unbroken Jewish presence in Judea/Palestine/the Holy Land despite innumerable conquests and persecutions for nearly two millennia.

9 The legal argument is that Israel is a state recognized under international law by virtue of a UN resolution.

10 The Hasidic Master Simcha Bunam of Pzhysha, 1765–1827, wrote: 'Everyone must have two pockets so that he can reach into the one or the other, according to his needs. In his right pocket are to be the words: "for my sake was the world created" and in his left: "I am earth and ashes".' Martin Buber, 1948, *Tales from the Hasidim: The Later Masters*, New York: Schocken Books, pp. 249–50.

11 *Supra* p. 306.

12 Deuteronomy 16.20. Interestingly, one major commentary explains the repetition of the word 'justice' as meaning that compromise will always be required. There has to be a measure of justice on both sides.

13 I want to acknowledge the immense contribution of Sister Margaret Shepherd who, back in the late 1970s, completed an MA in Jewish Studies at Leo Baeck College and has been, her stature notwithstanding, a towering influence on the Sisters of Sion over four decades.

14 *Supra* pp. 309–10.

15 See *supra* p. 314.

16 *Supra* p. 316.

17 *Supra* p. 315.

Concluding Thoughts

DAVID F. FORD

The four-year journey to complete this volume has been an extraordinary one for the authors. We have met as a group as well as in pairs, and have had intensive conversations with some very tense times. We decided on the title of our book after a long session of brainstorming during our final residential meeting and that was fitting: 'Deep Calls to Deep' rang true with the experience we had had together. It is from Psalm 42, which catches something of the dynamics of our four years: diverse longings for 'the living God'; probing and questioning; gratitude and disquiet; wrestling with the repeated question, 'Where is your God?'

As someone said during that last meeting, at the heart of our project has been coming together in one place to take part in one sustained conversation. There has been far too little of that in the history of our two traditions and even less that has been focused on issues related to theology. For the Council of Christians and Jews this theology project has been a new departure, and the painful times during our four years have shown why there has been a shying away from attempting it. Bring together a set of Jewish and Christian thinkers and practitioners of very different types (both of Jews and of Christians), divide them into pairs (most not knowing each other in advance) to tackle one chapter each, including many topics with a history of controversy, and it could be a recipe for any one of a wide range of outcomes, some of them disastrous. In fact, for all the difficulties, it did work. Partly this was due to Tony Bayfield. He conceived the shape of the project, which proved remarkably stable and gave a framework within which the Group could have honest and fruitful discussions. He also chaired it with sensitivity, humility and passion – a wonderful combination.

Like the others, I had no idea what to expect either in the Group or in being assigned to work on a topic with someone else. I was given 'The Legacy of our Scriptures' and paired with Rabbi Alexandra Wright, whom I had never met before. I describe in my contribution how we decided to study our Scriptures together, which led me into many fresh insights and immersion in a world of meaning shaped by Tanakh, Talmud and Jewish liturgy as well as by rich pastoral and cultural experience. Others had comparable experiences and it was fascinating to see how the various pairings worked out over the years.

In retrospect, four things especially stand out, each of them with implications for the future.

First, I do not think it is only because the topic assigned to Alexandra and me was our Scriptures that for me the most obvious conclusion from the project has been that these overlapping texts – and their subsequent reception and use in many ways to help form Jewish and Christian identities, understandings and practices – must be central to any deep engagement between Jews and Christians. Alexandra and I suggested to the wider group that we should all study Scripture together for a session at every meeting, on the model of Scriptural Reasoning. This not only worked well for our group: we see such joint study as a practice worth cultivating between our communities wherever practicable.

There needs to be a great variety of modes of interaction between Jews and Christians if we are to create a better 'ecology' of mutual understanding and cooperation and bring about a better interweaving of our narratives and orientations to the future. But one vital niche in that ecology must be conversation around our Scriptures and the traditions and practices that they have helped to generate. Just as within each of our traditions we rely on long-term practices of study, prayer, celebration, gathering for worship, and so on, so in our relationships with each other we need some such practices, and mutual hospitality around our Scriptures is one that has been shown to have great potential but happens far too rarely. There is now something like a wisdom tradition about how it can best be done with sensitivity, respect and alertness to what might go wrong, and this should be developed further if we want to strengthen and deepen the bonds between Jews and Christians.

Second, these four years have brought home how mutually beneficial interreligious and intrareligious engagement can be. Gathering a group of diverse Christians to meet with Jews means that the Christians have the chance to relate to each other afresh, and the same is true on the Jewish side. Strange to say, there are often more opportunities for sustained conversations between religions than there are between divided groups in a particular religion. Often, too, the passion invested in 'family quarrels' with members of one's own tradition can be greater than with those less closely related.

Within our group the most vocal intrareligious disagreements were among the Jews; but there were also some strong divergences among the Christians. Anyone who has read the publications of Alan Race and myself, for example, will be aware of how very far apart we are on many important questions of Christian understanding and practice, including interfaith engagement. We did not resolve these in the Group, but what in Scriptural Reasoning is called 'improving the quality of disagreement' certainly happened for me. And it was instructive to notice divisions among the Jews that are analogous to those between myself and Alan. In a pluralist world, deep disagreement within and between religions, and between the religious and non-religious, is in practice inevitable and ineradicable. The big question is how to live with it, and one valuable practice is the sort of mixture of inter- and intrareligious encounter that we have had in our group.

This is valuable far beyond the neuralgic points of most painful division. To be a witness at close quarters as another tradition displays its ways of coping with questions we all face is very educative, whether through contrasts or through parallels. On perennial issues about freedom and obligation, rights and responsibilities, tradition and innovation, minorities and democracy, men and women, particularism and universality, authority and reason, and many more, there is much wisdom to be learned by seeing how others debate and deliberate about them among themselves.

Third, there were the interpersonal relationships. It was by no means inevitable that the Group would work collegially at wisdom-seeking through conversation and there were some pivotal moments when it could have gone seriously wrong, to the point of disintegration. A challenge for the future is how such wisdom-seeking together can be built into long-term Jewish–Christian collegiality and interweaving of narratives. This is too important to be left to chance, hoping that others will do it. What was possible in our group was based on Jews and Christians sustaining the Council of Christians and Jews over decades so that it had the capacity and credibility to take this theological initiative. The older I get the more I appreciate those who have created and faithfully sustained organizations and institutions doing valuable work. We need these if good things are to last across generations. It is significant that our volume of essays is only the first stage in the CCJ conception: the next, crucial, phase is the wider communication of our understanding through educational materials and initiatives. For that the CCJ organization is essential. What we hope is that many Jews and Christians will be inspired by this process to improvise fresh forms of interfaith relationships and collegiality: the scope for these is virtually limitless.

Besides the organizational and group dimensions there are also the friendships. Over the years I have observed that, wherever there are examples of crossing deep divisions in good ways, there one usually finds daring friendships (though often they are quite hidden and only become apparent slowly). For most of us most of the time our friendships are with 'people like us'. Clearly, friendships cannot be planned or made to order – their 'chemistry' is complex, contingent and very particular. But we can be open to risking friendships that cross boundaries and we can prioritize them when the opportunity arises. The collegiality of our group created the conditions and understanding not only for inspiring further improvisations in collegiality and mutual learning but also for forming new friendships. A radical challenge for Christians and Jews is to go beyond our usual comfort zones in the friendships to which we are committed.

Fourth, there is the combination of urgency and importance for our twenty-first-century world. What we have been doing is not just significant for Jews and Christians but is also acutely relevant to the rest of the world. While writing this Conclusion I have been reading *Not in God's Name: Confronting Religious Violence* by Jonathan Sacks.[1] It is a wide-ranging, provocative analysis of religion-related violence, and a rallying call: 'For the sake of humanity and the free world, the time has come for people of all faiths and none to stand together and declare: NOT IN GOD'S NAME.' It draws perceptively on Scriptures, on history, on the human and social sciences, and on the lessons of anti-Semitism over many centuries. It also offers a prescription for action in response to the present situation that includes many of the things advocated in the essays of our volume. Above all, it is clear that the sort of action needed on religion-related violence, as on other fundamental issues facing our world, such as climate change and poverty, cannot be taken by one religion alone, or by one government or international organization alone. There has to be a concerted effort and if it is to be effective long term it has to be rooted in what is deepest and most important to the various traditions. Jews coming together with Christians in a way that deepens mutual understanding and helps to shape new collegiality and collaboration is just one part of what needs to happen; but, given their sibling relationship, their history and their roles in the contemporary world, it is crucial. As I do a final edit of this text in the aftermath of the UK decision in its June 2016 referendum to leave the European Union, there has been a surge of 'hate crimes' in this country. I am more convinced than ever that, if our society is to be healthily plural, that has to be a plurality of multiple depths that are in communication with each other for the sake of the common good. We have tried to give a sign of hope that that is possible between just two sets of depths, Jewish and Christian, and we hope others might find encouragement in this and go on to create their own analogous signs.

I have three further points to make.

CONCLUDING THOUGHTS

One is that ours is, I hope, a book for others to think with and then carry on the unfinished conversation, leading into better practice and cooperation. 'Thinking' and 'thought' have become increasingly important terms for me through the four years, as I noticed a range of variations in the literature of Jewish–Christian relations (and sometimes in our group's discussions and writings) on what I (and Tony Bayfield) find an unsatisfactory way of describing Judaism in contrast to Christianity. The usual form it takes is that Judaism is more practical and behaviour-oriented, while Christianity is more interested in doctrine and dogma. There is, as one might expect in an oft-repeated cliché, some truth in it. But for me as a Christian to think of my faith as more doctrinal than practical is simply untrue – for example, I am at present trying to write a commentary on the Gospel of John, the Gospel that has given rise to more doctrine than any of the others, and it has come home again and again how radically the imperative of love is embedded in it, reinforced even more emphatically by the First Letter of John. And my experience of Jewish textual interpretation, philosophy and theology is that they display some of the richest and most sophisticated conceptualities that I know. So thought and practice go together in each, though often in very different modes and genres. It has been part of the fascination of our group to see this interplay being performed among and between Jews and Christians, and I hope that the book will stimulate more of it.

Second, there is the sobering recognition of where we have most clearly failed: on the topic of incarnation and Trinity. This is not to be at all negative about the essays on the topic; it has, perhaps, been inevitable and intrinsic to the subject. Perhaps it was only by the end of our four years that we arrived at a place where we might have been able to deal more adequately with it together – given at least another four years. As a group, for various reasons we never quite got to the point of jointly discussing it in depth, and it is significant that the Christians were by no means united on it either. Patrick Morrow's thorough statement of the classic orthodox Christian position in a contemporary mode was answered honestly and sensitively from three Jewish standpoints, but somehow this massive topic remained in all its intractable insolubility. Tony Bayfield's commentary is very valuable in redescribing the Christian and Jewish approaches. The whole section is perhaps a healthy reminder of the depth of disagreement between our traditions, and yet it takes an important step towards improving the quality of that disagreement. This is above all achieved by how Patrick and Natan Levy handle the very reality of 'failure' in relation to God – there can be failure blessed by God. Natan's recovery of a suppressed text by Maimonides about Jesus and Muhammad surprised us all and, as Tony's commentary says, Natan's 'last two sentences are game-changing'. They are so not only by insisting on the necessity of continuing to wrestle with incarnation and Trinity, but also by being rooted theologically in Maimonides' daring Jewish conception of a role for 'failed' Christianity and Islam in the providence of God. Perhaps our group's failures too will be blessed with surprising outcomes.

Finally, Natan and Teresa Brittain provided us with a further instructive surprise on another topic that is often the subject of intractable disagreement: the Land. Natan's use of Levinas and Daniel Taub opened up the theological and ethical dimensions of the Land without advocating a particular solution. The striking central image was 'taking human faces for grasshoppers', with the accompanying testimony of Natan to his constant struggle 'to see faces'.[2] That position of responsibility before the face of the other, inseparable from accountability before the face of God, might stand as one of the two most essential elements in the sort of dialogue we tried to practise and want to advocate. The other element is summed up by Teresa as she describes the aftermath of *Nostra Aetate*: 'the dialogue began changing Christians from a deep place within their own identity'.[3] That, matched by Jews drawing on the depths of their identity, is the rationale for our title. Psalm 42 deserves to have the last word:

> As a deer longs for flowing streams, so my soul longs for you, O God.
> My soul thirsts for God, for the living God.
> When shall I come and behold the face of God?
> My tears have been my food day and night,
> while people say to me continually, 'Where is your God?' ...
> Deep calls to deep
> at the thunder of your cataracts;
> all your waves and your billows have gone over me.
> By day the LORD commands his steadfast love, and at night his song is with me,
> a prayer to the God of my life ...
> Why are you cast down, O my soul,
> and why are you disquieted within me?
> Hope in God; for I shall again praise him, my help and my God.

Notes

1 Jonathan Sacks, 2015, *Not in God's Name: Confronting Religious Violence*, London: Hodder and Stoughton.
2 *Supra* p. 305.
3 *Supra* p. 310.

Glossary

Absolutism An absence of relativism, ambiguity or changeability. In philosophical terms, absolutism holds that an objective, unconditioned and universal reality underlies all objects of perception. In contemporary theology it means claiming a monopoly on Truth.

Adversus Judaeos Genre of Christian writing setting opposition to Jews and Judaism, including triumphalism, polemic and character defamation. In particular, a series of homilies by John Chrysostom in the fourth century CE. Translated as 'against the Jews', these homilies are often cited as a 'decisive turn' in the history of Christian anti-Judaism.

Akhar ha-midbar Hebrew phrase used in Exodus 3.1. Means literally 'after' or 'behind the wilderness'.

Aggadah (Partner of halakhah) Those parts of Rabbinic literature consisting of homily, story and God-talk, rather than legal discussions.

Amidah The thrice-daily, central section of the Jewish service, recited standing (the Hebrew root means standing). Consists of 19 benedictions during the week and seven on Shabbat.

Anatheism Title of a 2010 book by American philosopher Richard Kearney. From the Greek *ana-theos*, indicating a return to God after God's death. It suggests that after the collapse of many traditional understandings of God, the way forward lies in hospitality given to the stranger and the 'Other'. To accept God is to accept the unfamiliar and the alien.

Aramaic One of a small group of related languages including Hebrew and Arabic. The Tanakh contains some Aramaic in later books; it was the language of ordinary people at the time of Jesus. The Talmud contains a mixture of Hebrew and Aramaic.

Ashkenazi From the medieval Hebrew for Germany. Jews and Jewish communities whose roots are in Northern and Central Europe.

Auctoritas Latin word, roughly translated as 'authority'. A term first employed in Ancient Rome to refer to the level of prestige or command one had in society. Here used as a contrast to the coercive power represented by *potestas*.

Bar Kochba revolt Jewish rebellion against Rome led by Simon bar Kochba *c.* 132–6 CE.

Bar mitzvah Name given since the fourteenth century for a coming-of-age ceremony for a boy aged 13, when he is called to read a section from the Torah. The corresponding ceremony for a girl is **bat mitzvah.**

Birkat HaMinim ('Benediction about apostates') The twelfth blessing of the Amidah.

Board of Deputies of British Jews Established in 1760, the main representative body of British Jews.

Cappadocian Fathers Basil the Great (300–79), Bishop of Caesarea; Gregory of Nyssa (332–95), Bishop of Nyssa; and Gregory of Nazianzus (329–89), who became Patriarch of Constantinople. These three figures were instrumental in the development of early Christian theology, including key contributions to the doctrine of the Trinity.

Church Councils Jerusalem: Conference of the Christian Apostles in Jerusalem *c.* 50 CE that decreed non-Jewish converts to Christianity were not required to observe the Mosaic Law of the Jews, except for the provisions of the so-called apostolic decree: abstention 'from what has been sacrificed to idols and from blood and from what is strangled and from unchastity' (Acts 15.29). **Nicaea:** Council of Christian bishops convened by Roman Emperor Constantine in 325 CE. Known for settling the christological issue of the nature of Christ and his relationship to God the Father, the construction of the first part of the Nicene Creed, establishing uniform observance of the date of Easter, and the development of early canon law. **Constantinople:** 381 CE. Known for lengthening and adopting the Nicene Creed (the profession of faith widely used in Christian liturgy) and for clarifying the relationship of the Holy Spirit within the Trinity. **Chalcedon:** 451 CE. Its ruling marked an important step in clarifying the nature of Christ and the doctrine of the Trinity for the Churches that accepted it (Oriental Orthodox Churches rejected it).

Confessing Church Movement within the Protestant Church in Nazi Germany that opposed, on ecclesiological grounds, the State's efforts to absorb the German Protestant Churches into National Socialism.

GLOSSARY

Council of Christians and Jews Organization established by Archbishop Temple and Chief Rabbi Hertz in 1941/2 to resist discrimination, encourage understanding and promote shared values.

Dat Yisrael Hebrew term for 'law' or 'custom' (and can also mean 'religion') 'of the people of Israel' (the Jewish people).

Diaspora Ancient Greek for 'scattered', this refers to a people no longer located in their original homeland. In this context used in connection with the dispersion of the Jews from the Land of Israel.

Docetism Early Christian heresy which argued Christ's body was not human but rather a phantasm or of real but celestial substance.

Ebionites Patristic term referring to a Jewish Christian movement during the early centuries CE.

European Convention on Human Rights International treaty protecting fundamental freedoms and human rights in all Council of Europe member states. Enacted 1953.

Ex nihilo Latin for 'out of nothing'. Often used in reference to creation, namely, that God created the universe *ex nihilo*.

Genizah Place where used Hebrew documents are stored, especially the Cairo Genizah, found in the Ben Ezra Synagogue, a collection of over 300,000 manuscript fragments.

G'mara Component of the Talmud which comprises Rabbinical analysis of and commentary on the Mishnah.

Gnosticism Prominent heretical movement in the Christian Church which flourished during the second century CE, partly of pre-Christian origin. Its adherents shunned the material world or treated it as irrelevant (which they believed to be evil or imperfect), and embraced the spiritual world.

Halakhah (Partner of aggadah) Law or rules of behaviour on a particular subject, as agreed by the Rabbis. English adjective: halakhic.

Halal Arabic for 'permissible', most often used in reference to food which adheres to Islamic law as stated in the Qur'an.

Hametz ('Leaven') Leavened foods are not eaten during Pesach (Passover).

Hanukkah Winter eight-day festival, on which candles are lit each night in the home to commemorate the rededication of the Temple in Jerusalem by the Maccabees in 164 BCE.

Havdalah Ceremony for the end of the Sabbath, with plaited candle, wine and spices. Its blessings emphasize the distinctions between the sacred and the ordinary, in particular with regard to the closing of the holy day and the arrival of a new, ordinary weekday.

Hellenism Refers to the culture of Ancient Greece, especially between the time of Alexander the Great and the annexation by Rome.

Historical criticism Also known as the 'historical-critical' method or 'higher criticism', this branch of literary criticism seeks to discover the origins behind a historical text so as to understand the 'world' behind the text.

Ioudaioi Greek term in classical and biblical literature which means 'Judean' or 'Jews'.

Kabbalah (adj. kabbalistic) Body of esoteric literature, including the *Zohar*, which uses (sometimes openly but often in a concealed fashion) the imagery of *sefirot* (powers or potencies in the Godhead) to describe aspects of God. The *sefirot* are ten aspects of God, sometimes arranged in diagrammatic form.

Kaddish A prayer in praise of God, written in Aramaic and recited regularly by mourners since the time of the Crusades.

Kallipolis Greek term meaning 'beautiful city'.

Kitniyyot ('Legumes') Name given to foods that are not leaven but that expand when cooked, thereby imitating leavened foods. *Kitniyyot* are not eaten by Ashkenazi Jews during Pesach (Passover).

Kiv'yakhol Hebrew phrase meaning 'so to speak', 'as if'.

Koine Greek Common form of Greek spoken during Hellenistic and Roman antiquity. It is the language of the Christian New Testament as well as the Septuagint (third-century BCE translation of Hebrew Bible).

Latin Vulgate Late fourth-century Latin translation of the Bible that eventually became the Catholic Church's officially promulgated Latin version of the Bible.

Marian Of or relating to the Virgin Mary.

Mashal Short parable with an ethical lesson or religious allegory, called a *nimshal*.

Midrash ('Enquiry') Term which describes (1) a homiletic comment or story which quotes a biblical text or texts to make its point; (2) a compilation of such comments on a particular theme or biblical book; (3) the whole body of such Rabbinic literature. Plural *midrashim*.

GLOSSARY

Minhag ('Custom')   As distinct from halakhah, 'law', customs (plural: *minhagim*) may vary from one Jewish community to another.

Mishnah   Earliest and most important compilation of Rabbinic teaching, thought to have been compiled by Rabbi Judah Ha-Nasi about 200 CE. Conflicting opinions are frequently cited. About 800 pages long in English translation, the Mishnah is divided into 6 separate sections (orders), and 63 smaller divisions (tractates).

Monism   Doctrine that ultimate reality is one, indivisible and simple in such a way as to be beyond the characteristics of personhood; in philosophy, it also denotes the theory that denies the existence of a duality in a particular sphere, such as that between mind and spirit, or God and the world.

Nakba   Arabic for 'disaster' or 'catastrophe', this term refers to the 1948 Palestinian exodus during which more than 700,000 Palestinians left or were forced to leave their homes during the 1948 war.

N'ginot ('Melodies')   Special signs used in biblical Hebrew texts to indicate the way the text should be chanted. Different traditions and melodies can be applied to the same signs.

Ninth of Av   In Hebrew *Tisha B'av*, this day in the Jewish calendar commemorates the destruction of the Temples and of Jerusalem, as well as other major calamities that have befallen the Jewish people.

Noahide Laws ('Seven Laws of Noah')   Set of seven imperatives based on Genesis 9.1–7 developed in Rabbinic tradition as binding on all humanity. In their earliest form, they are: to administer justice; not to worship idols; not to blaspheme; not to engage in forbidden sexual relationships; not to shed blood; not to rob; not to eat a limb taken from a living animal.

Nostra Aetate   Latin term meaning literally 'in our time', referring to the 1965 Roman Catholic Declaration on the Relation of the Church with Non-Christian Religions of the Second Vatican Council (Vatican II). Especially known for opening a new chapter of dialogue with Jews, repudiating the charge of Jewish responsibility for Jesus' death and condemning any form of anti-Semitism.

Ochlocracy   'Government' by mob rule.

Parashah or *sedra* or *sidra*   A weekly Torah portion. Plural *parashiyot*.

Perichoretic   Term referring to the close relationship of the three Persons of the Trinity to one another as interpenetrating, without any isolation. The analogy of persons engaged in a dance is often used.

Pesach Passover. Spring festival celebrating the Exodus of the Israelite slaves from Egypt.

Pharisees (Hebrew *P'rushim*, probably meaning 'separatists') Popular party in first-century Judaism, who believed the written law should be expanded and modified by the oral tradition, a view that was to become the norm in Rabbinic Judaism.

Phenomenology Philosophical method of inquiry developed largely by German philosophers Edmund Husserl and Martin Heidegger. Based on the premise that reality consists of objects and events ('phenomena') as they are perceived and understood in human consciousness, and are not independent of human consciousness. The study of what and how we experience.

Pluralism Term used to mean: (1) the objective reality of religious diversity in society; (2) a theoretical welcome of this diversity; and/or (3) the belief that the proper response to this diversity is to hold that some or all the faiths in question are substantially equal.

Postliberalism Theological movement emphasizing the importance of culture and language for discerning the meaning of all experience and thought.

Potestas Latin word meaning (coercive) power as distinct from *auctoritas*.

Purim Term used in Esther 3.7 meaning 'lots'. The annual festival in the last month of winter, Adar, of which the origin and celebration are described in the book of Esther.

Rabbinic Judaism The expression of Judaism developed by the Rabbis at the same time as Christianity, providing religious continuity when the four former pillars of Judaism – the Temple, the Sacrificial Rite, the Priest and the Land – were ended by Roman destruction and expulsion. The Rabbis were teachers not priests, the term 'rabbi' being a respectful form of address, meaning 'my master'.

Rosh Hashanah ('Head of the Year') The Autumn New Year festival, which begins on the 1st Tishri, developed by the Rabbis into a day of solemnity and reflection on God's kingship and judgement of the world.

Sadducees (Hebrew *Tzedukim*, perhaps from Zadok the Priest) Priestly party in first-century Judaism, who gave no special authority to oral traditions.

Second Temple Period Period of Jewish history from 530 BCE to 70 CE, when the Second Temple in Jerusalem existed. During this period, the sects of Pharisees, Sadducees, Essenes and Zealots were formed. This was also the time in which Jesus lived and taught.

Second Vatican Council Considered one of the most important events (1962–5) in the modern era of the Catholic Church. Significant for the way it inaugurated renewal in several key areas of the Church's identity and practice.

Sefer Torah The scroll on which the Five Books of Moses are written on parchment. The *Sifrei Torah* (plural) are kept in the Ark (*Aron HaKodesh*) in the synagogue.

Seleucid Greeks Those making up the Hellenistic State ruled by the Seleucid dynasty from 312 to 63 BCE.

Sephardi From the medieval Hebrew for Spain. Jews and Jewish communities whose roots are in the Iberian peninsula (Spain and Portugal).

Septuagint Third-century BCE translation of the Hebrew Bible into Koine Greek. Often designated with the Roman numeral acronym 'LXX' referring to the 70 Jewish scholars who by tradition undertook the translation.

Shavuot ('Weeks') Pentecost. Harvest festival 50 days after the first day of Passover, described in Leviticus 23.16–21, later considered by the Rabbis to be the anniversary of the giving of the Torah at Sinai.

Sh'khinah Feminine Hebrew term denoting God's indwelling presence on earth, a term which later became one of the *sefirot* used in kabbalistic literature.

Sh'ma (Hebrew for 'hear') Denotes the three paragraphs beginning with this word, recited twice daily in prayer: Deuteronomy 6.4–9; 11.13–20; and Numbers 15.38–41.

Shoah ('Devastation') Word first found in the book of Jeremiah and used for the Nazi Holocaust. Jews often use Shoah rather than Holocaust because a holocaust was a burnt offering and therefore carries sacrificial overtones.

Shtetlach Small Jewish towns in Eastern Europe prior to the Nazi destruction (singular *shtetl*).

Simkhat Torah Festival of the Rejoicing of the Torah, a medieval innovation following the conclusion of the festival of Tabernacles. The annual cycle of Torah readings is completed and the new cycle begun.

Sisters of Sion Founded in 1843, the Sisters of the Congregation of Our Lady of Sion is a Catholic congregation that teaches God's continuing love for the Jewish people and also seeks to hasten the fulfilment of God's promises concerning the future of the Jews and Gentiles.

Supersessionism Doctrine that Christianity renders Judaism null and void in all aspects of religious life.

Synoptic Gospels Matthew, Mark and Luke, called 'Synoptic' because they include many of the same stories, often in the same sequence and with similar wording. The Gospel of John is not counted as a Synoptic Gospel because of its distinct contents.

Tallit Fringed shawl worn during prayer. Plural *tallitot*.

Tanakh Hebrew term for the Hebrew Bible. An acronym of *Torah* ('Teaching'), *N'vi'im* ('Prophets') and *K'tuvim* ('Writings').

T'shuvah Hebrew term for repentance, meaning literally 'return'.

Theophany The appearance of God or a deity to a human being.

Torah ('Teaching') Used in various senses: (1) The Pentateuch (the written Torah); (2) the traditions embodied in the Rabbinic literature of late antiquity (the oral Torah); (3) the whole body of Jewish religious literature.

Torat Yisrael 'Teaching of the Jewish People', that is, Judaism.

Totum Dei Latin for 'all of God'.

Totus Deus Latin for 'all God', or 'wholly God'.

Transactional Analysis (TA) Psychoanalytic theory originated by Canadian Eric Berne, based on the idea that one's behaviour and social relationships reflect an interchange between parental (critical and nurturing), adult (rational) and childlike (intuitive and dependent) aspects of personality established early in life.

World Council of Churches Worldwide, inter-church organization founded in 1948. Its members today include the Churches making up the Anglican Communion, most jurisdictions of the Eastern Orthodox Church, most mainline Protestant Churches and some Evangelical Protestant and Pentecostal Churches. The Roman Catholic Church is not a member, although it sends accredited observers to its meetings.

Yahrzeit German and Yiddish word meaning 'year-time', 'anniversary'. Term borrowed by Jews from the Catholic Church to denote the anniversary of the death of a relative.

Yom HaShoah Day fixed by the State of Israel in 1953 for remembering the Nazi Holocaust, now observed throughout the Diaspora. It falls on 27 Nisan, 12 days after the first day of Passover. Distinct from Holocaust Memorial Day, which falls on 27 January and was instituted by the British Government.

Z"l Abbreviation for *zikhrono/zikhronah livrakhah* ('may his/her memory be a blessing').

Zohar The founding literary work of Jewish mystical thought known as Kabbalah, the *Zohar* is an Aramaic commentary on sections of the Bible which appeared in Castile in Northern Spain in the 1280s CE.

www.ingramcontent.com/pod-product-compliance
Lightning Source LLC
Chambersburg PA
CBHW021932290426
44108CB00012B/809